Beneath a Turkish Sky

Beneath a Turkish Sky

THE ROYAL DUBLIN FUSILIERS AND THE ASSAULT ON GALLIPOLI

PHILIP LECANE

The History Press Ireland

First published 2015

The History Press Ireland
50 City Quay
Dublin 2
Ireland
www.thehistorypress.ie

© Philip Lecane, 2015

The right of Philip Lecane to be identified as the Author
of this work has been asserted in accordance with the
Copyright, Designs and Patents Act 1988.

British Library Cataloguing in Publication Data.
A catalogue record for this book is available from the British Library.

ISBN 978 1 84588 865 7

Typesetting and origination by The History Press
Printed and bound in Malta, by Melita Press.

Dedicated to
my wife Kate (*née* Grant); my father Philip;
my mother Eileen (*née* O'Brien) 1932–1994;
Nora Byrne; Rita and Donal O'Driscoll;
Gaye and Norman O'Neill, friends who stood beside me.

The book is also in memory of two Dubliners
who wrote of men caught up in war:
my inspiration, Cornelius Ryan 1920–1974,
author of *The Longest Day* and *A Bridge Too Far*,
and my friend, Patrick Hogarty 1926–2005,
author of *Remembrance* and *The Old Toughs*.

''Twas better to die 'neath an Irish sky
than at Suvla or Sud-el-Bahr.'

'The Foggy Dew'

Contents

Acknowledgements

Holding down a full-time non-academic job, this book has taken me nine years to write. Many people have helped me over that time and I am very grateful to them all. My wife Kate's love and support sustained me when the going was tough. She has always believed in the book. She was a war widow during the lengthy periods I spent on the computer – writing or on the internet. I know she will be glad that I have returned from V Beach.

Life blessed me with amazing parents, my father, Philip, and my late mother, Eileen. My father showed me that life can contain magic and my mother showed me it can contain joy. Being the son of a wholesale newsagent gave me access to an Aladdin's cave of books and my mother took me to the cinema from a young age – both fuelled my imagination.

Nora Byrne, Rita and Donal O'Driscoll, Gaye and Norman O'Neill were there for me when I most needed support and I will always be grateful for this. It is a very great honour to have Dr Jeff Kildea, the holder of the Keith Cameron Chair of Australian History at University College Dublin, write the foreword to this book. The author of the excellent *Anzacs and Ireland*, he is a rarity among Australian historians, in having a knowledge and understanding of Irish participation in the Gallipoli campaign. 'The Gallipoli Three', Mike Lee, Michael Robson and Dave Neenan helped me in so many ways. As well as being excellent company, the two Michaels were very generous with their time and always willing to help with research. Both were there for me during the final push towards publication. Mike and Sally Lee are incredibly hospitable and I have come to think of their house as my second home. Also excellent company, Dave helped me over rough terrain in Gallipoli prior to my hip replacement operation and over the metaphorical rough terrain that was the final phase of the book. He assembled an exercise bike to keep me going on rainy days and a television table to ensure I did not get too much exercise. I am very grateful to Ken Kinsella, author of *Out of the Dark 1914–1918*, who was amazingly supportive during my push towards publication. With their encyclopaedic knowledge of the Royal Dublin Fusiliers, my good friends Liam and Conor Dodd displayed terrier-like persistence in tracking down numerous items of information for me. Special thanks are due to my fellow Royal Dublin Fusiliers Association committee members: Tom Burke MBE, Nick Broughall, Seán Connolly, Captain Séamus Greene (retired), and Brian Moroney. Tom was a trailblazer in commemorating the Irish who served in the First World War; Nick has always shared with me a particular interest in Gallipoli; Seán mans the association's website and put me in contact with the relatives of some of the V Beach men; Séamus was hugely supportive in seeking out photographs and illustrations, for which I am very grateful; and Brian plans the association's overseas expeditions, ensuring everything runs on time. Unusual for a regimental sergeant-major, he does amazing work on keeping up our morale and makes us laugh until our sides ache. I owe a very particular debt of gratitude to the late Pat Hogarty, who was also a committee member. His book *Remembrance: A Brief History of 'The Blue Caps' – The 1st Battalion Royal Dublin Fusiliers 1914-1922* was an invaluable source for my book. Chris Holland and Tony Jordan's book *The Story Behind the Monument: The 29th Division in Warwickshire and North Oxfordshire January-March 1915* was another invaluable source. I would also like to thank Tony Jordan for his very great kindness to me during my research. Thanks too to my fellow author Denise Deegan for her forensic editing of much of the book. Her comments and suggestions were most helpful. I am deeply grateful to Professor Lucienne Thys-Şenocak of Koç University, Istanbul, Turkey, for her very great kindness to me in sharing aspects of her research. The information she gave me on the castle at V Beach added greatly to the story. To Dr Piotr Nykier for taking the time and trouble to send me high quality photographs from his excellent website www. navyingallipoli.com and giving me permission to use them.[1] Unfortunately, pressure of space did not allow their publication, with priority being given to photographs of men mentioned in the text. To Steve Chambers for his kindness in providing photographs from his personal collection. To Peter Hart for his kind permission to reproduce his map of Gallipoli.

To members of The Great War Forum website, I owe a very great debt of gratitude, a matter I address in greater detail in my author's preface. For now, I will particularly mention three members of the Forum. Kate Willis for the eight-year loan of one of her valuable books, to a First World War researcher she has never met; Simon Riches for his research in the Liddle Archives on the trail of Captain John Kerr, original captain of the *River Clyde*; John Hartley for sharing his research on the footballer-musician Samuel Clough. The Great War Forum not only gave me very valuable information for this book but it also introduced me to some good friends: the previously mentioned Michael Robson, Eric Goossens who, with his wife Özlem, runs by far the best accommodation on the Gallipoli peninsula (see www.thegallipolihouses.com). Eric provided me with much valuable Gallipoli information and accompanied Mike Lee, Michael Robson, Dave Neenan and me on very interesting field trips on the peninsula. The Forum also introduced me to Lyn and Keith Edmonds, who were hugely supportive as I worked towards publication. They surely merit the Gallipoli Long Service Medal as the people who have visited the peninsula the greatest number of times. My thanks to David Buckley of the Royal Dublin Fusiliers Association for the extended loan of material from his collection and to Austin Fennessy of the Medal Society of Ireland for the extended loan of *The Incomparable 29th and the River Clyde*.

With the names of their relatives in brackets, I am very grateful to the following for personal stories: Jim Bowskill (Leading Stoker William Bowskill); Linda Carter (Edward Nugent); David Christmas (Arthur Wright); Michael Constant (Interpreter Maurice Constanini); Brian Filbey (Stephen Filbey), unfortunately, loss of contact with Brian meant I was unable to get the story of Stephen's later life; Ray Ludford (Michael Ludford); Letitia Pollard (Gerald Pollard); and Pam Smith (Harry Fox). My particular thanks to Hilary Tulloch (*née* Grimshaw) for inviting me to her home, where she shared information and family mementoes of Cecil Grimshaw. I greatly appreciate her patience with my many detailed questions, I am very grateful for her generous assistance in the final push towards publication. Brian Dodds for the tour of the parts of Newry associated with Sam and Jack Mallaghan. Roger Hutchinson, for his ongoing kindness and helpfulness with my queries about Sam and Jack. Gloria Hutchinson for her eleventh-hour dash to solve a riddle. Warrant Officer (retired) Myles Smyth for his unfailing courtesy, patience and humour in answering my many queries about Nicholas Smyth. Again, pressure of space did not always allow me to include all his information in the book. While uncertain whether I would be interested in his story, because her grandfather was not an Irishman, Lyn Edmonds readily gave me her research on Benjamin Hurt. He was a 'Dub' and fought at V Beach, Lyn, so he is part of the story. Thank you to Captain Howard Cook for information on his grandfather Ormond Cook, owner of the *SS River Clyde*.

My thanks are due also to the following people: Michael Carraher, author of *San Fairy Ann: Motor Cyles and British Victory 1914-1918*, for interesting discussions on relevant topics; Jean Prendergast for information on Royal Munster Fusiliers combatants with Cork connections and for telephone conversations and email communications that are always both interesting and amusing; Stephen Nulty for ongoing research support on a wide range of topics; Historian Mary Long for information on the Rooth family; Family Researcher Pam Stepney for information on the family of Royal Dublin Fusilier Officer Tom Frankland; Jimmy Taylor for his unfailing kindness in answering my ongoing research queries; Michael Pegum of irishwarmemorials.ie for ongoing support. I consider Michael to be one of the finest of the army of unsung heroes, who labour without recognition to commemorate Ireland's First World War dead; Mal Murray of the Gallipoli Association for answering my research queries and particularly in shedding some light on the riddle surrounding interpreter Maurice Constantini; Martin Staunton for ongoing research, advice and encouragement; Torquay Reference Library for the first names of the mayor and mayoress in 1915, my cousin Karen Phillips for work on photos, Joe Byrne and Philip Jackson whose always enjoyable company helped sustain my morale on the long road to complete the book. Special thanks to Ronan Colgan, Beth Amphlett, Chris West and the staff at The History Press. Thank you also to anyone I may have inadvertently forgotten and to those who provided information that, for reasons of space and structure, did not make it into the book.

Foreword

As an Australian I have lived all my life in a country where Gallipoli is a word that resonates with meaning, as it does in New Zealand. Elsewhere, those with a reasonable knowledge of the history of the First World War will recognise it as the name of the 1915 campaign to knock Turkey out of the war. But for Australians it is much more than that. For the Gallipoli campaign is widely regarded in Australia as the crucible of the nation, a period in our history when the inhabitants of the six former British colonies that had federated in 1901 were forged into citizens of the Australian nation. At an Anzac Day lunch in London in 1919 Prime Minister Billy Hughes told his audience that Australia was 'born on the shores of Gallipoli'. Many Australians challenge that view: in 2008 former Australian Prime Minister Paul Keating described Hughes' idea of the nation born at Gallipoli as 'utter and complete nonsense'. But the passion which the debate arouses in Australia confirms that Gallipoli, the place and the event, is well ingrained into our national psyche. If further evidence is needed, an examination of a bibliography relating to the Gallipoli campaign will turn up hundreds of titles covering Australia's participation in the campaign written by Australians and/or published in Australia.

Yet, for all that, Australians remain ignorant of many of the details of the campaign. They tend to think we and our New Zealand partners were the only ones there, apart from the Turks of course. Some Australians would be aware that British troops were there, but few would know that they included men from Irish regiments, and fewer still that many of those Irishmen fought alongside the Anzacs in battles such as Second Krithia, Lone Pine, Chunuk Bair and Hill 60, and at places iconic to Australians such as Quinn's Post, or that on the first day of the campaign more Irishmen were killed at the landing beaches than Anzacs.

But it is not only Australians who have forgotten the part played by their Irish cousins-in-arms; the collective amnesia extends to the Irish themselves. In Ireland, especially the Republic, the Dardanelles campaign is largely unknown and, except for commemorations organised by Australians and New Zealanders, the anniversary of the landing on 25 April passes almost unmarked in Ireland, notwithstanding that about the same number of Irishmen as New Zealanders died there. For, although the Irish were as gallant in battle as the Anzacs, their sacrifice at Gallipoli in the Empire's cause came to be portrayed at home as a betrayal of the Irish nation and its struggle for independence. In the words of the nationalist song 'The Foggy Dew', which commemorates those who died in the Easter Rising: ''Twas better to die 'neath an Irish sky than at Suvla or Sedd el Bahr.'

While a number of books on the Irish at Gallipoli appeared during and immediately after the war, such as Michael McDonagh's *The Irish at the Front* (1916), Bryan Cooper's *The Tenth (Irish) Division in Gallipoli* (1918) and Cyril Falls' *The History of the Royal Irish Rifles* (1925), the field soon dried up and remained so until the early 1980s. But over the past three decades academic and journalist historians have rediscovered the part played by Irish soldiers in the First World War. Although the figures vary, it is commonly accepted that about 200,000 Irishmen fought in the war and about 35,000 were killed or died as a result of their war service. Spurred on by a growing interest in genealogy and the advent of the decade of commemorations the Irish have emerged from their social amnesia with a hunger to know more and more about the part which the Irish played in the war.

It is in this context that Philip Lecane's *Beneath a Turkish Sky* comes to be published at such an important time. A number of books appearing in the last few years have discussed the Irish at Gallipoli, but often as part of more general works such as Myles Dungan's *Irish Voices from the Great War* (1995) or Tom Johnstone's *Orange, Green and Khaki* (1992) or concentrating on the Suvla Bay landing in August 1915, such as Philip Orr's *Field of Bones* (2006). *Beneath a Turkish Sky* is the first book to be published specifically on the landing of the 1st Battalion Royal Dublin Fusiliers and 1st Battalion Royal Munster Fusiliers at V Beach, Gallipoli on 25 April 1915. Its concentration on that one event in a campaign that lasted nine months, demonstrates the level of sophistication that Irish interest in the Gallipoli campaign has reached. While these days many sources will give an interested reader an overview of Irish involvement in the campaign, it is only works such as this that will enable the Irish people to develop a deeper understanding of the important part the Irish played at Gallipoli and the suffering they endured.

As with his earlier book on the 1918 sinking of RMS *Leinster*, the mail boat from Dublin's southern port of Dún Laoghaire (then Kingstown) to Holyhead in Wales (*Torpedoed* (2005)), Philip approaches the subject from the level of the individuals involved. While painting the broader picture so that we fully understand the significance of the Gallipoli campaign and the context of the involvement of the Irish in it, he peels the onion layer by layer so that we gain an intimate understanding of the momentous events from the viewpoint of those involved. As such it is a work of prodigious research, interrogating a wide variety of sources both obvious and obscure.

Under Philip's tutelage we travel with the men of the Dublin and Munster Fusiliers back from their colonial postings in India and Burma, we join them in the camps in England as they train for the new war they have been recalled to fight, we embark with them on their voyage to the Greek island of Lemnos in preparation for the landing at Gallipoli and we spend two days with them, 25 and 26 April, sharing their ordeal in the landing at V Beach and its immediate aftermath.

Any good historian, and Philip is one of them, must have a sense of place if he or she is going to give the reader a true understanding of the events described. Philip has visited Gallipoli on a number of occasions and many times has walked along V Beach, contemplating the terror which infused the soldiers as they huddled under the sandbank to avoid the hail of Turkish bullets, has crawled into the crumbling ruins of Sedd el Bahr Fort from which the Turkish defenders unleashed a withering fire on the hapless troops disembarking from the *River Clyde*, has stood on the heights above V Beach envisaging the landing from the point of view of the Turkish riflemen and has wandered through the narrow streets of Sedd el Bahr village, through which the exhausted Munsters and Dublins cautiously advanced the next day, constantly harassed by snipers. As an Australian brought up on tales of the courage and tenacity of the Anzacs in their landing at Z Beach (now called Anzac Cove), I am humbled by Philip's account of the Irish at V Beach. While over 700 Anzacs were killed in the first few days of the campaign, the landing itself at Z Beach was largely unopposed. Most were killed in the fighting in the hills and gullies above the beach once the Turkish reserves arrived to repel the invaders. For the Irish the slaughter occurred mostly on the beach itself, with many being killed as they sat helpless in open boats or when they emerged from the sanctuary of the *River Clyde* onto the gangways saturated with Turkish fire. If the gallantry of the Anzacs who stormed the heights above Anzac Cove deserves to be remembered, as it is and undoubtedly does, then that of the Irish at V Beach should never be forgotten either. Publication of *Beneath a Turkish Sky* is an important step in ensuring that will not happen.

Jeff Kildea
Keith Cameron Chair of Australian History
University College Dublin

Author's Preface

'On a recent UK quiz show with university graduates, not one member of either team knew the location of Gallipoli.'

Helles Landing: Gallipoli, by Huw & Jill Rodge (2003)

In November 1914, the British cabinet effectively gave responsibility for overseeing war operations to the War Council, a sub-committee of the cabinet. The War Council consisted of Prime Minister Herbert Asquith, Secretary of State for War Lord Herbert Kitchener, First Lord of the Admiralty Winston Churchill, Chancellor of the Exchequer David Lloyd George, Secretary of State for Foreign Affairs Sir Edward Grey, and Secretary of State for India Robert Crewe-Milnes, Marquis of Crewe. Particular meetings of the War Council were also attended by other cabinet ministers and army and naval officers. In practise, the War Council was dominated by Asquith, Kitchener and Churchill.

At the beginning of 1915, British and French armies on the Western Front found it impossible to break through the approximately 350 miles of heavily fortified German trenches that stretched from the English Channel to the Swiss border. Some British strategists, including Winston Churchill, felt the stalemate could only be broken by attacking Germany's ally, Turkey. The War Council decided a combined British-French fleet should force its way up the Dardanelles, the narrow seaway that leads from the Aegean Sea to the Sea of Marmara. The fleet would then cross the Sea of Marmara to the Turkish capital of Constantinople (Istanbul). It was believed this would bring about a Turkish surrender. This in turn would allow Britain and France to establish a supply route across the Black Sea to their ally Russia. It would also provide an opportunity to attack Germany and her ally, Austro-Hungry, on their eastern flank.

The attack on Turkey was badly planned and poorly executed. In March 1915, a combined British-French fleet was unable to force its way through the Dardanelles, because the narrow seaway was mined and both of its shores defended by artillery. The War Council therefore decided troops would be landed on the Gallipoli Peninsula, on the European side of the Dardanelles. Their objective would be to seize part of the peninsula and capture or immobilise the Turkish guns that dominated the Dardanelles. It was believed this would enable the seaway to be cleared of mines and allow the combined British-French fleet to sail to Constantinople.

Early on Sunday morning, 25 April 1915, British troops (including Irish battalions) landed on five beaches on the Gallipoli Peninsula. Australian and New Zealand troops landed on another beach and French troops landed on the Asian side of the Dardanelles. Some of the landings met with strong resistance from the Turks and – apart from the French landing – the Allies failed to achieve their initial objectives. This failure was followed by a protracted campaign, involving trench warfare similar to that on the Western Front. In August 1915, a further landing at Suvla Bay, further up the Gallipoli Peninsula, failed to break the deadlock and, in January 1916, the Allies withdrew from the peninsula.

ಬಇ

The Special Commissions (Dardanelles and Mesopotamia) Act 1916 established the Dardanelles Commission to investigate the planning and conduct of the Gallipoli campaign. The report of the Dardanelles Commission makes it clear the decision-making processes that led to the invasion of Gallipoli were gravely flawed. Military and naval 'expert advisers' who attended meetings of the War Council told the Dardanelles Commission they felt their role was to express their views only if called upon to do so, and they were rarely called upon. The political members of the War Council, however, told the Commission that the silence of the 'expert advisers' implied agreement with the plans under discussion. Apart from any other flaws in the decision-making process, this confusion on the role of 'expert advisers' alone was surely a recipe for disaster.

According to the report, the Commission was:

> struck with the atmosphere of vagueness and want of precision which seems to have characterised the proceedings of the War Council ... Some of those present at the meetings of the Council left without having any clear idea of what had or had not been decided.

While the War Council's objectives remained unchanged during the Gallipoli campaign, views on how to attain these objectives gradually underwent a profound change.

> The necessity for employing a large military force became daily more apparent. The idea of a purely naval operation was gradually dropped ... It does not appear that either the Cabinet or the War Council ever definitely discussed and deliberately changed the policy. General Callwell (Director of Military Operations) says that it would be very difficult to assign any date at which the change took place. 'We drifted,' he said, 'into the big military attack.'

According to the Commission's report, 'After March 19th (1915) there was no further meeting of the War Council until May 14th, and we are unable to ascertain any precise date on which, after the failure of the naval attack, military operations on the Gallipoli campaign were definitely decided on' The Dardanelles Commission issued its report in 1919, after the war was over. The report concluded the campaign was poorly planned, difficulties had been underestimated, delays after the first attack had wasted precious time and there had been insufficient artillery and ammunition. The final report was published in 1919, after the war was over. While various decision makers were mildly censured, publication of the report per se does not appear to have had a negative impact any of their careers.[1]

ॐ

Apart from the *Official History of the War: Military Operations: Gallipoli Vol. 1*, most books on the Gallipoli campaign tend to fall into one of three broad categories. The first is comprised of personal memoirs written shortly after the campaign. The second and third are comprised of more recent books that either look at the entire campaign or focus on aspects of the Australian experience.[2] The fact the Gallipoli campaign was relatively short meant that authors, including those writing memoirs, were in a position to examine the overall campaign (or the Australian aspects of the campaign) within a single book. So the initial landings, on 25 April 1915, are usually briefly covered as part of the overall story. With the exception of the landing at Z Beach, now popularly known as Anzac Cove, the story of the initial landings has yet to be covered in the detail it merits. The fact that participants from both sides are no longer available for interview means a book such as *The Longest Day* – Cornelius Ryan's epic work on the Second World War D-Day landings – will never be written about the 25 April 1915 Gallipoli landings.[3] Long tantalised by the all-too-brief references to the V Beach/Sedd el Bahr landing in books on Gallipoli, I set out to research the story of what happened there on 25 April 1915. The story has never been – and probably never will be – told in the detail deserved by the men of both sides who fought there. But some attempt at a detailed account is long overdue.

My research into the Sedd el Bahr landing was hampered by the lack of a war diary for the 1st Battalion Royal Dublin Fusiliers for the period of the landing.[4] However, the availability of two excellent sources allowed the telling of a part of the story not accessible through official documents and battalion histories. Patrick Hogarty's *Remembrance* and Chris Holland and Tony Jordan's *The Story Behind the Monument* tell the little-known story of British troops billeted on England's civilian population in the early part of the First World War. The authors of both publications researched local newspapers (Hogarty in Torquay and Holland & Jordan in Warwickshire and North Oxfordshire) for information on the soldiers who were billeted in these areas in late 1914 and early 1915. This book has also greatly benefited from Denis Stoneham's article 'Steamship River Clyde – How Britain Failed to Save a Hero of Gallipoli', published in *World Ship Review* (No. 40, June 2005).

The myth that there are no Turkish sources available on the Gallipoli campaign was strongly dispelled by Dr Edward J. Erickson, Lieutenant-Colonel US Army (Retired), in *Ordered to Die: A History of the Ottoman Army in the First World War* and *Ottoman Army Effectiveness in World War 1: A Comparative Study*. His works are invaluable sources on the Turkish experiences at Sedd el Bahr. During the writing of this book Dr Jeff Kildea made me aware of research being carried out by the Australian War Memorial on Turkish records of the Gallipoli campaign. Harvey Broadbent, Director of the Gallipoli Centenary Research Project and Senior Research Fellow, Department of Modern History, Macquarie University, New South Wales, very kindly briefed me on the scope of the project. Unfortunately my book went to print before the project's findings were published.

The V Beach landing took place below the village and the old fortress of Sedd el Bahr. I was most fortunate to be able to consult with Professor Lucienne Thys-Şenocak of Koç University, Turkey. She very generously made available to me a pre-publication draft of *Defending the Dardanelles:*

The Fortresses of Seddülbahir and Kumkale and the legacy of Turhan Sultan, Chapter 4 of her book *Ottoman Women Builders: The Architectural Patronage of Hadice Turhan Sultan.* I am deeply grateful for her kindness and assistance to me. The Great War Forum website, http://1914-1918.invisionzone.com/ forums/, and some of its members have been an amazing resource to me in the writing of this book. Like me, the vast majority of the Forum's members are non-academic First World War historians. The depth of their combined knowledge is matched only by the breath of their helpfulness and, indeed, their great kindness. I highly recommend the site to all who are engaged in First World War research.

∾

The major part of the force that landed at Sedd el Bahr on 25 April 1915 comprised of two-and-a-half British infantry battalions i.e. the 1st Battalion Royal Dublin Fusiliers, the 1st Battalion Royal Munster Fusiliers and two of the four companies of the 2nd Battalion Hampshire Regiment.[5] This book uses the Royal Dublin Fusiliers as the primary focus of the story.

∾

What is now modern-day Turkey was part of the Ottoman Empire in 1915. Although the men who opposed the landing at Sedd el Bahr were officially known as Ottomans, they were commonly known to their enemies – and often to themselves – as Turks. In this book the terms Ottoman and Turk are used interchangeably. Although the current Turkish name for the place where the 25 April 1915 landing took place is Seddülbahir, I decided to use the contemporary spelling most used by British sources (which at the time included Irish sources), i.e. Sedd el Bahr.[6] Though the Turkish name for their capital was Istanbul, I have referred to it as Constantinople, the name by which it was known in the English speaking world at the time of the Gallipoli campaign.

∾

Starting in 2005, and still continuing, one of the 'hottest' topics on the online Great War Forum has been a discussion as to whether or not the Turks had machine guns at the landing beaches on 25 April. On the one hand are numerous British and Australian accounts of having been fired at by machine guns, on the other are claims that the Turks had very few machine guns. The debate has included discussions on what exactly constitutes a machine-gun. For example, was a pom-pom gun a machine-gun? Not having any particular authority to comment on the issue, I have not entered the debate in this book. Where particular witnesses have stated they were fired on by machine guns, I have quoted this without comment.

There is an unresolved issue around casualties sustained by the Royal Dublin Fusiliers and Royal Munster Fusiliers during the landing at V Beach. Possibly because the landing has not previously been studied in any great depth, statements regarding the casualties sustained by both battalions on 25 April 1915 have been lacking in clarity. Several books appear to imply that hundreds of men from the Dublins and Munsters were killed during the landing at V Beach. Yet online Commonwealth War Grave Commission records show only approximately sixty Dublins and approximately fifty Munsters being recorded as killed on that day.[7]

One cannot conclude from this, however, that the landing was a minor action or that heavy casualties were not sustained. The quoted figures pose a problem when compared with the figures for the strength of both battalions just four days later. Out of the twenty-five officers and 987 men of the Royal Dublin Fusiliers who had gone to Gallipoli, the battalion had only one officer and 344 men fit for service on 29 April. The corresponding figures for the Munsters are that of the twenty-eight officers and 1,002 men who had gone to Gallipoli, only twelve officers and 588 men were available for service on 29 April. Because of their numerical deficiencies, both battalions were amalgamated for a short period, until reinforcements arrived. Given that the two battalions were in action only on 25 April and 26 April, why was there such a huge difference in the strength of the Dublins and Munsters between their arrival in the Mediterranean and on 29 April? There are two possible answers. Either the number of deaths cited for 25 April (based on figures supplied by both battalions) are incorrect or huge numbers were wounded during the landing. With no medical facilities available ashore, the wounded were quickly evacuated. Those who died aboard hospital ships or in hospitals around the Mediterranean would not have been recorded as having died in Gallipoli. Knowing that Lieutenant Raymond de Lusignan of the Dublins, recorded as killed on 26 April, was actually killed the previous day, I would tentatively suggest that perhaps at least some of the Dublins recorded for 26 April were in fact killed the previous day. In a letter home, Lance-Corporal John Walsh of the Munsters said that Private James Searles was killed on 25 April. Yet he is recorded as having been killed on 27 April. This whole issue would certainly merit further study.

∞

'The Foggy Dew' is a song about Ireland's 1916 Rising. Some sources attribute the song to Peadar Kearney, composer of the national anthem of the Republic of Ireland. Other sources attribute it to Canon Charles O'Neill, a parish priest of Kilcoo and later Newcastle, both places in County Down, Northern Ireland.[8] The confusion about authorship is hardly helped by the fact that there are a number of versions of the song. All versions contain the lines: ''Twas better to die 'neath an Irish sky, than at Suvla or Sud-el-Bahr' (note the spelling). One version of the song says that if the Irishmen who died in the First World War had died in the 1916 Easter Rising, 'Their graves we'd keep where the Fenians sleep,' while in another version it is 'Their names we'd keep where the Fenians sleep.' Until recently, the Irishmen and Irishwomen who served in the First World War were written out of their country's history. Many of the men who died at V Beach were Irishmen. In telling their story – and that of their British comrades – I hope to restore to memory some of those who died beneath a Turkish sky.

∞

A brief outline of the structure of the book might benefit the reader. With some mention of the 1st Battalion Royal Munster Fusiliers and the 2nd Battalion Hampshire Regiment, the early chapters of the book focus on the 1st Battalion Royal Dublin Fusiliers. We meet them in India, follow them on their journey to England, look at their time in England and their departure from Avonmouth. Their story is interspersed with events occurring elsewhere, such as meetings of the War Council and the naval attacks on the Dardanelles. These events are introduced to give a sense of the slowly unfolding disaster that led to the deaths of hundreds of men in the sea and on the beach below Sedd el Bahr village at the tip of the Gallipoli Peninsula. As the Royal Dublin Fusiliers leave Avonmouth, the focus of the story switches to Turkey, the country they are about to invade. The book then returns to the Royal Dublin Fusiliers and other units as they voyage from Avonmouth to Egypt. It looks at their time in Egypt and their voyage to Mudros harbour on Lemnos.

The following chapter tells of the gathering of the invasion force at Lemnos Island and the journey of the V Beach contingent to the Gallipoli Peninsula.

The story of the landing at V Beach is then told. The next two chapters cover the aftermath of the landing and the rest of the Gallipoli campaign. The final chapter tells the stories of some of the survivors of V Beach in the years that followed, as well as relatives of some of those who still lie beneath a Turkish sky. It might be helpful for readers to refer to Appendices 1 and 2 while reading the main text.

ঙ্গ

I would very much like to hear from any reader who has further information on the SS *River Clyde* or any of the men – Irish, British or Turkish – who fought at Sedd el Bahr. I can be contacted at the email address below or through the email address of the Royal Dublin Fusiliers Association: rdfa@eircom.net Please ask that your email be forwarded to me. The Royal Dublin Fusiliers Association promotes remembrance of the Irish men and women who served in the First World War. The association's highly informative website is at www.greatwar.ie. I also highly commend the site www.royaldublinfusiliers.com to the reader. As previously mentioned, I very highly recommend the site of The Great War Forum http://1914-1918.invisionzone.com/forums/.

Philip Lecane,
rmsleinster@gmail.com

About the Author

Philip Lecane was educated at Christian Brothers College, Cork, and University College Cork. Now living in Monkstown, County Dublin, he has written many articles on local history and Irish involvement in the First World War. A member of the Royal Dublin Fusiliers Association and the Gallipoli Association, he is the author of *Torpedoed! The RMS Leinster Disaster.*

'What I write about is not war,
but the courage of man.'

Cornelius Ryan,
author of *The Longest Day* and *A Bridge Too Far*

'This war has fallen heavily on some regiments.
Scarcely any has suffered more severely, none has
won greater distinction, than the Dublin Fusiliers.'

Winston Churchill, in *London to Ladysmith via Pretoria*

Prologue

The Lonely Graves

'In this generation we redeem their memory,
acknowledging their service
and the pain of those who loved them.'

President Mary McAleese,
remembering Ireland's First World War dead,
at Messines, Belgium, 11 November 1998

V Beach Cemetery, Sedd el Bahr,
Gallipoli, Turkey, 24 March 2010

The cemetery lies at the tip of the Gallipoli peninsula in Turkey, just yards
from where the men were killed. A few miles away, a steady stream of people
come from the Southern Hemisphere to visit the graves of the Australians
and New Zealanders who were killed in the Gallipoli campaign. But few
come to visit the lonely cemetery on the seashore. For almost a century the
men of the Royal Dublin Fusiliers and the Royal Munster Fusiliers who
died on the beach and in the sea have waited for Ireland to remember them.
Their voices seem to echo in the still air. Lieutenant-Colonel Richard Rooth,
the Dublins commanding officer, who died leading his men: 'We are an Irish
battalion, and we are far from home.' Father William Finn, the Dublin's chaplain, who came ashore in the same boat as Rooth: 'The priest's place is with
the dying soldier.' The ghosts of the Royal Munster Fusiliers are also here:
'I turned to a chap on my right. His name was Fitzgerald. He was from Cork,

but soon he was over the border' [i.e. dead.][1] 'Jimmy Searles was killed on the 25th April and was buried by the seaside.'[2]

But today the amnesia will end and remembering will begin. A woman enters the cemetery with her husband. Accompanying them are Turkish and Irish dignitaries, together with members of the media from both countries. All eyes are on the dignified woman. Mary McAleese, President of the Republic of Ireland, has come to tell the ghosts their long wait is over; she has come to hear their story and to bring it back home across the sea.

The President laid a wreath in memory of all who died at V Beach. She was then shown a number of particular graves and special memorials and was told about the men who are buried or commemorated there. For one brief moment the men who died at V Beach have attracted media attention. But one moment is all that is needed. Later that day a film of President McAleese's visit to the remote cemetery is shown on Irish and Turkish television. The following day, the visit is given front-page coverage in Irish and Turkish newspapers. In Ireland people began to discuss the coverage and some start to speak about their relatives who served in the disastrous Gallipoli campaign.

CHAPTER 1

India:
At the Empire's Front Gate

'The East India Company maintained its own army, composed of a few *"European"* regiments – white men, mostly Irish – and a growing number of *"native"* regiments.'

Queen Victoria's Little Wars, by Byron Farwell

Ahmednagar Barracks, Deccan, India, 1910-1913

The elephant and tiger on the buttons of their khaki British Army uniforms showed the men were members of the Royal Dublin Fusiliers, a regiment with a history dating back to the early days of British involvement in India. The soldiers were from the Dublins 1st Battalion. They had been taught the battalion's history; learning it had not been established as part of the British Army, but as part of a private army formed in India by the East India Company in the 1660s. After the Indian Mutiny, the battalion – and the rest of the East India Company army – had been taken into the British Army. Like most battalions in the army, it subsequently underwent a number of name changes, eventually becoming, in 1881, the 1st Battalion, Royal Dublin Fusiliers. The battalion had its own traditions, its own motto – *Spectamur Agendo* (We are known by our deeds) and its own nickname – The Blue Caps (originally Neill's Blue Caps, named after Commanding Officer James Neill, who supplied the men with blue coverings for their caps during the Indian Mutiny).

Comprised of between 800 and 1,000 officers and other ranks, the battalion was the British Army's basic infantry tactical unit. Membership of the 1st Battalion, Royal Dublin Fusiliers was 80 per cent Irish and 16.9 per cent English. While the recruiting area for the Royal Dublin Fusiliers was comprised of counties Carlow, Dublin, Kildare and Wicklow, 61.7 per cent of the 1st Battalion were born in Dublin city or county.[1] Like London and Liverpool, Dublin was designated a special recruiting district outside the territorial system. The three cities 'acted as magnets for large numbers of men … who came to them in search of work and who, if they could not find it, might enlist.'[2] The Inspector-General of Recruiting often directed that recruits from the three cities should be sent to regiments in need of men, whose own recruiting districts could not supply them.

Most British infantry regiments had two battalions. One tended to be based 'at home' (England, Scotland, Wales or Ireland) and the other overseas. The priority was to keep the overseas battalion up to strength. New recruits would be sent to the 'at home' battalion for a period of training, following which they would be sent to the overseas battalion as part of a draft (i.e. reinforcements). Having spent a number of years overseas, a battalion would come 'home' and its sister battalion would go overseas.

ॐ

Stephen Filbey and Harry Fox were firm friends. Their friendship was doubtless cemented by the fact that both had been placed in the Foundling Hospital, London, and it seems likely they would have known each other while at the institution.[3] Fox was a few years older, born on 10 July 1878. As his single-parent mother was unable to care for him, he was placed in the Foundling Hospital. The hospital named the infant Henry (known as Harry) Fox and later fostered him with the Clarke family in Hadlow near Tonbridge, Kent. Many families from the surrounding area took in foundlings from the hospital. Given the fact he maintained contact with them when he joined the army, Harry seems to have had a very good experience with the Clarkes, a couple who over many years fostered more than forty children. When aged five or six, foundlings were usually returned to the hospital to attend school. Some sang in the chapel choir and attracted large congregations whose collections helped to fund the hospital. Some were taught to play musical instruments and many of the boys went on to serve in military bands. On 10 April 1893, at the age of fourteen, Harry Fox joined the Royal Dublin Fusiliers as a drummer.[4] Of low stature; he eventually grew to 5ft 3in. Queen Victoria, who was not exactly a tall person herself, once spotted the boy drummer on parade and asked for him to be presented to her. Harry served in the Boer War and later in Malta, Crete, Egypt and the Sudan. He eventually attained the rank of band sergeant.

Stephen Filbey was born on 2 May 1884, to twenty-two-year-old Emily Higgs, a shirtmaker. Charles Pugh, the boy's father, worked in a drapery. The month the boy was born, his father gave notice to his employer. He abandoned Emily and their son, fleeing to New Zealand and then Australia. Emily's father, Edward Higgs, and her five brothers worked as lightermen in London's Docklands. (A lighter is a flat-bottomed barge used to transfer goods to and from moored ships. Unpowered, they were moved and steered using long oars, with their motive power provided by water currents.) Ironically, lighters would play a significant part in the landing at Sedd el Bahr on 25 April 1915.

Sergeant Stephen Filbey and Sergeant Harry Fox, 1912.

By the time of his grandson's birth, Edward Higgs's health had deteriorated. He was unable to financially support Emily and the boy. Emily continued to work in the shirt factory, while her mother Eliza cared for the boy during working hours. In January 1885, Eliza died. With no one to care for her son during the day, Emily was forced to stop working, leaving herself and her father with no income. By this stage, her brothers either had their own families to support or were unemployed. Emily petitioned the Foundling Hospital to take care of her baby. However, entry was conditional. The hospital would only accept a firstborn or only child, the mother had to be of good reputation, the mother and child had to have been abandoned by the father and the child had to be admitted before its first birthday. Representatives of the hospital interviewed Emily, her family, her former employer and the sister of the boy's father. Emily and her father were deemed to be 'most respectable people of their class' and her petition was accepted by the hospital. On 14 April 1885 Emily Higgs walked to the Foundling Hospital, where she gave up her child Charles Higgs, half a month before his first birthday. Foundling tokens (coins, buttons, jewellery, poems) were given by mothers leaving their babies, allowing the hospital to match a mother with her child should she ever come back to claim it. But, like the majority of children at the hospital, Charles never

saw his mother again. On the day he was admitted, Charles Higgs' identity
was wiped clean. An identity tag was placed around his neck with Foundling
Hospital identity number 22014. Infant number 22014 was bathed, wrapped
in a clean blanket and taken to the institution's chapel, where he was baptised
into the Church of England and given the name Stephen Filbey. Stephen
was fostered by Ellen and George Underwood (a farm labourer) in Chertsey,
Surrey. While Ellen, aged sixty, was the official foster mother, it is likely her
daughter Ellen Stevens, aged thirty-five, helped care for the several foundlings fostered by her mother. From 1885 to 1889, Stephen lived in a pastoral
setting with his foster parents and several other foster children. Like Harry
Fox, Stephen was returned to the hospital at about the age of five. This would
have been an extremely traumatic experience for him. The first few days and
nights in the institution would have been a nightmare for a young boy whose
only memories would have been of his Underwood parents and life in the
country. Newly returned foundlings were housed in a special area of the institution until they could be integrated into the boys or girls wing. Like Harry
Fox, Stephen was chosen for the Foundling Hospital band. Learning to play
a number of instruments, he became proficient at the cello. Even if Harry
and Stephen had not known each other before, due to the difference in their
ages, it seems likely they would have become familiar – and possibly friendly –
while in the band. There was an overlap period, from 1889 to 1893, when both
attended the Foundling Hospital and younger boys learned to befriend older
boys for protection against bullying. Perhaps Filbey and Fox teamed up for
mutual support: Fox being older but of small stature, Filbey being younger
but bigger.

Most foundlings never left the grounds of the institution, although they
could hear and partially see everyday London life in the vicinity of the hospital. The institution had an indoor pool, where they were taught to swim,
an uncommon skill for the time. The fact they could swim would serve both
Harry and Stephen well on the day they landed at Sedd el Bahr on 25 April 1915.

On 6 April 1899, aged fourteen years and eleven months, Stephen Filbey
joined the Royal Dublin Fusiliers in London, as a boy soldier. He was 5ft 1½in
in height, with fair complexion, blue eyes and brown hair. He had scars on
the back of his head and on his left shin. He gave his profession as musician.
He signed on for a period of twelve years and was assigned as a drummer,
with regimental number 6662. On 18 November 1902, he was one of a draft
for the 1st Battalion Royal Dublin Fusiliers in Malta. Doubtless he was glad
to see fellow ex-foundling Harry Fox welcoming him to the battalion. Like
Harry, Stephen became a member of the 1st Battalion's band.

Subsequently serving in Cyprus, the battalion later returned to Malta. In late 1905, it moved to Alexandria in Egypt, in 1907 to Khartoum in the Sudan and in 1908 to Cairo in Egypt. At Malta, on 3 March 1905, Stephen passed classes of instruction for rank of corporal. On 10 March, he was appointed lance-corporal. Two and a half months later, on 2 March 1906, at Alexandria, he was reduced to the rank of private, presumably for some misconduct of the type to which soldiers are regularly prone. However, he was again appointed lance-corporal on 30 October 1906. The following year saw the battalion based at Khartoum in the Sudan, where they rode camels in the desert. On 3 September 1909, in Cairo, Stephen signed on for a further period of service with the Dublins, for a term that would give him a total service of twenty-one years. The following year found the battalion back in India, the land of its birth, where it was based at Ahmednagar.

ꩌꩌ

One of Stephen Filbey's favourite off-duty pursuits was snake hunting. He and some of his pals, quite likely including Harry Fox, would leave the barracks at Ahmednagar and head for town. There, they would seek out local Indian mongoose owners and bargain with them for their hire and that of their animals. The soldiers had to keep a number of factors in mind. While trying to acquire the 'best' mongoose of the bunch, each man was also trying to hire the animal for the lowest possible cost. Having completed the transaction, the men had to calculate how much money to bet on their hired mongoose. Then, the party of Indians and off-duty soldiers would head off into the bush, each mongoose on a long leash.

In the bush, the party would search for snake holes in the ground, particularly those of the deadly cobra. Once a snake's lair was located, a mongoose would be sent in, its long leash being slowly played out. The men eagerly awaited the sounds which indicated the mongoose had found a snake and that mortal combat had ensued. Meanwhile, the men kept careful watch on the snake holes in case an agitated cobra emerged. Most times the mongoose emerged from the hole, a dead cobra in its mouth. The winner of the snake hunt was the man whose mongoose had killed the largest or the most snakes. These hunts would appear to have been the lower-rank equivalent to the tiger hunts in which officers engaged.

Harry Fox and Stephen Filbey were members of the battalion's band and both were eventually promoted to the rank of sergeant. Stephen had a luxurious moustache, of which he was very proud. One night, presumably after a few drinks, Harry and others cut off half of Stephen's moustache while he was asleep. Furious when he discovered what had happened, Stephen was unable to discover the culprit. To prevent ridicule in the sergeants-mess, he had to shave off the other half of his moustache. Presumably, however, this still did not save him from an unmerciful ribbing. A few months later, Harry was seeing Stephen off at a railway station. As the train pulled out Harry shouted that it was he who had cut his friend's moustache. The train disappeared with Stephen shaking his fist in anger at Harry.

Stephen had a talent for tennis that resulted in his being invited to play with the battalion's officers. When his present-day family first heard of this fact they found it very difficult to believe, because of the strict protocol that officers did not socialise with other ranks. Stephen's grandson Brian Filbey, however, subsequently acquired a photograph showing his grandfather wearing tennis clothes, with officer tennis players, their wives and Indian ball-boys seated in front.

On 29 February 1912, the men of the regimental band participated in a *Programme of Sports* held at South Lines, Ahmednagar. Entries, heats and places were published in a brochure printed after the event. Stephen Filbey and Harry Fox were mentioned several times.

∾

Private James Burke was from Kilkenny City.[5] The seventh of eight children, his mother died when he was nine. His father deserted the family soon afterwards. At the age of ten, James left the family home. Sleeping in a barn near the village of Ballyragget, he was discovered by farmer Sam Thorpe. On hearing his story, Thorpe and his sister Dolly took him to live with them and their housekeeper, Martha Ruddock. A Protestant family, the Thorpes ensured the Roman Catholic Burke attended mass every Sunday. Burke stayed with the Thorpes for four years. He then returned to his family home, to find it deserted and subsequently worked at various jobs, including behind the scenes at a circus.

In late 1908, Burke joined the Special Reserve as a part-time soldier at the Royal Dublin Fusiliers depot at Naas. Presumably he enjoyed the experience because, three months later, in early 1909, he transferred to the regular army, enlisting for a period of seven years with the colours to be followed by five years with the reserve. Posted to the 2nd Battalion Royal Dublin Fusiliers in England, he went absent without leave in February and April 1910, returning voluntarily on both occasions. His absences probably occurred following failure to report to the barracks on time following periods of leave, or possibly followed times spent drinking.

British Army battalions stationed at home would periodically send drafts (i.e. reinforcements) to battalions from the same regiment serving abroad. On 8 August 1910, Burke was posted to the 1st Battalion, which was stationed in India. Led by the battalion band, playing 'The Wearing of the Green', Burke and a draft of about thirty men, marched out the gates of Aldershot Barracks on their way to the railway station. Among the draft was Private Benjamin Hurt. Born in Milford, Derbyshire in 1884, he had worked on a farm as a waggoner and as a collier, before joining the Dubs in Birmingham on 7 June 1909. A week later he was at the regimental depot in Naas, County Kildare. On 29 September 1909, his training completed, he was transferred to the 2nd Battalion in England.[6]

James Burke, Benjamin Hurt and the rest of the Royal Dublin Fusilier draft docked at Bombay on 8 September 1910. From there they boarded a train to Ahmednagar. The train consisted of a series of roofless wagons, akin to horse boxes, pulled by an engine travelling at about 5 miles per hour. The wagons did not have seats and the men sat on the floor, which was strewn with banana skins, orange peel and red spittle, deposited by betel-chewing travellers who had previously been in the wagon. After a week under the blazing sun, the train pulled into Ahmednagar station. The station stood in a jungle, without another building in sight. The ground outside was covered by rice fields. A crowd of Indian men, women and children stood begging in the station with outstretched hands. The soldiers later learned the village of Ahmednagar was further back in the jungle.

The sergeant in charge of the draft lined up the men and addressed them. He said the journey had been hard on them all, but when they left the station, the locals would be watching. He asked the men to straighten up and not to let down 'the old Dubs'. He said the barracks was about a mile away and he did not want to see any man fall out. As the draft emerged from the station they were met by about six *Blue Cap* bandsmen, who had volunteered to play the draft back to the barracks. One of the musicians called out to a friend in the draft, telling him the first ten years were the worst! It was the hottest part of the day and the band played a slow march. The draft set off at a slow pace, all out of step. After they had travelled about half a mile, they lagged about fifty yards behind the band. The band halted until the draft caught up. Soon afterwards the sergeant sank to his knees and passed out. He was put on a bullock-cart which was following the column. Then another man collapsed, then another and yet another. Thinking those who had collapsed were weak, James Burke determined to arrive at the barracks on his own two feet. When the draft arrived at the barracks, however, he was one of those on the bullock-cart. At the barracks the whole of the battalion had turned out to greet the new arrivals. After the men had bathed, they were given a meal of curried stew. As they had never eaten anything like it before they were initially cautious, but soon began to eat with enjoyment.

James Burke, Benjamin Hurt and the rest of the newly arrived men found discipline was not as strict as it had been in England. They had fewer parades and route marches. Those who were not on guard duty could go to bed in the afternoon and sleep until tea-time. They found the afternoon was the best time to sleep, as sleep at night was very difficult. The afternoon heat was dry, whereas at night it was damp. Lizards and mosquitoes came out at night. The lizards ran along the rafters and up and down the straw window-blinds and the mosquitoes buzzed around the nets that surrounded the soldiers' beds, trying to find an opening. Thursday was 'bug-hunting' day. Each man took his bed onto the veranda, held it chest high and let it drop. The moment it hit the ground swarms of red, fat bugs were ejected from the crevices. The soldiers killed the bugs by stamping on them, resulting in an incredible stench.

Soldiers in India had much higher economic and social status among the local population in India than they had in England or Ireland. In India the locals addressed even private soldiers as Sahib, or Sir. They could afford to keep a servant, and most of them did. Burke paid his servant two annas a week, which was equivalent to two pence in English money. The servant cleaned Burke's boots and buttons, made his bed, ran messages, brought him early morning tea in bed and was always on hand in case he was needed. A barber came to the barracks every morning and shaved the men before reville, for which each man gave him a penny (an anna). Soldiers were paid five rupees (5s 10d) per week (roughly equivalent to £25.20 or €30.36). There were 14 annas to the rupee and 12 pye to one anna. A soldier could buy thirty-six cigarettes in the bazaar for one pye. Food was very cheap. Four annas would buy a large plate of curried stew, sago pudding, tea, bread and butter. A pint of beer could be bought for one anna.

Having always been interested in music, James Burke applied to join the battalion band. He was accepted and, following a year's training, he was playing clarinet. He also joined the battalion's dramatic society. Being a good singer, he teamed up with Joe Gallagher, a fellow bandsman and dramatic society member. Gallagher taught him to dance. Burke played the part of a toff and Gallagher that of a tramp. They travelled all over India entertaining troops, putting on shows at hospitals, regimental functions and once appeared at a command performance for the Viceroy of India.

ುುು

There were a number of skilled footballers among the battalion's band and drummers. A photograph taken at Ahmednagar in 1913 shows the Band and Drum team that won the 1st Battalion Inter-Company Football League in the 1912-1913 season. Included in the photo are Lance-Corporal Samuel Clough, Lance-Corporal Michael Ludford, Private Richard Richards and Bandsman Harry Whitham. Clough, from Cheshire and Richards, from Shropshire appear to have joined up at the same time, in 1905, as they both enlisted in Lichfield and were given sequential regimental numbers. Clough was the first-cornet soloist in the battalion band. Like Stephen Filbey and Harry Fox, he appears to have been the

Lance-Corporal Edward Nugent.

child of a single mother. He attended a certified industrial school – 'for destitute and neglected children requiring education.'[7]

Ludford joined the battalion in the same year as Clough and Richards, though he enlisted in Stratford. Born in Cottage Place, Lambeth in 1889 to Irish parents, like Clough, he had attained the rank of Lance-Corporal.[8] Bandsman Harry Whitham was from Mile End, Middlesex. Apparently the best footballer of the quartet, he was also a member of the battalion football team. With two exceptions, those in the photograph taken at Ahmednagar were dressed as footballers. The exceptions are Band-Sergeant Harry Fox and lance-corporal Edward Nugent, who appear in army uniform. It seems likely that Fox was the team manager and Nugent assistant-manager. Edward Nugent was born in Leigh, Lancashire. Following the death or desertion of his father, Edward and his older sister Mary ended up in the workhouse at Atherton. His enlistment as a drummer with the Royal Dublin Fusiliers presumably was his key to escape from the workhouse. Though Private Benjamin Hurt, who had arrived in the draft with James Burke, was an accomplished footballer, no record has yet been found of any of the battalion teams he played for during this period. It seems likely, however, in the light of his subsequent army footballing record, that he was on one of the 1st Battalion Inter-Company Football League teams beaten by the Band and Drum Team in the 1912–1913 season.[9]

Fort St George, Madras, 1913

In 1913, the battalion was moved to the city of Madras, on the east coast. Madras was the city where the battalion had originally been established as part of the East India Company Army. The climate was cooler than it had been at Ahmednagar and thousands of Europeans of various nationalities lived in the city. James Burke and Joe Gallagher were in great demand at the big house parties, garden parties and other social events. They also played with the battalion band on the marina every Sunday afternoon.

Also in the band, one of the battalion's sixteen drummers, was Private Samuel (Sam) Mallaghan. Sam's younger brother John (Jack) was stationed at an outpost at Bellary. Sam and Jack Mallaghan were a long way from their family home in Newry, County Down. The house, on Stream Street, is part of a terrace on one side of a narrow street. Facing the house is an open field where Sam and Jack had played boyhood games just a few short years before. St Patrick's church, where the family worshipped, overshadows the field and the row of terraced houses. The first Church of Ireland to be built in Ireland, it earned fame of sorts when Jonathan Swift penned a short ditty mentioning it. 'High church, low steeple. Dirty streets and proud people.' Still living in the Mallaghan family home were the boys' older sister Minnie, younger sister Ethel, mother Annie and father John.

Sam and Jack had joined up together. Their lives had changed completely since they had walked the short distance from their home to the Linen Hall Barracks, entered the archway and taken the King's shilling. Assigned to the 2nd Battalion Royal Dublin Fusiliers in England, Sam had been given the regimental number 10732 and Jack 10733. Like James Burke, the Mallaghan brothers had been sent to India as part of a draft. In 1913 or early 1914 Sam sent an undated letter to his parents in Newry, County Down.[10]

Sam Mallaghan.

Reg No. 10732
Pte. S. Mallaghan
1st Bn RD Fus
Drums
Kings Barracks
Madras
India

Dear Father and Mother,

Just a few lines to let you know I am well, as I hope it leaves you all the same. I was a long time in answering your last letter but I hadn't got time as I was [next word is word illegible. Looks like 'having'] my course. It is terrible hot here at present. It goes up to 102 in the shade but the place where Jack is it is a 115. I suppose you wonder why he was shifted from me. Well I will tell you. One bugler a company was sent to Bellary to do duty. Four companies was sent also. So he is in a different Coy [Company]. He is in E Coy [E Company]. Well we were sent to Madras on account of it being a swanky place. It is a town. So the drums is in Madras. This is where the regiment was formed. I go to church every Sunday night and I am on the tack. My chum Albert Bowsher put me on it. He is a Church of England to[o]. He is a nice we[e] fellow. He says to me every week come on Sammy give me your pay and I will keep it in my [next word is illegible. Looks 'bop.'] and you wont go to the canteen then and if I ask for a pint he says no. He is the same age as me. He was born in the same year, same date. He is always looking at Ethel on the wall and saying roll on till she grows up big. He took the photo and I took it back of[f] him again. Me and him goes home together. I am going to bring him to Newry for a while. Tell Minnie to send him a postcard. How is my father getting on in his new job. Owl [old] Wilson must have been a stingy old Devil. Never gave him a pice. Don't forget the we[e] bit of tobbacco. I am nearly pegging out smoking the stuff here. And here, Minnie should be glad now – I have got her a boy. How is Willie and Ethel getting on and Herbert are they well. I think I will close this letter now for I cant say any more at present. Don't forget the we[e] bit of tobbacco.

This is Jack's address Reg No 10741, Pte. J. Mallaghan, E Coy, Plassey Bks, Bellary, India.

This is Albert's address Reg No 10190 Dr. Albert Bowsher, Drums, 1st RD Fus, Kings Bks, Madras, India. Tell Minnie not to forget the p.c. and he will send her a present. Goodbye write soon. Don't forget the tobbacco.

The letter was unsigned.

ॐ

Twenty-seven-year-old Lance-Corporal Nicholas (Nicky) Smyth came from a family of nine children in rural County Meath. Like the Mallaghans and several others in the battalion, he appears to have joined the army to escape the grind of working as an agricultural labourer. Initially serving with the 2nd Battalion in England, he had subsequently been sent to India. His brother Christopher (Christy) had followed him into the Dubs and was now serving with their 2nd Battalion in England. Interestingly, the 1911 census form for the Smyth family home recorded Nicky's maternal grandfather, John Mitchell, living with the family. At eighty-seven years old, he was still working, with his occupation given as an agricultural labourer. Mitchell had served with the 41st Foot (later the Welsh Regiment) and fought in the Crimean War at Alma, Inkerman and Sevastopol. Presumably having escaped the life of an agricultural labourer by joining the army, his post-army life had condemned him to returning to this work.

ॐ

Milton Barracks, Gravesend, Kent, May 1914

Forty-eight-year-old Major Richard Rooth was serving with the 2nd Battalion Royal Dublin Fusiliers. Gazetted into the Dubs as a Second Lieutenant at the age of nineteen, he had spent all his adult life with the regiment, serving in both battalions. During the early 1890s he had been attached to the regimental depot in Naas, County Kildare. Promoted to captain in 1894, he spent a period as adjutant of the 2nd Battalion. This was an experience he enjoyed and which he subsequently repeated on detached duty as adjutant of the Poona Volunteers from 1897 to 1902. He returned to the Dublins in 1903, in time to serve in the Aden campaign with the 2nd Battalion. In November 1903, the 2nd Battalion returned to Ireland, where it was stationed at Buttevant, County Cork. Promoted to major in 1906, Rooth commanded the regimental depot in Naas, County Kildare from 1907 to 1910, following which he rejoined the 2nd Battalion. Born in London, he was the son of a barrister who had been born in Wales, and the grandson of a landowner who had been born in Ireland. Educated at Highgate School and in France, he subsequently attended the Royal Military College at Sandhurst. In 1895 he married Amy Mary Cann of Dawlish, Devon, daughter of a surgeon. They had two children, Richard and Nancy.[11] As the second highest-ranking officer in the 2nd Battalion, Rooth had taken command of the battalion during Lieutenant-Colonel Arthur Mainwaring's honeymoon in June 1912. Now his hour had come. Lieutenant-Colonel Downing,

Blue Cap Commanding officer
Lieutenant-Colonel Richard Rooth.

commanding officer of the 1st Battalion, was about to retire. Rooth, as the senior major in the regiment, was appointed to take over his command. On 13 May 1914, he left Milton Barracks with Captain William Higginson.[12]

While sailing from London, Rooth received a message telling him to ask the captain of the ship to slow down off Gravesend. A tender put out from Gravesend containing every officer, N.C.O. and man from the 2nd Battalion who could find standing room on the vessel. The regimental band played as the tender steamed alongside the ship, finishing up with *Auld Lang Syne*. It is nice to think Rooth and Higginson would have been happy as the battalion bid them farewell. Both men had less than a year to live.

ന്ദ

Fort St George, Madras, July 1914

Lieutenant James Grove from Letterkenny, County Donegal was stationed at the fort, but in a different capacity to his fellow officers. Assigned as aide-de-camp to the Governor of Madras, he was, however, still in contact with his battalion. On 24 April 1914 he wrote to his mother (Lucy Georgina Grove, who had been born in India) at Castle Grove, Letterkenny, County Donegal.

My dearest mother, This is only a short note. I have at last finished my exam I'm
glad to say and the only thing to do now is to wait for about 3 months for the
result. I'm off to [next word is illegible. Looks like 'duty'] tonight and am fairly
busy packing etc. So I won't write any more. In case there is no news. I have
been doing nothing except exam for the last week and am heartily sick of it.
However I think I ought to have passed all right. Although of course one never
can tell. Love to you and Monsieur, Your affec son, James R. W. Grove. [13]

Written examination regulated promotion from lieutenant to captain and
from captain to major. Promotion to lieutenant-colonel was by practical
examination in tactics.

ممم

Like his older brothers, Ewing and Herbert, and his younger brother Roly,
Dubliner Cecil Grimshaw had served part-time in the 5th Battalion Royal
Dublin Fusiliers (Dublin County Militia), a reserve battalion.[14] He and his
eldest brother, Ewing, subsequently went on to serve with the 1st Battalion.
Captured by the Boers near Talana Hill on 19 October 1899, Cecil was
brought to a prison camp at the Staats Model School in Pretoria. One of his
fellow prisoners was War Correspondent Winston Churchill. In his book
London to Ladysmith via Pretoria Churchill says: 'A very energetic and clever
young officer of the Dublin Fusiliers, Lieutenant Grimshaw, undertook the
task of managing the mess …' Grimshaw, however, in his own diary made
critical comments about Churchill's subsequent escape from the camp.[15]
Grimshaw and two other officers later made an unsuccessful escape attempt.
In January 1900, while he was still in the prison camp, Grimshaw's father
Thomas died in Dublin.[16] In June, the British captured Pretoria and the
prisoners were released. According to the diary of fellow prisoner Captain
Malcolm Lonsdale, 2nd Battalion Royal Dublin Fusiliers:

At about nine o'clock two men, who turned out to be the Duke of
Marlborough and young Churchill, galloped up to us.[17] Then we cheered
and shouted ourselves hoarse. We rushed out of the enclosure (both
Churchill and Grimshaw said the prisoners overpowered the camp guards)
and Grimshaw of the Dublin Fusiliers, climbed up the flag-staff with the
Union Jack in his mouth and fastened it to the top. This Union Jack had
been kept by us all the months of our imprisonment, having been manufactured out of a Transvaal flag, which had been cut up for the purpose.[18]

Grimshaw was twice mentioned in despatches and was awarded the Distinguished Service Order (DSO). He subsequently served in the Aden campaign with the 2nd Battalion (1903) and returned to Ireland with the battalion in November 1903. The following month he crossed to England where, on 18 December at Buckingham Palace, he was among a group of officers presented with the DSO by King Edward VII. On 30 April 1904, 100 men and the 2nd Battalion band, under the command of Captain Mainwaring, Lieutenant Grimshaw DSO and Lieutenant Haskard, formed a guard of honour at Lismore railway station, County Waterford to receive King Edward VII and Queen Alexandra who were visiting the Duke and Duchess of Devonshire at Lismore Castle. The band played at the castle every day during dinner and a guard of honour was mounted at the station when the King and Queen departed on 4 May. The year continued to be eventful for Cecil Grimshaw, with his promotion to captain and transfer to the 1st Battalion in Malta. In 1905, he moved with the battalion to Alexandria, Egypt, where the officers of the Blue Caps played an important part in the social life of the British community.

In Alexandria, Cecil Grimshaw became attracted to Agnes Violet Alderson, from a socially prominent expatriate family. Known to her family as Violet, she was not short of male admirers. Both she and Cecil were keen horse riders.

Relief of Pretoria Prison Camp. Cecil Grimshaw climbs the flagstaff on left.

During the year, Cecil received orders assigning him to duty at the regimental depot in Naas. He sent word to Violet, asking if he could call on her. She sent him a note on paper with her initials embossed, giving her consent. He came, told her he loved her and asked her father for her hand. Having received her father's consent, Violet went to the ship to see Cecil off. He put an engagement ring on her finger aboard ship. The couple were married on 3 October 1906 at St Mary Abbot's Church, Kensington. The wedding went ahead despite the fact that Violet's mother had died the previous week: Cecil's difficulties in getting leave and other family considerations being the deciding factors. They left for Ireland soon after the wedding, as Cecil had to return to duty at the regimental depot.

The first years of married life were difficult for Violet. While she enjoyed hunting and horse riding, she found it difficult to acclimatise to the cold and damp of Ireland, having lived all of her previous life in Egypt. Following an upbringing where she could have anything she wanted, she and Cecil now had to live on a captain's pay. The birth of their son Tommy, in 1907, curtailed her horse riding and limited her social life. But as Cecil's family lived in Carrickmines, County Dublin, and he had relatives in Belfast, the Grimshaws were not lacking in family contact. Circumstances changed yet again when Cecil was posted to the 1st Battalion at Ahmednagar, near Poona in India. Violet and Tommy accompanied him. The family was provided with a bungalow at Ahmednagar and a household of Indian servants. Violet was able to take up horse riding again and the Grimshaws had an active social life that included dinner parties, bridge parties and the meeting of wives for afternoon tea. In September 1910, George, the Grimshaws' second son, was born. The following year, Cecil was made battalion adjutant and was present at the Delhi Durbar when George V was enthroned as Emperor of India.[19]

The two Grimshaw boys were cared for by Rosie O'Neill, a uniformed Irish nanny. As he possibly feared losing her as nanny, Cecil Grimshaw did not approve of Rosie O'Neill's courtship with the battalion's Sergeant-Major Arthur Duffy, a Boer War veteran. He was, however, unable to prevent their engagement and subsequent marriage in Ireland. Following the marriage, Duffy appears to have transferred to the Dublins 2nd Battalion and the couple settled in England.[20]

അ

On 28 June 1914, the heir to the Austrian throne, Archduke Franz Ferdinand and his wife Sophie were assassinated during a visit to the Bosnian capital

Sarajevo. In the weeks following the assassinations, European politicians made a series of decisions that plunged the major powers into global warfare. On 3 August, Germany declared war on France. As a stepping-stone to striking at France from the north, Germany invaded Belgium on 4 August. Supporting Belgian neutrality, Britain declared war on Germany at 11 p.m. (Greenwich Mean Time) that night. The British Cabinet held its first Council of War on Wednesday 5 August. The following afternoon, it authorised the dispatch of four infantry divisions and a cavalry division to France. More troops would follow as soon as they became available.

On 1 August 1914, the British Army's active strength was 247,798. Just over 46 per cent were serving overseas and were not immediately available to join the force going to the continent. Excluding nine battalions of Foot Guards traditionally based at home, exactly half of the 148 Regular infantry battalions were abroad, as were twelve out of the thirty-one cavalry regiments. By far the greater part of those abroad were stationed in India, with fifty-one infantry battalions and nine cavalry regiments being stationed there.[21] Orders went to all parts of the British Empire calling most of the troops home. They were replaced with Territorial units.[22] Britain's declaration of war in 1914 automatically meant her colonies were also at war. Australia, New Zealand and Canada sent troops to assist the motherland.

ನನ

French mobilisation plans required the transportation of the XIX Corps from their Algerian colony, in North Africa, to France. In an attempt to disrupt these plans, on Tuesday 4 August 1914, the German battle-cruiser *Goeben* shelled the Algerian port of Philippeville, while the light-cruiser *Breslau* shelled the port of Bône. Then, under orders from Berlin, the ships, commanded by Rear-Admiral Wilhelm Souchon, began to make their way towards Constantinople in neutral Turkey. Britain did not declare war on Germany until the night of 4 August and the Royal Navy subsequently failed in its attempts to prevent the German ships reaching Turkey.[23]

ನನ

At 5 a.m. on 10 August 1914, the *Goeben* and *Breslau* arrived at the entrance to the Dardanelles, the narrow channel that led, by way of the Sea of Marmara, to Constantinople. The *Goeben* hoisted a flag requesting a pilot. A Turkish torpedo boat emerged from the Dardanelles and guided the German ships through. On their port (left) side as the ships passed the entrance to the Dardanelles was a small beach overlooked by an old fort and a village. Just over eight months later many soldiers who were now based in India would lose their lives on the beach, in the fort, and in the ruins of the village of Sedd el Bahr.

As Turkey was neutral, international law stipulated the German ships should be detained. The day after the ships arrived, however, Turkish sources falsely announced they had been bought by the Ottoman government. The *Goeben* was renamed the *Yavuz Sultan Selim* and the *Breslau* renamed the *Midilli*. According to American Ambassador, Henry Morgenthau, 'The German officers and crews greatly enjoyed this farcical pretence that the *Goeben* and the *Breslau* were Turkish ships. They took particular delight in dressing themselves up in Turkish uniforms and Turkish fezzes.' Rear-Admiral Souchon was appointed Commander-in-Chief of the Turkish navy. Meanwhile, British ships of the Eastern Mediterranean Fleet on station outside the Dardanelles were ordered not to take hostile action against Turkey, but to prevent the *Goeben* and *Breslau* leaving the Dardanelles.

ନ୍ଧ

Eleutherios Venizelos had been prime minister of Greece since 1910. He believed Ottoman territories inhabited by ethnic Greeks should be ruled by Greece. With the assistance of Britain and France, Venizelos modernised the Greek armed forces. He also assisted in the creation of the Balkan League, which defeated the Ottomans in the First Balkan War 1912-1913. As a result of this, and the Second Balkan War (against Bulgaria), Greece doubled her territory. Many ethnic Greeks, however, continued to live in Ottoman territory and Venizelos believed Greek support of the Allied cause would bring them under his country's rule. His plans were strongly opposed by Greek King Constantine I who, having married Princess Sophia of Prussia, was brother-in-law to the Kaiser. Constantine's opposition, together with concerns that Bulgaria might attack Greece if the latter was engaged in fighting Turkey, prevented Greece coming into the war on the Allied side until 29 June 1917. In the meantime, however, the country had a significant influence on the Gallipoli campaign.

ନ୍ଧ

On the outbreak of war with Germany A, B, F, G and H Companies and battalion headquarters of the 1st Battalion Royal Dublin Fusiliers were stationed at Fort St George, Madras. C, D and E Companies were at Bellary under the command of Captain Edward Molesworth. On 1 August 1914, in line with Special Army Order 26 of September 1913, the battalion's eight companies were reformed into four larger companies: A, B, C and D. According to *Neill's Blue Caps*, 'There being a considerable number of Germans and Austrians resident in the city of Madras, the duties became at once more than usually heavy owing to the necessity which arose for safeguarding the water-supply, the oil tanks, and all the public buildings and telephones ...' Jack Mallaghan and the men of E Company were recalled from Bellary, arriving in Madras on 9 August. Apart from extra guard duty, the outbreak of war had little effect on the life of the battalion. On 11 August, it was announced Lucknow Week would be postponed until further notice.[24] On 25 August, an order was published that 'certain German and Austrian subjects will shortly be interned in the new Supper Room, Fort St. George, pending their despatch to Ahmednagar.' The order said they were to be treated with 'as much consideration as orders on the subject allow, and soldiers should avoid doing anything to aggravate their unfortunate position'.

On the night of 22 September 1914, the war suddenly arrived on the Dublins doorstep. At about 9.30 p.m. Madras harbour came under bombardment from the German cruiser SMS *Emden*. According to the *Madras Mail* of 23 September:

The German cruiser *Emden*, which has been creating such havoc among the merchant shipping at the mouth of the Hooghy and on the Burma coast, is still at large in the Bay of Bengal, as the citizens of Madras now know to their cost, for she visited Madras between 9 and 10 o'clock last night, accompanied by [her collier] the *Markomania*, stood in the offing to the south east of the harbour within range of the beach, and proceed to bombard the port ... Subsequent shots set the [Burmah Company's] petroleum tanks on fire. The oil in the tanks immediately blazed up, rending the sea face of the town as brilliant as day, aided probably by the short cannonade that took place; but this was hardly necessary, as the *Emden* was using a particularly brilliant searchlight, under which every detail of the sea face was visible. That the visit was altogether unexpected may be judged from the fact that the lighthouse was working as usual, and undoubtedly helped the cruiser to take up its bearings and fire with the accuracy with which it did ... The call was paid early enough to find the shore lights all ablaze, the trams working, and all the business of the town at that time of the night going on as usual. As far as we can make out from personal observation, and from information received, she fired the guns of both broadsides before she extinguished her searchlight, in response, we believe, to return fire from the shore, and vanished silently in the darkness with all her lights extinguished.

A few shots fell on the town. Some hit the British India steamer SS *Chupra*. Apart from the material damage done to the city, five people were killed and about a dozen wounded. The attack 'had an injurious effect on public opinion in India'.[25]

That night James Burke and Joe Gallagher had returned to barracks after doing a show in Madras. As Burke prepared for bed the barracks was shaken by three explosions in quick succession. His room mates jumped out of bed in their underwear and grabbed their rifles. They thought they were under attack by Indian nationalists. A bugler sounded the fall in and the battalion was soon on parade. The Dublins occupied defensive positions all night. By this time, it was realised the Germans had shelled Madras and it was feared they might invade. Over the next month parades were held several times a day and extra guards were posted on the magazine where ammunition was stored. There were parades for inoculation and parades to hear the King's Regulations in time of war.

 app

On 26 September, British ships at the entrance to the Dardanelles turned back a Turkish torpedo boat. The following day, Turkey closed the Dardanelles to international shipping.

app

In early October 1914, in his parish in Yorkshire, Roman Catholic priest Father William Finn received a letter from his bishop:

St George's
York.
11 Oct. '14

My Dear Fr Finn,

Apropos of your 'ambition' to go to the front as chaplain, I am willing to re-consider my decision on one condition and one condition only. Namely that when the war is over and for one reason or another you cease to be chaplain to the troops *tempore belli*, that you at once report yourself to me or the Bishop in your own Diocese; and that you will not use this leave of absence as a means of seeking release from your own Diocese.

If you will write across this letter your acceptance of this condition in its plain and obvious sense and return it to me, I will give you leave of absence.

With a blessing
Yours Always
Bishop Lacy

Father Finn wrote across the letter, 'I agree to the condition in its plain and obvious sense. William Finn.'

∞

There were strong rumours among the Blue Caps that they would be sent to France. As they awaited orders, they suffered the inevitable deaths of troops stationed in a tropical country. In October Privates Edward Heffernan and Edward Coughlan died and were buried in Madras.[26] On 31 October, battalion orders contained the names of sixty-five NCOs and men who, for reasons of ill health or employment on important duties, were not to go with the battalion to England. When the time for departure came, however, some of the sick were found to be fit to travel.

∞

On 27 October 1914, on the orders of Turkish Minister for War, Enver Pasha, the *Goeben* and *Breslau* left Constantinople and sailed into the Black Sea accompanied by Turkish ships. Navy Commander-in-Chief Rear-Admiral Wilhelm Souchon was under secret orders to provoke a war with Russia. The fleet split into four task forces and shelled Odessa, Sebastopol, Theodosia and Novorossiysk. All of the Turkish and German ships returned to port safely.

Although Russia did not actually declare war on Turkey until 2 November, her army crossed the eastern Turkish frontier the previous day. By the end of November the Turkish Army managed to stabilise the position, though the Russians still held Turkish territory. Meanwhile, on 31 October, despite the fact that Britain had yet to make a declaration of war, Winston Churchill sent an order to all Royal Navy ships in the Mediterranean: 'Commence hostilities at once against Turkey.' Though Turkey had declared war on them on

31 October, Britain and France still had not declared war on Turkey when, on 3 November British and French ships shelled forts at the entrance to the Dardanelles. A shell from one of the British ships hit a magazine at Sedd el Bahr causing a massive explosion. Never in subsequent bombardments of the Gallipoli peninsula were Allied ships to cause so much damage. Britain declared war on Turkey on 5 November.

ᖇᖇ

On 5 November 1914, Father William Finn was appointed Army Chaplain 4th Class, equivalent to the rank of captain.

ᖇᖇ

On 12 November, battalion orders for the 1st Dublins contained the long-awaited announcement:

Orders have been received for the Battalion to embark for passage to England. The Battalion will parade at 4 p.m. tomorrow to march to the rail-way station. Dress — Marching Order. Officers to carry the colours (cased)

Lieutenant (Lawrence) Bousted and Second-Lieutenant (Reginald) Corbet.[27] The battalion will entrain in two trains: 1st Train — Headquarters, Band, A, B, and E Companies. 2nd Train — F, G and H Companies.[28]

On the afternoon of Friday 13 November, the 1st Royal Dublin Fusiliers marched out of Fort St George for the last time. Madras was the city of the battalion's birth. Many times in its history the battalion had marched forth to fight on behalf of the East India Company and the British Empire. Now it was going to fight in a war from which few of the battalion would return. Shortly after the war's end, the regiment would cease to exist.

Cecil Grimshaw.

The Dubs left on two trains for Bombay. Among the battalion's officers were Captains Cecil Grimshaw DSO and James Grove – the latter had passed the promotion examination he had sat in April and been promoted on 2 September. Among the ranks were the two friends and former residents of the Foundling Hospital, Sergeants Harry Fox and Stephen Filbey; performers James Burke and Joe Gallagher; brothers Sam and Jack Mallaghan; Sam's friend Albert Bowsher; Nicky Smyth from Meath; Benjamin Hurt, who had travelled to India in the same draft as James Burke; and the quartet of football-playing musicians Samuel Clough, Michael Ludford, Richard Richards and Harry Whitham. Missing from the battalion were Captain Denis Anderson and a party of one sergeant and four privates who had left for Bombay to meet the 4th Battalion Somerset Light Infantry – a territorial battalion that was replacing the Blue Caps – and escort it to Madras. Pending their arrival, garrison duties at Fort St George were taken over by the Madras Volunteer Guards.

ဢ

On 19 November, the battalion left Bombay. Lieutenant-Colonel Richard Rooth, battalion headquarters and six companies sailed on the British India steamship, *Malda*'[29] while second-in-command Major Edwyn Fetherstonhaugh[30] embarked on the P. & O. steamer *Assaye*[31] with A and B companies. The ships formed part of a convoy escorted by the French cruiser, *Dupleix*. Two days later, they were joined by seven ships from Karachi, making up a fleet of thirty-two ships in all. Aboard ship the men played games to pass the time. James Burke and Joe Gallagher organised concerts to entertain the officers and men. In his memoirs, Burke said that the soldiers did not know their destination.

ဢ

Cabinet Room, 10 Downing Street, 25 November 1914

The defence of Egypt was among the issues discussed at the first meeting of the recently established War Council. As Egypt was considered vulnerable to attack from Ottoman territory, First Lord of the Admiralty, Winston Churchill said the best way to defend the country was to make an attack on the Turkish coast. He suggested an attack on the Gallipoli peninsula that, if successful, would give control of the Dardanelles to the Allies and put them in a position to dictate terms to the Turks. He said it would be a difficult operation, requiring a large force. Secretary of State for War, Lord Herbert Kitchener agreed it might be necessary to make a diversionary attack on Turkey but felt it was not yet time to do so. The idea of an attack on Gallipoli was not further progressed.

ฌ฿ฌ

On Thursday 26 November, Corporal Mark Adams of the Royal Dublin Fusiliers died aboard the *Malda* and was buried at sea.[32] On Wednesday 9 December, football enthusiast Private Benjamin Hurt was promoted to Lance-Corporal. At Suez those aboard the convoy ships learned of the sinking of the German cruiser *Emden*. While at the port, one of the Blue Caps officers received a visit from his brother. Captain Cecil Grimshaw's older brother Ewing – who had previously served in the 1st Dublins – was now commanding the 62nd Punjab Regiment stationed at the Suez Canal. Ewing mentioned the visit in a postcard and letter sent to his wife Geraldine in Dublin. Both dated 15 December 1914, the postcard said: 'Wrote to you to-day … Saw Cecil and the R.D.F. on their way through.' According to the letter: 'Yesterday several transports passed through and stopped here, most unusual except to pick up or put down a pilot. I went on board and saw Cecil and the old Regiment: only three that I knew: [Lieutenant-Colonel Richard] Rooth, [Major Edwyn] Fetherstonhaugh and Cecil.'

The convoy crossed the Mediterranean and sailed into the Atlantic. On Wednesday 21 December, the Dubs docked at Plymouth and disembarked that night. James Burke said that the soldiers were surprised and delighted to learn that they were in England, as they thought they were in France. A train waited at the docks. Burke and his fellow Dubs boarded. A whistle sounded and the train set off into the night, its destination unknown to the men. At two o'clock in the morning the train pulled into a darkened station and the men were paraded on the platform. Burke asked a guard the name of the place. 'Yer in Torquay now, mate,' he answered. The Blue Caps were billeted in Torquay. A local newspaper reported: 'They still wear their Indian uniform and pith helmets, with small green cockades at the side.' The paper said notification of the Dublins arrival had only been received late on Monday afternoon. As Torquay did not have a military barracks, Inspector Rees of the Torquay Police was assigned to secure billets in private homes. According to *Remembrance,* by Patrick Hogarty, 'By 10.30 p.m. 500 billets had been secured. On Tuesday morning the remaining necessary accommodation was obtained. The requirements of the Military Authorities were announced at the picture houses, and applications came in with remarkable promptitude.' The Dubs arrived in two parties on Wednesday night. The following morning the battalion assembled on the Strand and marched to the Recreation Ground for parade. Lieutenant-Colonel Richard addressed the men. He asked them to behave themselves during their stay in Torquay and to show that, despite their reputation to the contrary, Irishmen were capable of behaving well, as well as fighting well. The battalion band, comprised of almost sixty men, was billeted in the Belgrave district of Torquay. James Burke said that he and several others were billeted with people who owned a butcher's shop and who had stayed up until three o'clock in the morning to welcome them. After a hot bath, the soldiers were given a meal and plenty of cigarettes. They then went to bed 'with white sheets, eiderdown, and, would you believe it? – a hot-water bottle.'

Remembrance by Patrick Hogarty quoted local papers as reporting, 'The men are being allowed to proceed home to Ireland and elsewhere for four or five days' furlough. The first batch, about 200 in number, left on Monday, and others departed yesterday.' Present-day relatives of the Mallaghan family believe that Sam and Jack did not get home on leave to Newry. Relatives of Nicky Smyth also believe he did not get home on leave to County Meath.[33] Hopefully the recently promoted Lance-Corporal Benjamin Hurt had the opportunity to visit his widowed mother, Mary, in Milford, Derbyshire. Band-Sergeant Harry Fox had maintained contact with his foster family. It seems likely that he visited the family at some point during the battalion's time in England, as Charlotte Clarke gave him a prayer book inscribed, 'To my darling son Harry from his ever loving mother Lottie. With God's blessing for protection always. 1915.' His pal, Stephen Filbey, was not so fortunate. His foster parents, the Underwoods, had been in their early sixties when they had fostered him during the 1880s. George Underwood had died, aged seventy-six, in 1899 and Ellen Underwood, aged seventy-seven, in 1901. It appears Stephen may have kept in contact with the Underwoods daughter Ellen Stevens. Unlike his pal Harry Fox, he did not have a home to visit on his return to England.[34]

∞

On 19 November 1914, it had been decided that Australian and New Zealand troops, on their way to England, would be landed in Egypt to complete their training. By 15 December, the disembarkation was complete. On 22 December, the Turkish Third Army began an attack designed to drive the Russians from their Eastern borders and cross into Russian territory in the Caucasus. Despite initial success, the Turks suffered a major defeat at Sarikamiş and by 7 January 1915 were in full retreat.

જાજ

In early 1915, General Sir John French, the British commander in France and Flanders, sent an appraisal to Secretary of State for War, Lord Herbert Kitchener. He said that a decisive result could not be achieved in France or Belgium. Ultimate victory could only be attained in the east, on the Russian Front. On the other hand, he said that if the French suffered defeat the consequences would be disastrous. Therefore he said that no troops should be moved from France or Belgium.

CHAPTER 2

England:
Coming Home to Blighty

*'Some 73 infantry battalions were garrisoning the Empire,
of which 35 were in India. Their soldiers, having fulfilled two years home
service, were part of their way through their five year stint overseas and
represented the most experienced and fittest soldiers in the Army.'*
The Story Behind the Monument,
Chris Holland and Tony Jordan

Present-day relatives do not believe the Mallaghan brothers had an opportunity to visit their family home on Stream Street, Newry, County Down. It seems that Annie and John Mallaghan did not get to meet their two older sons following their return from India. Sam did not get a chance to tease his older sister Minnie about his friend Albert Bowsher. Nor did young Ethel have the opportunity to be enthralled by her brothers' stories of faraway exotic places. But the official letter received shortly before Christmas may have been a minor compensation for the fact that Sam and Jack did not make it home. Stamped 'Privy Purse Office, Buckingham Palace', the letter was dated 15 December 1914 and addressed to 'Mr John Mallaghan'.

Sir, I have the honour to inform you that The King has heard with much interest that you have at the present moment four sons in the army. I am commanded to express to you The King's congratulations and to assure you that His Majesty much appreciates the spirit of patriotism which prompted this example, in one family, of loyalty and devotion to their Sovereign and Empire. I have the honour to be, Sir, Your obedient Servant, [Signature illegible], Keeper of the Privy Purse.

The letter was prompted by the fact that Sam and Jack's younger brothers Herbert (Herbie) and William (Willie) were also regular soldiers, serving with the Royal Irish Fusiliers.[1] It must have been a source of justifiable pride to John and Annie Mallaghan, both of whom had signed the Ulster Covenant in 1912, pledging with 471,412 others 'to defeat the present conspiracy to set up a Home Rule Parliament in Ireland.' While understanding John Mallaghan's paternal pride in the letter from Buckingham Palace, one might wonder how he, a gardener who had spent all of his life working in the vicinity of his birthplace, viewed his sons' occupation. The boys had travelled to exotic places and seen sights he would never see, nor could possibly have imagined.

ന്മ

On 2 January 1915, the British Government received a telegram from its ambassador to Russia. The telegram said the Russian army was coming under intense Turkish pressure in the Caucasus and expressed the hope, on behalf of the Russian Government, that a demonstration would be made against the Turks in some other quarter. The following day, a reply was sent to the ambassador, asking him to assure the Russian Government that a demonstration would be made. As has already been shown, the situation reported by the British Ambassador was soon overtaken by events. Five days later, the Turkish Third Army was in full retreat, having suffered a disastrous defeat at Sarikamiş on its eastern frontier.

On 3 January 1915, the same day that a reply was sent to the British Ambassador in Russia, Winston Churchill sent a message to County Tipperary-born Vice-Admiral Sackville Carden, commanding the Eastern Mediterranean Squadron, asking whether he considered it would be possible for his fleet to force their way through the Dardanelles. Carden's reply arrived on 5 January. 'I do not consider Dardanelles can be rushed. They might be forced by extended operations with large number of ships.'

ന്മ

James Burke said that the stay in Torquay consisted of 'one round of parties; we were invited to private houses, and to hotels where parties had been arranged for us. Joe Gallagher and I had been engaged for a week at the theatre and the people loved the Irish songs and dancing.' He said that Gallagher got engaged to three different girls while there, while Burke himself 'proposed to several and was accepted'. He said that nearly every man in the battalion was engaged before they left. He was aware of one man who survived the war, went back to Torquay and married.[2]

At a meeting of Torquay Town Council on 5 January 1915, Mayor Charles Thomas Towell reported that the Royal Dublin Fusiliers would shortly leave the town. Usually when a battalion went to war, its colours were stored in a cathedral or prominent building associated with the battalion. Lieutenant-Colonel Rooth had asked Mayor Towell if the town would take charge of the battalion's colours until it returned from the war. The mayor said this would be a very great honour, as Torquay was not a military town. Rain was falling the following day as, shortly before noon, 100 officers and men from the 1st Royal Dublin Fusiliers, led by the battalion band, marched to Torquay town hall under the command of Lieutenant-Colonel Richard Rooth and Major Edwyn Fetherstonhaugh. On reaching the town hall, the men formed a guard of honour under the command of Temporary Major Edward Molesworth, with the regimental colour carried by Lieutenant Henry Desmond O'Hara and the King's colour by Lieutenant George Dunlop. O'Hara was the only son of W.J. O'Hara, Resident Magistrate, Oriel House, Ballincollig, County Cork. He had been commissioned in the regiment in September 1912.[3] George Dunlop was the youngest son of the late Archbishop Dr Archibald Dunlop of Holywood, County Down.[4] His older brother, John, had been the first Royal Dublin Fusiliers' officer to be killed in action during the war.[5]

A large crowd watched as the contingent was greeted by Mayor Towell and many dignitaries. Among the invited guests were Lieutenant-Colonel Holmes, former commanding officer of the 2nd Royal Dublin Fusiliers, Dr Dunlop, Borough Medical Officer of Health, a cousin of Lieutenant George Dunlop and W.J. Labett, a Crimean War veteran wearing his medals. Standing in front of the colours, Lieutenant-Colonel Rooth addressed the mayor:

> As we are proceeding shortly to the front, I will ask you to take care of these colours. We are, as you know, an Irish Battalion, and we are far from home. In fact, I may say we are a long way from Tipperary [Laughter]. But I cannot conceive of a better home for these colours than this county of fair women and brave men. [Rooth's wife Amy was a native of Devon.] When I tell you that these colours, or rather the colours of which these are descendants, have been at the head of the regiment for 250 years, you will understand that they constitute one of our proudest possessions. [Applause.] On the regimental colours are recorded some of the battles in which we have fought, and if you study them carefully, you will find that

they are the history of India. Some day, I hope, some of us will come back to Torquay and reclaim these colours at your hands, and then we hope that we shall have fresh honours to add to them. [Loud Cheers.]

Handing over the colours in Torquay.

The mayor expressed his appreciation of the great honour that had been conferred on Torquay. He hoped and prayed that when the men went to the front, they would have God's blessing in all their times of trouble and danger, and that many of them would return. As the band played 'God Save the King', the colours were carried into the town hall. In the vestibule, as if it were a portent of what the battalion would soon face, the flag bearers passed a number of wounded soldiers under the care of nursing staff from the local Red Cross Hospital. In the Mayor's Reception Room, the flags were placed on either side of the carved oak mantelpiece.

꧁

On 6 January 1915, the day the Dublins colours were handed over to Mayor Towell, Winston Churchill sent the following telegram to Vice-Admiral Sackville Carden. 'High Authorities here concur in your opinion. Forward detailed particulars showing what force would be required for extended operations. How do you think it should be employed, and what results could be gained?'

꧁

During their stay in Torquay, the band of the Royal Dublin Fusiliers gave a number of concerts. Entertainments were laid on for the troops, including a billiard match between the Dubs and a team from the Lower Chelston area of Torquay. As if to prove that their duties did not allow them to spend too much time at the billiard table, the Blue Caps team was decisively beaten. Seven of the Lower Chelston eight-man team each had a score of 100, with the other man attaining a score of 76. The only Dub to obtain a score of 100 was the battalion billiards champion, Private Joe Murphy. Lower Chelston had a total score of 776. The Dubs scored 622.

ഇരു

On 11 January, orders arrived for 1st Royal Dublin Fusiliers to move to Nuneaton in Warwickshire. That night, shortly before 11 p.m., Jack Mallaghan and his fellow buglers sounded 'fall in' in various parts of the town. A misty rain was falling as men made their way to the Recreation Ground. Soldiers on picket duty went through the town directing men (some of whom had imbibed too freely) to the assembly area. A few men were found to have mislaid their rifles and kit. In the darkness of the Recreation Ground, hundreds of soldiers and their civilian friends were mixed in noisy confusion. There were hoarse calls of 'Fall in!' and companies began to hold roll calls. Finally, the order was given to march to the railway station. Civilians cheered as the soldiers marched out.

At the railway station, taxis screeched to a halt. Some of the inevitable latecomers clambered out, carrying their rifles and kit. More stragglers arrived on foot, some of them singing and accompanied by friends. In a corner of the railway station, a youthful bandsman was trying in vain to calm a girl of about fifteen who was sobbing bitterly. At the entrance to the station, a tall Dub was surrounded by a group of female admirers, one of whom asked him to write to her. He handed her a notebook for her address. The notebook returned, he placed it in his pocket beside a protruding small bottle of whiskey. As if to balance the whiskey, a long clay pipe protruded from the pocket on the other side.

Many older women had also come to the station. Presumably they were landladies, come to see 'their' boys off. The marching column arrived from the Recreation Ground, accompanied by a crowd of supporters. A group of about twenty men had spent several hours in the station waiting room. Lying about on the floor, on benches and on a table, the men were prisoners who had been transferred from the cellars of a building that had been used as battalion headquarters. They were serving sentences of between seven to twenty-eight days for a variety of offences against military discipline. A reporter from *The Torquay Times* possibly unearthed the reason the Mallaghan brothers from Newry and Nicky Smyth from County Meath did not get home on leave. When he expressed sympathy on the plight of the prisoners, he received the following reply. 'Sympathy,' said a sergeant, 'if you knew them, you wouldn't.' He continued:

These are the 'black sheep' of our flock. No sooner are they out of trouble than they are back in again. A few such men give a bad name to any regiment, and through their conduct, good fellows suffer. They are a regular nuisance to all grades, from the C.O. downwards. For instance, two batches of our fellows got away and some failed to turn up again at the proper time with the result that all leave was stopped and all the other men suffered! It is very selfish. I got word my mother was dying, but all the same, I could not get away to see her, because of the conduct of others. It is rather hard.

Presumably Lieutenant-Colonel Rooth was faced with the possibility of mass absence without leave among men who had been in India for several years. A difficult enough situation in peacetime, it would have been an appalling prospect for an officer about to lead his battalion to war. He must have felt that he had little option but to cancel all leave. The behaviour of a few 'black sheep' meant that many men who were soon to die were deprived of a final chance to be with their families. A plan to hold a farewell dinner for the Dubs had been cancelled due to the order for immediate departure. Instead, it was decided to send each man a tobacco box bearing the Torquay arms, the name of the battalion and the date. At the railway station, the mayor and other dignitaries, assisted by helpers, gave each soldier a pasty. It would be their only food on the journey to Nuneaton. In the crowded station, farewells were made. Promises were given to keep in touch by letter. Men cheered, laughed and sang. Officers and NCOs cursed as they tried to create order out of confusion. Finally a bugle sounded and the men fell in. A few minutes later many of them climbed aboard a train. At 1.10 a.m. a guard blew his whistle. The first train, containing Lieutenant-Colonel Rooth and about 500 men, moved off to loud cheers. The remaining companies boarded another train at 1.45 a.m. and left soon afterwards.

ळ्थ

On 11 January 1915, the day the Blue Caps received orders to move to Nuneaton, Dr Henry Speldewinde de Boer was officially granted the rank of temporary Lieutenant in the Royal Army Medical Corps. Born in Ceylon, he had qualified as a doctor in 1913. He would soon join the Blue Caps as their medical officer.

ळ्थ

Cabinet Room, 10 Downing Street, 13 January 1915

Winston Churchill informed the War Council that a reply had been received to the message sent to Vice-Admiral Sackville Carden. The Vice-Admiral said that it might be possible to force a passage in a four-part operation: **i** Destroying the defences at the entrance to the Dardanelles; **ii** Clearing the defences inside the straits; **iii** Destroying the defences at the Narrows; and **iv** Sweeping the minefield at the Narrows, advancing through the Narrows, reducing the forts further up and sailing into the Sea of Marmora. Carden estimated that it would take a month to carry out these operations. The War Council meeting took the following decision. 'The Admiralty should prepare for a naval expedition in February to bombard and take the Gallipoli Peninsula, with Constantinople as its objective.'

తఌ

Mayor Charles Towell of Torquay received the following letter in mid-January 1914.

Attleborough Hall,
Nuneaton,
January 14th 1915

Dear Mr Mayor,

I find it very difficult to express to you and the inhabitants of Torquay my gratitude for the way in which you treated the men of my battalion during our stay in your beautiful town. Neither I, nor the officers, non-commissioned officers, and the men of the Battalion will ever forget our much too short stay in Torquay. I hope you and the people of Torquay will understand and forgive any unfortunate excesses on the part of individuals, when I tell you the men have been absent from home for many years, and that, at Christmas time, in billets, it was impossible to maintain the rigid discipline to which my men are accustomed. I should take it as a great favour if you would express to all, the thanks of myself and my officers, for the great kindness and hospitality we received from everyone, and I should like to thank you personally, and the Mayoress [Alice Edith Towell] for your many kindly thoughts and actions.

Believe me to be,
Yours very sincerely,
R. Rooth
Lt-Col. Commanding 1st Royal Dublin Fusiliers

∞

Between 12 and 17 August, four British infantry divisions and a cavalry division landed in France and quickly crossed the Belgian frontier to face the
invading German Army. As battalions returned to Britain from overseas, they
were brought together to form new divisions and sent to Belgium and France.
By the end of 1914, there were ten British regular divisions in action. The 1st
Royal Dublin Fusiliers and the 1st Royal Munster Fusiliers were assigned to the
29th Division, which was formed in the Midlands of England in early 1915.

The 29th Division was one of the last divisions to be formed from regular troops.[6] The final eleven regular battalions returned to England in
December 1914 and January 1915. They were assigned to form the major part
of the 29th Division. Six battalions, including the 1st Royal Dublin Fusiliers
and the 2nd Hampshire Regiment, had returned from India.[7] Three battalions, including the 1st Royal Munster Fusiliers, were brought back from
Burma.[8] One battalion came from Mauritius and one from Tianjin, China.[9]
As the division was a battalion short, the unusual step was taken of adding a
Territorial battalion, the 1st/5th Royal Scots from Edinburgh. All of the 29th
Division's support units were Territorials, the majority coming from divi-
sions that had been sent on garrison duties to India and Egypt.

Commanded by Major-General Sir Frederick Shaw, the 29th Division's
headquarters was established in the Manor House Hotel in Leamington Spa
by 18 January 1915. Wounded at the First Battle of Ypres in November 1914,
the recently promoted Shaw was at home recuperating when he was given his
new command. He and his staff began the task of assembling and mobilising
the 29th Division. The eleven regular battalions at Shaw's disposal were almost
all at full strength. Any replacements required were brought from regimental
depots. The battalions were integrated into brigades and a divisional frame-
work created. The 29th Division's infantry brigades were numbered 86th, 87th
and 88th. The 1st Royal Dublin Fusiliers and the 1st Royal Munster Fusiliers
were attached to the 86th Brigade (with the 1st Lancashire Fusiliers and the
2nd Royal Fusiliers). Known as the Fusiliers Brigade, the 86th was commanded by Brigadier-General Steuart Hare, with Thomas Frankland of the
Royal Dublin Fusiliers as his brigade-major.[10] The 2nd Hampshire Regiment

was assigned to the 88th Brigade (along with the 1st Essex Regiment, the 4th Worcestershire Regiment and the 1st/5th Royal Scots). Brigadier-General Henry Napier, of the Royal Irish Rifles, commanded the 88th Brigade, with Captain John Costeker, DSO of the Royal Warwickshire Regiment as his brigade-major. The division's 87th Brigade was known as the Union Brigade, as it contained battalions from Ireland, Wales, Scotland and England. Commanded by Brigadier-General Sir William Marshall, it was comprised of the 1st Royal Inniskilling Fusiliers, the 1st King's Own Scottish Borderers, the 1st Border Regiment and the 2nd South Wales Borderers.

∽

Passing reference has been made to the 1st Battalion Royal Munster Fusiliers and the 2nd Battalion, Hampshire Regiment. As the fate of these battalions would be bound up with that of the Blue Caps, it is opportune to introduce them at this point in the story.

Like the Royal Dublin Fusiliers, the 1st Battalion Royal Munster Fusiliers was descended from a regiment in the East India Company Army and, like the Dublins, they had undergone a number of name changes. They also had their own nickname, The Dirty Shirts[11] The outbreak of war found the 1st Battalion Royal Munster Fusiliers stationed in Burma, under the command of Lieutenant-Colonel Henry Tizard. The battalion was ordered to occupy the forts and posts on the Rangoon River and place them in a state of defence. This was difficult work, as it was the monsoon season. The battalion was still organised in eight companies, with a Vickers machine-gun section commanded by Lieutenant Edward Dorman. Five companies were based at Rangoon, two at Thayetmyo under Captain Guy Geddes DSO and D Company, under Major Roger Monck-Mason at Port Blair in the Andaman Islands. In October 1914 the battalion was reorganised into four companies.

The regular battalions based in India and Burma had to wait for relief by Territorial battalions from Britain. The 1st Royal Munster Fusiliers was not relieved until November 1914. On 21 November, with D Company remaining in the Andaman Islands, nineteen officers and 879 other ranks from the battalion left for Calcutta. Reaching the city on 25 November, the Munsters remained there until 4 December. They then crossed India by rail for Bombay, from where they embarked on 9 December. Sailing aboard the *Corsican*,[12] they formed part of a convoy of thirteen ships. On Sunday 10 January 1915, the Munsters arrived at Avonmouth. Among the Munster's officers was Second Lieutenant Norman Dewhurst. He had joined the 2nd King's (Liverpool Regiment) as a private in

September 1906. Working his way up the ranks, he had been commissioned and transferred to the Dirty Shirts shortly before they sailed for England. Having attended a machine-gun course for sergeants at the School of Musketry, Changli Gali, he was assigned to the battalion's machine-gun section under the newly promoted Captain Edward Dorman.

∞

The Hampshire Regiment had been established in 1881, with the coming together of the 37th North Hampshire Regiment of Foot and the 67th South Hampshire Regiment of Foot. The former became the 1st Battalion of the new regiment, while the latter became the 2nd Battalion. On the outbreak of the First World War, the 2nd Battalion was stationed at Mhow, in the central Indian state of Madhya Pradesh. The battalion was commanded by Lieutenant-Colonel Herbert Carington Smith, who had spent most of his military career in the Royal Dublin Fusiliers and was listed on their strength until he took command of the 2nd Hampshires in 1913.[13]

On 31 August, the 2nd Hampshires, nicknamed The Tigers[14] made the three-day train journey to Bombay. Upon arrival, they marched to Colaba Barracks in the south of the city. There they relieved the 1st Battalion Sherwood Forresters, who, to the great envy of the Hampshires, sailed for Britain and the war. The Tigers were worried that the 'scrap' in Europe would be over before they could take part. Soon after arrival, the Hampshires faced their own drama when a ship containing ammunition caught fire in Bombay docks and they were ordered to move the ammunition to a safe location on the dockside. On 10 November, the Hampshires were told that they were to return to Britain. Four days later, they boarded the SS *Gloucester Castle*.[15] On 16 November 1914 the twenty-one officers, forty-three sergeants, fifteen drummers and 816 other ranks of the 2nd Battalion Hampshire Regiment left Bombay, travelling as part of a large convoy of troop transports and merchant ships. The Tigers arrived at Plymouth on 22 December. They immediately entrained for Romsey, near Southampton. Upon arrival, they were billeted in local houses, schools, church buildings and tents. Most of the men were given leave.

∞

By January 1915, Britain was awash with soldiers. There was insufficient barrack accommodation for the wartime army, even when the space allowance per man was reduced by a third. A programme of hut building had been started, but had run into difficulties. Those living under canvass often faced appalling conditions after the weather broke in mid-October 1914. During the winter of 1914–1915 the situation was addressed by billeting 800,000 soldiers on the civilian population. The soldiers of the 29th Division found themselves allocated to billets in Warwickshire and north Oxfordshire. In Warwickshire, troops were sent to the major towns, apart from Birmingham. The 1st Royal Dublin Fusiliers and the 1st Lancashire Fusiliers were billeted in Nuneaton, with the former's battalion headquarters in the Congregational Hall.[16] The 1st Royal Munster Fusiliers and the 2nd South Wales Borderers went to Coventry. The 2nd Hampshire Regiment was based in Stratford upon Avon. Communities were notified a week or two prior to the arrival of the troops.

The Story Behind the Monument uses the town of Banbury in north Oxfordshire to illustrate the procedure that was followed in billeting troops. On 8 January 1915, the mayor was notified that the first contingent of troops (the 1st Essex) would arrive on 18 January. On 11 January Brigade-Major John Costeker DSO, of the 88th Brigade, met with Chief Constable Wilson, who was acting as Billet-Master for the town. The town was divided into three areas and army billeting forms were served on the tenants of houses in designated localities. The forms required tenants to provide quarters for a stated number of officers or men: usually between two and four per household. Householders could make an objection to the Billet-Master. In some cases, the objections were upheld, especially in cases where there was no male living in the household. In general, however, objections appear to have been overruled. The *Branbury Advertiser* reported that 'in the event of the excuses being frivolous' the householder could find that the 'number of men billeted might be doubled'. *The Story Behind the Monument* says, 'Although such measures now seem draconian, it does not appear to have been too difficult finding the required accommodation. Apart from the call of duty, there was a billeting allowance for which many households were more than grateful.' A weekly allowance of 17s 6d was paid for each private soldier. This was calculated on the basis of 9d a night for bed and 1s 9d a day for food. Officers were billeted at 3s per night, but paid separately for their food. On the afternoon of 21 January, the 1st Essex Regiment arrived in Banbury on two trains. The men from the first train were played into the town by a Territorial unit band and were greeted by a crowd of locals. After reaching an assembly area, they were shown to their billets by police assisted by boy scouts. Buglers from the battalion band met the second party: otherwise the procedure was essentially the same. Similar scenes occurred throughout the division's billeting area. Arriving troops would receive the assistance of police, special constables and/

or boy scouts. In Nuneaton, entertainer James Burke of the Royal Dublin Fusiliers was billeted with the Turner family, of whom the husband and three sons worked as coal miners. He said that he was very well fed but that his pay did not have the spending power it had in India. So on pay day the husband, wife and three sons would club together to provide him with enough spending-money to last him until *their* next pay-day.

∞

On 16 January 1915, Private Michael Byrne of the Royal Dublin Fusiliers died at his home in New Row, Naas, County Kildare as a result of heart failure following bronchitis. Forty-seven years old, he had been a bandsman in the Dublins a few years previously. On retiring from the army, he took up hackney-car work. Following the outbreak of war, he rejoined the Dublins and was attached to the regimental depot in Naas. He was buried with full military honours the day after his death. Preceded by an outrider, his coffin was covered by a Union Jack flag and carried on a gun carriage drawn by two horses provided by the Royal Field Artillery. A firing party, with rifles reversed, accompanied the cortége. All the men attached to the depot marched in procession led by Major Shadford and Captain O'Meagher. Michael Byrne was survived by his wife Mary and a large family. His sons, Sergeant Laurence Byrne and Private Michael Byrne, were serving in the 1st Battalion, Royal Dublin Fusiliers.[17]

∞

The 1st Royal Munster Fusiliers arrived in England, docking at Avonmouth on Sunday 10 January 1915. According to Norman Dewhurst, 'We landed still clothed in our Indian uniforms, and stood on the quay shivering in our shorts. We were on active service and we entrained with full equipment and rifles for Coventry, where, in the dark early hours of the winter morning the Mayor, Aldermen and other leading citizens of the city were waiting to welcome us. It was a fine welcome, tea and other refreshments being immediately available.'[18] A photograph in the *Coventry Graphic* showed a group of Dirty Shirts still wearing the tropical uniforms they had worn in Burma. Within a short time the soldiers were out exploring the town, 'like schoolboys on breaking-up day,' according to the *Coventry Herald* Norman Dewhurst, however, said the soldiers had a more immediate priority than exploration of the town. The Munsters had been billeted in early morning darkness.[19] At 8 a.m. the pubs opened and most of the men rushed inside. Before long many of them were a little the worse for wear.

Few of them had taken note of where they had been billeted. 'Those that could stand, wandered around aimlessly and finally bunked down for the night in the local police station – it was days before they were all found and sorted out. It is well to record that these men were mainly old stagers who had done a long stretch in India following their participation in the South African War.' [20]

Despite the thirst quenching, the soldiers were reported to be well-behaved and this helped win local goodwill. According to, *The Story Behind the Monument,* 'The examples of mutual regard between soldiers and the local press

Norman Dewhurst,
Royal Munster Fusiliers.

seem far too numerous to be simply wartime propaganda.' The *Nuneaton Observer* described the Royal Dublin Fusiliers as 'manly, breezy fellows, full of their Indian stories and experiences.' *The Story Behind the Monument,* says that, 'Traditionally, men returning from a long spell of service overseas were entitled to a lengthy period of leave. However, this seems to have been reduced to a mere four days, as priority was given to getting the new division organised and trained ... . Where men found themselves in billets and communities in which a genuine welcome was extended, there must have been some element of compensation for those fleeting or forfeited family contacts.' In some cases, family members or fiancées travelled to visit soldiers. In January, a father visiting his Royal Dublin Fusilier son was knocked down and seriously injured in Nuneaton.

The battalions of the 29th Division were brought up to strength by reservists who had been recalled to the colours. Unless they signed up for further service, British soldiers served for a period of seven years in the army, followed by five years in the reserve. While in the reserve they were liable to be called back to service in the event of an emergency/outbreak of hostilities. On the outbreak of war in 1914 the army reserve numbered 145,000. This was slightly above the designated number required. Brothers, Robert (Bob) and Peter Jordan had previously served with the Royal Munster Fusiliers. Now living in New York, they travelled to England to rejoin their old regiment,

which had in the meantime come back from Rangoon in Burma. Bob and
Peter's father, John, had been born in County Limerick in 1836. He had joined
the 57th Regiment of Foot at Tralee, County Kerry and served with them in
the Crimean War. Despite marrying late – he married twice (his first wife
died) – he had nineteen children. Returning to Ireland, he became a recruit-
ing sergeant for the Royal Munster Fusiliers. Among those he recruited were
four of his sons. Following his death in 1906, his family emigrated to America.
Now Bob and Peter had voluntarily returned to serve with the old regiment.
The *Coventry Evening Telegraph* of 13 February 1915 announced that five Royal
Munster Fusiliers Warrant Officers and NCOs had been promoted to Second
Lieutenant. The men were Sergeant-Major William Cooch, Quartermaster
Sergeant Stephen Watts, Company Sergeant-Major Timothy Sullivan,
Company Sergeant-Major John Watts, and Sergeant Gerald Joseph Griffin.

Voluntary committees ran recreational facilities for the soldiers. Church
halls and local clubs were made available and provided with chairs, tables,
pianos, gramophones, billiard tables and games. Locals often gave furniture
on loan. Books, newspapers, magazines and writing materials were also
provided. Local communities bore the costs incurred, with people agreeing, for example, to pay for the daily papers provided at recreational centres.
Cigarettes and refreshments were often sold to soldiers at cost price. Concerts,
musical evenings, dances, whist drives and billiards matches were arranged.
Funds were established to which locals could contribute. In larger towns,
soldiers had access to music halls, theatres and cinemas. Nuneaton had
The Palace, The Picturedrome, The Royal and The Hippodrome. The presence of the troops was of huge economic benefit to the area. According to,
The Story Behind the Monument, 'For a period of about two months, roughly
£9,000 a week was going into the hands of local grocers, bakers, butchers,
dairymen and the like. Presumably, some of the modest profit which households made on billeting (also passed) into the local economy.' A private's basic
pay was a shilling a day and it was estimated that they were spending about
5s a week. 'This was principally to the benefit of local tobacconists, publicans
and places of entertainment, though soldiers also bought a lot of sweets and
fruit.' Nuneatonians were urged to 'Feed our Gallant Soldiers on Matthews
Sausages'. 'Haselwood — Specialists in Soldiers Necessaries' proclaimed their
wares under the heading, 'Presents for Soldiers'. The presents included gloves
and mittens, scarves, pants and vests and khaki handkerchiefs. The firm also
sold the badges of the regiments billeted in the town.

Church parades became a regular feature in the region. In January,
the *Midland Counties Tribune* reported 'huge crowds' turning out to watch

the troops go to church, preceded by their bands. Regimental bands were in great demand. In Coventry, the band of the Royal Munster Fusiliers played at services and football matches. They also played at the funeral of a young Kenilworth soldier who had died of pneumonia. The influx of thousands of young men into the area caused problems. Given the numbers involved, however, the problems appear to have been relatively minor. Consumption of alcohol, inevitably, caused difficulties. This, however, was a likelihood the authorities had foreseen. Locals were informed that the Defence of the Realm Act made it an offence to buy alcohol for soldiers. The act was also used to restrict opening hours of public houses and registered clubs. Following their first night in Coventry, six Royal Munster Fusiliers appeared before the courts on charges of drunkenness. They were handed over to the military authorities for punishment. Private John Moore of the Royal Dublin Fusiliers was arrested for being drunk and disorderly in Coton Road, Nuneaton and for fighting with a civilian. Appearing before Nuneaton Police Court, he defended himself by claiming that he had not drunk beer for eighteen months and had been overcome by the amount he had consumed. Amazingly, his defence was accepted and the case was dismissed! A Nuneaton newspaper reported that, Lieutenant Lawrence Boustead of the Royal Dublin Fusiliers (whose family lived at nearby Ascot) had run foul of the local police force. He was fined for driving a motorbike in Nuneaton without a light.

After hearing reports that soldiers were leaving their billets late at night to meet up with girls in the back streets of Nuneaton, 86th Brigade Chaplain, the Revd Oswin Creighton, mounted a one-man street patrol. To his relief, he found nothing untoward. Given the influx of so many young men, it was inevitable that romances and even marriages would occur. Royal Munster Fusiliers John (Jack) and William (Paddy) Long were from Glanworth in County Cork. Paddy was billeted with the Allen family in Lord Street, Chapelfields, Coventry and began courting the eldest of the family's three daughters. Royal Munster Fusilier Reservist Bob Jordan, who had returned from New York with his brother Peter, met Elsie Fleming. She was twenty-one-years-old and convalescing from a cycling accident. In March, the *Coventry Graphic* ran a picture story on the marriage at St Osburg's of Royal Munster Fusilier Second Lieutenant Timothy Sullivan and Maud Bates. From Bantry, County Cork, the thirty-one-year-old groom had served in the Boer War and on the North West Frontier in India. The *Coventry Evening Telegraph* had recently announced that Company Sergeant-Major Timothy Sullivan had been promoted to second lieutenant. His best man, Nova

Scotia-born John Watts, had also been recently promoted from sergeant-major to second lieutenant.

Training got underway as soon as the soldiers were settled into billets. The Warwickshire countryside mostly comprised of small enclosed-fields. This, and the widespread dispersal of the billeting areas, prevented large-scale manoeuvres at divisional or even at brigade level. Training was, therefore, confined to company and battalion-level exercises. As regular soldiers already had most of the required martial skills, much of the emphasis was on fitness training. Route marches were common and provided a novel spectacle for the local population. Battalions, preceded by their bands, marched along the roads and lanes of Warwickshire and north Oxfordshire. Whole villages would turn out to watch their passing. On 1 February, the Revd Oswin Creighton recorded in his diary: 'I went [on] a long route march with the Dublins in the morning, about twelve miles. The Colonel [Richard Rooth] rode part of the way, but walked a good deal, and was very pleasant and talked away quite a lot. Many of the officers are very pleasant, but I don't feel they very much care whether one exists or not. After all why should they? Again I marched just behind the band, and enjoyed the music. It is very amusing watching whole villages turn out to see us and the general excitement we arouse.'[21] The soldiers also undertook night marches and local newspapers warned motorists to be on the look-out. A soldier carrying a white light preceded the nocturnal marchers, while one carrying a red light brought up the rear of the column. Route marches allowed the division's transport and field kitchens to be tested. Troops regularly engaged in trench-digging and shooting practice. Machine-gun crews, using their weapons 'under modern conditions', were photographed for local newspapers. A bomb-making and explosive school for officers was established at Rugby. Participants practised their newly acquired skills on trenches and wire entanglements. Lieutenant Guy Nightingale of the Royal Munster Fusiliers found it all 'very dangerous' and thought throwing grenades at night 'more dangerous still'. He seemed relieved that there was only one casualty on the course he attended: this was an officer from the Royal Inniskilling Fusiliers.

ௐ

On 23 January 1915, at Bulford Camp on the Salisbury Plain, Father William Finn was medically examined and found fit for active service.

ௐ

The War Diary of the 1st Royal Dublin Fusiliers recorded a medical inspection of 'A' and 'B' Companies on 25 January and 'C' and 'D' Companies the following day. In total, one NCO and two men were declared to be unfit. On 1 February, 'new rifles arrived' and 'mobilisation stores and equipment began to arrive'. A draft of 110 men arrived from the 4th Battalion, based at Sittingbourne, Kent. The following day seventy men arrived from the 3rd Battalion, based at Queenstown (now Cobh), County Cork. Among the men who arrived from the 4th Battalion was Private Thomas Hughes. Moved to Cork upon mobilisation, the battalion had been based at Aghada until October 1914, when it had moved to Sittingbourne. At some point before their departure Hughes had written to his wife, Margaret at Upper Abbey Street, Dublin. (The house number is illegible on the envelope.)

Pte Hughes, Reg No. 6979
C Coy 4th R.D. Fus.
Aghada Camp

Dear [he started to write Mother and crossed it out. He then started to write Sister and also crossed it out] Wife,

Just a line hoping to find you in the best of health as this leaves me at present. I received the parcels alright which I was very glad to get. James is getting tried by the civil police on Tuesday as the Sgt. told me. As it is the first I heard about him only for the Sgt. of the constabulary told me I would not know yet. He is getting tried in Middleton [County Cork]. You can tell [next word is illegible. Looks like 'Ceomy.'] what I am telling you now. When you are sending the tobacco to me on Monday get it in the same place as it was very good. We are out of this on the 20th of this month. You need not write to me any more till I send you word where we are going to. It is somewhere about London. What is the reason you wont let me know what money you are getting or what is the reason of it because I do have a row [next word is illegible. Looks like 'down.'] here with the Captain over it. As I want to find out the proper money to pay back let me know in the next letter you send that they are only giving [The next word is illegible] 1/- per week and they are sending home the remainder. I am expecting to go to the front and I have left the whole lot over to you and the children. We are going straight out when we land in England. The first chance I get I shall write and let you know where

I am. Let me know how Mary and Tommy is getting on. I would like to see their face before I go out. I am sorry that I cant. I hope they shall be alright again I come home. If I ever do. Write as soon as you hear from me. Don't forget and send the tobacco not matter where I am. Your loving husband. Goodbye. [He did not sign his name. The letter closed with about twenty kisses.][22]

Among the seventy men who arrived from the 3rd Battalion was Private John Sullivan (5798). Thirty years of age, he was married with three children. John and his wife Kate Cowhig[23] were born in the summer of 1884 in neighbouring lanes on the northside of Cork City. They were married on the 7 October 1907 in the Cathedral of St Mary and St Anne, referred to by locals as the North Chapel. They both came from families long established in this area that have been traced to Blarney Street, Boyces Street and the many narrow lanes in the area, most of which have long since disappeared. The surrounding locality was once dotted with cattle markets, slaughterhouses, hide and skin merchants, cooperages, family butchers, shoe repair shops, and other businesses connected to the cattle and leather trade. Locals also worked as blacksmiths, seamstresses, carpenters and masons, trades and skills passed down from generation to generation.

Following their marriage, the young couple lived at Arch Lane where their first child, John, was born in 1908. They subsequently moved to Kellys Lane where a daughter, Ellen, was born in 1910. The family later moved again and rented rooms in a large tenement house in Boyces Street where their daughter, Margaret, was born in May 1914. At the outbreak of the war John was working for a printing company as a bill poster. On 26 October he enlisted at Victoria Barracks (now Collins Barracks). Being found medically fit, he was sent to the 3rd Battalion Royal Dublin Fusiliers. Moved to County Cork upon mobilisation, it was based in Queenstown.[24]

On the day that John Sullivan and his sixty-nine comrades arrived at Nuneaton to join the 1st Royal Dublin Fusiliers, Major Roger Monck-Mason and his company of Munsters, who had been stationed at Port Blair in the Andaman Islands at the outbreak of war, arrived at Coventry to rejoin the 1st Royal Munster Fusiliers. The following day, Captain Denis Anderson rejoined the Dublins. Having commanded the party that escorted the 4th Battalion Somerset Light Infantry to Fort St George, Madras, he had subsequently travelled to England.

∾∾

The Cabinet Room, 10 Downing Street, 28 January 1915

A meeting of the War Council was held at 11.30 a.m. Churchill said that he had informed Russian Grand Duke Nicholas and the French Admiralty of the proposed attack on the Dardanelles. The French had agreed to send ships and the Russians subsequently sent the cruiser, *Askold*. While First Sea Lord Fisher expressed doubts, Prime Minister Asquith said that, because of the steps which had already been taken, the matter 'could not be left in abeyance'. Support for the naval attack was also expressed by Lord Kitchener, Arthur Balfour and Sir Edward Grey. Churchill said that the naval commander-in-chief of the Mediterranean had expressed his belief that the attack could be successfully carried out and that he required from three weeks to a month to accomplish it. The necessary ships were already on their way to the Dardanelles.

A further meeting of the War Council was held at 6 p.m. the same day. Churchill later told the Dardanelles Commission that, 'I announced finally on behalf of the Admiralty … that we had decided to undertake the task with which the War Council had charged us so urgently. This I date as the point of final decision. After it, I never looked back. We had left the region of discussion and consultation, of balancings and misgivings. The matter had passed into the domain of action.'

≈

While Captain Cecil Grimshaw DSO was among the Blue Caps settling into Nuneaton, his older brother – and ex-Blue Cap – Lieutenant-Colonel Ewing Grimshaw was commanding the 62nd Punjab Regiment in Egypt. There was little light from the moon at 3 a.m. on 3 February 1915 as a Turkish force attempted to cross the Suez Canal near Tussum, at the southern end of Lake Timsah. They brought boats made of galvanised steel, each capable of carrying about thirty soldiers. The boats had been hauled across the Sinai Desert mounted on wheels. The banks of the Suez Canal are 50ft high at Tussum. Ewing Grimshaw's 62nd Punjabs didn't spot the Turks until they had launched the first boat and were sliding others down the slope. Supported by the 5th Egyptian Battery and six platoons of the 2nd Rajputs, the 62nd Pubjabs opened fire, forcing the Turks to abandon most of the boats. Three boats did manage to cross the canal, but their occupants were either killed or captured. Daylight attacks in the same general area also failed. Turkish losses were estimated to be about 1,400, half of them taken as prisoners of war.

British casualties were about 150. According to *Gallipoli,* by Eric Bush, 'This victory had the unfortunate effect of giving our troops a false impression of the fighting qualities of the Turkish soldier, which was to prove a handicap at Gallipoli.' Two and a half months later, Ewing Grimshaw's younger brother Cecil would be among those who would face a determined Turkish defence at Sedd el Bahr.

∾

On 5 February, Admiral Sackville Carden, Commander of the Eastern Mediterranean Squadron, was sent formal orders and told, if possible, to begin operations ten days later to force a passage through the Dardanelles. The following day, Winston Churchill ordered the Plymouth and Chatham Battalions of the Royal Marine Light Infantry from the Royal Naval Division to be sent to the Eastern Mediterranean to assist with the naval operations.

∾

On 10 February, in Coventry, Father Thomas Harker reported for duty as chaplain to the 1st Royal Munster Fusiliers. On the same day Private James McGhee of the Royal Dublin Fusiliers died of pneumonia at Tuttle Hill Hospital in Nuneaton. Thirty years old, he was a reservist who had been recalled to the colours. He had only been in Nuneaton for a week, being one of the seventy men who had come from the 3rd Battalion in Cork. His mother Elizabeth travelled from Glasgow for the funeral and he was buried with full military honours from St Joseph's church at Nuneaton (Our Lady of the Angels) Roman Catholic Cemetery. The *Nuneaton Observer* reported: 'this is the only record which we believe exists for a purely military funeral within the borough.'[25]

On 11 February, Major-General Cooper CB, the Colonel of the Royal Dublin Fusiliers, came to Nuneaton and inspected the 1st Battalion.[26] On 16 February, thirty-nine Royal Dublin Fusiliers were sent to the 3rd Battalion in Cork. According to the War Diary, they were 'immature soldiers and temporarily unfit'. The same day, 'all sea kitbags and spare clothing (were) sent to Embarkation Officer, Southampton'. It appears, at that point, the battalion was preparing to go to France, as Southampton was an embarkation port for troops going there.

∾

On 16 February 1915, some of the ministers on the War Council held an informal meeting. Decisions reached at the meeting were eventually incorporated into those of the War Council. One of the decisions was that the 29th Division, previously intended to form part of Sir John French's Army in France and Belgium, was to be despatched to Lemnos Island in the Mediterranean as soon as possible. The intention was that the division would support naval operations if necessary, but only by providing small-scale landing parties or garrisoning any land areas taken by the navy. It seems possible, however, that Kitchener had realised, from the outset, that a large military landing might be necessary to force the Dardanelles. It had been decided that Lemnos Island in the eastern Mediterranean would be used as a base for military operations against the Turks on the Gallipoli peninsula.

Also on 16 February, Rear-Admiral Rosslyn Wemyss (pronounced 'Weems') was appointed Senior Naval Officer for Lemnos Island. Two days later the remaining battalions of the Royal Naval Division, under the command of Major-General Archibald Paris, were ordered to follow the two battalions of marines that had been ordered to the eastern Mediterranean. The French had decided to send a division of mixed troops from depots in France and North Africa. Named the Corps Expéditionnaire d'Orient, the division was commanded by General Albert d'Amade.

On the night of 16 February, hours after the ministers of the War Council had held their informal meeting, in Nuneaton the Revd Oswin Creighton attended a dinner given by a wealthy mill-owner for the officers of the Royal Dublin Fusiliers. The dinner was held in the mill-owner's home, where Lieutenant-Colonel Richard Rooth was billeted. It was attended by 'the General and Brigade-Major and about sixteen Dublin officers'. As Creighton said that 'the General' had previously commanded a territorial brigade, this suggests that he was Brigadier-General Steuart Hare, commanding officer of 86th Brigade and the brigade-major was Dublin Fusilier Officer Tom Frankland. Creighton recorded that '[Colonel Rooth] made me play auction bridge afterwards, and they were very nice when I demurred about playing for money, and they let me off. It was a very pleasant evening, a good way to get to know the officers.'[27]

∞

Among the letters sent by Blue Caps from Nuneaton was one written by Lance-Corporal Nicholas Smyth to his sister Katie Bennett in County Meath. Their brother Christy was serving with the Dubs 2nd Battalion.

Thursday 18/2/1915.
7 George Elliott Street,
Nuneaton, Warwickshire.

My Dear Katie,

I am just writing you a couple of lines hoping to find you are keeping well, also
the baby [Katie's daughter Jane] and Mick and Paddy [Katie's sons]. I am not
so well for the past week, I was laid up with a bad cold, but I am getting on
alright again. I suppose you had a letter from my mother, I told her to send
my letter to you as the one would do the two of you. I think we are going away
next week for certain, we sent all our kit way to France on Monday last. So that
looks as if we are going. Shortly to [presumably this means 'soon'] I believe
we are getting three days leave before we go, but I don't know whether we will
get the chance of going to Ireland or not for that three days, so if I do get the
chance I will go home for a day. Do you know Willie Rafferty,[28] he told me to
tell you he was asking for you. I suppose you were wanting me down again
before I came back, I would have gone down only I had too many people to
see. When did you hear from Maggie or is she in Navan yet? Dear Katie, I have
no more to say for the present, hoping this finds you all in good health.

Your loving Brother, Nicholas.
P.S. Write soon and don't forget, Write by return in case I might have gone
to France.[29]

∞

Private James Burke was in his billet one morning when his sergeant arrived
and told him to report to Lieutenant-Colonel Rooth. Not having been up on
a charge for years, he was very worried as to what he might have done wrong.
Rooth soon put his mind at rest, by telling Burke that he had been selected as
batman to Brigadier-General Steuart Hare, commanding officer of the 86th
Brigade. Rooth told Burke to immediately report to Hare. He wrote down
an address, gave it to Burke and wished him the best of luck. Brigadier Hare
was staying as a guest in a big house just outside the town and according
to Burke, he was a tall, broad-shouldered man of about sixty-five, with gray
hair and grey moustache. He told Burke that while they were in England,
his duties would solely consist of polishing Hare's boots and leggings and
cleaning his buttons. He would be excused all parades and he would receive

an extra guinea a month. Hare asked Burke what was his name. When told, Hare smiled and said 'Burke and Hare. I hope we are not going to end up like our predecessors.' As Burke was, at the time, unaware of the infamous murderous duo, Burke and Hare, he did not comment.[30]

∾

The Dardanelles is a narrow seaway linking the Aegean Sea in the Eastern Mediterranean with the Sea of Marmara in Turkey. The Allied plan called for a fleet of British and French ships to sail up the Dardanelles, into the Sea of Marmara and from there to the Turkish capital of Constantinople. The Dardanelles defences had three zones. At the entrance, the outer defences consisted of guns located at Sedd el Bahr on the European shore and Kum Kale on the Asiatic shore. The intermediate defences commenced about 6 miles in from the entrance and consisted of five lines of mines stretching from shore to shore, with batteries of mobile howitzers and field guns ready to fire on any ships attempting to clear the mines. About 2 miles beyond the fifth line of mines, the shores of the Dardanelles came closer to each other, at a point known, as The Narrows. This area was protected by five further lines of mines overlooked by field guns and a number of forts. On 19 February, Vice-Admiral Carden's ships opened fire on the forts at the entrance to the Dardanelles. Initially firing from long range, the ships did not receive any counter fire. When the ships moved closer, however, the guns in the forts opened fire. The attack concluded as daylight failed. Plans to resume the attack the following day were hindered by bad weather that continued for several days.

∾

Since December, Australian and New Zealand troops had been based in Egypt completing their training before their planned deployment to France. On 20 February, Lord Kitchener ordered General Sir John Maxwell, who commanded the troops in Egypt, to send as many of them as possible to Lemnos Island. Ships would be sent from England to transport the rest. Lieutenant-General Sir William Birdwood, an Englishman who had served in India, commanded the Australian and New Zealand troops. Kitchener asked Birdwood, when he reached Lemnos, to give his personal opinion as to whether troops would need to be landed to support the naval assault on the Dardanelles.

∾

The naval attack on the Dardanelles resumed on 25 February. By the end
of the day, the guns of the outer forts, at Sedd el Bahr and Kum Kale, had
been silenced, the forts abandoned and the entrance swept clear of mines.
The possibility of the Allied ships forcing their way through the Dardanelles
threw Constantinople into panic and preliminary preparations were made
to move the Ottoman government into the interior of Turkey. The following
day, the Royal Navy landed parties at Sedd el Bahr and Kum Kale to complete the destruction of the forts' guns. After initial success, both parties
evacuated in the face of stiffening resistance. There was a heavy gale the next
morning. Rain reduced visibility so that little progress could be made inside
the Dardanelles. A landing party was put ashore at Sedd el Bahr, however,
and some guns destroyed. The weather on 28 February was again stormy and
all operations were postponed.

ळ

Gallipoli was discussed at meetings of the War Council on 19, 24 and
26 February. On 24 February, Lord Kitchener said he felt that if the Fleet
could not get through the Straits unaided, 'the Army ought to see the business through.' At the same meeting, however, he asked Churchill whether he
contemplated a land attack. Churchill said that he did not, 'but it was quite
conceivable that the naval attack might be temporarily held up by mines,
and some local military operation required.' After the meeting Kitchener telegraphed General Sir John Maxwell, the British Commander in Egypt. 'It is
proposed that the Navy should silence the guns and destroy the forts with
gun fire. It is not intended that parties should be landed on the Gallipoli
Peninsula, except under cover of the naval guns, to help in total demolition
when the ships get to close quarters ...' On 26 February he sent a telegraph,
by way of Maxwell, to Lieutenant-General Sir William Birdwood. 'The forcing of the Dardanelles is being undertaken by the Navy, and as far as can be
foreseen at present the task of your troops, until such time as the passage
has actually been secured, will be limited to minor operations, such as final
destruction of batteries, after they have been silenced, under the covering
fire of the battleships ...' In the meantime, in accordance with the decision
taken at the meeting on 16 February, the Admiralty had been preparing
transports to bring the 29th Division to the Mediterranean. It was envisaged their departure would begin on 22 February. On 20 February, however,
Colonel Oswald Fitzgerald, Kitchener's Personal Military Secretary, called
to the Admiralty and said it had been decided the 29th Division would

not be sent. This decision led to 'an acute difference of opinion' between Kitchener and Churchill at the meetings on 24 and 26 February. Churchill made 'the strongest possible appeal' for the immediate despatch of the 29th Division. Kitchener said that the Australians and New Zealanders, whom it was proposed to send from Egypt, and the Royal Naval Division and Marines, who had already been dispatched, would constitute a sufficient force. At the time of the discussion, Kitchener apparently still thought that the Navy could force the Dardanelles unaided. According to the report of the Dardanelles Commission, it had been decided on 16 February to employ troops on a large scale. The decision still held good, but its execution was to be delayed. At the same time, the idea of forcing the Dardanelles with the Fleet alone had not been abandoned.

The French and most of the British high command saw the Western Front as the place where the war would be won or lost. Kitchener's commitments to the French required him to send every available man there. Thus the allocation of the 29th Division had assumed a symbolic importance. If the British sent the division to Gallipoli, it would signal a change of policy. At a meeting of the War Council held on 3 March, Kitchener's opposition to sending the 29th Division appears to have weakened. He told Churchill that he proposed to leave the question open until 10 March, when he hoped to have heard from General Birdwood. On 5 March, Birdwood telegraphed Kitchener from the Dardanelles. 'I am very doubtful if the Navy can force the passage unassisted ...' A further telegram the following day expressed similar views. On 10 March, Kitchener told the War Council that he felt the situation on the Western Front was now sufficiently secure to justify the despatch of the 29th Division.

When ministers of the War Council met on 16 February, there were two options open to them. The first was to conclude that commitments elsewhere precluded sending an expeditionary force to Gallipoli. The second option was to immediately commit troops to the venture. Yet, for at least three weeks, the War Council vacillated and came to no definite decision. Forewarned, the Turks were given time to prepare for an attack. Even when the decision to dispatch the 29th Division was taken, it was still hoped that the troops might be confined to 'minor operations.'

The time for the 29th Division's departure approached, though its destination was still not known. Battalions were moved closer together to form brigades, with four battalions to a brigade. On 26 February, Major-General Sir Frederick Shaw inspected the 86th Brigade (1st Royal Dublin Fusiliers, 1st Royal Munster Fusiliers, 1st Lancashire Fusiliers and 2nd Royal Fusiliers) at Shilton, Oxfordshire. On 5 March, the 2nd Hampshires were moved from Stratford to Warwick. On 6 March, the Dublins were scheduled to move from Nuneaton to Kenilworth, about 17 miles to the south-west. Shortly before departure, Private Ephraim Dyball was apparently cleaning his rifle in an outhouse at his billet in Edward Street. The weapon discharged, shooting him in the knee. As Dyball had a good record, it was assumed that the shooting was a genuine accident. However, the mystery remained as to why the gun was loaded. Dyball was taken to Nuneaton General Hospital. His injuries prevented him from embarking with his battalion.[31]

The Story Behind the Monument says that the Dubs' departure from Nuneaton 'was the occasion of considerable emotion'. Crowds began to gather more than an hour before the departure at 9.30 a.m. The Dubs marched past a crowd that was several thousand strong and predominantly comprised of young women. The *Nuneaton Observer* reported, 'It was the age of youth – the moment of youth.' The soldiers were in high spirits. 'Tipperary' was sung as the Blue Caps marched out. When the battalion reached Coventry, they and the 2nd Royal Fusiliers, who had followed them, were greeted by large crowds. As the troops marched behind their regimental bands, members of the crowd pressed sweets, cigarettes and oranges into their hands.

The Royal Fusiliers took up billets in Coventry, where the 1st Royal Munster Fusiliers were stationed. The Dubs continued their march to Kenilworth. For many of the Dublins, the initial experience of Kenilworth was not a happy one. Men complained of overcrowding, with one soldier quoted as saying that he had been forced to sleep on boards and another that he was not allowed into the sitting room of the house where he was billeted. The town's response was that the men of the Army Service Corps had no complaints when billeted there, that overcrowding was caused by the authorities asking the town to take a greater number of troops than actually materialised and that the initial problems were soon cleared up. The *Warwick Advertiser* said that the soldiers were probably disappointed to leave Nuneaton which had 'several places of amusement', as well as a bigger population for the men to mix with. On the evening of their arrival in Kenilworth, and on the following day, many of the Dubs expressed their disappointment by returning to the houses where they had been billeted in Nuneaton. 'Their re-arrival generated almost as much excitement as their departure!' Matters were resolved, however, and the discontented Dubs bade another farewell to Nuneaton. They soon settled into Kenilworth, being described in the *Warwick Advertiser* as 'right good company – always full of humour'.

On 10 March, the 29th Division learned that its commander, Major-General Sir Frederick Shaw, was to be replaced by Major-General Aylmer Hunter-Weston. On 11 March, the 86th Brigade staged a mock battle on the banks of the River Avon. The battle had to be curtailed, however, as the Division was scheduled for inspection by the King the following day. Early on 12 March, the Dublin Fusiliers moved by train from Kenilworth to the village of Brandon, about 8 miles to the east. From there, they marched to the London Road where, under the command of Major-General Sir Frederick Shaw, the soldiers of the 29th Division began to assemble along the London Road between the Fosse intersection and Dunchurch, with the left of the Division almost reaching the railway bridge at Dunchurch. According to *The Story Behind the Monument* 'The line of review must therefore have been over two miles long.'

The troops had not been officially told the purpose of the gathering. The weather was dry, but without sun. The soldiers had a lengthy wait, as the royal train appears not to have arrived at Dunchurch station until mid-morning. Wearing khaki uniform, King George V left the station on his horse Delhi. His entourage rode slowly down the ranks of soldiers, who came to attention as the King approached. As each battalion was reached, its colonel walked the King's horse down the line of his troops. The King proceeded to the Fosse Way-London Road crossroads, where he was joined by various dignitaries. By this time, an estimated crowd of between 1,000 to 1,200 civilians had gathered. The King's arrival was cheered by the civilians and the Warwickshire Yeomanry, who were drawn up near the crossroads. Then a march-past commenced, led by the Warwickshire Yeomanry, a local unit that was not part of the 29th Division. Next came the Division's artillery, followed by the infantry marching eight abreast. *The Story Behind the Monument* describes it as follows. 'Twelve splendid battalions, each at war strength in personnel, with fixed bayonets, filling the broad roadway from edge to edge and constantly flowing onward under the canopy of gigantic elm trees, was a splendid spectacle, and His Majesty was obviously greatly impressed by it.' The Revd Oswin Creighton wrote of 'the long line of silver bayonets winding through the trees like a stream' and said that the Division 'seemed vast, and the men were magnificent'. At least one of the participants held a less poetical view. Lieutenant Guy Nightingale of the Royal Munster

Fusiliers complained of the 8½ mile march from Coventry along a 'beastly hard road', followed by a long wait in the cold. But even he admitted that the Division 'looked a fine crowd'.

∞

On 12 March 1915, the day the King inspected the men of the 29th Division, General Sir Ian Hamilton, Commander of Home Forces, was working in his office at Horse Guards Parade, London. At about 10 a.m. he received a message that Secretary of State for War Lord Kitchener wanted to see him. Ian Hamilton was a decent, courteous and kindly man, who was also an intellectual and gifted writer. He had served as Kitchener's deputy during the Boer War and was somewhat in awe of him. According to Hamilton, he found Kitchener writing at his desk. 'After a moment, he looked up and said in a matter-of-fact tone, "We are sending a military force to support the fleet now at the Dardanelles, and you are to have command." Kitchener then resumed writing. At last, he looked up and inquired, "Well?" Hamilton began to ask questions about his assignment. K[itchener] frowned; shrugged his shoulders; [Hamilton] thought he was going to be impatient, but although he gave curt answers at first he slowly broadened out ...'

Kitchener told Hamilton that he would be given the Australian and New Zealand Army Corps (about 30,000 men), the 29th Division (about 19,000), the Royal Naval Division (11,000) and a French contingent (size unknown at the time, but believed to be of about division size). As Kitchener's directions for the force's use was extremely vague, presumably he hoped that Hamilton would come up with a workable plan. Hamilton met Kitchener again the following day. He was told that Turkish strength at Gallipoli was estimated at about 40,000 and it was believed that they were commanded by Jevad Pasha. It was not known how many heavy guns they had. Kitchener gave Hamilton written instructions of less than 1,000 words which said that landings by troops were only to be considered if the fleet failed to break through the Dardanelles. Kitchener did not wish Hamilton luck. As Hamilton picked up his cap from the table, Kitchener said, 'If the fleet gets through, Constantinople will fall of itself and you will have won, not a battle, but the war.' At 5 p.m. Hamilton and his staff left London by train. Crossing the Channel by destroyer, they travelled by train to Marseilles, where they boarded the cruiser *Phaeton* and set out for the Eastern Mediterranean.

∞

Meanwhile, having subdued the Dardanelles outer defences, in early March, the Allied navies began to attack the intermediate defence zone. As they moved forward, they came under fire from Turkish mobile guns on both shores. Due to their mobility, the guns were very difficult to locate. The failure of the ships to silence the mobile guns meant that minesweeping – carried out by trawlers with civilian crews – was hindered. The low-speed trawlers made little headway against the current. They were forced to sail upstream beyond the minefield and then sweep downstream. Attempts to use destroyers for minesweeping failed. As the civilian crews of the minesweeping trawlers were unable to cope with the intensity of fire from both shores, daylight minesweeping was abandoned. On 12 March, Vice-Admiral Carden added naval personnel to the trawlers' crews. But the trawlers' lack of power continued to impede progress.

ୠ

86th Brigade was scheduled to leave for Avonmouth, the port of embarkation, on 15 March. As the time for the troops to depart drew nearer there were stories of a number of Dublins marrying local girls. Tobacconists in Kenilworth were practically cleared out of their stock as townspeople made up parting gifts for the Blue Caps. On the afternoon of 15 March, the Dubs left for Avonmouth on three trains. The first train left at 5.30 p.m. and reached the port at 9.50 p.m. The final train arrived at Avonmouth at 6.10 a.m. on 16 March.

In Coventry, there was a flurry of presentations as the time approached for the departure of the 1st Royal Munster Fusiliers. The battalion was presented with an English bull-terrier as a mascot. 'Buller' was given a khaki coat for weekdays and a braided emerald-green one for Sundays, sporting the arms of Coventry and Munster. He was put on the Battalion roll and drew billet-money – half that of a soldier. The Coventry Irish Club presented the battalion with a flag inscribed *Erin go Brágh* (Ireland for Ever). Accepting the flag on behalf of the Munsters, Sergeant Robert O'Donaghue said that he hoped to carry the flag to Berlin (showing that he believed that the 29th Division was bound for France or Flanders). The city of Coventry presented the battalion with an illuminated scroll commemorating its stay. But some apprehension must have lurked beneath the air of joviality. On 14 March, Limerick man Company Sergeant-Major David Danagher of C Company drew up his will. The Boer War veteran left all his possessions to his wife Margaret. After the soldiers were issued with new boots, ten-year-old Elsie from the fruit shop in Earlsdon Street heard another Limerick man, Private Martin O'Malley, say quietly: 'I expect that these are for my grave.'

According to *The Story Behind the Monument*, 'The departure of the Munsters from Coventry was a tumultuous and emotional affair. It was meant to be a dignified march to the station but the good citizens of Coventry would have none of it. These sons of Ireland had been adopted as their sons, their lovers. Children weaved their way in and out of the marching ranks, women hung around the necks of soldiers. The police tried to control things, but were no match for the high emotion of the people. Through the night, there continued to be the tears and embraces. Three trains came and went, carrying away their cargo of men, until, in the cold dawn, there was nothing but silence – and waiting.' Shortly before departure, Bob Jordan, who had returned to the colours from New York, went to the Nursing Home where Elsie Fleming was convalescing. Charming the stern matron, he secured her permission to see Elsie and asked her to wait for him to return from the war. Elsie said that she could not promise, but that she would be straight with him and let him know if she met someone else.

Father William Finn, the Blue Caps Chaplain.

The 1st Royal Dublin Fusiliers left England with most of the officers who had come from India. Apart from Lieutenant-Colonel Richard Rooth and Major Edwyn Featherstonhaugh, the battalion had twenty-four officers. There were ten captains, twelve lieutenants and two second lieutenants. Captain Arthur Broadhurst-Hill and Lieutenant James Shine had been transferred to the 3rd Battalion in Cork. Four officers had been assigned to the battalion: Lieutenants William Andrews[32] and Cuthbert Maffett and Second Lieutenants Joseph Hosford and John Walters.[33] Also attached to the Dublins were Chaplain Revd Father William Finn and Royal Army Medical Corps Lieutenant Henry Speldewinde de Boer.[34] While Finn's service file does not record the date he took up duty with the Blue Caps, Revd Oswin Creighton recorded in his diary on Wednesday 17 February: 'Father Finn, the R.C. chaplain, came to see me and seemed very pleasant.' As Creighton did not mention Finn among the attendees at the dinner for Dublins officers the previous evening, it seems likely that Finn called to Creighton on the day he reported for duty with the battalion. Presumably Dr de Boer joined the battalion shortly before they left England, given that he had officially been commissioned as recently as 11 January 1915.

∾

On 1 April 1908, for home defence, Britain established the Territorial Force, comprised of part-time volunteer soldiers. Modelled on the Regular Army, the Territorials included artillery, engineers, medical and supply formations. On the outbreak of war many Territorial units volunteered to serve abroad. The 1st West Riding Field Company of the Royal Engineers was raised in Sheffield. Assigned to the 29th Division during February, the company was stationed at the village of Long Itchington, Warwickshire for about ten days. Among the company was Lance-Corporal George Beverly Smith who had been called up from his job in Sheffield Steel Works on 4 August 1914. On their final night in the village, the men of the unit were given a final hot meal at their billets. At 10.30 p.m. they paraded on the village green. Then, to the accompaniment of best wishes from the villagers, the company marched off into the night on their way to Leamington and an early morning train to Avonmouth.

∾

As suggested by its name, Avonmouth is located at the mouth of the River Avon. The river flows into the Bristol Channel at the town. Avonmouth became one of the major ports of departure for British troops embarking for France. Now the 29th Division was departing from the port, bound for the Middle East. The 29th Division's brigades left from Avonmouth in numerical order. On 16 March, a few hours before the 86th Brigade departed, the Revd Oswin Creighton, Church of England Chaplain to the brigade, took the opportunity to get off the *Alaunia*, where he had slept the previous night, and went shopping in Bristol. There he happened to run into Lieutenant-Colonel Richard Rooth of the Dublins, who was also on a shopping expedition. Rooth told him that his servant had left all his kit behind on the railway platform, necessitating his having to replace it.[35]

Upon arrival at Avonmouth, Second Lieutenant Norman Dewhurst of the Munsters was put in charge of a party of men with orders to get thirty horses on board the *Mercian* and nine vehicles on the *Ausonia*. The job took all night and it was early morning before he got to his cabin. Meanwhile, the 1st Dublins boarded the *Ausonia*. Brigade Headquarters was also aboard: Brigadier-General Steuart Hare, Brigade-Major Thomas Frankland and Staff Captain Harold Mynors Farmar (known as Mynors). Brigade-Major Thomas Hugh Colville Frankland was a Royal Dublin Fusiliers officer who had been captured with Winston Churchill during the Boer War.

A, B and C Companies of the 1st Royal Munster Fusiliers travelled on the *Anson*, while D Company was aboard the *Alaunia*, with the 1st Lancashire Fusiliers and the 2nd Royal Fusiliers. Battalion transports and horses were aboard the *Haverford* and *Mercian*. One Royal Dublin Fusilier Officer and seventy other ranks travelled on the latter ship with regimental horses and mules.

When the Revd Oswin Creighton returned from shopping he found those on the *Alaunia* 'were wearing life-belts and being shown where to stand in case of being torpedoed'. After lunch he wandered onto the *Ausonia*. He described the ship as 'a very small, uncomfortable boat, and they are very crowded, four officers in a tiny cabin and a miserable little dining-room'. He tried to persuade Brigadier-General Steuart Hare to transfer to the 13,405 ton Cunard-liner *Alaunia* with his staff. Hare said that it would not look well to transfer now that they were setting off on active service. At 7.30 p.m., the ships containing the 86th Brigade put to sea, escorted by two destroyers.

ର

On 16 March, the day 86th Brigade left Avonmouth, Vice-Admiral Carden, overcome by the strain of the past weeks, was placed on the sick list. The next most senior officer in the theatre of operations was Rear-Admiral Rosslyn Wemyss, who was involved in establishing a base for Allied troops at Lemnos Island. Expressing the view that he ought to remain where he was, Wemyss indicated his willingness to serve under Carden's second-in-command. So on 17 March, St Patrick's Day 1915, Carden was succeeded by fellow Irishman Rear-Admiral John de Robeck. Promoted to acting Rear-Admiral, the County Kildare man indicated that, weather permitting, operations would continue the following day.

ର

Cecil Grimshaw with George (left) and Tommy, taken before his departure for Gallipoli.

87th Brigade sailed from Avonmouth on St Patrick's Day. The 2nd Hampshire Regiment arrived at Avonmouth on 20 March. Y and Z Companies set sail on the *Manitou* the same day, with the battalion transport on the *Tintorette*. The following day, Battalion Headquarters and X and W Companies sailed on the *RMS Aragon*, with one company of the 4th Worcestershire Regiment.

∞

As the men of the 29th Division set out from England, it is appropriate to look at the country about to be invaded.

CHAPTER 3

Defending their Homeland: The Turks, the Dardanelles and Gallipoli

'Surrounded by hostile states and greedy empires, and with international
tensions unlikely to allow a long period of reconstruction, Turkey could
not afford diplomatic isolation in 1914, and the regime sought a protective
alliance with one of the major European power blocs.'
The Macmillan Dictionary of the First World War,
by Stephen Pope and Elizabeth-Anne Wheal

Many English language books on the Gallipoli campaign tend to portray the
Turks as powerless victims of German scheming. Based on recent research,
David Fromkin's *A Peace to End All Peace* suggests the reality was completely
different. Having reached its pinnacle in the sixteenth and seventeenth centuries, the Ottoman Empire began to go into decline in the eighteenth century
and lost a significant amount of territory in the nineteenth century. The loss of
further territory in the Balkan Wars of 1912-1913 was followed by a coup d'état
in 1913, by a group nicknamed *The Young Turks*. The new rulers struggled
to reform and modernise the disintegrating empire.[1] While the government
was composed of a number of factions, all agreed that Turkey's most urgent
need was to secure a powerful European ally. Attempts to secure an alliance
with Britain, France or Germany were unsuccessful. On 24 July 1914, Kaiser
Wilhelm II ordered that the Turkish offer of an alliance be explored. Secret
talks began in Constantinople. Despite the Kaiser's views, German Prime
Minister Chancellor Theobald von Bethmann Hollweg was unenthusiastic
about an alliance. He told Ambassador-to-Turkey, Hans von Wangenheim,
not to sign a treaty of alliance unless Turkey had something significant to
offer. On the face of it, the Turks had little to offer. Yet, on 1 August, a secret
treaty was signed. Why?

On 31 July, the British cabinet agreed that, for possible use against Germany, the Royal Navy should seize two ships that were being built in Britain for the Turkish navy. Records in German diplomatic archives show that, on 1 August, the Turks offered to give Germany one of the ships, the battleship *Sultan Osman 1*. Von Wangenheim accepted the offer. But why would the Ottomans offer to give away Turkey's prize battleship, whose construction was paid for by a national collection among the Turkish people? It transpires that, on the day the offer was made to the Germans, Minister for War, Enver Pasha, told fellow Young Turk leaders that Britain had seized the battleship.[2] So the Turks offered the ship to the Germans knowing that they would never have to meet the offer. The Germans never discovered that they had been fooled. They believed the Turks intended to keep their side of the bargain and were only prevented from doing so by the British seizure of the ships.

The 1 August treaty pledged Germany to defend the Ottoman Empire if it were attacked. The Ottomans were only required to go to war if Germany were required to enter the fighting under the terms of her treaty with Austria-Hungry.[3] The Ottoman government ordered a general mobilisation the day after the treaty was signed, but proclaimed neutrality in the European conflict. In conversations with Allied representatives, Enver Pasha went so far as to suggest that Turkey might join the Allies. The treaty with Germany remained a secret. On 1 August, Enver held a private meeting with Hans von Wangenheim, German Ambassador, and Otto Liman von Sanders, head of the German Military Mission to Turkey. They discussed how their countries might collaborate if Turkey were to enter the war on Germany's side. They decided that the German Mediterranean fleet, consisting of the *Goeben* and the *Breslau* should come to Constantinople to strengthen the Ottoman Black Sea fleet. On 3 August, the German Admiralty ordered Rear-Admiral Souchon to sail his ships to Constantinople, with consequences previously outlined. What has not been outlined is the Turkish side of the story.

∾

On 6 August, Ottoman Foreign Minister, Prince Said Halim held discussions with the German Ambassador. In the Mediterranean, the *Goeben* and the *Breslau* were being hunted by the Royal Navy. Said Halim said his government had decided to allow the ships enter the Dardanelles, subject to six conditions, including some of the spoils of victory if Germany won the war. The German ambassador had no option but to agree to the conditions. Von Wangenheim had barely recovered from these demands when, three days later, Said Halim told him that the Ottoman Empire might join Greece and Romania in a public pact of neutrality in the war. If so, something would have to be done about the presence of the *Goeben* and the *Breslau* in Turkish waters, if Turkish neutrality was not to be compromised. The Ottomans proposed to make a fictitious purchase of the ships. The German ambassador rejected the Turkish proposal. The Ottoman government immediately issued a public statement claiming it had bought the ships. In the face of public rejoicing throughout Turkey, von Wangenheim advised Berlin on 14 August that Germany had to go along with the 'sale.' If they disavowed it, they would risk turning Turkish public opinion against Germany. As the Turks did not have crews trained to operate the ships, Admiral Souchon was appointed commander of the Ottoman Fleet and his sailors given Turkish uniforms and fezzes. Britain viewed the episode as one of German duplicity. Even today, many historians repeat that view.

On 26 September, British ships turned back a Turkish torpedo boat at the entrance to the Dardanelles. The following day, the Turks closed the Dardanelles to international shipping. Yet they made no move to declare war. This passive hostility baffled and frustrated First Lord of the Admiralty, Winston Churchill. Unknown to Churchill, German representatives in Turkey were equally frustrated at their failure to push Turkey into the war. They hoped, in vain, that the presence of *Goeben* and *Breslau* might provoke Britain to declare war on Turkey. At the same time that Rear-Admiral Limpus, head of the British naval mission to Turkey, was informing Churchill that Turkey was almost completely in German hands, General Liman von Sanders, head of the German military mission, told the Kaiser that the atmosphere made it almost unbearable for German officers to continue serving there. The Kaiser refused von Liman's request to be allowed to return to Germany. Germany's hope of a quick victory on the Western Front had been stopped at the first Battle of the Marne. Germany now desperately needed Turkey to enter the war on her side.

Despite the benefits derived from the policy of non-intervention, Enver Pasha began to scheme against the policy and its supporters. Previously his policy had been driven by fear of Russian conquest of Turkish territory, but following German successes against the Russians, he seems to have hoped that Turkey might seize Russian territory. In autumn 1914, rival factions struggled for control of the Turkish Government. Enver Pasha stopped trying to persuade his government to come into the war. If he could not get Turkey to declare war on the Allies, he might provoke the Allies to declare war on Turkey. Secret orders were given to Admiral Souchon to attack Russian vessels in the Black Sea, under the pretext the Russians had attacked. Souchon decided to push matters by bombarding the Russian coast. The result brought Turkey into the War on Germany's side.

ໜ

Gallipoli: The Battleground

According to a British military intelligence report in September 1914,[4] the Gallipoli peninsula is 52 miles at its longest point and 14 miles in width at its widest. At its narrowest, it is less than 3½ miles wide. The peninsula had been fortified for several hundred years. At Bulair, at the narrowest point, the British and French had built fortifications during the Crimean War. Work on its modern defences had begun during the 1880s. Until 1912, they mainly consisted of coastal defence guns, searchlights and under-water minefields. In 1912, during the Balkan Wars, the Ottoman General Staff ordered fortification of the peninsula to defend against possible Greek landings. Strong points were built on key terrain features overlooking the peninsula's beaches, trenches were dug, gun pits built and a roads and communications network developed. Despite these preparations, the Dardanelles defences remained weak. This was due to the poor condition of the fortifications, the fact that many of the guns were old and the scarcity of ammunition and supplies. In 1913, troop levels on the peninsula reverted to peacetime levels. What the Turks termed 'The Çanakkale Fortified Area' (the land on either side of the Dardanelles), was commanded by Brigadier-General Cevat. His command consisted of a string of old forts, mostly at the mouth of the Dardanelles and at The Narrows and a brigade of three heavy and medium artillery regiments. Sedd el Bahr came within Cevat's area of responsibility.

In late autumn 1914, in an attempt to address the weakness of the Dardanelles defences, the Germans sent Vice-Admiral Guido von Usedom, an authority on seacoast defences, to Turkey. He was accompanied by about 500 German specialists in coastal artillery, communications, and mines, including defense specialist army engineer Colonel Weber.

ໜ

Gallipoli Peninsula, Late July 1914

Brigadier-General Esat, commander of 111 Corps, was a graduate of the Ottoman and Prussian War Academies and a hero of the Balkan wars.[5] While the average age of Turkish corps commanders was forty, Esat, in his early fifties, was the oldest. His white bushy moustache gave him a somewhat grandfatherly appearance. But his appearance belied his active nature and aggressive command style. He was known as a 'teacher of teachers', because he had served in several military schools as an instructor and had been the Dean of the Military Academy. Nearly all of his divisional and regimental commanders were his former students. According to the memoirs of one commander, Esat continued to act as an instructor during the Gallipoli campaign, by teaching his subordinates about the art of war. His experienced command team were also veterans of the Balkan wars. 111 Corps had fought in every major battle of the Balkan Wars in the Thracian theatre. In a war that destroyed large portions of the Ottoman Army, 111 Corps was the only corps to survive organisationally intact. Of the thirteen Ottoman Army corps in 1914, it was the only one that was able to concentrate exclusively on operations and training. It was the most experienced and well-prepared corps in the Ottoman Army.[6]

Though Turkey had not entered the war, the Turkish General Staff decided to mobilise the army, which included calling up the reserves. At 1 a.m. on 2 August 1914 they sent out mobilisation orders. The orders arrived at Esat's 111 Corps headquarters at 2.45 a.m. and he immediately got out of bed to read them. Meanwhile, captains of the Reserve (the Redif) sent out mounted gendarmes to alert the men of the army reserve. Reservists were not assigned to specific units. They reported to mobilisation depots and were assigned to units as required. In Çanakkale province, twenty-two-year-old Serif Ali Arslan was working in the fields near Çan-Malli village when the word came. Harvest time was approaching, it was a Friday and the weather was very hot. Serif Ali had served in the 7th Division in the Balkan Wars. He had lost four of his friends fighting the Bulgarians. Upon discharge from the army he had reported to the captain of the Reserve, handed in his uniform and been registered as a member of the Redif. Now, the chief of the village came and told him that he was to report to the military authorities in the town of Kepez, near Çanakkale. 'Set out quickly, otherwise I will get in trouble,' the chief told him. Serfi Ali Arslan set out with other men from the village. In Kepez he was assigned to the 1st Battalion, 25th Regiment, 9th Infantry Division, part of Esat's 111

Corps. The 25th Regiment spent August and September training its soldiers. On 17 November 1914 it was moved forward to defend the beaches at Kum Kale on the Asiatic side of the Dardanelles.

Esat's 111 Corps began to mobilise on 3 August, the day following receipt of the mobilisation order. Composed of the 7th, 8th and 9th Infantry Divisions, defensive plans required the corps to reinforce Cevat's Çanakkale Fortified Area Command, as well as providing troops to defend the Gallipoli Peninsula.[7] The 9th Infantry Division was commanded by forty-nine-year-old Colonel Halil Sami, who had commanded the 5th Rifle Regiment in the Balkan Wars.[8] Following mobilisation, the 9th Division was assigned to act as a mobile reserve for the Çanakkale Fortified Area Command. While the division still technically reported to Esat's 111 Corps, to all intents and purposes it now came under the command of Cevat's Çanakkale Fortified Area Command, of which Sedd el Bahr formed a part.

The 9th Infantry Division was composed of three regiments: the 25th, 26th and 27th. The 26th Regiment was commanded by Major Hafiz Kadri. The regiment's 1st Battalion was on detached duty at Basra when mobilisation was ordered. So the 2nd and 3rd Battalions proceeded with mobilisation. By 15 August, the regiment had 381 serving soldiers, 2,092 reservists and 199 untrained conscripts on its rolls. The following day it began to organise a new 1st Battalion. Four days later, the regiment was ordered to occupy coastal observation posts and to prepare defensive positions by stationing a company at Sedd el Bahr, a platoon at Gaba Tepe (near Anzac), a company further up the coast at Ece Limani, north of the Gulf of Saros,[9] and the rest at Ecebat (Maidos).[10] On 4 October, in cooperation with artillery[11] located at Alçi Tepe (meaning Plaster Hill, it was known to the British as Achi Baba or Archie Barber), Major Kadri developed plans for covering fire for his troops. Troops from his regiment would oppose the landing at Sedd el Bahr on 25 April 1915.

လလ

Aegean Sea Entrance to the Dardanelles, 3 November 1914

Turkey declared war on Britain and France on 31 October. Though the Allies had not made a reciprocal declaration, on 3 November, the British battle-cruisers *Indefatigable* and *Indomitable* and the French battleships

Suffren and *Vérité* opened fire on the forts guarding the entrance to the Dardanelles. The British ships shelled Sedd el Bahr on the European shore, while the French ships shelled Kum Kale and Orkanie on the Asiatic shore. The forts on both sides of the straits were manned by Turkish regular soldiers from the two battalions of the 5th Heavy Artillery Regiment. Although none of the Allied ships came within range of their guns, the Turkish gunners replied to the attack. The encounter lasted about half an hour. During the exchange, troops in the Sedd el Bahr Castle began to move ammunition and black powder for the castle's guns out of the line of fire. While this was still in progress a shell from the *Indominitable* landed behind the fort. It ignited powder that had leaked onto the ground in the vicinity of a cart that was being loaded with ammunition. According to a survivor, this resulted in a massive explosion. Eighty-six Turkish officers and men were killed in the detonation. All the casualties were buried outside the castle wall.[12] French shelling of the Asia shore did not produce any significant results.

☙❧

The Turkish Army's 8th Artillery Regiment, consisting of mobile 150mm howitzers, was sent to the Dardanelles by mid-February 1915, to defend against attacks by British and French ships. The regiment's twenty-two artillery pieces were divided into three groups and deployed in hidden positions covering the entrance to the Dardanelles. They were later reinforced by fourteen mobile howitzers. By February, the Fortress Command had on the Gallipoli Peninsula over 34,500 soldiers, armed with 25,000 rifles, eight machine guns and 263 artillery pieces. By the time of the Allied naval attack on 18 March 1915, the Turks had eighty-two fixed guns and 230 mobile guns and howitzers on the peninsula.

☙❧

On 26 March, German General Otto Liman von Sanders arrived at the port of Gallipoli (Gelibolu) to take command of the Fifth Army, that was being established for the defence of the Dardanelles. His command consisted of III Corps (stationed on the Gallipoli Peninsula), XV Corps (stationed on the Asian side of the Dardanelles), the 5th Infantry Division and a cavalry brigade (the infantry division and cavalry brigade were kept as reserves). Over the following four weeks Liman von Sanders put his troops to work, improving the road network, camouflaging troop concentrations and artillery and improving fortifications at the landing beaches. They commandeered tools and barbed-wire fences from local farmers. In between the gruelling periods of building fortifications, at night, and in inclement weather, the troops were endlessly subjected to anti-invasion alarms and drills. The invading British and Irish soldiers of the 29th Division would meet Turkish defenders who were very well prepared and very determined.

CHAPTER 4

Voyagers:
Sailing to the Mediterranean

'We were on the first boat of the whole Division to leave. Very strict orders
were given. No lights were allowed. We had to sleep in our clothes with
life-belts at hand. At 10.30 I went on deck. It was very dark. The boat was
steaming ahead in perfect darkness and silence. I could just dimly make out
the form of a destroyer accompanying us with no lights.'
     With the Twenty-Ninth Division in Gallipoli by Revd O. Creighton

Off Avonmouth, Bristol Channel, 16 March 1915

On board the *Ausonia*, the Blue Caps were settling down for a long voyage.
The 8,133-ton Cunard line ship had been built six years previously. Despite the
Revd Creighton's critical comments about the ship, its cuisine was reported
to be of first-class hotel standard. As the convoy of four ships and two escorting destroyers made their way down the Bristol Channel, a suspicious craft
was spotted. The merchant ships altered course and the destroyers gave chase
to what was presumed to be a German submarine.

The following day was St Patrick's Day and one would have expected the Irish
to have celebrated it in style. However neither *Neill's Blue Caps* nor *History of the
Royal Munster Fusiliers* mention the Irish holiday in their accounts. Munsters
officer Norman Dewhurst recorded the day as being quiet. He said that on
the afternoon of 16 March everyone on his ship received vaccinations and on
18 March they had a lecture, on the poop deck, about guns. It became foggy at
7 p.m. The ship sailed through the night with its fog siren blowing, apparently
fearless of possible submarine attack. Later the soldiers heard that they were
bound for Constantinople and from there through Austria to Berlin.[1]

Officers of the Blue Caps, taken immediately prior to embarkation for Gallipoli. From left to right, back row: 2nd Lt J. Hosford, 2nd Lt J.P. Walters, Lt R.H. de Lusignan*, 2nd Lt R.V.C. Corbet*, Lt H.D. O'Hara*, 2nd Lt W. Andrews*, 2nd Lt C.W. Maffett, Lt QM J. Jennedy, Revd Finn*, CF, Lt H. de Boer RAMC, Capt. G.M. Dunlop*, Lt F.S. Lanigan-O'Keeffe, Lt R. Bernard*, Lt C.G. Carruthers, Lt L.C. Boustead*. Front Row: Capt. D. French, Capt. J.R.W. Grove, Capt. J.M. Mood, Capt. A.M. Johnson, Capt. W.F. Higginson*, Maj. E. Fetherstonhaugh*, Lt-Col. R.A. Rooth*, Capt. C.T.W. Grimshaw*, DSO, Capt. E.A. Molesworth, Capt H.C. Crozier, Capt. A.W. Molony, Capt. D.V.F. Anderson*, Lt. H.M. Floyd*. Those killed in action are marked with an asterisk.

Cecil Grimshaw, Adjutant of the 1st Dublins, copied the following notice into his notebook on St Patrick's Day:

Published on Board SS Ausonia
March 17th 1915

Complimentary orders are forbidden by the Kings Regulations & therefore the commanding officer is unable to make any reference to the fact that owing to his promotion to Field rank Major Grimshaw DSO had to give up his appointment as adjutant to the Btn. [Battalion]

There is however no objection to Coy [Company] officers telling the NCO's & men of their Coys [Companies] that the CO has the very highest appreciation

of the services rendered to the Btn [Battalion] by Major Grimshaw. Major Grimshaw has worked with untiring energy during the full time that his term of office has lasted. No officer has had the interests of the Btn [Battalion] more at heart & it is greatly his work that the Battalion has earned such a good name in peace time & that it is so well prepared for service.
Complimentary Memo By Lt: Col: Rooth
1st R.D.F.

Captain William Higginson – who, in May 1914, had left Milton Barracks in Gravesend to travel to India with the then Major Richard Rooth – succeeded Grimshaw as adjutant. He had previously spent a period as adjutant of the 2nd Battalion.

The following message from the King was read soon after departure:

Buckingham Palace

Message from the King to the 29th Division

March 12, 1915

I was much struck with the steadiness under arms and marching powers of the splendid body of men composing the 29th Division.

The combination of so many experienced officers and seasoned soldiers, whom I particularly noticed on parade, will, I feel confident, prove of inestimable value on the field of battle.

That the 29th Division, wherever employed, will uphold the high reputation already won by my army in France and Belgium, I have no doubt.

Rest assured that your movements and welfare will ever be in my thoughts.

The diary of the Revd Oswin Creighton gives some idea of shipboard life. 'Life on a troopship is wonderfully orderly and smooth. Everything follows a carefully arranged programme. I am usually up by 7.15, when the officers of one regiment do physical drill and I join them … Then there are rounds at 10.30, when the Colonels inspect their battalions and the Captain goes round his ship, followed by drill and probably a lecture for the officers … In fact the day goes very quickly. Supper at 7p.m …' Of the soldiers he says:

The men are really just like so many children. They have been writing reams of mawkish sentimental letters to the Nuneaton girls, which the officers have had to censor. I don't know a single man who thought of buying a book or magazine for the journey … They behave extremely well, give no trouble, and are perfectly docile. You very rarely hear them slanged by either officers or NCOs. They take everything for granted as it comes along, grumbling a little and longing to be back with Susy or May in Nuneaton. They are always very friendly and responsive. The tone among the officers seems very high, and they strike me as a nice, clean-living, straightforward, moderate lot of men. One or two are quite intelligent and have interests outside the army, but the younger ones are mostly interested in sport. None of them put the least bit of side on, and they all work hard at their jobs and have a strong sense of responsibility.

∽

The Dardanelles, 18 March 1915

The fleet resumed its assault at 10.30 a.m. The ships sailed in three columns, with the British in the first and the third (Reserve) and the French in the second. The fleet came under howitzer fire from the shore as ships made their way to their assigned positions. At about 11.30 a.m., the British ships opened fire on Turkish forts at The Narrows. It appeared that the bombardment was having an effect, as the guns in the forts for the most part remained silent.

At 12.06 p.m., Vice-Admiral de Robeck ordered the French ships to pass through the British line and shell the forts from closer range. As the French ships began to move forward, more and more of the Turkish batteries and forts opened fire on the British ships. The French ships reached a range of 10,000 yards and began a tremendous duel with the forts. At 1.45 p.m., the Turkish fire slackened. To allow the battleships to move closer to the forts, de Robeck ordered minesweepers to begin clearing a passage through the minefield the Turks had laid across the Dardanelles. He also ordered the reserve British ships to replace the French ships, as the latter had been repeatedly struck by fire from the forts. At 2 p.m., as the French battleship *Bouvet* approached the British line she was rocked by an explosion. To those aboard the Royal Navy ships it was not clear whether the explosion was caused by a shell or a mine. Almost immediately there was a second, bigger explosion, which seemed to suggest a magazine had exploded. As the smoke cleared the *Bouvet* was seen to have taken a heavy list. About two minutes later the ship turned over and sank. Only forty-eight of her crew were saved, with over 600 lost.

The reserve British column sailed forward, replaced the French ships and continued the duel with the forts. Though the forts ceased firing from time to time, it was obvious that they had not been put out of action. At 4.11 p.m., the battle cruiser *Inflexible* struck a mine on her starboard bow. Taking on water, she attempted to sail for Tenedos Island, outside the Dardanelles. Three minutes later the battleship *Irresistible* struck a mine. With ten volunteers, including the captain, being left aboard, twenty-eight officers and five hundred and twenty-eight men were taken off by the destroyer *Wear*. At 4.50 p.m., the *Wear* reached De Roebuck's flagship, the battleship *Queen Elizabeth*. Only then learning that a mine was the source of *Irresistible*'s problems, he ordered the ships that had accompanied her to fall back.

After Captain Hayes-Sadler of the battleship *Ocean* and Captain Dent of the battleship *Irresistible* decided it was not possible for the former to tow the latter, the *Irresistible*'s remaining crew were evacuated. At this point Vice-Admiral de Robeck hoisted the 'General Recall' signal and began the return to Tenedos Island for the night. The *Ocean* withdrew under heavy fire. At about 6 p.m., when she was about a mile from the *Irresistible*, a heavy explosion on her starboard side announced that the *Ocean* had struck a mine. Almost at the same time, a shell struck her aft on the same side. Under fire from both shores, the crew were evacuated by three destroyers, one of the destroyers later returning to pick up four men who had been inadvertently left aboard. After reporting to the Vice-Admiral at Tenedos, the captains of the *Irresistible* and the *Ocean* returned with a group of destroyers and minesweepers. But though they searched until almost midnight, neither ship could be located. They both lay beneath the Dardanelles.

Meanwhile, in spite of the damage she had sustained, the *Inflexible* had managed to reach Tenedos. It was soon evident that she would require assistance to sail to Malta for repairs. It was also found that the French battleships *Suffren* and *Gaulois* would have to undergo extensive repairs before they would be fit for further service. Of the sixteen ships involved in the attack, three had been sunk and three put out of action for an indefinite period. Of the whole Allied battle fleet, one-third had been put out of action in one day. On 19 March, de Robeck suspended operations, because of uncertainty over the cause of the sinkings. The following day a return of bad weather put an end to an immediate resumption of the attack.

∞

In the meantime, Captain Reginald Hall, Director of Naval Intelligence, had instigated secret negotiations in an attempt to persuade Turkey to cease hostilities. The negotiators were authorised to pay a large sum of money to the Turks. The negotiations failed because the British were unwilling to give assurances that the Turks could retain Constantinople, having previously promised it to the Russians.[2]

∞

Aboard the Ausonia, *at Sea, March 1915*

On 19 March, battalion orders for the Royal Dublin Fusiliers directed that A, B, C and D companies would henceforth be designated W, X, Y and Z companies. *Neill's Blue Caps* records that during the voyage helmets were issued and all ranks were given silk handkerchiefs, a present from the citizens of Madras. Three days later, Lieutenant-Colonel Richard Rooth reached his forty-ninth birthday. Also on that day, Dubliner Robert Roleston from C Company wrote a letter to his mother Elizabeth at 2 Grants Row, off Lower Mount Street, Dublin.[3]

British Expeditionary Force
Pte. R. Roleston
11174 C Company
1st Royal Dub Fus
86th Infantry Brigade
29th Division

22nd March

My Dear Mother

I am writing to you hoping you and all at home are well as I am myself at present. I am not landed yet or I don't know where I am going to land.

But I hope I will get out of this war alright. If you watch the papers closely you will know whether I am wounded or killed. I hope it will be neither. I hope you will write as soon as you get this letter. I hope Billy[4] is working and also Mr. Chambers and aunt [the next part is illegible]. You will know if I am killed because the money will be stopped. You will want to be on the watch if I am killed. You will have a few pounds to get belong to me that is my credit.

No more. Write soon. Good Bye. I hope it will not be forever.

R. Roleston [ten kisses followed the signature]

Good Bye. I hope it will not be forever. Tell all the people I was asking for them and Mrs Brown.

About two weeks later, Royal Dublin Fusilier John Sullivan, who had left his job as a bill poster upon the outbreak of war, wrote to his wife Kate in Cork.

Dear Kate

I write you these few lines hoping you and the children are in good health as this leaves me at present and thank God for it. Dear Kate I was fine until we got to the coast of Spain then an awful seasickness came on us, but I was only sick an hour. We have four priests with us, grand gentlemen they are we had Mass, Confession and Holy Communion on Sunday morning April 3rd and I received and we had Mass every morning on the ship. Dear Kate this is a good ship for travelling but we are going very slow on account of the mines. While I am writing this I am sitting in my hammock waiting to have the ship to call at Gibraltar for the post. Dear Kate I suppose the children are lonesome after me, they are very often running in my mind as you are. But dear wife whatever you do look after yourself and the children and always pray for me and also light two candles every week to St. Anthony's Altar in Broad Lane Chapel for the safe return of your loving husband. Kate we don't know what is before us when we get out here but with the help of God I hope we will get through it. Dear Kate I will let you know more when I land having no more to say at present …

න

On the morning of 24 March, the *Ausonia* docked at Malta for re-coaling. As it did not depart until 7.30 a.m. on the morning of 26 March, it would be nice to think that those aboard would have been allowed some time ashore. Munsters officer Norman Dewhurst, however, reported that on his ship – which docked at 10 a.m. on 23 March – only officers were allowed ashore. He said that he had lunch at the Osborne Hotel and in the evening went to the Alambra Theatre. He went ashore again the following day and had a two-hour drive around the island on a hired carriage. That evening, he attended an Italian company's pro- duction of *Faust* at the Opera House. He said his ship left Malta at 7 a.m. on 25 March, in company with the troopship *Adania*. As the two ships sailed out, they passed the inbound *Sudan*, which Dewhurst said contained wounded sailors from the Dardanelles.

On Sunday 28 March, while the *Ausonia* was in the eastern Mediterranean, twenty-seven-year-old Private Peter Kavanagh of the Royal Dublin Fusiliers died of pneumonia in the ship's hospital and was buried at sea at noon.[5] Sergeant Joseph Skerritt from Birr, County Offaly, Corporal James Ennis from Swords, County Dublin, and Privates Patrick Dunne and Thomas Ryan, both of Dublin, may have felt a particular sadness at Peter Kavanagh's death. The records show that they had all joined the regiment in Dublin at the same time as Kavanagh and had been given sequential regimental numbers. (Peter Kavanagh 9843, Joseph Skerritt 9844, Patrick Dunne 9846, James Ennis 9847 and Thomas Ryan 9848.)[6] In just over a month all would be dead.

ରେ

The men of the 29th Division were bound for Egypt. The country, nominally part of the Ottoman Empire, had run up huge debts during the 1870s. Under a plan prepared by an international commission, a new cabinet was installed with a British Minister of Finance and a French Minister of Public Works. A coup against the ruling Khedive Tewfik was crushed at the Battle of Tel- el-Kebir, by a British Army led by Dublin-born General Sir Garnet Wolsey. The British agreed to leave Egypt, subject to certain conditions. French and Russian pressure on Ottoman Sultan Abdul Hamid prevented his agreeing to the British terms. Ironically, this had the effect of the British remaining on, an outcome that did not please the French, Russians nor Turks. The British were still in the country at the outbreak of the First World War.

ରେ

The *Ausonia* docked at Alexandria, Egypt in the early hours of 29 March, but the troops remained aboard. The *Anson* carrying Headquarters, A, B and C Companies of the Munsters docked the same day. The *Alaunia,* with D Company of the Munsters and the 1st Lancashire Fusiliers and the 2nd Royal Fusiliers aboard, had arrived the previous day, having docked at Malta on 23 March and sailing for Egypt on 25 March.

On the day following the arrival of the Blue Caps Lieutenant Francis Lanigan-O'Keeffe was brought to hospital.[7] At 4 p.m., the battalion began disembarking and marched to Mex Camp about 5 miles east of Alexandria, where the 29th Division's 86th and 87th Brigades were based.[8] The camp was situated on a strip of desert between a salt lake and the sea. Not a pleasant spot, it had two redeeming features: a tram link to Alexandria and the nearby sea, in which soldiers could swim. The War Diary of the 1st Royal Inniskilling Fusiliers recorded that the water supply at Mex Camp was insufficient and the sanitary arrangements poor. Norman Dewhurst said that his ship docked at Alexandria on 29 March. The harbour was full of ships of every description, transports, cargo boats, supply vessels, warships and captured enemy ships. The Munsters disembarked the following day and marched to Mex, where they erected tents and slept on bare hard ground.

Neill's Blue Caps records the strength of the Dublins as twenty-five officers (excluding the chaplain and medical officer) and 987 other ranks. Each man had 220 rounds of ammunition. The battalion had four machine guns, with 11,500 rounds available for each gun, fifty-three draught horses, eleven riding horses, nineteen wagons and sixteen tool carts. The two brigades at Mex Camp practised disembarking from small boats and forming up and advancing rapidly after landing. *The History of the Royal Munster Fusiliers* says that ship's whale-boats were used in the training. Norman Dewhurst said the Munsters returned to camp each day wet and covered in sand. The men were not allowed into Alexandria, but he visited it once or twice at night. 'At first you took a donkey from the camp to the nearest terminus, but soon train tracks had been laid from the camp to the tram point and we went that way. I did not go into town until 10 in the evening as that was the time when things really began to warm up.' Dewhurst said he last visited Alexandria on the evening of 3 April, when he went to the Kursaal and Belle Vue nightclubs. He got back to camp at 4 a.m., on what was now Easter Sunday. He said that after about a week at camp he stopped going to Alexandria 'as it meant dressing up each time'. So after the heat and exertions of the day, he had dinner at 8 p.m. and went to bed at 10 p.m. He said the ground at the camp was so bad, the officers' mess tent was moved five times in seven days.

Around this time Corkman John Sullivan wrote to his wife Kate.

5798 Pte John Sullivan RDF
W Coy 86 Brigade 29th Division
Mediterranean Expeditionary Force.
Dear Kate,
Just a few lines hoping to find you and the children are in the best of health
as this leaves me at present thank God for it. You must excuse me for not
writing before now as notepaper is very scarce out here but things will be
better after a while. I hope you did the little favour I asked you to do for me
and hoping you will light some more candles. Dear Kate send me out a box
of woodbines and a prayer book. Tell Mrs Fox I made enquires about her
son but the fellows tell me they know nothing about him except that he is
in France … [Remainder missing].[9]

On 6 April, General Sir Ian Hamilton inspected the 86th and 87th Brigades
of the 29th Division at Mex Camp. Afterwards he wrote in his diary: 'There
was a strong wind blowing which tried to spoil the show, but could not – that
Infantry was too superb! Alexander, Hannibal, Caesar, Napoleon: not one of
them had the handling of legionaries like these. The Fusilier Brigade were
the heavier. If we don't win, I won't be able to put it on the men.' *Neill's Blue
Caps* says that orders were received on 7 April to march to Alexandria harbour that afternoon. At 4.30 p.m., twenty-six officers (including the chaplain
and the Medical Officer) and 939 other ranks[10] re-embarked on the *Ausonia*,
while one officer and forty-six men[11] boarded the *Marquette* which carried
fifty-two horses[12] and nineteen vehicles belonging to the Dublins. Four-
thousand-eight-hundred gallons of drinking water in 1,200 kerosene tins
were taken aboard, also timber for the construction of piers. The *Ausonia*
sailed from Alexandria at 11 a.m on 8 April.[13] The Blue Caps left Lieutenant
Francis Lanigan-O'Keeffe and six men behind, in hospital. The War Diary
recorded that one man was absent.

The Munsters also received their disembarkation orders on 7 April.
Norman Dewhurst was ordered to bring the battalion's transport carts to the
quay. At 3 p.m. the Munsters boarded the *Caledonia*. Dewhurst described it
as a beautiful ship, with good accommodation. It had large smoking rooms
and splendid dining rooms. It is necessary to keep in mind that the facilities
available to officers differed to those available to the rank and file. The 1st
Lancashire Fusiliers and the Anson Battalion of the Royal Naval Division
were also aboard the *Caledonia*. The ship left Alexandria at 10 a.m. on 8 April.

The sea was rough. Dewhurst mounted his battalion's four Vickers machine guns at the bow of the ship. The following day, he was orderly officer. After lunch he had HQ-company running up and down ladders in full kit. Other officers kept their companies running up and down the ladders all night. On 10 April, the ship anchored in Mudros harbour on the island of Lemnos. Dewhurst said there were between 200 to 300 ships in the harbour, including the battleships *Queen Elizabeth* and *Implacable*. The *Ausonia*, with the Dublins aboard, arrived at 11 a.m. the same day.[14] Dewhurst said troop ships were anchored in pairs and that the *Ausonia* – which he mistakenly called the *Ansonia* - was anchored with the *Caledonia*.

ཉༀ

The 29th Division had three field ambulances, each attached to one of its brigades. Each field ambulance was commanded by a lieutenant-colonel, had nine officers and 224 other ranks and answered to an assistant director of medical services, a colonel, at divisional headquarters. Lieutenant George Davidson, from Aberdeen, was a doctor attached to the 89th Field Ambulance, 86th Brigade, 29th Division. He kept a diary of his experiences. On 6 April, he met two of his fellow officers who had come from the Excelsor Hotel, the headquarters of the 29th Division in Alexandria, with the news that the unit's stretcher bearers had to set off before morning and that Davidson was one of the three officers who were to accompany them. Davidson and his colleagues 'hung about' the following day, waiting for a phone call from headquarters, but none came. At 9 p.m. an officer arrived from Brigade HQ, asking why they had not boarded their ship. After making a number of phone calls they discovered that they had been overlooked. They were ordered to leave at once, as their ship was due to sail at 7 a.m. the next morning. It was now past 10 p.m. and the men had to be roused from their tents and the mules yoked. Three officers and 124 men fell in and set out on the 4-mile march to Alexandria. They reached the docks about 1.30 a.m. and boarded the *Ausonia*. Twenty-six officers and 953 men of the 1st Royal Dublin Fusiliers were already aboard. According to Davidson, the *Ausonia* sailed at 10.45 a.m. the following day (8 April) and reached Lemnos about noon on 10 April.[15]

CHAPTER 5

Lemnos:
The Invasion Force Gathers

'The destination of all these troops was the natural
harbour of Mudros on the island of Lemnos.'
Defeat at Gallipoli, by Nigel Steel and Peter Hart

The island of Lemnos lies about halfway between the western coast of Turkey and the mainland of Greece. Measuring about 19 miles east to west, the island's unusual shape means its north to south distance varies. Mudros, a small town at a large harbour, is on the south coast. Much of the island is mountainous. The climate is Mediterranean, with warm dry summers and mild winters. Lemnos had been Ottoman territory until the First Balkan War. In late 1912 the Greeks captured it – and the islands of Imbros, Tenedos, Samothrace, Thasos and Strati. They still held the islands on the outbreak of war between the Allies and Turkey. When the Allies needed bases from which to launch their invasion of Gallipoli, the pro-Allied Prime Minister of neutral Greece, Eleutherios Venizelos, came up with a devious plan. Though the Greeks occupied the islands, Turkey had not renounced her claim to them. The Greek garrison was withdrawn from the vicinity of Mudros harbour in Lemnos, while continuing to occupy the capital, Kastro, on the west of the island. This allowed the Allies to occupy the harbour area, on the grounds that it was territory claimed by Turkey, a country with which they were at war.

∞

In London, on 16 February 1915, Winston Churchill told Rear-Admiral Rosslyn Wemyss it had been decided an attempt would be made to force the Dardanelles. The island of Lemnos would be the operational base for the attempt. Wemyss was to be Governor of the island and was to leave immediately. His orders would follow. They never did. On his way to Mudros, Wemyss met Vice-Admiral Sackville Carden at Tenedos Island at the mouth of the Dardanelles. Carden told Wemyss that he would not, in fact, have authority over Lemnos, but only of the harbour and the town of Mudros. He said that about 10,000 troops were expected to arrive shortly, but he did not know how these troops would be used. Wemyss arrived at Mudros harbour on 24 February and went ashore the following morning. Mudros was a small town, with one small wooden pier used by fishing boats. Lacking piers, cranes or facilities for unloading ships, the town had a church, between sixty to eighty houses and a poor-quality road leading to Kastro, the capital at the other side of the island. Wemyss summed up his situation as follows. 'Appointed in London Governor of an island which on my arrival I found being governed by its own legitimate officials, administering a town over whose inhabitants I had no legal authority, commanding a base situated in a territory that was in theory if not in fact neutral and for whose well-being I was responsible, my task was rendered none the easier from my entire ignorance of the actual political situation. Was Greece a secret ally? Or was she a neutral, whose neutrality was being flagrantly violated?'

తించ

Wemyss recorded his experiences in *The Navy in the Dardanelles Campaign.* The book is interspersed with extracts from his contemporary diary. It provides a vivid picture of a competent officer doing his best in an impossible situation. He said, 'I was still chafing at the ignorance I was being kept in, never realizing that the plan of campaign, the knowledge of which I believed would be of such assistance to me, did not exist' and 'I think I have got over most of my worst difficulties, but certainly not with the assistance of the Admiralty. Like nearly all public departments they won't take any strong line to help their people.' He also observed, 'The confusion that has been caused by the slipshod manner in which the troops have been sent from England is something awful. The ships packed anyhow, things that belong to one battalion stowed at the bottom of a ship carrying another and so on all through …The same old story, I suppose, nobody knowing what anybody else is thinking of and at the head of affairs men ignorant of all technique who think they have only to say 'do this' and it is done. And so the thing is done but in such a manner that it had much better be left undone.' Wemyss informed the

Admiralty that, due to the lack of facilities at Mudros, the troop ships would have to be sent to Egypt for unloading.

∞

As the island's supply was only sufficient for the locals, Wemyss was concerned about the shortage of fresh water on Lemnos. He asked the Admiralty for condensing ships. He was told none were available. He arranged to have water sent on every ship that came to the island from Malta. On 1 March, Lieutenant-General Sir William Birdwood, Commander of the Australian and New Zealand troops, arrived from Egypt aboard the light cruiser *Dublin*. There to inspect Lemnos before his men arrived, he told Wemyss that the number of troops to be expected was nearer to 40,000 than 10,000. He said that 'so far no decision as to their employment had been reached, that this decision would probably rest upon the result of the naval bombardment of the forts.' Wemyss and Birdwood landed on Lemnos looking for areas where troops could camp. While they found many suitable sites, water shortage meant that few men could be landed and most would have to remain aboard ship. Wemyss felt a military landing would require many steamboats, tugs, lighters etc. On 4 March, 5,000 Australians arrived from Egypt. Of these, 1,000 were landed and encamped near the town of Mudros. The rest remained aboard ship because of the water shortage. On 9 March, a French general arrived at Lemnos. Wemyss recorded that: 'He is the precursor of a French Army and has apparently been told that I will supply him with all that they need.' When the French troops arrived they went ashore. Wemyss was merely called upon to mark out the area of their encampment.

∞

For generations Greeks had a dream of a great Greek empire with Constantinople as its capital. Prime Minister Venizelos saw an alliance with the Allies as a way of bring this about. On 1 March 1915, he proposed that three Greek Divisions should land on the Gallipoli peninsula. The following day the Russian Government informed their Minister in Athens that they could not agree to Greek participation in the Dardanelles campaign. On 3 March, the Greek General Staff declared that the time for successful military action on the peninsula had passed and King Constantine refused to consent to Venizelos's proposal, possibly because the Greeks had become aware of the Russian stance. Around the same time it emerged that Britain and France had promised Constantinople to Russia in the event of an Allied victory. His plans in ruins, Venizelos resigned. He did, however, return to power in 1920, 1924, 1928-1932 and 1933.

∞

An anti-submarine net was installed to protect Mudros harbour and three old torpedo boats were used to control entry and exit. British and French troops formed a cordon that nominally placed the eastern part of the island under Allied control. But the western side of the harbour remained open to observation by what Wemyss called 'spies, secret agents, mischievous neutrals, babblers, and adventurers of all sorts'. Among the Royal Navy ships that arrived at Mudros were the *Hussar,* captained by Commander Edward Unwin, and the *Imogine* captained by Commander Harold Escombe. According to Wemyss 'their energy, ability and cheerfulness helped us to overcome our difficulties. We were all living on board the *Hussar* and the *Imogine* for convenience sake moored alongside of each other'. To facilitate the invasion of Gallipoli, the Admiralty commissioned a Maltese named Vincent Grech to purchase boats, lighters etc., wherever available in the Mediterranean. Unable to contact Grech, Wemyss employed agents of his own to buy the required craft, which arrived at Mudros in batches. Many of the boats were manned by Greeks, who insisted they should be allowed to operate them. Wemyss, however, doubted their ability and hoped to replace them with Royal Navy crewmen.

According to Wemyss, French uniforms of every description mixed with British khaki and the colourful clothes of the local peasants and fishermen. Moving among them was 'the wily Greek, avaricious and plausible, ... hawking every sort of commodity from onions to Turkish Delight and Beecham's pills. Through all this motley crew there was a steady stream of Australians carrying stores and pushing improvised carts ...The natives are in the seventh heaven of delight, money pouring into their pockets. We are getting very full up now; transports, supply ships, colliers of both nationalities fill the harbour and with each fresh arrival the work increases.'

On 16 March, Wemyss was summoned to meet Vice-Admiral Sackville Carden aboard the battleship *Queen Elizabeth* off Tenedos. Carden was ill and about to give up his command. Wemyss was next in seniority, but Wemyss reluctantly decided he should remain in charge at Lemnos. He felt that, given his experience of shelling the Dardanelles forts, Rear-Admiral John de Robeck should take command of the attacking fleet. Wemyss telegraphed his decision to the Admiralty, saying if they considered it desirable to promote de Robeck to vice-admiral, he would serve under him. In his memoirs Wemyss said he felt bitterly disappointed, but felt he had made the correct decision.

On 17 March, Wemyss attended a Council of War called by the now Vice-Admiral John de Robeck aboard the *Queen Elizabeth* at Tenedos. Also attending were Army Commander Sir Ian Hamilton, Commander of the Corps Expéditionnaire d'Orient General Albert d'Amade, Hamilton's Chief of Staff Major-General Walter Braithwaite, Hamilton's Military Secretary Captain Stephen Pollen, Contre-Admiral Émile Guépratte of the French Navy and Commodore Roger Keyes of the Royal Navy. According to Hamilton: 'The Admiral asked to see my instructions and Braithwaite read them out. When he stopped, Roger Keyes, the Commodore, inquired, "Is that all?" And when Braithwaite confessed that it was, everyone looked a little blank.' The conference decided another attack would be made on the forts the next day, to cover a further attempt to clear the minefield. The decision on how the army would be used would be dependent on the result of the attack. The following day, Hamilton cabled Kitchener, telling him that equipment had been incorrectly loaded on transport ships and that, as Lemnos did not have the necessary facilities, it would be necessary to use Alexandria in Egypt as a base. Hamilton then sailed aboard the cruiser *Phaeton* to inspect the Gallipoli Peninsula. On the way, he compiled his first report to Kitchener, saying that Gallipoli 'looks a much tougher nut to crack than it did over the map [in Kitchener's office].' Having sailed up to Bulair, the narrowest point of the peninsula, he decided the defences there were too strong to permit a landing. Sailing down the coast, the *Phaeton* arrived at the entrance to the Dardanelles. There the sounds of the bombardment of The Narrows could be heard. The *Phaeton*'s captain decided to sail into the Dardanelles, thus giving Hamilton sight of the disaster that followed.

ॐ

Many of the lighters in Mudros harbour were damaged by a gale on 19 March. Some sank at their moorings, though most were later recovered. On 22 March, a strategy meeting was held aboard the *Queen Elizabeth* in Mudros harbour.[1] According to Hamilton, 'The moment we sat down de Robeck told us he was now quite clear he could not get through without the help of all my troops'. The situation was reviewed and the pros and cons of immediately landing troops on the Gallipoli Peninsula were discussed.

Hamilton recorded that the naval representatives said armour-plated light-ers that could carry 500 men were being built, 'and probably are now built'. Hamilton thought if he could contact Churchill 'we would very likely be lent some and with their aid the landing under fire will be child's play to what it will be otherwise'. Protocol, however, required him to deal directly with Kitchener. With the approval of the naval representatives, he drafted a cable to Kitchener asking if the Admiralty would 'send us out post haste 20 to 30 large lighters'. It was agreed a landing would not be made until plans were finalised, the 29th Division arrived and the army's equipment aboard ships was reorganised in Egypt. In the meantime, the naval bombardment would continue. In addition to his duties at Lemnos, Wemyss was assigned to plan the naval part of the Gallipoli landing. The *Official History of the War: Military Operations Gallipoli Volume 1* recorded, 'Sir Ian Hamilton and his General Staff had been engaged in a study of the problem from the date of his arrival at the Dardanelles, and on the 23rd March he approved an outline plan completed on the previous day'.[2] On 24 March, Hamilton left for Egypt. On 26 March, he received a despatch from Kitchener. It included the phrase 'Bullet-proof lighters cannot be provided'. Also on 26 March, the Maltese Vincent Grech arrived at Mudros. Assigned by the Admiralty to purchase boats, lighters etc., he told Wemyss he had been unable to buy any because of governmental embargoes in the countries he visited. Wemyss's decision to make his own purchases had proved wise.

൚

On 31 March, in Alexandria, Hamilton recorded in his diary that he had com-plained to the British High Commissioner about the Egyptian press reporting the Gallipoli Peninsula as the destination of the Allied Expeditionary Force. The Commissioner told Hamilton he had no control over the Egyptian press and did not wish to get into a quarrel with the Egyptians. On 2 April, Hamilton had lunch with officers of the Plymouth Battalion, Royal Naval Division, whose men had landed at Sedd el Bahr and Kum Kale to blow up the Turkish guns at the entrance to the Dardanelles. In his *Gallipoli Diary*, Hamilton said that he learned five times as much about Sedd el Bahr and Kum Kale from the face-to-face meeting as he had from the officers' des-patches. 'The Turks lie close within a few yards of the water's edge on the Peninsula ... At Sedd-el-Bahr, the first houses are empty, being open to the fire of the Fleet, but the best part of the other houses are defiladed by the ground and a month ago they were held ... The thought of all that barbed wire tucked away into the folds of the ground by the shore follows me about like my shadow.' On 4 April, he cabled Kitchener 'I should much like to have some hint as to my future supply of gun and rifle ammunition. The Naval Division has only 430 rounds per rifle and the 29th Division only 500 rounds which means running it fine.' The following day he recorded in his diary 'We are struggling like drowning mariners in a sea of chaos; chaos in the offices; chaos on the ships; chaos in the camps; chaos along the wharves ...'

಄

On 10 April, Hamilton arrived at Mudros harbour aboard the *Arcadian*. He met Vice-Admiral de Robeck, Rear-Admiral Wemyss and Commodore Keyes and outlined his invasion plan. In the north, in an attempt to deceive the Turks, the fleet would bombard the Bulair Lines, the defences at the narrowest point of the Gallipoli Peninsula. Transport ships of the Royal Naval Division would then act as if they were about to land troops. Further south, a bombardment would be followed by a landing of the Australian and New Zealand Army Corps. At the foot of the peninsula, a bombardment would be followed by a number of landings by battalions from the 29th Division. Meanwhile, ships of the French Fleet would shell the Asian side of the Dardanelles, to be followed by a brief landing by French troops. In *Gallipoli Diary* Hamilton said 'From the South Achi Baba mountain is our first point of attack, and the direct move against it will start from the beaches at Cape Helles and Sedd-el-Bahr. As it is believed that the Turks are there in some force to oppose us, envelopment will be attempted by landing detachments in Morto Bay and [on the west coast] opposite Krithia village. At the same time, also, the A[ustralian] and N[ew] Z[ealand] Corps will land between Gaba Tepe and Fisherman's Hut to try and seize the high backbone of the Peninsula and cut the line of retreat of the enemy on the Kilid Bahr plateau.' He also said, 'The backbone of my enterprise is the 29th Division. At dawn I intend to land the covering force of that Division at Sedd-el-Bahr, Cape Helles and, D.V.[3] in Morto Bay. I tack my D.V. on to Morto Bay because the transports will there be under fire from Asia unless the French succeed in silencing the guns about Troy or in diverting their aim.' While, unfortunately, Hamilton's *Gallipoli Diary* never spelt out exactly why he decided to land the 29th Division on the south of the peninsula and the Australian and New Zealand Army Corps on the west coast, the path to that decision may possibly be inferred from his quoted comments.[4] With the general plan agreed, the next two days were spent working on the specifics. On 11 April, de Robeck and Wemyss came aboard the *Arcadian* to work with the General Staff on technical details, Wemyss having been appointed to command the ships covering the landings of the 29th Division. On 12 April, de Robeck invited Hamilton aboard the *Queen Elizabeth*. Following engine trouble, the ship had been overhauled and was about to undergo steam trials along the Gallipoli coastline. Hamilton brought about thirty-five divisional and brigade officers with him. This gave them their first look at the peninsula.

In *Defeat at Gallipoli* Nigel Steel and Peter Hart said that between 10 and 12 April the naval and military staffs discussed the details of the landing. On 14 April 'Force Order No. 1' was issued, giving the initial objectives for the 29th Division and the Australian and New Zealand Army Corps. Steel and Hart said the 29th Division was to capture 'the ridge of high ground running through the hill of Achi Baba, six miles inland from Cape Helles.' ANZAC's objective was 'a similar ridge of ground running through the hill of Mal Tepe, about five miles to the east of the beach on which they were to land to the north of Gaba Tepe'. Steel and Hart said that, as a result of the discussions between 10 and 12 April, four changes were made to the original plan.[5]

Firstly, in order to speed up the landing of the first wave of troops, it was decided they would be landed from warships rather than transport ships, with the troops being transferred from the latter to the former on the eve of the landing. Secondly, instead of keeping the French Corps Expéditionnaire D'Orient on standby while the 29th Division landed, one infantry regiment and an artillery battery were to be landed near Kum Kale on the Asia shore, to prevent the Turkish guns there from shelling the troops landing at Sedd el Bahr. It was hoped that the French landing would also persuade the Turks to keep troops on the Asian side of the Dardanelles rather than land them on the Gallipoli Peninsula to resist the invasion there. Thirdly, Hamilton proposed an additional landing on the west coast (at a place designated Y Beach). The purpose of this landing would be to threaten communication between Helles and Krithia and to harass troops retreating from the Helles landing. Landings would be made at five beaches at Helles, from Morto Bay in the east to Hamilton's extra landing site due west of Krithia. The beaches were lettered (from east to west) S, V, W, X and Y. The beach farther up the west coast where the Anzacs would land was given the letter Z. The final change of plan was of huge importance to the landing at V Beach, Sedd el Bahr. At all beaches troops would land from ships' boats. Once the initial landings were made, the boats would return to their ships to pick up a second wave of troops. There would be a long delay between the initial landings and the arrival of the reinforcing troops. Royal Navy Commander Edward Unwin suggested that, to get a second wave of soldiers ashore quickly, a specially modified merchant ship could be filled with troops and run ashore on a beach. It was decided that this ship would be used at V Beach.

ﬦﬦﬦ

In a despatch dated 1 July 1915, Vice-Admiral de Robeck reported that: 'Immediately upon the arrival of the Army Staff at Mudros, committees, composed of officers of both services, commenced to work out the details of the landing operations...' Unwin's proposal to use a merchant ship to carry troops was put forward at one of these meetings. Imperial War Museum File IWM 13473 05/63/1 contains two undated accounts by Commander Edward Unwin of his time aboard the *River Clyde*. The first appears to have been prepared for Wemyss and the second as a record for general readership. Unwin said that 'on or about 15 April,' a meeting, chaired by Captain Hope of the *Queen Elizabeth*, was held aboard the *Arcadian*.[6] As Rear-Admiral Wemyss told him he would be in charge of the lighters used during the landing, Unwin requested that he be allowed to attend the meeting. According to Unwin 'Various matters were discussed but they all cantered around boats and tows. Captain Dent turned to me and said, "what do you think about it Unwin?" I said "My idea would be to land the men in a specially prepared ship, right on the beach." I had come to the meeting without any plans at all, only on hearing what had been said it seemed to me that if the beach was properly defended by an enemy at only 200 yards, who reserved their fire till the boats were about 100 yards from the beach not many would get ashore.'[7]

Unwin believed that those in attendance were impressed by his proposal, but they did not express an opinion. He said Captain Hope was against the idea, fearing that the ship might be sunk and a lot of men lost. Unwin said that he left the meeting soon afterwards. According to Wemyss, who later joined the meeting, 'The staff did not view the proposal favourably; they thought it entailed too great a risk, for if the ship were sunk before she reached her destination, the sacrifice would be too great. When the scheme was laid before me, however, I was at once attracted by the promise it held out of overcoming the disadvantage under which we were labouring from the shortage of boats for landing sufficiently large numbers of men at one time. Further examination convinced me that the risk of the ship being sunk was not so great as it appeared, and I was able to win over the military authorities to my views and the scheme was adopted with their full consent.' Wemyss told Unwin that he could have any ship in Mudros harbour. According to Unwin, the only ship in the harbour that was suitable for his purpose was the *River Clyde*, a British merchant ship under charter to the French. The ship had about a hundred tons of stores aboard. The French Military Officer in charge of the stores objected to Unwin taking over the ship, but Contre-Admiral Émile Guépratte of the French navy facilitated the handover.[8]

Maritime Researcher Denis Stoneham has traced the history of the *River Clyde*.[9] The 3,913 gross ton ship was 345ft in length. Built by shipbuilders Russell and Company for the firm of Ormond Cook and Company of Glasgow, the ship was completed in March 1905. On 4 April, she sailed with a cargo of coal from Barry in South Wales. Her voyage took her to Salif, in the Yemen and Calcutta and Karachi in India.[10] During 1905 and 1906, the *River Clyde* was captained by Robert Bryce, with John Kerr as first mate. In 1907, Kerr took over as captain. Born in Glasgow in 1874, he was the son of Master Mariner Angus Kerr of 149 North Street, Glasgow, 'a native of Arran in the county of Bute'. On 5 June 1890, at the age of sixteen, he signed an apprenticeship with Henry Grierson, ship-owner of 101 St Vincents Street, Glasgow. At Antwerp on 17 January 1894, Don Campbell, master of the ship *Milton Park*, certified that Kerr had served on the ship for four years and ten months, with the final ten months at the rank of third mate. At Liverpool on 7 September 1896, George Williams, master of the barque *Salamanca*, certified that Kerr had served with him for two years at the rank of second mate. On 29 September 1899, Certificate (No. 027603) of Competency as a Master of a Foreign Going Ship was awarded to John Kerr, 149 North Street, Glasgow, having passed an examination at Greenock on 25 September 1899.

Kerr was still in command of the *River Clyde* in 1915, when the ship was in Japan at the outbreak of war.[11] She subsequently sailed to Australia, visiting Newcastle in New South Wales, Adelaide and Sydney. Then moving north, she docked at Haiphong in French Indo-China, what is now Vietnam. On the last day of 1914 she sailed from Haiphong bound for Marseilles, arriving on 11 February. It seems probable that the French chartered the ship either in Haiphong or in Marseilles. In any event, the ship subsequently sailed from the latter port and docked in Alexandria on 31 March. Denis Stoneham says that the Admiralty purchased the *River Clyde* on 12 April 1915. *VCs of the First World War: Gallipoli*, by Stephen Snelling says that 'under Wemyss' direction Unwin <u>chartered</u>' (my underlining) the *River Clyde*.

Without giving a date, Unwin said 'The stores [from the *River Clyde*] were landed that night by us, and at 9 a.m. the next morning I took her alongside the repair ship [*Reliance* to have her fitted out for her mission]'.[12] Just 423 tons, the *Reliance* had been the civilian-owned *Knight Companion* when purchased by the Royal Navy on 14 November 1912. She had been used as a repair ship since 1913. Wemyss says that the *Reliance* 'had on board' Engineer Captain Henry Humphreys, 'whose resourcefulness, tact and ability were worth his weight in gold.' Presumably the men who carried out the modification to the *River Clyde* worked under the direction of Humphreys, who had joined the navy as an Assistant Engineer in 1885. He was serving as Senior Engineer of Halifax Dockyard, Nova Scotia when, on 15 March 1897, a crane gave way and five men were thrown into deep water, surrounded by floating ice. Four of them were quickly rescued, but W. Tout (fifty-eight) was badly injured in the fall and had been submerged when Henry Humphries, pausing only to take off his heavy sea-boots, jumped in and supported Tout until rescue arrived. For this action he was awarded the Royal Human Society's Bronze Medal. Appointed Engineer Captain on 26 January 1913, on the outbreak of war he was on the staff of Admiral Sir Berkley Milne, Commander-in-Chief of the Mediterranean. Subsequently appointed for special duties at Malta, he was later assigned to Lemnos.

While owned – and presumably crewed – by the Royal Navy, the *Reliance* had civilian workshop staff.[13] The staff was divided into three departments: the Constructive Department (thirty-four men), the Electrical Department (twenty men) and the Engineering Department (one hundred and sixteen men).[14] Despite the skill of the workshop staff, at least one man was drafted in from another ship to carry out the modifications to the *River Clyde*: Leading Stoker William Bowskill, of the cruiser *Bacchante*. From Church End, Arlesey, Bedfordshire, he was aged twenty-two when he left home on 26 December 1905. Never having left his village previously, he walked to Whitehall in London with 3*d* in his pocket, sleeping in a barn on the way. He signed on to the navy on 30 December 1905, was given a half a crown and a train warrant to Chatham. Joining the crew of the stokers training ship *Acheron* on 5 January 1906, he served in the navy until 30 December 1910. Missing the service, he signed on again in June 1912. Now aged thirty-one he was assigned to work on modifying the *River Clyde*.[15]

In a letter to his father, twenty-year-old Midshipman George Drewry RNR of the *Hussar* said, 'I got tired of doing nothing so asked the Captain [Unwin] for more work, which I got with a vengeance. He took me aboard this ship [the *River Clyde*] and gave me thirty Greeks and told me to clean her. Well she was the dirtiest ship I've seen. She was in ballast and had just brought French mules up from Algiers, they had built boxes and floors in the tween decks and carried the mules there without worrying about sanitary arrangements. We knocked the boxes up and cleaned her up for troops, painted the starboard side P&O [Peninsular and Oriental Steam Navigation Company] colour. [P&O ships had brown funnels] A large square port was cut on each side of each hatch in the tween decks and from the No. 2 ports I rigged stages right round the bow.'[16] Drewry's letter would appear to suggest that, while on her way to Alexandria, the *River Clyde* had docked in Algiers, to collect mules.

Leading Stoker William Bowskill worked on converting the *River Clyde*.

According to Norman Dewhurst, most of the *River Clyde*'s internal partitions were removed and her hull was reinforced. She would carry troops in her holds. To enable the fully-equipped soldiers to exit the holds, eight large holes were cut at lower deck level in the forward sides of the ship, four on either side. Doors were then constructed to cover the holes. The resulting exits were termed sally-ports. Wooden gangways, three planks wide were hung from both sides of the ship, just below the doorways. They allowed men exiting the sally-ports to step on to the gangways and move forwards towards the bow of the ship. About halfway to the bow each gangway had a hinged extension allowing it to drop at what appears to have been about a 45° angle. The hinged gangways would allow the men to make their way to a boat to be anchored in front of the *River Clyde* and from there to the shore.[17]

As the originator of the *River Clyde* plan, fifty-one-year-old Commander Edward Unwin was assigned by Wemyss to command the ship during the landing.[18] Unwin was born in Hampshire. At the age of fourteen he joined the Mercantile Marine's training ship *Conway* on the River Mersey. His two years on the ship must not have been happy, as they culminated with his receiving two-dozen strokes of the birch. He subsequently served fifteen years in the Merchant Navy, first aboard a clipper owned by Donald Currie and then with the P. & O. Line. On 31 October 1895, he transferred to the Royal Navy with the rank of lieutenant. In 1897, he married Evelyn Carew, the daughter of a major-general. Soon afterwards he took part in land operations against the West African kingdom of Benin, during which he commanded a successful defence of a supply camp attacked by Edo tribesmen. After serving on the port guardship HMS *Thunderer*, he later served in the Boer War. In 1903 he was promoted to lieutenant-commander. He retired six years later with the rank of commander. Recalled to active service shortly before the outbreak of war, he was appointed fleet coaling officer on Admiral Jellicoe's staff aboard the *Iron Duke*. In February 1915 he was given command of the *Hussar*.[19]

Unwin said that he hoped to achieve three objectives by using the *River Clyde*. The first objective was to get the troops to V Beach 'in a sort of protected fort, with 12 maxims round my bows'. The second objective was to carry '700 tons of water for immediate use and able to condense 100 tons a day'. The final objective was to use the ship as a temporary hospital for the wounded, until they could be sent to a hospital ship.[20] Unwin said that he addressed the crew of the *River Clyde*, told them about the mission and asked for volunteers. He said that the captain of the ship (John Kerr) said: 'we will do all we can to help you prepare the ship but I don't think you can expect us to be there when the bricks begin to fly about'. Unwin then went to his own ship, the *Hussar*, and called for volunteers to man the *River Clyde*.[21] As his second-in-command, Unwin appointed twenty-year-old Midshipman George Drewry.

The third of four brothers, Essex-born Drewry had packed much drama into his short life. With his younger brother Ralph, he had fallen into a bog, sinking up to their necks. Their cries were heard by a passer-by who hauled them to safety. On another occasion he was knocked over by a car. At the age of fourteen he joined the Merchant Navy. During his early training he fell from the mast of the sailing vessel *Indian Empire*. He was saved when the ship's mate dived into the sea and rescued him. On a subsequent voyage the ship was wrecked on a remote island in the Pacific Ocean. Drewry and his fellow crewmen survived on roots and shellfish for fourteen days, before being picked up by a Chilian gunboat. Like Unwin, Drewry had served on P & O Line ships. He joined the company in 1912, serving as an officer on the Australia and Japan routes. In 1913 he joined the Royal Naval Reserve. On 3 August 1914, while at Port Said, he was called up and posted as a midshipman to HMS *Hussar*.

In his report to Wemyss, Unwin said, as crew for the *River Clyde*, he also selected six seamen, six engine-room ratings and the ship's carpenter. He said that the *Hussar*'s engineer lieutenant was keen to go, but Unwin took the warrant engineer, as he had the necessary experience 'to convert the condensing plant into use for distilling to the shore'. Unwin said that Wemyss later supplied him with 'some' petty officers. He also said 'a leading seaman [William

Williams] came up to me and asked if he could not come. I told him I was full up and that I did not want any more petty officers, to which he replied 'I'll chuck my hook [meaning he would give up his rating] if you let me come and I did, to his cost but everlasting glory. I shall never forget the way he died.'[22]

In his second account, Unwin refers to the seamen as deck hands and the engine-room ratings as stokers. He also mentions that he took Naval Surgeon Peter Burrows Kelly to the *River Clyde*. He said that two or three days before leaving Mudros, several of the *River Clyde's* original crew approached him. They said that the ship's captain had spoken without consulting them and they asked if they might come along. Unwin, however, had enough men by this time. His account for Wemyss said that the ship's original steward was part of the crew during the landing, but unfortunately did not mention the circumstances of his volunteering. Of interest is the fact that the steward was the brother of the *River Clyde's* captain. Unwin said that 'apparently having more guts than his brother, nobody stood the shelling better than he did'.[23] As Unwin made no mention of a radio operator, or radio messages, it seems that the *River Clyde* did not have a radio aboard.

∞

Among the thousands of men gathered in Mudros harbour were some fairly exotic units. One of the most unusual of the British units was the Royal Naval Armoured Car Division. Formed shortly after the outbreak of war, the division was manned by members of the Royal Naval Air Service (RNAS) and operated a mixed collection of armoured cars, lorries, Ford cars and motorcycles with side cars. When the Gallipoli landings were decided upon, No. 3 and No. 4 Armoured Car Squadrons and No. 10 Motor Cycle Machine-Gun Squadron were sent to the Mediterranean to assist the army.

While hoping that there would be an opportunity to use the armoured cars and motorcycles after the landings, General Sir Ian Hamilton saw a more immediate use for the machine guns and their crews. He ordered

Josiah Wedgwood.
(Courtesy of Keele University)

Lieutenant-Commander Josiah Wedgwood of No. 3 Armoured Car Squadron
to report to Commander Edward Unwin. Unwin and Wedgwood agreed
that Wedgwood's Maxim guns would be mounted on the forecastle of the
River Clyde and manned by men from No. 3 Armoured Car Squadron. Unwin
said there were twelve maxims.[24] In a letter to Winston Churchill, Wedgwood
said there were eleven.[25] Given that Wedgwood was in charge of the guns – and
that his letter was written soon after the landing, whereas Unwin's appears to
have been written several years later – it seems more likely that he had the
correct number. Under Wedgwood's direction, RNAS mechanics put steel-
plate and sandbag protection in place around the machine-gun positions and
along the whole of the upper deck and bridges. According to Wedgwood 'our
mechanics built casemates, armed her with maxim guns, and lined her bridges
with boiler plate and leaky sand-bags.'[26]

ಬಬ

The final April 1915 entry in their war diary shows that, on 10 April,
the 1st Battalion Royal Dublin Fusiliers arrived in Mudros harbour at 11 a.m.,
aboard the *Ausonia*. The 1st Munsters also arrived that morning aboard the
Caledonia. Munster Second Lieutenant Norman Dewhurst said troop transports were anchored in pairs and the *Ausonia* and *Caledonia* anchored next
to each other.

> For the next three days, we aboard the *Caledonia* practised, as did all the
> troops on the other transports, disembarking down rope ladders in full
> kit. All around the ships small craft ran in and around, to and fro, every-
> thing was in movement and spirits were high ... The Lancashire Fusiliers
> (who were also on the *Caledonia*) now began practising landing ashore
> from row boats towed by naval cutters and I had my machine gun team out
> in a rowboat too.

For this period the *History of the Royal Munster Fusiliers* records: 'Everyday
was spent in practising embarking in whale boats by means of ladders, in full
marching order.' *Neill's Blue Caps* says, 'The ten days following the arrival
of General Hunter-Weston's command at Mudros Bay were passed by the
brigade and battalion leaders in reconnoitring the coast and by the troops in
practising getting up and down rope ladders and in rowing and landing from
boats.' The 2nd Hampshires, aboard the RMS *Aragon* arrived at Mudros on
13 April.

According to the Revd Oswin Creighton 'All kinds of boat-drill has been going on. The men are not much good at rowing, and the boats are very heavy and cumbersome. But they are as a rule towed in strings of five or six by a steam pinnace.' *Military Operations Gallipoli* says that 'Every chance was seized to exercise the troops in harbour in getting noiselessly into small boats, in rowing, and in landing silently and quickly. Whenever the water at Mudros was calm enough for these exercises, which unfortunately was not often, the harbour was alive with ships' boats crowded with laughing men, and this training did much to keep them healthy and in good spirits during their enforced idleness.' It also says that 'As few naval ratings would be available for the boats, eight of the men told off for each boat were to be detailed to row her ashore from the point where the water became too shallow for towing.' The battleship *Cornwallis* 'practised landing troops from transports at Mudros, and gave them some training in getting ashore from boats to beaches, rehearsing all manner of evolutions in the face of a make-believe enemy.'

On 11 April, aboard the *Ausonia*, Scottish Lieutenant George Davidson of the 89th Field Ambulance, 86th Brigade, wrote in his diary: 'When I looked through my porthole at 6 o'clock this morning the surrounding countryside looked very fresh, and free from all haze, and the bright green of the crops and grass on the hill-sides would have done credit to old Ireland. After lunch I met Lt-Col. Rooth of the Dublins, who gave me some authentic information concerning the proposed military landing in Gallipoli.' Davidson said that the Munsters and Lancashires were on the *Caledonia*, which was lashed to the port side of the *Ausonia*. The next day a number of officers from the *Ausonia* visited the battleship *Queen Elizabeth*. They returned with alarming reports. The *Lizzie* had taken part in the shelling of the Turkish forts and the officers were told that 'the whole of Gallipoli swarms with Turks, and the whole coast is covered with trenches and barbed-wire entanglements 6ft high'. It was believed that the landing would probably take place on 14 April or the following day at the latest. 'A very warm reception from the enemy on shore is expected, as I gather from the way the Dublins officers talk. It is also said that we will have to make a dash for it under the cover of night.' That night Davidson noted 'all our officers were unusually quiet and serious ... while they discussed the situation no doubt'. According to *Military Operations Gallipoli*, 'From the 11th April onwards a hostile plane flew over Mudros harbour, where there was unfortunately no suitable machine to set against it, and Turkish headquarters was thus kept well aware of the growing size of the British armada.' Davidson recorded that, on 12 April, disembarkation practice was held on the *Ausonia*, with units lining up in the stations that had been allocated to them. Apart from their rations, which had not yet been issued, the soldiers carried their full marching-order loads. He said that while landing, each man would also carry about 5lbs of rations. Davidson thought that none of the men he spoke with held out any hope of returning, all believing that their landing cutters would be 'peppered with shot and shell'. During landing practice that day 'we had to appear with the straps of all our equipment outside our shoulder straps, and the ends of our belts free, ready to whip open and get rid of it at a moment's notice ...' He said that the *Queen Elizabeth* had gone to the Dardanelles that day, carrying the commanding officers of the battalions which were to land on the beaches. 'We saw her return to harbour about 6 p.m., and we hear she was fired on.' On 15 April, Davidson said that 'Just after breakfast I met a naval man on the stairs leading down to the saloon, looking for the O.C. the troops, Col Rooth, and he sent a message through me, introducing himself as the commander of our covering ship. Looking over the rail I found HMS *Cornwallis* painted on his steam launch.' [27]

According to *Military Operations Gallipoli*, aerial reconnaissance on 14 and 15 April 'reported numerous trenches above Helles and Sedd el Bahr'. According to *The Immortal Gamble* at least half a dozen transports arrived daily at Mudros. To save space in the harbour they were tied up in pairs. The authors believed that, apart from warships, there were about a hundred and sixty other craft, from many shipping companies, in the harbour. There were at least forty large ships in the outer harbour, including French transports. The Revd Oswin Creighton believed that there were over a hundred transports, supply ships, hospital ships, twenty man-of-war, colliers, minesweepers, water boats, and all types of tugs in the harbour. He said that it was very difficult to locate particular ships.

The *Official History* said that naval wireless was practically non-existent and it was impossible to establish an intercommunication service between the many transports in the harbour. Visual signalling was only possible between adjacent ships. The water was often too rough, and the distances too great for the use of rowing boats. Steam launches were used to communicate between ships, but these vessels were in short supply. It was very difficult for commanding officers and their staffs to consult with their superiors, to attend conferences, or to visit the units under their command. This was very frustrating to a land force, accustomed to the use of telephones, cars, and cyclists for the prompt despatch of orders and communications.

For soldiers with cash to spare, there were two sources available to supplement the food provided aboard ship. The first was the ship's canteen. But, as one Australian said, while items such as tobacco, cigarettes, chocolate and condensed milk were soon out of stock, the canteen 'fortunately remained fully stocked with the things that really mattered – macaroni, mixed spices and boot laces'. The second available source was islanders selling from boats in Mudros harbour. According to *25 April 1915: The Inevitable Tragedy* by Denis Winter 'Fresh loaves, thickly crusted, could be bought for a shilling; figs, threaded on coarse grass, for sixpence a pound; and walnuts for sixpence a hatful. Apples and Turkish delight were always available.' *Koniak* was a potent drink that had posed many problems for the military authorities when the troops were in Egypt. It had been banned, as was the fierce jet-black wine of Lemnos. Enterprising men, however, easily managed to bypass the prohibitions.

On or about 15 April, Lieutenant Francis Lanigan-O'Keeffe – who had been hospitalised in Alexandria – rejoined the Dublins. Munsters Second Lieutenant Norman Dewhurst said that by 16 April 'we were all impatient to get going – we had been issued with two days emergency rations and 200 rounds of ball ammunition. But we still waited, and then we had our first real rehearsal of what was to become a legend in British military history. We were packed like sardines on the SS *River Clyde* which was to carry us to the landing point at Gallipoli … The next three or four days were spent in rowing in small boats around the harbour and in swimming. Our C.O. Colonel (Henry) Tizard had another trip up the Dardanelles…'[28]

Irishman Lewis Weldon had spent fourteen years working in the Survey Department, in Egypt. Travelling home on leave when war broke out, he was offered a commission in the Dubs or the Leinster Regiment. About to accept, he had received a cable ordering him to return to Egypt. There, he was made a temporary captain, attached to the General Staff Intelligence. He was assigned to the *Aenne Rickmers*, a captured German merchant ship (formerly owned by the Rickmers family: Aenne was the owner's daughter). The ship was renamed HM Sea Plane Carrier *Anne*, given French seaplanes for observation duties and to drop agents behind enemy lines. Damaged by a Turkish torpedo, the ship was ordered to Mudros for repairs, arriving on 12 March. Repairs were delayed due the arrival of the damaged HMS *Inflexible*. According to Weldon:

By the middle of April there was no mistaking the signs that the big adventure would not be long delayed. At that time I ran into various old friends belonging to the 29th Division, and I was fairly often a guest on the transports which carried them. One of these, the *Ausonia*, was tied up alongside the now famous *River Clyde*, and I saw the working parties cutting the

rectangular openings in her sides through which the gangways were to
be lowered. On the morning of the 17th April I watched the Dublins and
Munsters filing into her. I remember one man called to a pal, 'Come on,
Mike: come into your coffin,' a jest which was to come very nearly true
for many of them. I was so bored sitting doing nothing on the old *Aenne*
that I asked Colonel Rooth, who commanded the Dublins, if I might go
with him. At first he said 'yes', but afterwards refused on account of the
questions which might be asked later. It was lucky for me that he had that
afterthought.[29]

∞

Wemyss would command the ships covering the landing on the south of the
peninsula. He was assigned twelve naval officers to act as Beach Masters during
the landings. Preparations began for the landing of 100,000 men, guns, ammunition and stores. An armada of over 200 ships would leave Mudros harbour,
accompanied by lighters, pontoons etc. On the two nights preceding the invasion, the waters separating Lemnos from the peninsula would be filled with
craft moving back and forth. As ships would not be carrying lights, the greatest
of care would have to be taken in timing their movements, so as to prevent
accidents. Hamilton recorded that a conference was held aboard the *Queen
Elizabeth* on 18 April. He said that he did not attend, as the purpose was to go
point by point into orders already approved. The date of the landing was set for
23 April and the naval landing orders were read out and discussed. Hamilton
said, 'The Naval and Military Beach Personnel is in itself a very big and intri-
cate business which has no place in ordinary soldier tactics. The diagrams of
the ships and transports: the lists of tows; the actions of the destroyers; tugs;
lighters; signal arrangements for combined operations; these are unfamiliar
subjects and need very careful fitting in.'

   According to *Military Operations Gallipoli*, the matter of a day or night
disembarkation was settled at the conference. Naval representatives said that
daylight would be required for the landings at Helles. The current flowing out
of the Dardanelles might cause tows to go off course and lose their way in a
night landing. There was also a danger from uncharted rocks. It was decided
that, following a half an hour bombardment at first light, the Helles landings would be made at about 5.30 a.m. (Eastern Mediterranean Time, i.e. two
hours ahead of Greenwich Mean Time). It was decided that the Anzac Corps
would land on the west coast while it was still dark, as it was believed that the
chosen beach was extensive, the current weaker and rocks less likely.[30]

Military Operations Gallipoli says details of the naval and military beach personnel were published on 19 April. For the three beaches at the south of the peninsula the military beach personnel would consist of a number of selected officers, the 2nd London Field Company Royal Engineers, and two and a half companies of the Anson Battalion, Royal Naval Division. The Engineers were to work in creating piers, jetties, water stations and exits from beaches. The Anson Battalion was to supply beach and working parties. V Beach was assigned ten naval officers, fifty naval other ranks, thirteen military officers and 300 other ranks for beach and working parties. Captain Robert Lambert, Royal Navy, was designated Beach Master V Beach and Commander Neston Diggle as Assistant Beach Master. With the exception of Y Beach, artillery observation officers would land with the leading troops, while others would be aboard ship. Communication from ship to shore was to be by visual signalling and wireless. The latter to be used as soon as stations could be established on V, W and X beaches. Shore signals would be repeated from ship to ship as required. It was hoped that aeroplanes, using wireless, would supplement observation and communication. Plans and arrangements being complete, Wemyss transferred his flag to the cruiser *Euryalus*. Irishman, Captain Lewis Weldon, of the *Aenne Rickmers* had received orders the previous day, assigning him to the *Euryalus*.

All was in readiness. There was, however, one factor over which the Allies had absolutely no control – the weather. In that part of the Mediterranean, settled conditions can generally be expected after mid-April. On the morning of 20 April, however, a strong wind developed. The following day brought no improvement. At noon operations were postponed. The next morning, Friday 23 April, St George's Day – the date originally set for the landing – conditions began to improve. It was decided that departure from Mudros would commence that afternoon.

ॐ

With one exception, books on the Gallipoli campaign imply that, once Commander Edward Unwin's *River Clyde* plan was adopted, it was always envisaged that the ship would be used to land troops at V Beach. While I have outlined the circumstances in which it was decided to use the ship, I have not, unfortunately, been able to establish when and why it was decided to use the ship in the V Beach landing and which troops would sail aboard the ship. Information in Denis Winter's *25 April 1915: The Inevitable Tragedy* would appear to suggest that, not only were the decisions made late in the day, but they were made only after the navy had offered the ship for a landing at another beach. Winter's book deals with the landing at the beach now known as Anzac Cove. He says that plans for the Anzac landing went through a number of drafts before final agreement was reached. He calls these drafts Plan 1, Plan 2 and Plan 3. Plan 2 was adopted on 18 April. On 22 April, plans having being made at divisional, brigade and battalion level, 'the men were given a sketchy outline of what was planned for the next day. Meanwhile, however, the weather had changed for the worst.' A meeting was held between Lieutenant-General Sir William Birdwood, commander of the Anzac troops, Hamilton's Chief of Staff Major-General Walter Braithwaite and Rear-Admiral Cecil Thursby, commander of the naval forces covering the Anzac landing. It had been decided that the landing at Anzac Cove would be made during darkness. Winter says that postponement of the landing to 25 April meant that there would now be little more than an hour between the setting of the moon and dawn, leaving insufficient time for the men to land by tows and achieve their objective in darkness. The navy offered the *River Clyde* as a solution. 'By sailing on a compass course and running them onto the beach, it could still land the 3rd Brigade's first wave before dawn … Birdwood turned this offer down.'[31] Winter says that Birdwood then drew up Plan 3. As plans to use the *River Clyde* at V Beach were well advanced by this stage, the forgoing scenario seems puzzling to say the very least. Given the shortage of boats to carry troops to the shore, if the *River Clyde* was diverted to Anzac Cove at the last minute, how was it proposed to convey the battalion of Royal Munster Fusiliers, the half battalion of the Hampshire Regiment, the company of Royal Dublin Fusiliers and the other assorted troops scheduled for passage on the ship, to V Beach? Indications that plans to use the *River Clyde* at V Beach were well advanced by the 22 April date of the Anzac meeting is shown by the war diary of the 1st Munsters and the diary of Lieutenant George Davidson of the 86th Brigade's Field Ambulance. The Munsters War Diary entry for 17 April reads: 'Practiced getting on board *River Clyde*. The entry for 20 April reads: 'Instructions for covering force issued.' The remarks column records: 'Order of landing from *River Clyde*. See Appendix No 1 (a).' The appendix records: 'Copy of preliminary order No 1 by Brig. Gen S.W. Hare commanding covering force. As regards the landing at 'V' from the collier *River Clyde* the O.C. Hants [Hampshire] Regt [Regiment] will arrange that troops are disembarked in the following order. 1st Rl. Munster Fusl., One coy 1st Rl. Dublin Fusl, 2nd Hants Regt. (less 2 coys), 1 Platoon Anson Batt., G.H.Q. Signal Section, W.[est] Riding Field Co.[mpany] R.[oyal]E.[ngineers], 3 Bearer Sub. Division.' The entry is signed 'H.S. Wilson Capt Adgt 1 Rl Munster Fusl.' Subsequent to recording receipt of the 20 April 'Order of landing from the *River Clyde*,' the *History of the Royal Munster Fusiliers* says 'As the battalion was given the place of honour in the vessel, Commander Unwin and Lieutenant-Colonel (Henry) Tizard went into the question of stowing the men on board. 'There was one rehearsal of it at Lemnos, but the detail of the troops was altered twice, and yet a third time just before the vessel left, so that others were put in who had never been on board before.' On 17 April, Lieutenant George Davidson of the 86th Brigade's Field Ambulance recorded that his unit breakfasted at 6.00 a.m. and paraded at 7.00 a.m. They then stood on deck until 10.45 a.m. awaiting their turn to cross to the *River Clyde*. 'The intention is to run her ashore at full speed, ploughing into the sands, when her load of 2,000 men are to get overboard as best they can on to floating gangways. By a long, circuitous route we all got into our place, and were packed close on the various decks which have had large square openings cut through the iron plates of the sides of the ship, and from these and the upper deck we have to decamp as quickly as possible.' Unfortunately neither *Neill's Blue Caps* nor *The Royal Hampshire Regiment 1914-1918* record when the 1st Battalion Royal Dublin Fusiliers or the 2nd Battalion Hampshire Regiment received orders for part of their battalions to travel to V Beach aboard the *River Clyde*.

ജ

On 20 April, Munsters Lieutenant Norman Dewhurst received permission to take a party ashore. The sea was a bit rough as they made their way across the harbour, but the sun was shining, and the green hills surrounding the cluster of white houses which formed the village of Mudros, looked well. The Dirty Shirts got ashore and marched around the island. Dewhurst said Lemnos was quite small, and had a population of about 10,000 living in four villages. By 4 p.m., their march completed, the Munsters were back on the beach. The weather had worsened, however, and they were unable to get a boat to take them back to their ship. Hours passed and the sun went down. As Dewhurst and his men shivered in their shirt-sleeves on the windy beach, he gave the order for 'games of movement' to keep them warm. Unfortunately Dewhurst gave his ankle a severe wrench when he stumbled on an uneven surface. At 10 p.m. a boat turned up and returned the 'sorry deflated' group to their ship. That night Dewhurst's ankle swelled up and next morning he was unable to get his boot on. He was in great pain and no treatment was available. He rested his ankle all day and was glad to hear that departure from Lemnos had been postponed.

On 21 April, Lieutenant George Davidson went on deck before breakfast
and found that everything had been arranged for an afternoon sailing at
4 p.m. Everyone was rushing about. But bad weather resulted in the landing
being postponed for another twenty-four hours. The 1st Munsters war diary
entry for 21 April recorded: '9 a.m. General Hunter-Weston held a conference for Brigadiers & Cos. Owing to storm move postponed 24 hours.' Also
on 21 April Lieutenant-Colonel Herbert Carington Smith, Battalion headquarters and Y and Z Companies of the 2nd Battalion Hampshire Regiment
transferred from the *Aragon* to the *Alaunia*. W and X Companies remained
aboard the *Aragon*. On 22 April, Davidson recorded that 'we gave the men
their Iodine ampules for use with their first field dressings'. He said that no
boats had been allowed leave his ship for two days, unless it was done to save
life. 'Water, which we were very much in need of, was brought on board last
night.' Davison said that he was given his service cap, 'helmets having been
recalled a week ago'.

Also on 22 April, the following messages were distributed to all soldiers of
the 29th Division.

Force Order
(Special)
General Headquarters
April 21st 1915

Soldiers of France and of the King.

Before us lies an adventure unprecedented in modern war. Together with
our comrades of the fleet we are about to face a landing upon an open
beach in face of positions which have been vaunted by our enemies as
impregnable. The landing will be made good, by the help of God and the
navy; the positions will be stormed, and the war brought one step nearer
to a glorious close. 'Remember', said Lord Kitchener when bidding adieu
to your commander, 'Remember, once you have set your foot upon the
Gallipoli Peninsula, you must fight the thing through to a finish.'

The whole world will be watching our progress. Let us prove ourselves
worthy of the great feat of arms entrusted to us.

Ian Hamilton
General

Personal Note from
Major-General Aylmer Hunter-Weston, C.B. D.S.O.
to each man of the 29th Division
on the occasion of their first
going into action together.

The Major-General congratulates the Division on being selected for an enterprise, the success of which will have a decisive effect on the war. The eyes of the world are upon us, and your deeds will live in history. To us now is given an opportunity of avenging our friends and relatives who have fallen in France and Flanders. Our comrades there willingly gave their lives in thousands and tens of thousands for our king and country, and by their glorious courage and tenacity they defeated the invaders and broke the German offensive. We also must be prepared to suffer hardships, privations, thirst and heavy losses by bullets, by mines, by drowning. But if each man feels, as is true, that on him individually, however small, or however great his task, rests the success or failure of the expedition, and therefore the honour of the Empire, and the welfare of his own folk at home, we are certain to win through to a glorious victory.

In Nelson's time it was England, now it is the whole British Empire, which expects that each man of us will do his duty.

Aylmer Hunter-Weston

One can but wonder what men like Sam and Jack Mallaghan and their comrades made of the line 'We also must be prepared to suffer hardships, privations, thirst and heavy losses by bullets, by mines, by drowning.'
  Of the lead up to the invasion Commander Edward Unwin wrote:

I have never spent such a time in my life as I did before the landing, the awful responsibility, for I wasn't just carrying out orders but carrying through a scheme of my own in which if I failed the consequences might be awful. The thousands of thoughts that flash through one's head at such a time as to what might happen and how to meet them, and top of it all the wonder as to how one will behave one's self, as I don't believe any man is quite sure of himself.[32]

On 22 April, 86th Brigade Chaplain Revd Oswin Creighton wrote in his diary:

> It seems a perfectly desperate undertaking. I can hardly expect to see
> many of my men alive again. My present feeling is that the whole thing
> has been bungled. The navy should never have started the bombard-
> ment without the army. Now there has been no bombardment for some
> weeks. Meanwhile the Turks, under German direction, have perfected
> their defences. The aerial reconnaissance reports acres of barbed wire,
> labyrinths of trenches, concealed guns, maxims and howitzers everywhere.
> The ground is mined. In fact everything conceivable has been done. Our
> men are to be towed in little open boats to land in the face of all of this ...
> We had a printed message from Hunter-Weston, our Divisional General.
> He said the eyes of the world are on us, and we must be prepared to face
> heavy losses by bullets, shells, mines, and drowning. Cheery, isn't it?
> People's eyes seem perfectly open. My brigade is to land first. At least three-
> quarters, it seems to me, will probably be casualties the first day.

On the same day, the Munsters War Diary recorded: 'Move again postponed.'
George Davidson's 89th Field Ambulance was joined by two officers, named
Assassiz and Thomson, and nineteen men, forming a tent-subdivision.

By Friday 23 April, stories from the navy and airmen had made their way
to the *Ausonia*. It was reported that Gallipoli was swarming with well-armed
Turks in trenches surrounded by wire entanglements of great width and height.
A feeling of strain and anxiety pervaded the ship. George Davidson spent most
of the morning aboard the *Caledonia* which was lashed to the port side of the
Ausonia. There he spoke with General Hare, whom he thought looked worried
and thinner than when Davidson had last seen him in Coventry.

> Col. Rooth of the Dublins does not look over happy. He came down to lunch,
> had a look at the table, and went up to deck with a cigarette, and at the present
> moment he stands near where I am writing with both hands in his pock-
> ets, peering down the side of the ship into the waters. Those of us with less
> responsibility are certainly less troubled; all are prepared for great sacrifices,
> and everyone is ready to play his part in what will certainly be a great tragedy.[33]

Orders issued by Vice-Admiral de Robeck said that two days before the
landings (i.e. on 23 April), the *River Clyde* was to leave Mudros at noon.
The *Fauvette* (carrying buoys etc.) would leave at 1.30 p.m. Beginning
at 5 p.m., the *Ausonia*, the *Caledonia* and the *Alaunia* were to leave the

harbour at half-hour intervals, each ship towing four lighters. The *Cornwallis*, *Euryalus* and *Implacable* were to leave at 6.30 p.m.[34] Given the magnitude of the operation, it was perhaps inevitable that there would be some change of schedule. It would, however, appear that perhaps Rear-Admiral Rosslyn Wemyss's memory failed him when he came to write his memoirs several years later. In these he said 'The first ships to leave [Mudros] were the three transports carrying the battalions forming the advance parties for Helles and Morto Bay, bound for an anchorage off Tenedos. They were followed shortly afterwards by the *Euryalus* [Wemyss's ship], *Implacacable*, *Cornwallis*, and the *River Clyde*.' One of Unwin's undated accounts, apparently written a few years after the event, says that the *River Clyde* left Mudros at noon on 23 April. In a letter to his father, written a few weeks after the landing, Midshipman George Drewry said that the *River Clyde* left at 1 p.m., towing three lighters, 'a steamboat' (pinnace) on the port (left) side and a steam hopper on the starboard. (A sketch he drew, however, shows a lighter on the starboard side and, on the port side, two lighters, a steamboat and, outside them, the hopper, *Argyle*. Given later accounts, the sketch would appear to have been correct.) He said that the crew of the *River Clyde* were Unwin, Drewry, Warrant Engineer Horend RNR, nine seamen, nine stokers, one carpenter's mate, the *River Clyde*'s original steward and Unwin's servant.[35] According to Wemyss, those aboard the ships in Mudros harbour cheered the departing warships and the *River Clyde*. As the cheers died away they were replaced by those of the men aboard French transport ships anchored in the outer harbour.

George Davidson was aboard the *Ausonia* with part of the 89th Field Ambulance and the 1st Battalion Royal Dublin Fusiliers. He recorded that the ship set sail from Lemnos at 4.57 p.m. He went on deck after dinner and saw three warships. They were said to be the *Swiftsure*, *Dublin* and *Euryalus*, all in line. Neither they nor the *Ausonia* were showing lights. The port-holes on the *Ausonia* were covered with cardboard and the iron shutters were down. Davidson and Lieutenant Graham Balfour[36] of the London Regiment, who shared his cabin, wondered if they should sleep on deck, as they believed the cabin would become uncomfortably warm. 'We drag three large barges alongside which prevent our going at much speed, and it is expected that we reach Tenedos about 3 a.m.'[37]

At 6 p.m., the *Caledonia* left Lemnos with the Munsters aboard. She steamed slowly out to sea between rows of British and French warships. The bands on the ships played 'Tipperary' and 'The British Grenadiers' and men cheered loudly. Among the Dirty Shirts, however, there was almost

complete silence and no reply was made. According to Boer War veteran
Captain Guy Geddes DSO: 'What struck me most forcibly was the demean-
our of our own men, from whom, not a sound, and this from the light hearted,
devil may care men from the South of Ireland. Even they were filled with a
sense of something impeding which was quite beyond their ken.'[38] Norman
Dewhurst recorded: 'I continued to nurse my ankle and when we finally left
Mudros harbour on the 23rd it was much better. All the ships' companies
in the harbour lined the rails and cheered us as we left, it was an exciting
moment and we were all ready to have a go.' Drewhurst's gung-ho retrospec-
tive comments on the lead up to the V Beach landing are in marked contrast
with sombre contemporary remarks recorded by Dr George Davidson and
the Revd Oswin Creighton.

Lieutenant-Colonel Herbert Carington Smith, Battalion headquarters and Y and Z Companies of the 2nd Battalion Hampshire Regiment
left Mudros harbour aboard the 13,405 ton Cunard-liner *Alaunia*.
In *The Dardanelles Campaign*, H.W. Nevinson said that the navy called
the transport ships (such as the *Alaunia*, the *Ausonia* and the *Caledonia*)
'the black ships,' as they were painted black. Presumably they had been
painted before leaving England.

∞

According to *History of the Royal Munster Fusiliers*, the *Caledonia* – and presumably the *Alaunia* and *Ausonia* – steamed slowly all night, with lights out.
Tenedos, about 40 miles away, was reached at 8 a.m. on Saturday 24 April.
'The sea had got up a good bit and rumour had it that "zero" [hour] would
have to be postponed.' George Davidson recorded that the *Ausonia* didn't
reach Tenedos until 9.30 a.m. on 24 April. 'We had been delayed by the wind
rising and the waves dashed over our lighters till they were nearly swamped.
On our east we have the coast of Asia with several high hills near the coast.'[39]

∞

Lieutenant-Colonel Charles Doughty-Wylie and Major Weir de Lancey-
Williams DSO, two members of Ian Hamilton's staff, left Mudros aboard
the *River Clyde*.[40] They were accompanied by an interpreter, Maurice
Constantinidi, an Englishman. Constantinidi's family had been Greek
subjects of the Ottoman Empire, who had moved to England from
Constantinople in the mid-nineteenth century.[41] According to Commander

Edward Unwin 'Col. Doughty-Wylie and Col. Williams had also wriggled on board, I never discovered quite why, but there they were.'[42]

Forty-six-year-old Charles Doughty-Wylie was an English officer on detached duty from the Royal Welch Fusiliers. He had served with his regiment in India, Crete, the Sudan, South Africa, China and Somaliland. The fighting in Somaliland in 1903-1904 was his last experience in combat until the Gallipoli campaign. In 1904, he married Lilian Wylie and changed his surname by deed poll from Doughty to Doughty-Wylie.

Interpreter Maurice
Stuart Constantinidi.

Wishing a change from traditional soldering, he applied for diplomatic work. In 1906, he was appointed British military vice-consul in Konia, a Turkish province in Asia Minor. In April 1909, more than 2,000 people were killed when Armenian Christians were attacked by their fellow Turkish residents in the town of Adana. The death toll would probably have been higher but for the intervention of Doughty-Wylie. Donning his army uniform he rode at the head fifty Turkish soldiers through the Christian quarter, restoring order. Shot in the right arm by an Armenian who thought he was a Turkish officer, Doughty-Wylie continued to police the town, quelling marauding gangs and sparing the Armenian Christian population further bloodshed. He was awarded a CMG for his actions. Promoted consul-general, he was posted to Addis Ababa, Ethiopia where he served until 1912. On the outbreak of the Balkan War he and his wife went to Constantinople, he as director of the Red Cross units and she as superintendent of Nursing Staff. He subsequently chaired a commission to decide on the Greek-Albanian frontier, service for which he was awarded a CBE. In 1913 he returned to the consulate in Addis Abba. In 1907, he met the archaeologist Gertrude Bell. They began a correspondence, which appears to have developed into an affair in August 1913. In February 1915, he was in Cairo, en route to England, where he hoped to resume active service. General Sir John Maxwell, British Commander-in-Chief in Egypt, requested permission to take him on to his staff, but Doughty-Wylie was assigned to the Intelligence Section of Sir Ian Hamilton's staff with the rank of lieutenant-colonel.[43] He went to London before taking up his appointment and again met Gertrude Bell. He joined Hamilton's staff on 18 March 1915. Without having previously mentioned him in his diary, on 24 March 1915 Sir Ian Hamilton made the following diary entry: 'Have sent Doughty Wylie to Athens to do *Intelligence*.' He did not record when Doughty-Wylie returned.

Forty-three-year-old Weir de Lancey Williams was a Welsh officer detached from the Hampshire Regiment. He had been awarded the DSO and mentioned in despatches for service in West Africa in 1898. He had served in the Boer War, during which he was severely wounded and again mentioned in despatches. He subsequently served in India, before becoming a staff officer with the Welsh Division. On 3 March 1915, he was assigned to the Operations Section of Sir Ian Hamilton's staff.[44]

Midshipman George Drewry said that when the *River Clyde* cleared Mudros harbour the lighters it was towing were dropped back and towed astern. According to Commander Edward Unwin, 'I had the hopper and three lighters in tow, and lengthened out the tow as soon as I was safely through the boom.' Apart from its human freight, the ship also carried two donkeys.[45] Drewry took command of the bridge while Unwin went for lunch. Upon Unwin's return Drewry went to lunch and later carried out 'the many things to be done.'[46] According to Unwin, 'We arrived at Tenedos just before the sun set, and anchored for the night, we worked till midnight getting things done.'[47]

ന

Tenedos Island, Saturday 24 April 1915

Tenedos was halfway between Mudros and the tip of the Gallipoli peninsula. Like Lemnos, it had been captured by the Greeks in the First Balkan War and was also being used as a base by the Allies.[48] The purpose of anchoring there was to transfer troops from their transports to the ships that would carry them to the peninsula. The venue was also used to prepare the open boats in which the troops would land on the beaches. According to Rear-Admiral Wemyss:

> These boats had to be towed to the rendezvous off Helles, and since there were ninety of them the utmost care had to be exercised that there should be nothing missing and that they should be in a perfect state of preparation on our arrival at the rendezvous ... The work was perfectly simple, but it was of the utmost importance that no detail, however slight, should be overlooked, for there would be no time to put matters right the next morning at the moment when the troops would be embarked and when so small a mistake might spell so great a disaster.[49]

George Drewry, *River Clyde*'s second-in-command, said 'About 6.00 a.m. a signal came to us telling us we were in someone's berth so we had to weigh and for an hour we wandered among the ships with our long tail (i.e. the lighters being towed) just scrapping along ships' sides and across their bows. We were nobodies dog nobody loved us. Finally we tied up to the stern of the *Fauvette* and we put the last touches to the staging on the bow.'[50]

George Davidson, aboard the *Ausonia*, recorded that, on the north side of Tenedos, the three transport ships (*Ausonia*, *Alaunia* and *Caledonia*) formed a little group among torpedo boats, destroyers, minesweepers, tugs 'and other small fry'. Eight battleships were drawn up in a line facing the open sea.

> The famous 'Horse of Troy', the *River Clyde*, lies near, and the thought of spending the coming night on her lowest deck is not attractive. She is painted khaki on one side (photos show this to be the starboard side – the right side – of the ship) I see, but only in patches, the idea evidently is to make her resemble a sandstone rock – all very ingenious not doubt, but she will make a good target in spite of her paint. I said yesterday that all the officers looked anxious, but in the evening all were their old selves exactly, and baccarat went on as usual among the younger officers who sang all their usual songs and yelled and laughed until midnight.[51]

The stormy weather continued on the morning of Saturday 24 April. Because ships towing boats moved at a low speed, departure from Tenedos could not be later than 10 p.m., if the landings were to be made on 25 April. Wemyss believed that if conditions did not improve by 2 p.m. there would have to be a further delay. At noon the wind began to die down. By 1.50 p.m. it had ceased and final preparations for the invasion commenced. It was probably after the go-ahead was announced that Father William Finn heard confessions, said mass and distributed holy-communion aboard the *Ausonia*.

Three lighters each were sent to the *Alaunia*, the *Ausonia*, and the *Caledonia*, and loaded with ammunition, supplies and beach equipment for the first wave of troops to go ashore. When the lighters were filled, they were assigned to tugs, which would tow them ashore after the landings had been made. Ship's boats from the *Cornwallis*, the *Euryalus* and the *Implacable* were organised into eighteen tows, each comprised of four boats pulled by a steam pinnace. Naval beach parties were sent to the ships from which they would land.

Aboard the *Alaunia*, the *Ausonia* and the *Caledonia*, the soldiers who would go ashore in the initial landing were given a hot meal. Then, each carrying his rifle, 200 rounds of ammunition and his pack with three days of rations, they lined up to await disembarkation to the warships that would carry them towards the Gallipoli shore. A small party from each battalion would be left aboard transport ships to take charge of regimental baggage and stores.

The log of the minesweeper *Newmarket* shows that at 4.20 p.m. she anchored alongside the transport *Caledonia*. At 6.04 p.m. she embarked troops (possibly the 1st Battalion Royal Munster Fusiliers; Captain Guy Geddes DSO said that 'At 4.30 p.m. we were transhipped to a cross channel steamer and went aboard the *River Clyde*, which we had previously inspected in Mudros harbour.' The *Newmarket* had been a cross-channel steamer, but note the time-discrepancy between the ship's log and the Geddes account.)[52] The *Newmarket* cast off at 6.20 p.m. and sailed to the *River Clyde*, where she disembarked troops. At 6.45 p.m. she cast off from *River Clyde* and anchored alongside the *Ausonia*. Her log contains the following entries: 'At 7.30 p.m. Darkened ship and posted armed sentry. 9.15 p.m. Embarked troops (possibly men from the 1st Battalion Royal Dublin Fusiliers). Left Transport B1 (the *Ausonia*) and proceeded course as ordered by *Cornwallis*.'

∽∾

History of the Royal Munster Fusiliers tersely records that 'at 3.15 orders were received to embark on the *River Clyde*; by 7.30 p.m. the embarkation was complete'. (Their War Diary says the order to embark was received at 3 p.m.) Norman Dewhurst is equally brief: 'At tea-time we were packed like sardines below deck on the *River Clyde*. We passed the night in anticipation of what was, to most of us, a great adventure.' Henry Denham was a midshipman aboard the battleship *Agamemnon*. He recorded that, on Saturday 24 April, the ship dispatched both its picket-boats, one to the *Euryalus*, and the other to the *Cornwallis*. Then a signal was received that a midshipman was needed to sail aboard the *River Clyde* as part of a beach party for V Beach. Denham prepared himself, only to be disappointed when the order was later cancelled. He said that landing conditions, which were now reported every few hours, seemed very favourable for a landing the next day. Second Lieutenant Reginald Gillett was aboard the *Alaunia*. Eight months previously, in August 1914, he had still been a pupil at Felsted School in Essex. Commissioned on 15 August 1914, he was now in command of No. 13 Platoon, Z Company, 2nd Battalion Hampshire Regiment. 'As evening approached we had orders to leave the *Alaunia* and to go aboard the *SS River Clyde*.'[53] Among the units transferred to the *River Clyde* was W Company, 1st Battalion Royal Dublin Fusiliers with Captains Herbert Crozier and Alexander Molony,

Lieutenants Lawrence Boustead and Henry Desmond O'Hara, Company Sergeant-Major Charles Smith and Company Quartermaster-Sergeant Patrick Curran. Lieutenant-Colonel Richard Rooth, Battalion Headquarters and the men of X, Y and Z companies of the 1st Battalion Royal Dublin Fusiliers spent the night aboard a minesweeper. (For reasons outlined in a footnote, there is conflicting evidence as to whether they were aboard one or two minesweepers.)[54] With the Dublins was No. 4 Platoon of the Anson Battalion, Royal Naval Division, under the command of Lieutenant John Denholm, RNVR.[55] The Royal Naval Division has previously been mentioned a number of times. As men from the Division took part in the V Beach landing, it is appropriate to take a brief look at their background.

෨෨

When Britain's naval reservists were called up in 1914 there were many more naval and Royal Marine personnel than could be accommodated on ships. Winston Churchill formed them into a Royal Naval Division (RND), for use on land. The division was made up of eight battalions of Royal Naval personnel and four battalions of Royal Marines. The Royal Naval battalions were numbered 1st to 8th and named after admirals (Drake, Hawke, Benbow, Collingwood, Nelson, Howe, Hood and Anson respectively). The Royal Marine battalions were numbered 9th to 12th and named after marine bases (Chatham, Portsmouth, Plymouth and Deal). The RND used naval ranks, were allowed to wear beards and remained seated during the toast to the King's health. Due to shortage of space at Mudros harbour, the RND and the French forces were sent to Trebuki Bay on the island of Skyros, 80 miles south-west of Lemnos.

The RND's commanding officer, General Archibald Paris, was asked to supply men to assist with the landing. Three hundred stokers (150 each from the Hood and Howe Battalions) were sent to Lemnos on 17 April under the command of Hood Sub-Lieutenants Dodge, Gammage and Trimmer. Sub-Lieutenant John Bigelow Dodge of A Company, Hood Battalion, was an American who was related by marriage to Winston Churchill. As he went ashore at V Beach, some background information might be beneficial. Known from childhood as Johnny, his parents on both sides were descended from the early settlers of Massachusetts. His paternal grandfather, General Charles Dodge, had been one of the youngest Union brigadier-generals during the American Civil War. His maternal grandfather, John Bigalow, was Lincoln's ambassador to France. Johnny's parents divorced and his mother, Flora, married Lionel Guest, a first cousin of Winston Churchill. At the outbreak of war Flora appears to have written to Churchill asking if a commission could be found for Johnny. Assigned to the Royal Naval Division, he took part in the unsuccessful attempt to prevent Antwerp from falling to the Germans. Having obtained British citizenship, he sailed for the Mediterranean with the Hood Battalion, Royal Naval Division, aboard the Union Castle liner *Grantully Castle*. He shared a cabin with the poet Rupert Brook during the voyage. On 23 April, after a period of illness, Brook died of septicaemia. As he wished to be buried on a Greek island, his fellow officers – including Johnny Dodge – buried him on the island of Skyros. A simple white cross bore the inscription: 'Here lies the servant of God, Sub-Lieutenant in the English Navy, who died for the deliverance of Constantinople from the Turks.'

∞

The *River Clyde* had four holds. From bow to stern these were designated No. 1 Fore Hold, No. 2 Main Hold, No. 3 Mizzen Hold and No. 4 After Hold.[56] Behind No. 2 Main Hold – and forward of No. 3 Mizzen Hold – was a Reserve Bunker, behind which were Port and Starboard Bunkers, the ship's engines and boilers. According to *History of the Royal Munster Fusiliers,* the troops on the ship were accommodated as follows. No. 1 Hold (Upper Deck)[57] Headquarters, four machine guns and X, Y and Z companies of 1st Battalion Royal Munster Fusiliers. No. 1 Hold (Lower Deck): W Company 1st Battalion Royal Munster Fusiliers and W Company 1st Battalion Royal Dublin Fusiliers. No 2 Hold: Four machine guns, Y and Z companies 2nd Battalion Hampshire Regiment and one company of the West Riding Field Engineers. In the aft of the ship, in No. 3 and No. 4 Holds: Two sub-divisions Field Ambulance, one signal section and No. 13 platoon Anson Battalion, Royal Naval Division. All the troops on the ship were under the command of Lieutenant-Colonel Herbert Carington Smith, Hampshire Regiment. *History of the Royal Munster Fusiliers* does not mention where the RNAS contingent was stationed. But, as they were to man the eleven Maxim machine guns on the upper deck, presumably they were stationed in the vicinity of that deck. They comprised of four officers, a doctor, and seventy-two men of No. 3 Armoured Car Squadron. The doctor was Surgeon Peter Burrows Kelly, Royal Navy, attached to the RNAS. The officers were Lieutenant-Commander Josiah Wedgwood and Sub-Lieutenants Hon. Arthur Coke, Douglas Illingworth and Charles Herbert Parkes. According to Wedgwood, when Coke saw his machine-gun position he said,

Sketch of RDF Sergeant. (Courtesy of Séamus Greene)

'This is my seat in the stalls, and there are many men in England would give £1,000 for it.'

Forty-three-year-old George Josiah Clement Wedgwood RNVR was the Member of Parliament for Newcastle-under-Lyme. Known as Josiah, he had served in the Boer War, commanding a battery of the Royal Artillery. Three times elected to parliament as a member of the ruling Liberal Party, he had taken a strongly independent line, in accordance with his conscience. In defiance of the government, he had supported the suffragettes. In 1913 he staged a filibuster against the government's Mental Deficiency Bill, believing it to be unjust. For two days, sustained by barley-water and chocolate, he tabled 120 amendments to the Bill and made 150 speeches. He only ceased when his voice gave out. Wedgwood married his first cousin Ethel Bowen in 1894. They had seven children but Ethel left him in 1913. A member of the RNVR, Wedgwood joined up on the outbreak of war and was attached to the RNAS. In *With Machine-Guns in Gallipoli*, Wedgwood expressed somewhat condescending views on the officers who commanded the *River Clyde*. Without naming them, Wedgwood said the ship 'was commanded by a dug-out half-pay captain who dreamed of lighters, a midshipman of Adonis-like beauty from the merchant marine and an engineer from the River Plate, who would describe with unnecessary zest how he was going to get two extra knots out of the old tub to "boost" her ashore by sitting on the safety valve.'

∞

On the eve of the landing, Brigadier-General Steuart Hare issued a statement to the men of his 86th Brigade: 1st Royal Dublin Fusiliers, 1st Royal Munster Fusiliers, 2nd Hampshire Regiment and 2nd Royal Fusiliers. 'Fusiliers, our brigade is to have the honour to be the first to land and to cover the disembarkation of the remainder of the Division. Our task will be no easy one. Let us carry it through in a way worthy of the traditions of the distinguished regiments of which the Fusilier Brigade is composed, in such a way that the men of Albuhera, Minden, Delhi and Lucknow may hail us as their equal in valour and military achievements, and that future historians may say of us, as Napier said of the Fusilier Brigade at Albuhera "Nothing could stop this astonishing infantry".'

The log of the battleship *Cornwallis* noted that at 7.30 p.m. three companies of the South Wales Borders were taken aboard. At 10.40 p.m. the ship weighed anchor and sailed for the Dardanelles accompanied by *Fleet Sweeper No. 1* and trawlers 'with tows of boats in company'. Given that the sweeper *Newmarket*'s log noted that she was sailing a course as 'ordered by *Cornwallis*', it would seem that she was *Fleet Sweeper No. 1*. According to *The Immortal Gamble*, 'Starting overnight from Tenedos anchorage, towing transport's life-boats, [the *Cornwallis*] steamed slowly towards the Gallipoli Peninsula.' Writing to his sister, Able Seaman Dick Ricus from the *Cornwallis* said that at 8.30 p.m. sailors from the ship got into boats which were tied up astern of the ship and were towed all night.[58]

Lieutenant George Davidson wrote in his diary on the night of 24 April.

10.30 p.m. Arrived on coal boat [*River Clyde*] at 6.30 a.m. Place in stern fitted up for officers' supper; two lime barrels and a few rough boards form table: whisky: tinned meat: biscuits: 2,200 of us on board: all happy and fit. We start in two hours: only 12 or 13 miles to go: then anchor 1½ miles from land and wait for daylight and bombardment: then at proper moment rush in: said that coast is to be battered with 150,000 shells. Supper finished some time ago and am writing this in the mess I have just mentioned. Some sleeping or pretending; others smoking; I doing latter and sitting on board after trying to snooze with head on a big box and less high one in small of back; but too uncomfortable for anything, so whipped out my 'bookie' and scribbled; light bad, only an oily lamp with glass smoked black, and nearly 20ft distant. Queer scene altogether.[59]

In a later entry Davidson said:

Before dark all the men were served with tea and food, which we were told was to be their last solid meal.[60] Soon after this the men retired to rest in a hold near the stern which had been allotted to the West Riding Engineers and ourselves. The officers took up their quarters in the stern deck house,[61] where we had cocoa, tinned meat, etc., after which we too tried to make ourselves as comfortable as possible in the most uncomfortable of all quarters, most shutting their eyes and pretending to be asleep.[62]

Commander Edward Unwin said that 'The troops came on board at about 6 p.m. in capital spirits and stored themselves away for the night. We had plenty of stores on board so I had a dinner party in my so called ward-room of all my crowd plus as many of the regimental officers as we could seat, for many of whom it was there [sic] last dinner.'[63]

Midshipman George Drewry said, 'At 11.30 p.m. all was ready and the Capt[ain] told me to snatch some sleep.' He said the ship set sail at midnight, towing a lighter on her starboard side and two lighters, a hopper and a small steam pinnace and on her port side.[64] Commander Edward Unwin said, 'It was a perfectly calm night and we could see the Chanak search light [to their right, inside the Dardanelles] the whole [the next word is illegible. Possibly time?] and most useful it proved to me as owing to the amount of iron I had put round the bridge my compass hadn't much idea where the North Pole was.'[65]

Second Lieutenant Reginald Gillett of the Hampshires was aboard the *River Clyde*:

> The night was dark and very silent, the sea which up to a few hours before had been rough was now very smooth. The night was bitterly cold. The holds were crowded and uncomfortable. Some of the officers went up on deck. I tried to get some sleep. I did find a warm sheltered spot near the engineers, but as I was dozing off a heavy sea boot was placed firmly on my face. I had overlooked the fact that I was lying across the doorway to the engine room. Later we were all ordered below.[66]

Lieutenant-Commander Josiah Wedgwood invited Royal Munster Fusilier Captain Guy Geddes DSO to sleep on the floor of his cabin. Geddes said 'I got a hot cup of chocolate, so had a very pleasant night's rest.'[67] At about 2.00 a.m. Midshipman George Drewry took over the bridge from Commander Edward Unwin. 'I found myself on the bridge very sleepy with only the helmsman, steering towards the Turkish searchlights on a calm night just making headway against the current, shadowy forms of destroyers and battleships slipping past me. Visions of mines and submarines rose before me as I thought of the 2 ½ thousand men in the holds and I felt very young.'[68] It seems unlikely that Unwin got any sleep. In his account to Wemyss some years later he said: 'I kept watch all night as it would have been impossible for me to sleep whereas Drewry might.' While Unwin's years-later account seems less accurate on minor details than Drewry's contemporary account, it seems likely that while Drewry took over the bridge at about 2 a.m., there was no question of Unwin getting sleep. The fact that he probably went to another part of the ship is supported by his comment that 'At 2 a.m. we whacked out cocoa to all hands and I think something to eat as well'.[69]

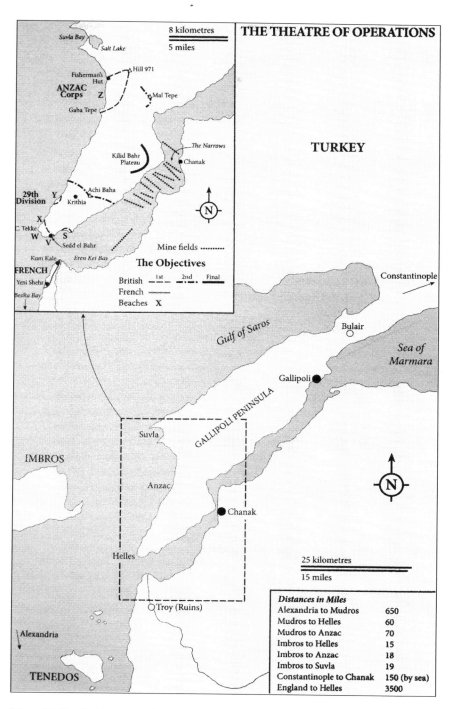

Map of Gallipoli. (Courtesy of Peter Hart)

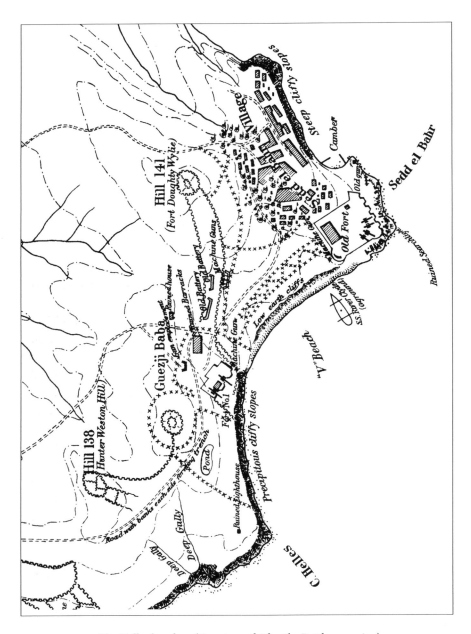

The Helles beaches. (Courtesy of *After the Battle* magazine)

CHAPTER 6

Ertuğrul Koyo – V Beach: 25 April 1915

'Every officer and man will carry on a string around his neck
an identity disc showing his name, number if any, unit and religion.'
Field Service Regulations Part 11, 1909 (reprinted 1914).

The Gallipoli peninsula is 52 miles at its longest point and 14 at its widest. At its narrowest, it is less than 3½ miles wide.[1] The ancient Greeks built a settlement on the peninsula. Named Kallipolis (Beautiful City), it became a major Greek trading port.[2] It later became known in the English-speaking world as Gallipoli and its name was applied to the whole peninsula. In 1658, work began on fortresses on both sides of the Aegean entrance to the Dardanelles, at Sedd el Bahr ('Barrier/Dam of the Sea') at the tip of the Gallipoli peninsula and Kum Kale (Kale means fortress) on the Asiatic shore.[3] The project was the brainchild of Hadice Turhan Sultan. The mother of boy Sultan Mehmed IV, she was known as Valide Sultan (Queen Mother).[4] The Ottoman chronicler Naima said the inhabitants of Sedd el Bahr objected to the proposed fortress near their village. They petitioned the Valide, saying that the fortress would be used as a refuge by bandits who would prey on the locals. (This would appear to suggest they believed the fortress would not be permanently garrisoned.) While sympathetic to their plight, the Valide was persuaded by her advisers that strategic necessities must prevail. Her foundation deed for the fortresses at Sedd el Bahr and Kum Kale said that 'inside both fortresses a grand mosque, a fine school, and a clean public bath should be built along with many houses, shops and markets for the guardians and protectors of the fortresses; these should all surpass those found anywhere else.'[5] The fort at Sedd el Bahr was built by 'all the prisoners of the navy, large landowners from islands in the Mediterranean, soldiers from the mountainous regions

Beneath a Turkish Sky

around the Dardanelles, many architects and approximately ten thousand peasants.'[6] At Sedd el Bahr 'the structures in the interior of the fortress were built of a variety of materials – wood, stone and mudbrick. As at Kum Kale, there was a mixed community of civilians of Turkish, Greek, Jewish and Armenian origins.'[7]

∾

The Valide's fort was garrisoned during the many wars that preceded the First World War. In 1854, Britain and France sent an expeditionary force to help Turkey against Russia. In April of that year, British troops sailed past Sedd el Bahr and safely entered the Dardanelles. Among them were thirty-year-old John Mitchell (41st Regiment of Foot), from County Meath and eighteen-year-old John Jordan (57th Regiment of Foot) from County Kerry. Reflecting the changing nature of alliances, just sixty-one years later Britain and France were allied to Russia and at war with Turkey. In April 1915, Mitchell's grandson Nicky Smyth and Jordan's sons Robert and Peter Jordan came with a British force to attack Sedd el Bahr. Smyth was serving with the Dublins and the Jordans were with the Munsters.

∾

Behind the Valide's fort and Sedd el Bahr village is a hill which the British called Hill 141. Approaching Sedd el Bahr from the sea, the fort is on low ground to the right of a small beach. On high ground overlooking the left of the beach is a fort built in the 1890s.[8] The fort and the beach are named after Ertuğrul, a warrior after whose son, Osman, the Ottomans were named. The harbour is Ertuğrul Koyo (Cove). The fort is Ertuğrul Tabyasi. The British called it Fort No. 1.

The Valide's fort (Sedd el Bahr Tabyasi, referred to by the British as Fort No. 3) and Ertuğrul Tabyasi (Fort No. 1) had been shelled several times by the Royal Navy. On 3 November 1914, five officers and eighty-one men had been killed as a result of a massive explosion caused by naval shelling. Following further shelling, on 26 February 1915, a force from the battleship *Irresistible* came ashore at Sedd el Bahr. Finding four of the six heavy guns in the Valide's fort undamaged, they blew them up. Approaching Ertuğrul Tabyasi (Fort No. 1) they came under attack. They destroyed two 12-pounder field-guns near the fort, but then had to retire to their ship's boats. The following day, another party landed from the *Irresistible*. Having destroyed a battery of six 6in Krupp mortars, the group withdrew. On 3 March, a group from the *Irresistible* surveyed the approaches to a harbour called The Camber, in Morto Bay, at the rear of the Valide's Sedd el Bahr Fort. After completing their survey, the party saw 'concealed in the arches under the fort, a battery of six 15-pounder guns of modern type. They were all destroyed, and then the party entered the fort, only to find that all the ammunition had been removed.'[9] On 4 March, a group from the *Inflexible* and the *Ocean*, landed at the Camber to carry out further demolition and to reconnoiter the area for a site where an aerodrome might be established. During the landing the group came under heavy attack. Three marines and a sailor were killed. A number of Turks were also killed, including a wounded man who flung himself down a cliff from a British stretcher. The heavy resistance met during this final landing was a portent of what would be faced at Sedd el Bahr on 25 April.[10]

The Gallipoli peninsula was home to thousands of people of Greek descent. Suspected of being a threat to Ottoman security, in early April 1915 soldiers of Brigadier-General Esat's III Corps began to evacuate them from the peninsula and move them to villages across the Sea of Marmara. By 10 April, most of them had been evacuated, about 22,000 in all.[11]

დდ

Colonel Halil Sami's 9th Infantry Division, with about 300 officers and 12,000 men, was stationed in the south of the Gallipoli Peninsula, with divisional headquarters in the town of Maidos (Eceabat). The division had an artillery regiment and three infantry regiments, the 25th, the 26th and 27th. Each regiment had three battalions. Sami placed the 27th Regiment's 2nd Battalion in the area later known as Anzac. Placed in reserve, under 27th Regiment's commanding officer Lieutenant-Colonel Mehmet, the 1st and 3rd Battalion were several kilometres behind Anzac. South of them, placed as a reserve for the Cape Helles area, was the 25th Regiment. This regiment, commanded by Lieutenant-Colonel Irfan, had been brought from Asia in March. Among its ranks was twenty-two-year-old Serif Ali Arslan from Çan-Malli village, who had been promoted to corporal.

The 26th Regiment had been stationed in the Cape Helles area since 19 August 1914 and so had eight months to prepare for the coming invasion. During this time the regiment, commanded by Major Hafiz Kadri, usually had two battalions in the beach defences and one in reserve. While it was in the vicinity during the shelling of 3 November 1914, no record has been found as to whether it sustained casualties on that date. It did, however, come under shelling during the allied naval attacks on 25 February, 3 March and 18 March 1915. The regiment lost four men killed and fourteen wounded during the 3 March attack. On 21 April, Colonel Halil Sami ordered that Major Kadri's entire 26th Regiment move into the Cape Helles beach defences. On the eve of the Allied invasion, there was a fully trained regiment of about 3,000 infantry men defending the southern tip of the Gallipoli Peninsula.[12]

On the morning of 22 April, Major Kadri and his staff finalised their defence plans. Kadri issued a regimental order describing in detail how the defences were to be occupied by his men. He played close attention to his artillery support and distributed a map with its details to his commanders, as well as to the adjacent Fortress Command. He stationed his 1st Battalion at Kum Tepe on the Aegean coast of the peninsula, roughly halfway between what the British would call Y Beach and Z Beach (Anzac Cove). He put his 3rd Battalion, of about a thousand men, commanded by Major Mahmut Sabri, in the Cape Helles-Sedd el Bahr region. Behind them he placed three of his 2nd Battalion's four companies in reserve. The final company (7 Company) was stationed to the north-west, linking his forces at Cape Helles-Sedd el Bahr with those at Kum Tepe. Kadri set up his regimental headquarters in the village of Krithia. Behind Kadri's 26th Infantry Regiment, Irfan's 25th Infantry Regiment waited in general reserve.

Under the command of Major Mahmut Sabri, the 3rd Battalion, 26th Infantry Regiment was stationed in the Cape Helles-Sedd el Bahr area. Sabri assigned two of his four companies, 10 and 12 Companies, to beach defence. He set up his command post about ½ mile from the beaches and stationed the two remaining companies, 9 and 11 Companies, and his attached engineering company as a reserve. The two companies on beach defence each had two of their three platoons in strong points, fortified by barbed wire and trenches, overlooking the landing areas of Ertuğrul Koyu (V Beach), Teke Koyu (W Beach) and Ikiz Koyu (X Beach). The third platoon in each company was positioned in reserve behind the strong points. On 23 April, told to expect an imminent enemy landing, Sabri wrote new orders for the 3rd Battalion. He ordered his platoon strong-points to engage enemy ships and landing craft at ranges of 200 to 300 yards. He told the platoons that they would be reinforced by reserves, once he knew the direction of the main enemy attack. He ordered them to make patient preparations and to be brave. He said that the battalion first-aid station would be at Harapkale, the ruins of a fort that had predated the Valide's fort and stood on Hill 141 (*Harap* means ruined and *Kale* means castle). He identified the best route to reach the first-aid station, safe from enemy fire. The battalion received the orders on the morning of 24 April.

Reconstructed Turkish trench overlooking V Beach. (Michael Lee)

The 9th Division's artillery, which provided support to its 25th, 26th and 27th Infantry Regiments, was commanded by Lieutenant-Colonel Mehmet Ali. Having attached some artillery to the 27th Infantry Regiment, in the vicinity of Z Beach (Anzac Cove), he was left with forty-four guns to support the defences in the southern part of the 9th Division's sector. Most of the guns were sited on the landing beaches. Ali also had priority call on three howitzer batteries from the nearby Fortress Command. He told these batteries that their priority was to fire on Allied ships forcing the Dardanelles, but if this was not happening they were to fire on enemy troops landing at Sedd el Bahr.

ۥ

The night of 24 April was quiet and moonlit. Turkish sentries reported that, despite a light breeze and waves, they heard enemy ships and, occasionally, aircraft. While Allied planes could fly on bombing missions at night, none were attempted on the night before the invasion and, as there would have been no point in reconnaissance flights at night, the sentries' reports of hearing aircraft must be doubted. At 3.20 a.m. 7 Company, 2nd Battalion, 26th Regiment sent a message to Brigadier-General Esat's 111 Corps headquarters at Gelibolu, saying there was enemy activity off Teke (Cape) Burnu.[13]

Aboard the SS River Clyde, *at Sea off the Dardanelles, Early Sunday 25 April 1915*

Sometime between 3 a.m. and 4 a.m., Commander Edward Unwin took over the bridge from Midshipman George Drewry. The latter had a brief sleep, before being called again at 5 a.m. Unwin then told him that he was to take command of the hopper (a barge for carrying materials like rocks, sand, soil or rubbish) *Argyle,* which the *River Clyde* was towing on the port (left) side. Also being towed on the port side, inboard of the *Argyle* and one-behind-the-other, were two lighters and a small steam pinnace. To get from the *River Clyde* to the *Argyle,* Drewry had to cross the first lighter. To crew the *Argyle,* he had six volunteer Greek sailors. Unwin said that Drewry had spent some years in charge of a Greek lighthouse and could speak Greek like a native. Also among Drewry's crew was twenty-six-year-old Scots Ablebodied Seaman George Samson, one of the *Hussar's* crew, who had answered Unwin's call for volunteers to serve aboard the *River Clyde*.[14]

ɷ

It was still dark when the twenty-four ship's boats assigned to the V Beach landing were organised into six 'tows'. Each tow comprised of four boats in line-ahead. A rope ran from the stern of the first boat to the bow of the second, from the stern of the second to the bow of the third and from the stern of the third to the bow of the fourth. Each tow was pulled by a steam-powered picket boat.[15] The tows were numbered from No. 1 to No. 6. Each boat was manned by a midshipman and about six seamen. No. 1 tow was pulled by a picket boat commanded by Midshipman Denis Last, from the *Cornwallis.* Travelling aboard the picket boat, in overall command of the tow and assigned as Assistant Beach Master for V Beach, was Royal Navy Commander Neston Diggle. The first boat in the tow was commanded by seventeen-year-old Midshipman Haydon Forbes, from the *Cornwallis.* His crew also came from the *Cornwallis*.[16]

Each tow was taken to a minesweeper,[17] from where they disembarked the men of X, Y and Z Companies of the Royal Dublin Fusiliers and No. 4 Platoon of the Anson Battalion, Royal Naval division. Under the command of Lieutenant John Denholm RNVR, No. 4 Platoon was to form a beach party. No. 1 Tow was taken to the minesweeper *Clacton.* Haydon Forbes went aboard and had a cup of tea while half of Major Cecil Grimshaw's Z Company, 1st Battalion, Royal Dublin Fusiliers disembarked. The soldiers in No. 1 Tow were under the command of Captain John Muspratt Mood and Lieutenant Raymond de Lusignan.[18] Major Cecil Grimshaw DSO travelled in a different tow, with the other half of Z Company.

The disembarkation of the troops took half an hour longer than had been envisaged. When completed, the six tows took up station, with No. 1 Tow on the right of the column. No. 2 Tow was on the left of No. 1, No. 3 Tow was on the left of No. 2 etc., all the way across to No. 6 Tow on the left of the column. Apart from No. 1 Tow, records have not been found as to who was in which tow. It is, however, possible to surmise. Given that half of Z Company was in No. 1 Tow on the right of the column, it seems reasonable to assume that the second part of the company, under Major Cecil Grimshaw DSO, would have travelled in the nearest tow i.e. Tow No. 2. As Grimshaw would have wanted to exercise command over his men, it seems reasonable to suppose that he might have travelled in the first boat in No. 2 Tow. With Captain John Mood and Lieutenant Raymond de Lusignan in No. 1 Tow, Grimshaw had only one remaining officer from his company available for his tow: Lieutenant Colin Carruthers. He also had Company-Sergeant-Major Michael O'Keefe and Company Quartermaster-Sergeant Thomas Brennan.[19]

Being in overall command, it seems reasonable to think that Lieutenant-Colonel Richard Rooth might have stationed himself in the front, in the middle of the column. This would have put him in the first boat in No. 3 Tow or No. 4 Tow. Major Edwyn Featherstonhaugh was not in the same boat as Rooth. Initially I speculated that, as second-in-command, he may also have been in the first boat of one of the middle tows. For reasons that will be outlined later, however, I deduced that he was in the third boat of No. 4 Tow. This in turn leads me to suggest that the most likely tow for Rooth was No. 3 Tow. Given that W Company of the Blue Caps was aboard the *River Clyde* and men from Z Company were in No. 1 Tow on the immediate right of the column of tows, it seems reasonable to suggest the troops may have travelled as follows: the second half of Z Company in No. 2 Tow, Y Company in No. 3 and No. 4 Tows (under the command of Captains David French and Arthur Johnson, Lieutenants William Andrews, Robert Bernard and Francis Lanigan-O'Keeffe, Company Sergeant-Major George Baker and Company Quartermaster-Sergeant James Bedding) and X Company in No. 5 and No. 6 Tows (under the command of Major Edward Molesworth, Captain Denis Anderson, Lieutenant Cuthbert Maffett, Second Lieutenants Joseph Hosford and John Walters, Company Sergeant-Major Harry Fox and Company Quartermaster-Sergeant Henry Baker). Lieutenant Henry Floyd, did not take part in the landing, remaining aboard the *Marquette* in charge of battalion transport.

Aboard the minesweeper that morning, Father William Finn said he wanted to go ashore with the Blue Caps. Lieutenant-Colonel Rooth tried to persuade him to remain aboard ship, where he could minister to wounded brought back from the beach. But Father Finn insisted, saying that the priest's place was with the dying soldier. Now Finn was in the same boat as Rooth and battalion adjutant Captain William Higginson.[20] The following officers were also in the tows: Machine-gun Officers Captain George Dunlop and Lieutenant Reginald Corbet, Signalling Officer James Grove, Quartermaster Lieutenant Michael Kennedy[21] and Medical Officer Lieutenant Henry de Boer. Also in the boats were Regimental Sergeant-Major William O'Mahoney, Regimental Quartermaster-Sergeant Joseph Thurlow and Orderly-Room Sergeant Percival Bonynge. As the steam-powered picket boats pulled their tows towards Sedd el Bahr, sailors and soldiers within the boats held oars vertically, their paddles pointed towards the night-sky.[22] In addition to their rifles, the Dubs each carried 200 rounds of ammunition. In their packs, they carried three days of rations, their great-coats and a waterproof sheet. The six tows heading for Sedd el Bahr were slowed by the current flowing out of the Dardanelles and by the trawlers carrying troops to S Beach.

∞

The nine ships of Wemyss's squadron responsible for supporting the troops with their fire during the landing were called the 'covering ships'. Under the immediate command of Rear-Admiral Stuart Nicolson, they were to be deployed as follows. *Prince George* off the Asiatic coast, *Lord Nelson* and *Vengeance* in the Dardanelles, *Albion* off V Beach, *Swiftsure* (Nicolson's ship) off W Beach, *Dublin*, *Goliath*, *Minerva* and *Talbot* off Y Beach and north of it. All located Turkish guns and trenches as far north as Achi Baba were to be kept under fire. The battleship *Cornwallis* was to support the landing of troops at S Beach in Morto Bay. When the landing had been made, the ship was to take up station off V Beach, with the *Albion*.

At 4.20 a.m., the battleship *Albion* entered the Dardanelles. At 4.30 p.m. the crew went to action stations. Seven minutes later the ship took up station off V Beach. The naval bombardment began at about 5 a.m., with the *Albion* opening fire at 5.04 a.m. The sun rose at 5.08 a.m. On an approximate bearing of N 75 E, it shone straight into the eyes of the gunlayers aboard the *Albion*. The rising sun put the shore in shadow and a haze covered the scene. The *Albion* ceased firing at 5.30 a.m., the time the tows were due to land at V Beach. By then the beach was shrouded in mist and smoke. As the tows had not appeared, the ship re-opened fire. Before the tows finally landed, the *Albion* had fired 900 6in shells, more than 1,000 rounds of 12-pounder ammunition and twelve 12in shells.[23]

∞

Major Mahmut Sabri, commanding officer of the 3rd Battalion of the 26th Regiment, said the shelling destroyed two 37.5 mm guns and 'some of the rifle trenches which had been dug to protect the soldiers' lives instead became their graves'. Wounded men who were able to walk gave their ammunition to colleagues, before reporting to the battalion first-aid post at Harapkale on Hill 141. Due to the shelling, the shore area was covered in bluish-black and greenish smoke, so that nothing could be seen. Stationed ½ mile inland, Sabri believed he knew where the landing would come. He decided, however, to await reports from the commanders of 10 and 12 Companies before taking action.

∞

Having sailed against a strong current all night, Commander Edward Unwin was worried when the *River Clyde* arrived off Helles behind schedule. There was no sign of the tows that were to beach before his ship. Unwin did not know whether they had still to arrive, or if they had gone on to the beach. As the *River Clyde* passed the cruiser *Euryalus*, Rear-Admiral Wemyss signalled 'Don't wait for the tows go right in'. But Lieutenant-Colonel Herbert Carington Smith, commanding officer of the troops aboard the *River Clyde*, told Unwin this would 'upset the whole arrangements'. Lieutenant-Colonel Doughty-Wylie and Major de Lancey-Williams agreed with Carington Smith.[24]

If Unwin slowed the *River Clyde*, the hopper *Argyle* and the lighters the ship was towing might get snarled up. Carrying human freight, rather than a cargo of coal, the *River Clyde's* propeller and rudder were out of the water. If Unwin reversed engines, the tow ropes could foul the ship's propeller. Not wanting to impede other ships, Unwin turned his vessel sharply to starboard (right), just managing to clear the stern of the battleship *Agamemnon*. On the starboard of the *Agamemnon* there were two destroyers with a mine-sweeping cable between them. Realising he would be unable to clear the destroyers, Unwin sailed between them 'knowing that they had plenty of time to slack down the wire and let us run over it'. As he still could not see the tows and was uncertain if they had gone ahead, Unwin decided to sail for V Beach. The sun was low in the sky, directly ahead, as the *River Clyde* steamed in slowly. Visibility was further reduced by smoke from bursting shells. Unwin found it difficult to locate the beach. A week previously he had visited the area and noted the location of 'a sort of gravestone on the beach in line with a conspicuous tree on the hill'. He took his bearings from these and sailed towards them.[25]

∞

V Beach is about 350 yards wide and about 10 yards in depth. Approaching from the sea, the Valide's fort is on low ground to the right of the beach. The left of the beach is overlooked by high ground on which stands Ertuğrul Tabyasi (Fort No. 1). Imagining the area as an amphitheatre, the beach would be located on the stage, overlooked on its left side, front and part of its right by high ground that climbs in a manner similar to tiered seating. The V Beach plan required two and a half companies of the Blue Caps to land on the beach from ship's boats, while a half company landed at the Camber, a small harbour in Morto Bay behind the Valide's fort on the eastern side of Sedd el Bahr. Operating on the right side of V Beach, the Dubs were ordered to capture the fort and the village of Sedd el Bahr. Soon after they landed, the *River Clyde* was to run onto the beach. W Company of the Dubs would come ashore to support their battalion in obtaining its objectives. The 1st Munsters would come ashore and operate on the left of V Beach, with orders to capture the remaining defences, including Ertuğrul Tabyasi. Two companies of the 2nd Hampshires were to be held in reserve. The plan called for the Blue Caps in their boats and the *River Clyde* to be ashore by 7 a.m. Then, if all went well, some units of the 88th Brigade would begin landing at about 8.30 a.m.

Able Seaman Dick Ricus from the *Cornwallis* wrote to his sister: 'About half an hour before daybreak our steam boats took us in tow and we went to get our troops at daybreak. All the warships which joined us in the night started to bombard and you never heard such a noise in your life. All the boats advanced under cover of the ship's fire. Landing in six different places, our steam boats slipped us about two hundred yards from the shore and we had to row the remainder.'[26] Contrary to plan, the tows and the *River Clyde* arrived at V Beach almost simultaneously. As the tows approached the beach, 'three to starboard and three to port of the *River Clyde*, a single shot was heard. Whether a prearranged signal or not, it was the immediate prelude to a shattering blast of Turkish small arms and automatic gun fire, soon to be a continuous roar.'[27]

A shell from Turkish batteries on the Asiatic shore fell just ahead of Midshipman Haydon Forbes' No. 1 Tow. Another exploded behind. From the

River Clyde at V Beach. (Copyright Stephen Chambers)

Gallipoli shore smaller shells rained down. Passing astern of the *River Clyde*, No. 1 tow overtook her on her starboard (right) side. About 50 to 100 yards from shore the steam picket boats slowed down and the towlines were slipped. Orders rang out 'Oars down! Give way together!' Those at the oars pulled hard for the shore. Breaking away from the tows heading for V Beach, No. 1 tow veered to the right and headed for the Camber. Shrapnel burst overhead, causing everybody in Forbes' boat to duck. Forbes looked around. Everyone in the boat was safe. The boat was peppered with shrapnel as it approached the shore. It pulled into the Camber and the Blue Caps leapt ashore.[28] They took cover beneath a wall without sustaining casualties. Forbes's boat was the first to leave the Camber and was again sprayed with shrapnel.

ൟ

None of the Dubs who survived the landing at the Camber left a published account of the fighting that followed. For that we have to rely on a number of other sources, of which the best is an eyewitness account contained in *The Immortal Gamble,* by Acting-Commander Archibald Stewart and Chaplain Charles Pershall of the *Cornwallis.*

> A party that landed at the Camber by the old fort got up to the village of Sedd-ul-Bahr as far as the windmills ... Advancing in a series of crawls and short runs, with backs bent double, across an open space between the cliff and a row of houses, our men sheltered as best they could, crouching low against the foundations of anything standing. Opposite them the Turks held a loop-holed wall. Sometimes one side and sometimes the other bobbed up, and a shot was fired – often not more than ten yards separated the adversaries. And all the while what impressed us breathless onlookers was the adroitness with which our men turned every projecting angle of a house, every fallen stone, every insignificant rise in the road, to account ... The brave little company was driven back, outnumbered; many cut off ...[29]

Major-General Callwell said:

> This camber ... was about three hundred yards from the south-eastern end of V Beach, and as it turned out this minor affair was quite distinct from the operations at that point. The half-company disembarked on the camber with less loss than might have been expected, and they tried to work across to Beach V, below the castle. This, however, they found to be quite impossible. They then strove hard to gain a footing in the village, but they found this also to be beyond them. The warships could give them little help, and in their isolated and very exposed position they naturally suffered heavy losses. Eventually the survivors were got away ... [The] camber was so near to Beach V that the defenders were in a position to collect troops very rapidly to bar the way to the half-company of Dublins ...[30]

According to the *Official History*: 'On the right, the two platoons ordered to land at the Camber were able to get ashore in safety, and a few men succeeded in reaching the village, where they were eventually overpowered. But the greater number was held up by the galling fire that met them and all the officers were killed'.[31] It later said, 'Remnants of the two platoons who attempted this flank attack eventually returned to the Camber, where all their officers being killed, they signalled to the flagship to be reembarked. They were eventually rescued by a picket boat from the *Queen Elizabeth*, which volunteered to run in with two cutters to bring them off.'[32]

The Official Naval History said:

[The] landing [at the Camber] had been unopposed, but when they attempted to advance up the steep and narrow approach which led to the village they were met by a blast of rifle and machine-gun fire that was quite impassable. Again and again, with the greatest gallantry, they strove to close the loopholed ruins of the fort, and so far did they push on that from the sea it looked as if they had actually reached the village. But it was, in fact, beyond human effort, and at last – reduced to a bare skeleton of the party that had come ashore – they had to be re-embarked …[33]

According to Eric Bush, 'Climbing the cliff in front of them, they advanced in short rushes as far as the windmills near the eastern corner of Sedd-el-Bahr village. Here, later, they were overwhelmed by a crowd of snipers. They lost all their officers, some NCOs and eighty-six men. A few survivors did get back to the Camber, while others tried to join the rest of their company which was due to land from the *River Clyde*. It was sad that the two platoons in No. 1 tow had fared so badly after an almost unopposed landing in the Camber. Much had been expected of this flank attack. Could not Commander Diggle have told someone of the existence of this comparatively safe landing place so that another wave of troops could be sent in there instead of on to V Beach, where they were slaughtered almost to a man? Perhaps he did. But nothing was done. The survivors of No. 1 tow who withdrew to the Camber were brought off to safety in two separate parties. The first was led by Lieutenant Francis Sandford, with Midshipman Lennox Boswell … Later in the day Midshipman Geoffrey Norman brought off the rest.' 'On the way back to the *Queen Elizabeth*', Norman wrote:

I received a good deal of back-chat from one of the soldiers in the stern of our boat, who merely sat tight with a pipe in his mouth. I was a bit curt with him as he would give orders and make no effort to move. When we got to the ship we helped out all the others, and at last he said, 'Come on, give us a hand,' and for the first time I saw that one of his legs was almost completely shot away. That night I went to the sick bay to find out how he was getting on and was told that he had insisted on the others being dealt with before him. His first words on getting over his anaesthetic were to ask for his pipe, the stem of which he had already practically chewed away.'[34]

The first group of survivors were evacuated by boats commanded by Royal Navy Lieutenant Francis Sandford. On 26 and 27 February, he had commanded demolition parties that had landed at Sedd el Bahr.[35]

The statements (by the official military history and Eric Bush) that all the officers of the Camber contingent were killed are puzzling. *Neill's Blue Caps* says the troops who landed at the Camber were commanded by Captain John Muspratt Mood and Lieutenant Raymond de Lusignan. While de Lusignan was killed, Mood survived the war and was serving in the 2nd Battalion at the time of its disbandment. It is a pity an account of the action at the Camber was not obtained from him for *Neill's Blue Caps*. In a witness statement at the Military Hospital, Devonport on 29 July 1915, Acting Colour-Sergeant James Finnegan, 9992, Z Company, said de Lusignan was also of Z Company and '…. he saw Lieut de Lusignan killed by shell fire whilst placing a screen to show the ships they had captured the position. Dardanelles April 25th.'[36] In a statement at Ward 34, Royal Infirmary, Edinburgh, Private Joseph Cruise, 11293, X Company, 1st Royal Dublin Fusiliers said that he 'was beside this officer about half-an-hour after they landed, standing on the cliff. He was hauling up a casual screen (signal for stop firing) to stop the ships from shooting. He saw him killed and he was left out until the following morning, when he was buried with other officers.' It is a pity that the statement is undated, because, given that the troops who landed at the Camber were from Z Company, the fact that Cruise was a member of X Company is a bit of a puzzle. (Possibly he may subsequently have transferred to X Company.)[37] At approximately 8.30 a.m. on 25 April, the battleship *Queen Elizabeth* arrived off V Beach, where she received the message: 'Do not shell the forts and the village of Seddulbahir. Our troops are there.' Possibly the signal followed from Lieutenant Raymond de Lusignan's raising of the 'casual screen'. Captain John Mood gave an account of de Lusignan's death that differed from that of Finnegan and Cruise. On 8 May 1915, Mood wrote to de Lusignan's mother from hospital.[38]

Anglo-American Hospital,
Regina,
Cairo.
8-5-15

Dear Mrs Lusignan,

I am writing to express my deepest sorrow for your loss and to let you know that he died like a gallant gentleman. He and I and 100 men had a special job apart from the rest of the Battalion. We had to land round the south side of Sedd-el-Bahr and Captain Johnson to the north of it. I sent him to the left with a party of men to join up with Johnton who I afterwards heard was held up with the [battalion] on the beach and never reached the village at all, while I went [to the] right according to orders.[39]

By midday we were kicked out of the village back to the fort at the end of it. His party was also out numbered and a wounded man lay in the middle of the street being sniped to death when the dear old prince tried to pull him back into cover and was at what no one else dared to do. I feel sure you would like to know the splendid manner of his death. I heard all this from one of his men who survived. I feel very much for you and also for myself because he was a friend of mine.

Yours very sincerely,
John Mood

ෆ

The first reports from his company commanders began to arrive at Major Mahmut Sabri's 3rd Battalion headquarters at about 6 a.m. While they did not give him any definite information, he decided to send a situational report to Major Hafiz Kadri's 26th Regiment command post in the village of Krithia, outlining the strength of the naval forces bombarding his positions.

Contemporary drawing. (Courtesy of *After the Battle* magazine)

He finished his report with the words 'The battalion is ready and will perform to the final degree'. Meanwhile, at 6 a.m., the men of 10 Company saw a flotilla of boats approaching Sedd el Bahr. They were amazed to also see a steamship (the *River Clyde*) heading towards the shore. At the four hundred meter mark they 'began to engage the enemy with machine guns and light artillery'.[40] At 6.30 a.m., they saw 'five' of the enemy boats separate from the rest. (This was the tow heading for the Camber. The tow actually had four boats.) They 'engaged them with very heavy rifle fire.'[41] The *River Clyde* continued on until it grounded in the surf. 'The ship immediately became a magnet for heavy Turkish fire as the company commander directed rifles and machine guns against it.'[42]

∞

The tows carrying X Company, Y Company and half of Z Company, 1st Battalion Royal Dublin Fusiliers were scheduled to arrive at V Beach before the *River Clyde*. Due to a delay, however, they arrived at the same time. They were met by a blistering fire from the Turkish defenders. The third boat of No. 4 tow beached just after the *River Clyde*. The bowman, Liverpudlian Able Seaman William Taylor (thirty-nine), jumped out with the painter, the rope for tying up the boat. He was immediately shot down. Subsequently brought to hospital in Malta, he died on 15 June 1915.[43] The few unwounded soldiers in the boat jumped into the water. Of the thirty-two *Blue Caps* originally aboard, only three got ashore. A major, a captain, and a lieutenant were killed or wounded with their men. Eric Bush said Major Edwin Fetherstonhaugh was mortally wounded before his boat reached the shore. *Neill's Blue Caps* said he died of wounds on 27 April. As he was the only one to fit the criteria, Fetherstonehaugh, second-in-command of the battalion, must have been the major in the third boat of No. 4 tow.

Having discharged its soldiers, the third boat of No. 4 tow needed to leave the beach. Leading Seaman Thomas Ford was at the tiller. Ablebodied Seaman Cragie and Boy Herbert Runacres were in the bottom of the boat dressing wounded men. Ablebodied Seaman Walter Lyne had been hit in the leg by a bullet which had first passed through the boat's side, and though he could not move, he dressed the wounded who were within his reach. There were only two sailors left at the oars, Ablebodied Seaman James Skitmore and Boy James Darling. Darling was hit and Ford took over his oar, while still manning the tiller. 'Cheer up, my son, it will soon be over,' he told Darling; and almost immediately a bullet struck his shoulder. He continued to row with one hand, and, between them, he and Skitmore backed the boat out. They met a steam-pinnace, which towed them to a minesweeper. After the wounded were put aboard, the three unwounded seamen were ordered to land more soldiers. They landed under less heavy fire, with fewer losses. Soon afterwards the boat was struck by a shell and rendered unseaworthy. The three sailors jumped overboard and swam to the *River Clyde*, from where they rejoined the *Cornwallis* in the evening.[44]

Able Seaman Dick Ricus from the *Cornwallis* wrote to his sister.

> The Turks waited until we got close and then opened a murderous fire. The troops started to fall like leaves. It was then I got hit in the right shoulder. Anyway we got the boat ashore, and those soldiers that could, got out. By this time all my boat's crew were either killed or wounded so we had to stop there under a hail of bullets from Maxims and rifles. This was 7 a.m. and we remained there for about nine hours. Every time one of us got up to try to get the boat off we were met by a hail of bullets. The poor old Dublins.[45]

Some of the boats headed for a narrow strip of partially submerged rock, about 25 yards in length, jutting out from the right side of the beach. (This line of rock played an important part in the landing. Called different names by various narrators, for the sake of uniformity I will refer to it in every account as 'the line of rock.') According to a Royal Dublin Fusiliers private:

> I jumped into the sea with my gun, and made towards the shore. When I got up on the rocky place I had my first bullet in my side. I felt as if I were struck with an iron bar in the back. It knocked me down. I put up my right hand to my head with the pain, when I got a bullet through that also. I had thus two narrow escapes. The first bullet just missed my lung and spine; it made a big hole in my back. The second one just missed my head.

Many of the Blue Caps who got out of the boats and attempted to swim or wade to the shore were entangled in barbed wire and drowned. The few who reached the shore crawled on their stomachs, or ran, reeling and staggering, to the shelter of a sandbank, about 4 feet high, which stretched across the beach. Most of the boats that carried the Dublins were destroyed. Others, filled with dead and dying men, drifted out to sea, where they were picked up by ships of the Royal Navy.[46] A Dubs officer said:

The line of rocks. (Michael Lee)

Shrapnel burst above our heads and before I knew where I was, I was covered with dead men. Not knowing they were dead, I was roaring at them to let me up, for I thought I was drowning. The guns still played on us till we got back to a minesweeper. I was simply saturated all over with blood, and I could feel the hot blood all over me all the way across. When they pulled these poor fellows off me they were all dead, and the poor fellows under me were dead also. The boat was awful to look at, full of blood and water.[47]

According to Private Robert Martin:

There were twenty-five in my boat, and there were only three of us left. It was sad to hear our poor chums moaning, and to see others dead in the boat. It was a terrible sight to see the poor boys dead in the water; others on the beach roaring for help. But we could do nothing for them. I must have had someone's good prayer for I do not know how I escaped.[48]

Captain Alexander Molony, W Company, who was aboard the *River Clyde*, wrote:

The boats came in; they were met by a perfect tornado of fire, many men were killed and wounded. Wounded men were knocked into the water and drowned, but they kept on. Survivors jumped into the water in some cases up to their necks, and got ashore; but the slaughter was terrific. Most of the officers were killed or wounded. Colonel (Richard) Rooth, the C.O., was shot dead at the edge of the water; Major (Edwin) Featherstonhaugh, second-in-command, was mortally wounded in his boat; Captain (Arthur) Johnson (Y Company) was badly wounded while still in his boat; Captain (David) French, the biggest man in the Battalion, got ashore with a bullet through the arm; Captain (Denis) Anderson (X Company) was shot dead on the beach, and many others were wounded. The machine-gun detachment worked desperately to get their guns ashore, but they were nearly all killed or wounded; both the officers, Captain (George) Dunlop and Lieutenant (Reginald) Corbet, were killed. It was a terrible affair, and a few minutes of such fire decimated the Battalion. The people who got ashore established themselves on the beach as best they could under a bank which ran along the shore for some distance and was four to five feet high.[49]

Captain David French, Y Company, was in the last boat of one of the tows:

About 6.30 a.m. we were quite close to the beach in a little bay. The *R. [iver] Clyde* had grounded before it was intended and a hot rifle fire was poured into her from the Turkish trenches. As soon as the 'tows' got into shallow water the picquet boats cast off & the bluejackets commenced to row. You can imagine how slowly we progressed – 6 men pulling a heavy boat with about 30 soldiers – each carrying over 60 lbs kit and ammunition on his body –!! At this moment the warships ceased cannonading – and a most appalling fire – machine gun, rifle and pom-pom was opened on us from the enemy, while concealed howitzer batteries from inland added to our discomfort with shrapnel. I was in the last boat of my tow and did not realize they had started at my boat until one of the men close to me fell back – shot. I realized immediately that having practically wiped out the other three boats ahead they were now concentrating their fire on us. I jumped out at once in the sea (up to my chest) yelling to the men to make a rush for it & to follow me. But the poor devils – packed like sardines in a tin & carrying this damnable weight on their backs – could scarcely clamber over the sides of the boat and only two reached the shore un-hit while the boat ahead of mine suffered as much – the same number escaping from that. The only other officer in my boat [evidence appears to suggest that this was Captain Arthur Johnson] never even got ashore being hit by five bullets. A picquet boat most heroically came right in close and towed the

boat back to the battleship *Albion* which was now anchored about 800 yds
from the beach. I had to run about 100-150 yds in the water and being the
first away from the cutter escaped the fire a bit to start with. But as soon as
a few followed me the water around seemed to be alive – the bullets striking the sea all around us. Heaven knows how I got thro' – a perfect hail of
bullets. The beach sloped very gradually – fortunately. When I was about
50 yards from the water's edge I felt one bullet go through the pack on my
back and then thought I had got through safely when they put one through
my left arm. The fellows in the regiment had told me I was getting too fat to
run but those who saw me go through that bit of water changed their opinions later – I ran like hell!! On reaching the shore I made for a bit of cover
and found one sergeant who bound up my wound. I then ran along the
beach to join another officer [possibly Lieutenant Cuthbert Maffett, whose
account comes later] and in doing so had to pass the mouth of a nullah.
Three bullets whizzed past and needless to say I did not expose myself for
some minutes. It was hot! I could find only 30 or 40 men and we commenced to dig ourselves into the low cliff. Why the Turks with their vast
preparations did not level this bank of earth down I cannot imagine. Had
they done so not one of us would have escaped. While the tows were being
pulled into the shore the Munsters began to disembark from the *R.[iver]*
Clyde & they too suffered terribly. I was about 50 yds from where she
grounded and as the men ran ashore they were 'mown' down. I counted
42 killed in one platoon not a single man escaping. And still they came
down the gangways. It was an awful sight but they were a real brave lot.
After a few minutes it became even harder for them to get ashore. After
passing down the gangways and across the lighters under a heavy fire they
had to run along about 25 yards of jagged rocks [the previously mentioned
partially submerged strip of rock jutting out from the right side of the
beach] – each side of the ridge now being covered with bodies.⁵⁰

Midshipman Maurice Lyoyd, from the *Cornwallis*, was in a boat in the third
tow, under the command of Midshipman Howard Weblin. 'We were twenty-
eight in all on board: some beach parties, some soldiers and the crew.' (Given
my theory as to which troops were in which tow, I would suggest that the
soldiers were from Y Company.) 'After leaving the picket boat, we had got
half-way to the shore, when we met [Midshipman Haydon] Forbes in his
boat, who shouted to us to go to the starboard side of the [*Argyle*].' (Forbes
was in the first boat in Tow No. 1, which landed at the Camber. It is unclear
whether they met him going to, or returning from, the Camber.)

Before we got there, all the men pulling at the oars were either killed or wounded. [Ablebodied Seaman] Leach, though wounded, was the only one still pulling. (Leach was the 'funny man' of the ship, full of real wit and always cheerful. None of us who ever saw him come up to the bridge, looking like a rat-catcher, with woolly headgear and an old plain-clothes coat, will forget the scene. He was wonderful too, in hospital at Malta, and kept everyone alive; the doctor in charge gave him a bottle of porter a day because he was such a cherry fellow and kept the others merry.) When we came within fifteen yards of the [*Argyle*], an R.N.D. officer shouted to us to jump out of the boat and swim for it. Weblin and I both jumped out and tried to swim to the [*Argyle*], but we found our packs too heavy, and returned to our boat. We hung on to the life-lines for a few minutes, as we could not get into her, she was so high out of the water. However, at last Weblin managed to push me over the gunwale: I then pulled him on board, but with the loss of his pack. While hanging on the lines I got hit, a bullet running under my vest and across my shoulders, just taking some flesh off my shoulder-blade. Also my cap was knocked off. All this time a very heavy fire was being kept up. Bullets were flying everywhere, some coming on one side and some the other. The boat was riddled, full of holes, and half full of water. We knew it was hopeless to stay there, so we sat at the bottom of the boat in the water, and rowed towards the [*Argyle*], pulling with our arms over our heads. We got there all right, jumped out and secured our boat. Here I got another bullet across the back of the hand. By this time we were rather exhausted, so sat down under what we thought was cover. But we soon found we were being sniped, so I moved round the corner [to the other side of the *River Clyde*]. Here I saw Lieutenant [Tony] Morse R.N. [The senior officer of the thirty-eight man *Cornwallis* party.] He called to me to lend him a hand in securing a lighter. [This would appear to have been the single lighter towed on the starboard side of the *River Clyde*.][51] So we hauled the lighter astern, giving the stern a kick out so as to meet the other lighters. We both jumped into the lighter: but she was moving. Morse said: 'Have you secured the hawser?' My reply was: 'No, sir, I thought you had.' So again I jumped out on to the [*Argyle*], before the lighter swung out, and secured the hawser round a bollard. Just in time, as I got another bullet through my lung. I spun round and fell down, managing to get more or less under cover. I lay where I was till about 11 a.m., when, coming under machine gun fire, I crawled round to the rear of the [*Argyle*]. At this time I saw twenty soldiers making a rush across the [*Argyle*] from a lighter. The Turks turned a machine gun on to them and

168 *Beneath a Turkish Sky*

killed the lot. Unfortunately for me, I, too came under this fire. The only bit of me that was exposed was my ankle, which caught another bullet. I was rescued by a seaman from the *Hussar* – [Ablebodied Seaman George] Samson [Who later got a V.C. for his work during the landing.] He came out of the engine-room [of the *Argyle*] and carried me below. Here I stayed till 10 p.m., knowing very little of what was going on, only hearing from time to time the sounds of the rushing feet of men who made attempts to ashore.[52]

In another example of differing accounts of the same event, Weblin said that their boat carried men from the Royal Naval Division. He said many of the men in his boat were killed. The survivors plunged into the water, holding on to the boat on the side away from the shore. As the firing continued, more of the men were hit. Eventually the boat was filled with water and the Turks shifted fire to another target. After sometime 'a Sub-Lieutenant, R.N.V.R., of the Naval Division' let go of the boat and started to swim for the shore, but Weblin did not think he reached it.[53] The boat finally drifted near the stern of the *River Clyde*. Weblin let go and swam to a ladder hanging from the stern, by means of which he climbed aboard the ship. He stayed aboard until the beach was secured the following day and he was able to leave.[54] But for the fact that Lloyd said Weblin was in the same boat, one might think from their accounts that they were in different boats. (Weblin's experiences were recounted by a third party and so would, inevitably, have been changed in the re-telling.)

Lieutenant Cuthbert Maffett, X Company, Blue Caps, was in one of the tows.

When the picquet boat cast us off we all rowed for the shore as hard as we could. The Turks let us get very close, and then they opened a terrible fire on us with machine guns and pom-poms, the shells of which contained an incendiary mixture. They began to hit the boat I was in very frequently, and killed many of my men as we were rowing ashore. We were also unlucky enough to lose several of the [sailors] who were rowing us in, and the men had to take over their oars, and as they did not know much about rowing the result was that we often got broadside on to the shore and presented a better target to the enemy. Just before we grounded the boat got hit once or twice with incendiary shells, and commenced to go on fire. She was also half full of water from the many holes in her by this time. Several of the men who had been wounded fell into the bottom of the boat, and were either drowned there or suffocated by other men falling on top of them; many, to add to their death agonies, were burnt as well. We then grounded, and I jumped out of the bow of the boat and got hit in the head by a machine-gun bullet, others going into a pack that I was carrying on my shoulders. I went under water and came up again, and tried to encourage the men to get to the shore and under cover as fast as they could as it was their only chance. I then went under again. Someone caught hold of me and began pulling me ashore, and as I got to dry land a [sailor] joined him. When I recovered a bit I found it was my platoon sergeant, Sergeant [W.] Willis. I did not see him again that day as far as I remember. Two men got ashore beside me, and then two more that were wounded. We took cover under a low sort of bank that was about ten yards from the water's edge, and bound each other up as best we could. Looking out to sea I saw the remnants of my platoon trying to get to the shore, but they were shot down one after another, and their bodies drifted out to sea or lay immersed a few feet from the shore. I found myself at the extreme left of the beach,[55] and put the men I had around me on the alert for a rush from the enemy: of course we could not have done any good … I lay under cover for the greater part of the morning, and tried to get in touch with some of the others. After a bit I crawled along towards the fort at Sedd-el-Bahr, and there found Captain [David] French. He had been hit in the wrist with a bullet which had driven bits of his wrist watch into him. I lay under cover with him for a time … I then went to the left of the beach to see if I could collect any men there, but all I found were either wounded or dead. At the part almost under the lighthouse I found a boat that was nearly all submerged, and in it were some of our machine gunners under Lieutenant [Reginald] Corbet; they were all dead as far as I could see, and the machine guns useless. I then went back to where Captain French was lying, and spent the rest of the afternoon under cover beside him. We had a man near us with a pocket periscope, which we put over the top of the bank from time to time to see if the Turks were coming down on us, but there was no move on their part. We had no food or water with us, as the sea water had destroyed it all … The whole beach was strewn with dead, and there were very few hale men amongst us. One had to keep down the whole time, as the Turks were firing at us all day.[56]

The sailing pinnace from the *Cornwallis* carried sixty Blue Caps. The tow rope was slipped near the *River Clyde*. Five men from the *Cornwallis* began rowing, supported by the unskilled efforts of some of the heavily laden soldiers. With the exception of Ablebodied Seaman Ward, every sailor at the oars was shot down.

As the boat beached, Petty Officer First Class William Medhurst, coxswain of the boat, shouted 'Jump out, lads, and pull her in!' There was only Ward and himself left to answer the call. Out they jumped, one on the port side and the other on the starboard. Only three soldiers are believed to have got ashore. With two exceptions, all the others were killed in the boat or in the water as they landed. Medhurst survived for a time, by sheltering behind the boat, but when the stern of the boat swung in the tide, he was exposed to the enemy's fire. He was not seen again until his body was recovered from the water on the following day.[57] Ablebodied Seaman Ward and two of the Dubs survived by remaining in the water, under the lee of the gunwale from 7 a.m. to 5 p.m. When the boat was picked up the following day, it was riddled with holes and filled with dead men.[58]

> In the leading boats most of the seamen and soldiers were killed or wounded. Some boats were so riddled with bullets that they sank. The survivors tried to gain the beach in water frequently too deep for wading, and of those some were killed, some wounded, while others were drowned by the weight of their equipment. In a few minutes nearly every man was a casualty. A lot of the boats could be seen drifting about helplessly, some broadside on with a few men in the water taking cover behind them: in others not a man was untouched; in one boat only two were still alive. Some boats disappeared entirely. Major Ferherstonhaugh, second-in-command was mortally wounded before his boat reached the shore. Lieutenant-Colonel Rooth was shot dead at the edge of the water.[59]

Michael McDonagh's *The Irish at the Front* was based on the letters of officers and soldiers of the Irish battalions and records compiled at the regimental depots. McDonagh said Father William Finn:

> … at once jumped out of the boat and went to the assistance of the bleeding and struggling men. Then he was hit himself. By the time he had waded ashore to reach the beach his clothing was riddled with shot. Yet disabled as he was, and in spite of the great pain he must have been suffering, he crawled about the beach, affording consolation to the dying Dublins. I have been told that to give absolution he had to hold his injured right arm with his left. It was while he was in the act of blessing one of his men that his skull was broken by a piece of shrapnel. The last thought of Father Finn was for his Dublins. His orderly says that in a brief moment of consciousness he asked; 'Are our fellows winning?' Amid the thunder of the guns on sea and land his soul soon passed away.[60]

In *At Antwerp and in the Dardanelles,* Anglican chaplain the Revd Henry Clapham Foster said that despite being severely wounded in the head, Father Finn 'continued his work of mercy until he lay down to die from sheer exhaustion and loss of blood'. Foster 'highly esteemed Father Finn as a friend'. The feeling was reciprocated by Finn, who had presented the Anglican cleric with a medal of *Our Lady of Mount Carmel* as a talisman to protect him. Like Finn, Foster was meant to land at V Beach. But he and three platoons of A Company, the Anson Battalion, were diverted to W Beach. Father William Finn was the first British or Dominion chaplain to be killed in action in the war.[61]

An extract from a letter written by Corporal James Colgan (10315) to his wife was published in the *Cork Examiner.*

> [I] am lucky to get away alive, as nearly everyone you know is killed, both sergeants and privates. All the heals were killed, including Fr. Finn. On the Sunday night there were only 115 left to answer their names. Whether there are any left or not now I don't know, but it was awful. There were thirty-two in a boat, and only six escaped alive, including [Private Arthur] O'Hanlon (10949) who had his hand blown off. He and I were trying to save another when he got hit again in the foot and fell back into the boat. Two bullets went through my pack, and I dived into the sea. Then came the job to swim with the pack, and one leg useless. So I managed out the knife and cut the straps and swim to the shore, about half a mile. All the time, the bullets were ripping around me. My God I'll never forget what we went through all day Sunday, and the Sunday night, lying waiting for someone to take us off, but no one came as it was too dangerous.[62]

Aboard one of the boats was Winston Churchill's cousin-by-marriage, Sub-Lieutenant Johnny Dodge of A Company, Hood Battalion, Royal Naval Division, who had been assigned as an Assistant Naval Landing Officer at V Beach. Under fire as his boat approached the beach, he was about to jump into the water when he was struck in the chest and felt pain in both his arms. He jumped overboard and swam about ten yards to the beach. He then scrambled ashore and took cover behind a sandbank.[63]

ɷɷ

Former resident of London's Foundling Hospital Company Sergeant-Major Harry Fox, X Company, managed to get ashore and take cover below the sandbank. According to Private Henry Thompson, 5615:

I was in the act of getting out of a small boat, when I was badly hit in the arm, chest and leg. This caused me to fall into the water, which at that point was between four and five feet in depth. I tried to wade towards the beach but was soon in difficulties, for in addition to my wounds, which caused me to be practically paralysed down the left side, I had my equipment which in my state of weakness, I was unable to abandon.

[Company Sergeant-Major Harry] Fox had previously landed and was already on the beach, under partial cover of a little ridge of sand, but when he saw my difficulty he left his cover and rushed to my assistance, over about twenty yards open space, and under heavy rifle fire and machine gun fire, finally assisting me to reach a place of safety, and certainly rescuing me from what would have meant certain death from drowning.[64]

Speaking of Harry Fox, Major Edward Molesworth wrote:

No. 4823 Coy Sergt Major H Fox 1st Bn Royal Dublin Fusiliers X Company, of which I was in command, displayed conspicuous courage and devotion to duty at the landing on V beach Gallipoli on 25th April 1915. When under fire he dressed wounded men, assisted two men wounded in the legs who were in danger of being drowned from rising tide and brought them to cover. He was wounded himself and remained on duty till the following day. He gave much assistance to wounded men. The Medical Officer

An Imperial War Museum diorama of V Beach, reproduced
in an unidentified post-First World War magazine.

[Lieutenant Henry de Boer] was himself badly wounded and unable to move.[65]

So, apart from dressing wounded men and bringing Private Henry Thompson to cover, Harry Fox had also brought another wounded man to cover. The former foundling may have been small in stature, but he had a very big and brave heart.

According to *Blue Cap* officer Captain Alexander Molony, W Company, aboard the *River Clyde*:

> Meanwhile the men on shore had attempted to advance, but any movement was impossible, for as soon a man showed himself he was bowled over. Captain [William] Higginson was shot through the head while endeavouring to knock out a Turkish sniper, and died instantly. By this time the beach was a harrowing sight; bodies were lying all over it, in some places in little clumps, in others half in and half out of the water. Wounded men were all over the place, and it was impossible in most cases to bring them aid.[66]

Hundreds of Blue Caps were casualties that day. While the Commonwealth War Graves Commission officially records only approximately sixty of the battalion as dying on 25 April 1915, out of the 25 officers and 987 men who had gone to Gallipoli the battalion had only one officer and 344 men fit for service on 29 April. This suggests that a huge number were wounded. With no medical facilities available ashore, the wounded were quickly evacuated. Those who died aboard hospital ships or in hospitals around the Mediterranean would not have been recorded as having died in Gallipoli. Thus, without further detailed study, it is not possible to say how many of the wounded died in the days, weeks and months following the landing, nor how many were never able to return for service with the battalion as a result of the severity of their wounds. What can be said is that the battalion was effectively destroyed at V Beach and subsequently had to be rebuilt.

Among the Dublins to die that day, the oldest recorded was forty-nine-year-old Lieutenant-Colonel Richard Rooth. The youngest was seventeen-year-old Private Alfred Verrent. Born in Nenagh, County Tipperary, he was the son of the gamekeeper of Kinnity Castle, just across the county boundary in County Offaly. Annie and John Mallaghan's eldest son, twenty-one-year-old Sam, was among those killed. He left his, no doubt grief-stricken, nineteen-year-old brother Jack to mourn his passing. Also from the battalion band, Harry Whitham, from Mile End, Middlesex was among the dead.

A footballer, as well as a musician, he had played for the Band and Drum team and the battalion team. Two brothers serving with the Dublins were killed during the landing. Private Samuel Smyth (twenty-eight) and Lance-Corporal William Smyth were from Londonderry. Unfortunately no information about their family was available at the time of writing. Twenty-one-year-old Dubliner Private Thomas Toohey had made his will that morning, leaving all he owned to his mother. He was killed a few hours later.

Men from the Royal Navy died side by side with the Blue Caps. According to a naval dispatch dated 1 July 1915, 'Able Seaman Lewis Jacobs, *HMS Lord Nelson*, took his boat in to V Beach unaided after all the remainder of the crew and the troops were killed or wounded. When last seen, Jacobs was standing up and endeavouring to pole the cutter ashore. While thus employed he was killed.'[67] Travelling in the second boat of No. 3 Tow, eighteen-year-old Midshipman Wilfred St Aubyn Malleson and seventeen-year-old Midshipman Arthur Hardiman were assigned beach party duties. According to the former, 'We arrived starboard side of the *River Clyde*. In coming in we only sustained about four or six casualties all due to stray rifle fire. Even in getting out of the boat we got off very lightly. It was in the act of getting out of the boat that [Midshipman] Hardiman was fatally wounded. That was about the nearest escape I had, as I was standing about 2ft away from him.'[68] According to Eric Bush, Hardiman was taken aboard the *Albion*. Unconscious, he was in great pain, delirious, tossing and groaning. Unable to do anything for him, the fleet surgeon asked the chaplain to take care of him. He died soon afterwards.[69] Having reported on the fatal wounding of Midshipman Arthur Hardiman, Midshipman Wilfred Malleson continued, '[Sub Lieutenant] Waller and Mr Spillane (Bosun) stayed in the boat with the crew and took her round to the stern of the *River Clyde*. We lost sight of them. Our remnant of the Beach Party was now on its face in the lighter. Nothing very much was possible as bullets were whistling over our heads and the lighters were all isolated and forward on account of the current. After about an hour of inaction, during which time occupants of the lighter sustained about one casualty every ten minutes, I observed a lighter on the starboard side, manned by [Lieutenant Tony] Morse and [Midshipman George] Drewry, being pushed from behind by our 2nd picket boat (Midshipman Voelcher). This lighter was pushed into place between my lighter and the next, a very skilful performance, owing to the numerous shoals, constant rifle fire and general unwieldiness of the lighter. The fore end of the new lighter was secured, but the near end began to drift away owing to the current.'[70]

Commonwealth War Graves Commission records show that nine sailors who were killed at V Beach on 25 April are buried in the cemetery near the beach and two others (one whose body was not recovered and one who appears to have been buried at sea having died of wounds) are commemorated on the Chatham Naval Memorial.

ண

Aboard the SS River Clyde, *on the Approach to V Beach*

Commander Edward Unwin told Rear-Admiral Wemyss that as the ship approached the beach, Turkish guns on the Asiatic shore began firing. The *River Clyde* was struck by 5.9in shells and a few men were killed. One shell peeled the covering off the main steam pipe, 'quite near enough for those down below'. He said the ship beached at about 6.30 a.m. and the Turks then opened fire with rifles and machine guns.[71] In an illustration of how people can report the same events differently, Major Weir de Lancey Williams said that all was quiet as the ship approached the beach. He made the following note '6.22 a.m. Ran smoothly ashore without tremor. No opposition. We shall land unopposed. 6.25 a.m. Tows within a few yards of shore. One boat drifting to the north, all killed. Others almost equally helpless. Our hopper [*Argyle*] gone away.'[72]

The 1st West Riding Field Company of the Royal Engineers was on the *River Clyde*. Their war diary recorded 'Beached under heavy fire off the fort of Sedd-El-Bahr. Casualties two killed and five wounded by shell fire from the Asiatic coast and rifle fire from the forts.'[73] Unable to see what was going on from his station in one of the holds, George Davidson went on deck. When the ship was about 200 yards off shore he went down to warn his men to lie down in case the ship struck rock. Davidson clung to a stanchion. The ship had beached before he became aware of the fact. According to Private William Flynn of the Royal Munster Fusiliers 'When we woke up on the *River Clyde* in the morning and looked out of the portholes and saw land, they told us it was the Dardanelles and we had to make a landing there. It was called Cape Helles. We couldn't see anybody. All we could see was this piece of land shaped like a saucer which gradually went up to a little hill, which was called 141. That dominated the whole beach.'[74]

Norman Dewhurst said:

As we approached the shore everything was calm and the boats [with the Dublins] moved ahead of the ship. As these boats got within a few yards of the beach the *River Clyde* touched land, but leaving still an expanse of water between her and the shore. At this moment the Turks, whom everyone had thought dazed and routed by the preceding naval bombardment, opened fire with everything they had, the range was short – something like one hundred yards frontally and up to three hundred yards on the flanks – for the cove where the landing was taking place was roughly bow shaped and quite small.[75]

W Company 1st Battalion Royal Dublin Fusiliers was aboard the *River Clyde*. Lieutenant Henry Desmond O'Hara said:

The idea in the case of our ship, the *River Clyde*, was that she was to be run ashore at full speed, and then the sides were partly arranged on hinges which were to open, and then we were to get ashore and dig ourselves in. The rest of the regiment was to be towed ashore by steam pinnaces in boats. The latter arrived before we did, and you never saw such a shambles as that beach was when the boats got in. The whole of the high ground round was honey-combed with the enemy's trenches, and they waited till the boats, which were crammed full, got about five yards from the shore, when they let drive at them with rifles, machine guns, and pom-poms. Numbers of men were killed in the boats, others as they waded ashore, and more on the sand before they could take cover behind a sandbank some twelve or fifteen yards from the shore ... Meanwhile, our ship, instead of grounding as had been arranged, stuck about fifteen yards from the shore, and it was that that saved our lives, as we had to stay where we were.[76]

In a letter home, Irish Surgeon Peter Burrows Kelly of the Royal Naval Air Service said that 'a large shell had gone right through our after hold without exploding, but it killed several. Shortly after one got in the engine room. That ought to have finished us, but it did not.'[77]

Lieutenant-Colonel George Stoney had been assigned as a military landing officer for V Beach. His ship's boat arrived at V Beach after the *River Clyde* had beached. As they were under heavy fire, Captain Robert Lambert RN, the beachmaster, who was in the same boat as Stoney, said that there was no point in attempting a landing. Stoney said that he climbed a ladder to the *River Clyde* under fire from a maxim machine gun on the shore. 'One could hear the bullets hitting the ship's side all round.' He said that from then until dark there was little for him to do.[78]

Lieutenant George Drewry said that Commander Unwin was on the bridge of the *River Clyde* and Drewry was at the helm of the *Argyle* on the port side of the ship as they sailed towards the beach. Also being towed on the port side, inboard of the *Argyle* and one-behind-the-other, were two lighters and a small steam pinnace. Another lighter was being towed on the starboard side. Drewry said that the *River Clyde* beached at 6.10 a.m. The *Argyle* shot forward and 'grounded on her Port bow'. The *Argyle* had a line to the lighters and Drewry and his crew tried to haul them in. Unwin left two accounts of the landing. In one he said that as soon as the *River Clyde* beached, he ran to the port side of the bridge to see how matters were with the *Argyle*. He said that he was 'horrified' to see Drewry hacking at the tow rope with an axe, as he had told him to slacken the rope. The plan had been to put the stern of the *Argyle* at the bow of the *River Clyde*. Soldiers coming down the gangways on either side of the ship would board the stern of the *Argyle* and exit its bow by means of a small gangplank to the shore. (Should the gap between the shore and the *Argyle-River Clyde* combination be too wide, Unwin intended to use the lighters to form a bridge between the *Argyle* and the *River Clyde*.) But Unwin said the *Argyle* 'sheered off to port [the left] and was of no further use, except as a death trap to a lot of men who were trying to land in boats...' In his second account Unwin said that he 'looked over the side [as the *River Clyde* beached] and saw the [*Argyle*] sailing away at right angles to my line of keel, and at that angle she went ashore, and I realised she would be of no use to me'. Eric Bush said the Greek crew, who were on the deck of the *Argyle,* ran below as soon as shooting started. He said the men in the engine-room reversed the engines when the *River Clyde* beached, instead of going full speed ahead as ordered. In contrast, Rear-Admiral Wemyss (to whom Unwin reported) said the *Argyle*'s engine had stopped before the *River Clyde* beached. When the tow rope was cut, the *Argyle* was struck by 'a great gust of wind ... and swinging away failed to place herself between the ship and the shore'. Eric Bush said when the *River Clyde* grounded the flow of water across her bow (from right to left) would have increased. He said the *Argyle* should have been towed on the *River Clyde*'s starboard side 'from which position she should have swung across the bow, instead of away from her parent ship'.

Unwin said he 'dashed over the side', accompanied by Seaman William Williams and they managed to get the lighters into position under the bow of the *River Clyde*. He did not give details of how this was done, apart from saying that in retrospect he was astonished as to how they had achieved it. Drewry said that Unwin 'appeared on the lighters and the steam pinnace took hold of the lighters and plucked them in until she could go no closer'. This appears to suggest that Unwin and Williams pulled the lighters into position using the small steam pinnace which Drewry said the *River Clyde* towed with the *Argyle* and the lighters. Unwin, however, makes no mention of the pinnace in either of his accounts. In one of his accounts, Unwin said that having managed to get the two lighters into position and connected to the bow of the *River Clyde*, Williams and he tried to connect them to the beach (so as to form a bridge from the *River Clyde* to the beach). But he said that as there was no way to connect the lighters to the beach, Williams and he held on to the rope and shouted out to the troops on the *River Clyde* to disembark. The previously mentioned partially submerged line of rock jutting out from the right side of the beach formed a sort of pathway from where Unwin and Williams stood.[79] Unwin and Williams 'threw a gangplank across two of the lighters, and together they half-swam, half-waded ashore, pulling the lighters behind them. Within a matter of minutes they succeeded in dragging the first lighter to within a few yards of the beach. There they remained, waist-deep in water, holding the lighters in place under a murderous fire from the Turkish defenders dug in along the heights. It was at this moment, with the 'bridge' precariously linking ship to shore, that Unwin called for the disembarkation to begin.'[80]

It might be helpful to give again the layout of the *River Clyde*, together with the location of the different units aboard, as given in *History of the Royal Munster Fusiliers*. The ship had four holds. From bow to stern these were designated No. 1 Fore Hold, No. 2 Main Hold, No. 3 Mizen Hold and No. 4 After Hold.[81] According to *History of the Royal Munster Fusiliers* the troops on the ship were accommodated as follows. No. 1 Hold (Upper Deck):[82] Headquarters, four machine guns and X, Y and Z companies of 1st Battalion Royal Munster Fusiliers. No 1 Hold (Lower Deck): W Company 1st Battalion Royal Munster Fusiliers and W Company 1st Battalion Royal Dublin Fusiliers. No. 2 Hold: Four machine guns, Y and Z companies 2nd Battalion Hampshire Regiment and one company of the West Riding Field Engineers. In the aft of the ship in No. 3 and No. 4 Holds: Two sub-divisions Field Ambulance, one signal section and No. 13 platoon Anson Battalion, Royal Naval Division. All the troops on the ship were under the command of Lieutenant-Colonel Herbert Carington Smith, Hampshire Regiment. While the *History of the Royal Munster Fusiliers* placed the two Hampshire Regiment companies in No. 2 Hold, *The Royal Hampshire Regiment 1914-1918* said they were in No. 3 Hold. The matter of exactly where units were positioned on the *River Clyde* was further complicated by the account of Captain Guy Geddes,[83] who said the 1st Munsters were dispersed as follows. 'Forward main deck holds [presumably this equates with No. 1 Hold (Upper Deck)] X Company, commanded by Captain Guy Geddes and Z Company, commanded by Captain Eric Henderson.' While the *History of the Royal Munster Fusiliers* also put battalion headquarters, four machine guns and Y Company on this deck, Geddes made no mention of the first two and put the third in a different location. According to Geddes, W Company, commanded by Major William Hutchinson and Y Company commanded by Major Charles Jarrett were in the 'Forward lower holds' (presumably this equates with No 1 Hold Lower Deck)). While the *History of the Royal Munster Fusiliers* put W Company on this deck, it put the accompanying company as W Company, 1st Battalion, Royal Dublin Fusiliers. Geddes placed the Dublins and the two companies of the 2nd Battalion Hampshire Regiment in the 'After holds'. He did not mention the other units aboard. Therefore, while *History of the Royal Munster Fusiliers* has the most information of any source on the location of units, it has been challenged by at least two other sources on some of its detail.

The 1st Battalion Royal Munster Fusiliers was commanded by Lieutenant-Colonel Henry Tizard. He recorded that as the *River Clyde* and the tows carrying the men of the Royal Dublin Fusiliers came inshore they came under heavy fire from 'rifles, machine guns & pom-poms'. When Unwin and Drewry managed to get the lighters into position and the signal was given for the troops to disembark, Tizard was standing near 'the port exit' of No. 1 hold, presumably the door which had been installed to facilitate troops exiting No. 1 hold on the port (left) side of the ship. At about 6.45 a.m. the gangways on the sides of the ship were reported ready for the troops to land.[84]

Tizard said the plan of attack – which he said had been changed just before the troops embarked on the *River Clyde* – was that the Munsters would attack Hill 141 'and the redoubt on the hill to the left of the bay'. (Hill 141 was behind the village of Sedd el Bahr, the Blue Caps objective. The redoubt on the left would appear to have been Ertuğrul Tabyasi (Fort No. 1). So it appears that, while operating on the left of the beach and capturing the defences there, the Munsters were also ordered to move to the right behind Sedd el Bahr and capture Hill 141.) They would then link up with the troops coming from W Beach and, if necessary, launch a combined attack with them on Hill 138, located between W and V Beaches. Meanwhile, in conjunction with the rest of the Blue Caps, landed in ship's boats, W Company of the Royal Dublin Fusiliers was to go ashore from the *River Clyde* and attack the village of Sedd el Bahr. The two companies of the Hampshire Regiment and the 1st West Riding Field Company of the Royal Engineers were to be ready to support either attack if required. No. 13 Platoon, Anson battalion was to bring tools, stores etc. ashore after the beach had been secured.

Tizard ordered X Company of the Munsters (Captain Guy Geddes) to exit on the port side of the *River Clyde* and Z Company (Captain Eric Henderson) to exit on the starboard side. The companies were to go out by platoons, to avoid crowding on the lighters. Z Company began its exit slightly before X Company. Turkish fire, concentrated on the exits, hit some men 'before they left the vessel. I suppose it was due to the rush of men on to the lighters but after a few men got ashore [the lighter nearest the shore] broke adrift and slued round at right angles to the nearest [lighter] and the men had to jump into deep water. Capt. Geddes himself who was leading his company had to swim about 20 yards.' Geddes[85] said the reason for the slight delay in X Company exiting the ship was because the gangway on the port side jammed 'for a few seconds'. Then 'off [they] went the men cheering wildly'. Geddes said that, as they made their way down the gangway:

Man after man behind me was shot down, but they never wavered. Lieutenant [John] Watts, who was wounded in five places and lying on the gangway cheered the men on with cries 'Follow the Captain'. Captain [David] French of the Dublins told me afterwards that he counted the first forty-eight men to follow me, and they all fell. I think no finer episode could be found of the men's bravery and discipline than this, of leaving the safety of the *River Clyde* to go to what was practically certain death. Leaving the *Clyde* I dashed down the gangway and already found the lighters holding the dead and wounded from the leading platoons of Z Company (including 2nd Lieut O'Sullivan an ex C.S.M [Company Sergeant Major] a fine fellow.)[86] I stepped on the second lighter and looked around to find myself alone, and yelled to the men following out of the *Clyde* to come on, but it was difficult going across the lighters. I then jumped into the sea and had to swim some dozen strokes to get ashore. There is no doubt that men were drowning owing chiefly, I think, to the great weight they were carrying, a full pack, 250 rounds of ammunition, and three days' rations, I know I felt it. All the officers were dressed and equipped like the men.

Tizard said that many of the men who followed Geddes 'were drowned by the weight they carried although they could swim. The fire was very heavy and few got ashore without being hit.' According to Geddes:

There was a small rocky spit jutting out into the sea [i.e. the previously mentioned line of rock] which was absolutely taped down by the Turks [i.e. the Turks had guns pointed at the line of rock], and few if any, survived who attempted to land there. We all made, Dublins and all, for a sheltered ledge on the shore which gave us cover. Here we shook ourselves out, and tried to appreciate the situation, rather a sorry one. I estimated that I had lost about 70 percent of my Company, 2nd Lieuts (John) Watts and (Edward Josiah) Perkins were wounded and my C.Q.M. Sgt Killed. [Thirty-six-year-old Boer War Veteran, Company Quartermaster Sergeant Thomas Walsh, 5530, from County Waterford.]

Private William Flynn, accompanied Geddes on exiting from the *River Clyde:*

Our cue was when the Dublins came off the warship in cutters. We then had to run down the gangway across the two [lighters] and [the *Argyle*], and then we only had perhaps 10 or 20ft to go to the shore. But the [*River Clyde*] had been carried away towards [the line of rock] and the [*Argyle*] and one of the lighters had been cut away and drifted out to sea. The [lighter] that was tied to the bow of the ship was all right, but as we ran down the gangway, instead of having two separate gangways either side of the ship, they had connected them. [As mentioned in footnote 17 of this chapter, paintings and drawings of the landing – presumably based on research by the artists – show the gangways on both sides of the ship extending towards the shore, thus providing two separate pathways ashore. Flynn, however, appears to suggest that that the two gangways may have met somewhere near the bow of the ship, thus allowing only one pathway to the shore. His is the only account I have come across that appears to sug-gest this.] Unfortunately, the first batch had to run across into the lighter and what with us running down and them running across, and all the bodies piling up, it was like a barricade. They simply fell into the lighters. Some were dead, some were wounded, some weren't hit but got smothered in the pile-up. Captain Geddes and I managed to get on the first lighter, where the dead were. Captain Geddes said 'It's no good Flynn. Come on.' But I was weighed down by a big periscope I was carrying for him. We had double ammunition, double rations, double everything. He had the sense to tell everybody to throw off their coats before we made land. All the Dublins never had a chance to drop their coats. They went down, they sank – just disappeared. I followed Captain Geddes down the gangway and along the gunwale of the lighter, and we laid down in the bow with just enough cover to hide us. He looked back and called for the remainder of the company to come, but they couldn't. So he said 'Well, over we go, we're going to fall into the sea.' [i.e. They tumbled into the water.] I managed to come up once or twice for fresh air, then gradually drifted to my right until I came up by [the line of rock] which was piled high with dead. Anyway, I managed to crawl over the rock, exhausted. [The next piece is unclear, but appears to suggest they decided to go to one of the Dublins' boats and use it for cover.] There was about twelve feet of water to go through. The boat was facing ashore. So I dived into the water, crawled along the bottom and eventually came up behind the boat. It just hid us. Although when the waves wobbled a bit it turned the boat's stern into the shore and the enemy could just see us. We didn't realise this until I heard something go by and I said to Captain Geddes 'My that was close' and he said 'It was, wasn't it.' It was then that his ear was shot off and I don't know how it missed me, but it did. He said 'We'd better get ashore, but how can we?' I said 'We'll have to go underneath, if there's enough room. Wait till the waves lift the boat and shove your rifle in front of you.' Anyway, we managed to scramble for the shore with eight or nine feet to go, and we got behind a bank about five feet high, where we were safe for the time being.[87]

The first men from Z Company had exited the starboard (right) side of the *River Clyde* shortly before the men from Geddes' X Company began to leave on the port side. When Geddes reached the lighters, he saw dead and wounded men from the leading platoons of Z Company aboard. Among the wounded was thirty-one-year-old Boer War Veteran Second Lieutenant Timothy Sullivan, whose promotion from Company Sergeant-Major to Second Lieutenant had been announced in Coventry in February and who had married Maud Bates in that city in March 1915. He died of his wounds on 4 May 1915. Sullivan's best man, Second Lieutenant John Watts, had cheered the men of X Company as they followed Captain Guy Geddes down the gang-plank. Z Company Commander, thirty-three-year-old Captain Eric Hume Henderson, was a past pupil of Loretto, Scotland's oldest boarding school, just outside Edinburgh. According to the school's roll of honour 'Captain Henderson was the first officer to land, and early in the day his arm was shattered. He fought on, but was again wounded, in the side, and was removed to hospital. He died of these wounds at Alexandria on May 29th 1915. For his conduct at V Beach, Captain Henderson was mentioned in Despatches.' According to Captain Raymond Lane:

Henderson led his company (Z) [out the starboard side of the ship] ordering me to follow at the end of my first platoon. One by one they popped out, and then my turn. All the way down the side of the ship bullets crashed against the side. *[sic]*. On reaching the first [lighter] I found some of the men had collected and were firing. I mistrusted the second [lighter] and the track to the shore so I led them over the side [of the first lighter]; the water came nearly up to our shoulders. However, none of us were hit and we gained the bank. There I found Henderson badly hit, and heaps of wounded. Any man who put his head up for an instant was shot dead. Then came [Second Lieutenant Francis] Lee with his platoons and formed up on the left of mine. The bank we were under had a small nulla running up towards the barbed wire. I worked my way up under the right-hand wall and tried to cross it, running as fast as I could; a sniper at the top let fly at me, the bullet went through my right ankle and carried on sideways, smashing my left leg to bits. One of my platoon then came out very pluckily and pulled me into safety. I had only been on the beach five minutes and never saw a Turk.[88]

Tizard said the troops began exiting the ship at 6.45 a.m. Having described what had happened to Captain Guy Geddes and how the men who followed him 'were drowned by the weight they carried' and how 'few got ashore without being hit,' he said:

Three platoons from each company had gone out by now and [a] great many killed remained in the lighters. Those men that were wounded took cover. Captain Unwin and Midshipmen Drury and the crew who had not previously been hit now went out again to get the lighter into a better position with the help of some of the men who had got ashore. This was eventually done, a gangway being made by the 2 lighters and a ships cutter with planks towards [the line of rock] that ran towards the right of the shore near the vessel. This place was littered with dead from the boats which ran in at this point. The men who had managed to get ashore were crowded together under a bank that ran along the shore, the only place where cover from fire could be got. In front of this about 25 yards was a line of barbed-wire entanglement. Many of the wounded who had been hit at the edge of the beach managed to crawl up to this bank. I saw gallant deeds done but in most cases the men were killed. Only about half the 2 companies I had sent out were left fit for work, the rest were out of action & men who left cover of the bank were immediately hit, although the guns from the supporting ship *HMS Albion* and machine guns on board the vessel [the *River Clyde*] were firing rapidly on the fort and village and high ground to the left of the bay.

Royal Naval Air Service Surgeon Peter Burrows Kelly said that:

> All this time our fellows were dropping on their way to the beach, about
> two to every three. While arranging about a volunteer to assist me in rescu-
> ing a poor fellow shot in very narrow water, someone shouted: 'Take cover,
> you fool.' Almost simultaneously a bullet bit my cap, and one went either
> side of my head, shaving my ears. As I dropped flat one clipped me on the
> right shin and another entered my right foot, but came out again. I was the
> first of the staff to go, and was dragged to the chart room.[89]

Unwin said:

> The Turks seemed to concentrate [their fire] on the lighters [more] than
> on the River Clyde, and it was on the lighters and on the [line of rock] that
> the greatest number of dead and wounded lay. Of course many fell into the
> water and were drowned. We were literally standing in blood. For an hour
> we held on, and thinking I could be more use elsewhere I asked Williams if
> he could hang on without me but he said he was nearly done and couldn't.
> Just then a 6 [inch] shell fell alongside us. (I have it in my field at home).
> Williams said to me 'whatever is that.' I told him, and almost immediately
> I heard a thud and looked round and Williams said 'A shell has hit me.'
> I caught hold of him, and as I couldn't let him drown, I tried to get him on
> to the lighter and then for the first time I saw Drewry, who with somebody
> else helped me and I remember no more till I found myself stripped in my
> cabin in blankets, and [Peter Burrows] Kelly the Doctor, standing over me.

In his other account of the landing, Unwin said that after Williams and he
had been in the water for about half an hour:

> I thought I would try and make a better connection by getting one of the
> light brows [a ramp] ashore. [Presumably a ramp to connect the lighter to the
> shore or to the line of rock.] I knew there was one on the lighter but I couldn't
> make the troops understand what I wanted. So I asked Williams if he could
> hang on to the lighters himself whilst I got out of the water and placed
> the brow, but he said he was too cold and couldn't hang on alone, so there
> was nothing for it but to sit it out. A shell from Asia [Kum Kale] came and
> cheered us up by dropping within a yard of us. I have it now in my house. It is
> a 5.9 lydite shell. This was going on for about an hour when Williams gave a
> gasp. I asked him what was the matter and he said a shell had hit him. As he

was evidently becoming unconscious, and if he fell he would certainly drown I caught hold of him and he died in my arms. For some reason or other I collapsed at the same time, and somebody got me on board …

Meanwhile Drewry said that:

Samson and I tried to put a brow [ramp] out over the bow [of the *Argyle*]. The Greeks had run below and two of us could not do it. So I told him to get out of the rain, and I jumped over the bow and waded ashore, meeting a soldier wounded in the water. We (I and another soldier from a boat) tried to carry him ashore but he was again shot in our arms, his neck in two pieces nearby. So we left him and I ran along the beach towards the [line of rock]. I threw away my revolver, coat and hat and waded out to the Captain. He was in the water with a man named Williams wading and towing the lighters towards the [line of rock]. I gave a pull for a few minutes and then climbed aboard the lighters and got the brows [ramps] lowered onto the lighter. The Captain still in the water sang out for more rope. So I went onboard [presumably the *River Clyde*] and brought a rope down with the help of a man named Ellard. As we reached the end of the lighters the Captain was wading towards me carrying Williams. Pulled him onto the lighter and Ellard carried him onboard the ship [*River Clyde*] on his shoulders, but he spoiled the act by not coming down again.[90] Williams was dead however. Got a rope from the lighter to the [line of rock] and then with difficulty I hauled the Captain onto the lighter. He was nearly done and I was alone. He went inboard [i.e. he was brought aboard the *River Clyde*] and the Doctor had rather a job with him.

Aboard the *River Clyde*, Surgeon Peter Burrows Kelly had earlier been wounded in the right foot and brought to the chart room. 'I found I could carry on after being attended to. About 8 a.m. Commander Unwin was carried in, suffering from prolonged immersion and shock and hit badly. I attended him for two hours … ' From Athy, County Kildare, the surgeon was the son of Gilbert Kelly, Clerk of the Crown and Peace for Queen's County (now Laois). An officer in the Royal Naval Air Service, he had taken part in the defence of Antwerp. He was later sent to Gallipoli, from where he wrote home describing the landing on V Beach.[91]

Tizard said, at 7 a.m, Captain Guy Geddes 'tried to move his company off towards the right flank under cover of broken ground near the base of the fort ruins. I saw at this time it was impossible to carry out the original scheme, as to move out in any formation for the attack onto the objective given me meant certain death. Capt. Geddes led out 5 men towards the right to protect the flank, having to cross a short gap in the bank to do so. He himself was shot and 2 men killed and [one] wounded out of his party, about quarter of an hour after this another platoon attempted to cross but most were hit.' Geddes himself said that:

> Seeing that Sed-el-Bahr and the beach to our right was unoccupied, and fearing the Turks might come down, I called for volunteers to make a dash for it, and make good the right of the beach. [In doing this, he was taking over the task assigned to the Dubs, whose objective was to capture the right side of the beach and the fort and village of Sedd-el-Bahr.] The men responded gallantly. Picking Sergt. [Patrick] Ryan [Reg. No. 5130] and 6 men we had a go for it. Three of the men were killed, one other and myself wounded. However we got across, and later picked up fourteen stragglers from the Company of the Dublin's who had landed at [The Camber]. This little party attempted to get a lodgement inside the fort but we couldn't do it, so we dug ourselves in as well as we could with our entrenching tools.

At 7.30 a.m., the battleship *Albion*'s log recorded 'Boat came alongside with wounded'. It recorded that other boats arrived 'throughout the day'. At about 8 a.m., Tizard saw:

> Some men on the extreme point of the right of the bay near a small stone house under the fort, about four or five of them. These I found out afterwards were part of a party of fourteen men of the Dublin Fusiliers who survived from the boat landing at [The Camber] and who had managed to get round from that place. After a bit a few more came round and joined up with [about half of the Munsters X Company] over that side, they then proceeded to dig themselves in. I saw a patrol soon after move off over the ruins towards the fort and they disappeared from view. I now sent out half of Y Company under Major [Charles] Jarrett.[92] They had many casualties getting ashore. [The line of rock] running out into the bay over which the men had to pass was now littered with dead and to my mind appeared a veritable death trap … [At about 8.30 a.m., Tizard was] told by a staff officer

whose name I do not know, that there were many men in the lighters who were not hit and could get ashore. I went down to the lighter to see and found a few taking cover amongst the dead. There was one a lance corporal and I told him to get the men over, this after a bit of trouble he did, but three out of seven got over without being hit. The men crawled from one lighter to the other and then jumped into the water on the far side of the cutter [possibly the boat behind which Geddes and Flynn had sheltered] to get cover from view but directly they got onto the spit of rock they got shot at. I then came back to the vessel. The lighters were now covered with dead and wounded and a lot had been hit by pom-poms. It appeared useless waste of life to try and get the men across except under cover of darkness. I went back to ask [Lieutenant-Colonel Herbert] Carington Smith about it. My [Adjutant, Captain Harry Wilson] had been wounded in the leg while still on board and the senior Major [Roger Monck-Mason] had also been hit through the shoulder by this time. I heard about this time that [Brigadier-General Steuart Hare, commanding officer of the 86th Brigade] had been wounded [at W Beach] and that, [as a result, Lieutenant-Colonel Herbert] Carington Smith [now] commanded the brigade. [Presumably this information had been conveyed to Hunter-Weston, who was aboard the *Euryalus* off W Beach, and from there, by sea, to the *River Clyde*.] He agreed with me that it would be better to wait till dark and with that I went down to stop the men going out. My reason was that we had already lost a considerable number of men and that if I continued to send men over, our force would probably not be strong enough to drive the enemy back. I considered at the time it was the only thing to do to hold on and dig in which the men did under the bank. Lieut. [Guy] Nightingale then met me in the hold with a message from Major [Charles] Jarrett [of Y Company] who was on the shore with about half his company asking me not to send any more men down til later on. I then went out on the bows again to tell the men of No. 11 platoon who were on the lighters to hold on for a bit. I got scratched on the hand by a bullet from the left.

At 9 a.m. he noted that while 'in the hold at No. 1, Lieut. [Gerald] Pollard who was waiting order to advance was killed, many men had already been hit in there.' Referred to as Lieutenant Pollard in contemporary accounts and in the *History of the Royal Munster Fusiliers*, Pollard is recorded by the Commonwealth War Graves Commission and Norman Dewhurst's memoirs as captain, suggesting that official notification of his promotion to captain arrived after his death.

According to Norman Dewhurst:

> The exit ports were opened and as the men began to run down the gang-
> ways they were simply shot to pieces. I had my [Vickers] machine guns
> going all the time in an attempt to give covering fire. [Unfortunately he
> did not say where on the *River Clyde* the guns were stationed.] This confu-
> sion went on for hours, during which men were still being ordered down
> the gangways to death and mutilation. The gangways became blocked with
> men going down and the wounded attempting to return. Captain [Gerald]
> Pollard was killed before my eyes as he passed through the exit port onto
> the gangway.

Geddes said that Pollard was in Z Company. As Z Company exited the
ship on the starboard side and Pollard was killed before Dewhurst's eyes,
Dewhurst must have been on the starboard side of the ship.

> As I scribbled these notes I had fifty or so seriously wounded men lying
> around me. The scene was indescribable. The navy was now shelling to
> cover us and doing a fine job – it had been realized that the men could
> not be landed, and we still aboard kept under cover behind the protection
> offered by the ship's plates and sandbags. I kept my machine gun team at
> their posts and we continued to try to give some fire in return to the Turks,
> and at the same time assist cover the small group of some two hundred or
> so of our comrades who had managed to land on the beach and were shel-
> tering behind the scanty cover provided by a shallow sandbank.[93]

After describing how Unwin had been taken aboard the *River Clyde*, Drewry
said that 'All this time shells were falling around us and into the ship, one hitting the casing of one boiler but doing no further damage. Several men were
killed by two shells in No. 4 hold. I stayed on the lighters and tried to keep
the men going ashore but it was murder and soon the first lighter was covered
with dead and wounded and the [line of rock] was awful, the sea round it for
some yards was red. When they got ashore they were little better off for they
were picked off, many of them before they could dig themselves in.' He said
that, as the troops stopped coming off the *River Clyde*, he 'ran onboard' into
No. 1 hold where he saw dead and dying men lying near the exit ports. He went
up to the 'saloon' where he saw Unwin being treated. 'He murmured something about the third lighter [towed on the *River Clyde*'s starboard side], so I
went down again.' A few minutes later a picket boat [under the command of

Lieutenant Tony Morse] arrived on the starboard side of the *River Clyde* and pushed the lighter [that had been towed on that side of the ship] towards the *Argyle*. The lighters having drifted away from the line of rock, Drewry tried to connect them with the *Argyle*. Just then a piece of shrapnel hit Drewry on the head, knocking him down for a second or two and covering him with blood. 'However we made the lighter fast to the [*Argyle*] and then I went below in the [*Argyle*] and a Tommy put my scarf round my head and I went up again.' Attempting to make a link to the lighters which had drifted away, Drewry swam towards the lighters carrying a rope. 'But the rope was not long enough and I was stuck in the middle.' He called to Midshipman Wilfred Malleson (who was on 'the picket boat with Morse') to throw him a line, but the only available rope was that which 'had originally kept the lighters to the [line of rock]. He stood up and hauled this line in (almost half a coil) and then, as I had drifted away, he swam towards the lighter I had left and made it alright. Then I made for home, but had a job climbing up the lighters for I was rather played out.' Drewry went aboard the *River Clyde* where, he said the doctor dressed his head and rubbed him down, as he was 'awfully cold'. He said that the doctor would not let him get up. So he had to 'lay down and listen to the din'.[94]

Surgeon Peter Burrows Kelly said that Commander Unwin had been brought to him at about 8 a.m., 'suffering from prolonged immersion and shock and hit badly'. He said that he attended to Unwin for two hours 'and then he got on fresh clothes and returned once more to the beach, though hardly able to walk'. In one of his accounts, Unwin said that 'a little rubbing and a lot of brandy soon got me round again. As I left my cabin I found Drewry laid out in the cabin with a bullet graze on the head, a very near shave.' In his account to Wemyss, he said, 'I don't know how long I lay there but I soon felt alright again, and got up, and just then they brought Drewry in. He told me a bullet had grazed his forehead, a very near thing, they bound him up and he was soon about again.' In the sort of discrepancy often found between witness accounts, Drewry makes no mention of meeting Unwin at this time. Unwin goes on to say, 'Very soon after Kelly himself got hit in the foot. He bound himself up and was at work again at once, he was simply splendid all day.' This is at variance with Kelly's account that his wound occurred earlier, before he had treated Unwin. Combining information from Unwin's two accounts, it appears that Drewry told him that he had got the lighters into position. 'As I had no more uniform with me I got into a white shirt and flannel trowsers [*sic*], and went on the [*Argyle*] to see if I could do any good ...' [He said the *Argyle* was lying under the port bow of the *River Clyde* and filled with men, 'most of them were wounded and many were dead'. He said they were 'not men that came in with me, but they had pulled in in boats' i.e. they were Royal Dublin Fusiliers.] Aboard the *Argyle*, Unwin said that, with the help of 'an old merchant seaman, he looked at least 70, and a boy I got a line out, but I don't think it was ever used.' [It is not clear if the man and boy were Greek crew members of the *Argyle*.] Meanwhile, Drewry said, 'Then I heard a cheer and looking out of the port I saw the Captain standing on the hopper in white clothes. A line had carried away and by himself he had fixed it. Then I went to sleep ... '

Sergeant Christopher McCann, (9809) of W Company of the Dublins, was aboard the *River Clyde*. He incorrectly said that it was about 4.30 a.m. when the ship beached.

> Then came the dreary wait for orders; several times the order was passed down to get dressed and immediately countermanded. At about 10 a.m. someone came aboard from the beach with the sad news that our Colonel, Adjutant, and most of our officers were killed. The effect of the news of Colonel Rooth's death could be read plainly on the faces of all ranks, as they had such faith in him as their commanding officer and would have followed him to the ends of the earth.[95]

About 300 yards to the left of the ship, on high ground overlooking the beach, was a high projecting rock. According to Lieutenant George Davidson, 89th Field Ambulance:

> From here came that infernal shower of bullets that was causing such terrible havoc. From the *Clyde* one could easily tell where the bullets were coming from by their sputter in the water. [Royal Navy ships kept shelling this rock.] The whole rim of V Beach, as it stretched backwards for 500 or 600 yards, was searched time after time by high explosives, each shell bursting with accurate precision 5 or 6ft under the crest. But the mischief was not coming from this crest, it was from that infernal rock alone, but in spite of all their efforts our guns could not silence this machine-gunfire.[96]

⚬⚬⚬

Anchored about 1,000 yards off W Beach, aboard the *Euryalus*, 29th Division's commanding officer, Major-General Aylmer Hunter-Weston, knew the 1st Lancashire Fusiliers had landed on W Beach despite heavy fire. He had also received news of successful landings at S, X and Y beaches. A misleading

SS *River Clyde* at V Beach.
(Photograph by Dr Andrew Horne. Copyright Margaret and Patricia Horne)

message reported that troops from the *River Clyde* appeared to be 'ashore well' and a message from the *Lord Nelson* signalled that British troops could be seen in Sedd el Bahr village. At 8.30 a.m. Hunter-Weston gave orders for the landing of the second wave of troops on the beaches.[97] The original plan for V Beach had called for the Blue Caps and the *River Clyde* to have landed by 7 a.m. Then, if all went well, for units of the 88th Brigade to land at about 8.30 a.m. The units in question were 1st Battalion Essex Regiment, 4th Worcester Regiment, the remaining two companies of 2nd Battalion Hampshire Regiment and two companies of the 1st/5th Royal Scots. Hunter-Weston, however, decided to divert 1st Battalion Essex Regiment to W Beach to reinforce the success of the Lancashire Fusiliers.

In response to Hunter-Weston's order, the minesweeper *Newmarket* moved towards V Beach, carrying Brigadier-General Henry Napier and 88th Brigade's staff, W and X Companies of 2nd Battalion Hampshire Regiment and two platoons of 4th Battalion Worcestershire Regiment. Offshore, the sweeper awaited the return of the tows from V Beach which, according to the original plan, were to land Napier and his troops in the second wave. Soon after 9 a.m. a few of the boats from the earlier landing arrived alongside the sweeper. The boats were full of wounded and dead Royal Dublin Fusiliers and the sailors who manned them were well aware of the hopelessness of any further attempt to land on V Beach. But, the sailors were not in a position to challenge a plan drawn up by senior officers. The boats were emptied of the dead and wounded and Napier and his staff got aboard and headed for the beach with two platoons from 4th Battalion Worcestershire Regiment, followed by '50 men of W and X Companies' Hampshire Regiment under the command of Captains Hubert de Crespigny Wymer (Commanding Officer of X Company) and Richard Spencer-Smith. The shortage of boats to carry the second wave of troops to V Beach meant that three platoons of the Anson Battalion, Royal Naval Division and naval and military beach parties remained aboard the *Newmarket*, until 10.30 a.m. when they received an order to land at W Beach.[98]

∽

From aboard the *River Clyde*, Brigadier-General Napier's tow was seen to be heading for the beach. According to Private George Keen, 4th Worcestershire Regiment,[99] the tow was about to pass to the right of the *River Clyde*, but Carington Smith 'shouted from the bridge, "For God's sake go round the other side!"' Keen said that the Turks were concentrating their fire to the right of the ship. The naval officer in charge of the tow complied. With one exception, accounts of the V Beach landing say that Napier boarded a lighter on the port side of the *River Clyde*, where he was killed. Tizard, however, said, at 9.30 a.m., 'As the enemy fire had slackened down I sent a message by [way of] a man of the Worcester Regt., a platoon of which had come on board during the action to tell the men in the lighter to have a try getting over. About 5 men got across [the line of rock] without a shot being fired, when the Regt. came in for a very heavy burst & most were knocked over. About 10 o'clock Gen. [Henry] Napier came on board with a staff officer [Brigade-Major Captain John Costeker].' Meanwhile, the boats carrying Captain Hubert de Crespigny Wymer, Captain Richard Spencer-Smith and '50 men of W and X Companies' of the 2nd Hampshires arrived on the starboard of the *River Clyde*. 'A burst of fire met them, but they kept on and, jumping into shallow water and scrambling along a projecting spit of rock, the two officers and two-thirds of their men joined those Dublins and Munsters who were sheltering along the bank under the Sedd el Bahr cliffs.'[100]

∽

At 9.07 a.m., a report from the commanding officer of 10 Company at Sedd el Bahr reached 3rd Battalion, 26th Regiment commanding officer Major Mahmut Sabri at his command post about ½ mile inland. This 'indicated that the [*River Clyde*] was a *bankrupt operation*.' Nevertheless, Sabri felt that the presence of the ship confirmed that Sedd el Bahr was the enemy's main effort and he ordered his 11th Company, [then in reserve] forward to Sedd el Bahr. 'This would give him about 300 riflemen on his critical left flank. By 10 a.m., having sent his 9th Company towards X Beach, Sabri had committed his entire battalion to the fight.'[101]

Meanwhile, at 9.30 a.m., Major Hafiz Kadri, Commanding Officer of the 26th Regiment, based in Krithia, phoned 9th Division's headquarters in Maidos, urgently requesting reinforcements. He subsequently forwarded a stream of situational reports from Major Sabri that described the deteriorating situation in his sector.[102]

ॐ

At about 9 a.m., Hunter-Weston, still unaware of the desperate situation at V Beach, sent a message to the *River Clyde*, urging that its troops move leftwards to link up with the Lancashire Fusiliers coming from W Beach. In response to the order, Lieutenant-Colonel Herbert Carington Smith ordered one company of the Hampshires ashore from the *River Clyde*. A few men managed to get ashore, but after Captain [Caryl] Boxall, No. 9 Platoon, Y Company, was mortally wounded and twenty men hit, Carington Smith called off the attempt.[103] 'Meanwhile the [Hampshire's] machine guns on board the *Clyde* under Lieutenant [George] Rosser and [Wedgwood's] guns [continued to fire].[104] According to Lieutenant-Colonel Henry Tizard of the Munsters,

> [One company] of the Hampshire Regt. under Major [Arthur] Beckwith came over to the fore hold and went off.[105] As they got onto the lighter it appeared to drift away into deep water & only a few got ashore, the remainder laid down in the lighter and some came back along the bows into the hold. I don't know what happened, but I believe Gen. Napier with his brigade Major went down onto the lighter to try and get the men over not knowing what had happened. I saw him lying on the nearest lighter with the brigade Major near him. I afterwards heard he had been hit and he died soon afterwards, this brigade Major was also killed.

Tizard's statement that Napier boarded the *River Clyde* has been noted, as has the fact that no other account mentions this. As Tizard does not actually say that he met Napier, the balance of probability would appear to suggest that he was in error in saying that Napier boarded the ship. According to the *Official History*, 'General Napier, seeing the lighters choken with men, and not realizing that they were dead, sprung on board the nearest lighter, meaning to lead them ashore.

A warning voice from the collier shouted: "You can't possibly land!" But Napier shouted back: "I'll have a damned good try." At once there was a renewed burst of Turkish fire.'[106] Private Cecil Jeffries, 4th Worcestershire Regiment followed Napier. 'I saw three wounded Irishmen, wounded and hanging on to a small boat; one was shouting, "Oh, by Jesus save me!" I gave the General a leg-up on to the lighter, then his Brigade Major. Then I was pushed up and the deck of the lighter was covered with dead men. We started over the deck when the General went down, he never spoke. Then the Major went down but he raised himself on one knee and said, "Carry on, men!" Then he was dead.'[107] According to the *Official History*, 'Thus died the very man who, by his rank, his nerve, and his knowledge, would have been of priceless value to the troops in the southern area during the rest of that vital day.'[108] Private George Keen of the Worcestershires said, 'We were following the General. He got to the third boat and was killed; the Brigade Major followed him and got killed. Our Major [it is unclear to whom he was referring] said, "This is too risky!" and he got out of the way in the little boat. That caused us to stop and we all lay in the lighter, myself lying on another fellow. I was sorry for him but he said, "Never mind!" There we stayed till night came.'[109] The *Official History* says that Sir Ian Hamilton signalled Hunter-Weston at 10.21 a.m.: 'Not advisable to send more men to V Beach. We have 200 on shore unable to progress.' The remaining infantry intended for V Beach were then diverted to W Beach. These included the 4th Battalion Worcestershire Regiment and W and X Companies of Hampshires, less the fifty that landed with Napier.

Aboard the *Argyle*, Unwin heard Brigade-Major John Costeker yell at him to lie down, as he said that Unwin was drawing fire. Unwin had lain down when he hear Costeker shout, 'They've got me.' He said he believed that Costeker had been shot in the stomach.[110] A bullet then hit a stanchion near Unwin 'and spluttered over my face and neck.' Feeling that there was little point in remaining, Unwin ran up the gangway to the *River Clyde* and climbed in through 'the fore-most port [hole].' He later learned that a man who helped him in through the porthole was shot through the lung and died. Unwin went on deck, where he saw Lieutenant-Colonel Herbert Carington Smith and told him there was no point in trying to land more men. Unwin said that just

Lieutenant-Colonel
Herbert Carington Smith.

then, on the high ground to their left, the two men saw a party of British troops coming from W Beach. Carington Smith cheered, as did soldiers nearby. Followed by Carington Smith, Unwin climbed the ladder to the bridge of the *River Clyde*. Unwin then climbed to the upper bridge, which he said he had had 'surrounded with ¼ inch sheet iron, two thicknesses, through which no shot had penetrated'. Seeing Carington Smith 'standing on the lower bridge, which had no protection, looking towards the beach with his glasses,' Unwin shouted to him to come to the upper bridge. He said that Carington Smith replied, 'Oh I'm all right here.' Almost immediately, he was shot in the mouth. The officer's servant was nearby, but Unwin and he could do nothing as Carington Smith was dead.[111] Tizard said Carington Smith was killed at 10.20 a.m. (The *Official History* and *The Royal Hampshire Regiment 1914-1918* place his death at approximately 3 p.m.)

ʊʊ

Hamilton and de Robeck were aboard the battleship *Queen Elizabeth*. The ship had been stationed off Z Beach, as the Australian and New Zealand troops went ashore. Then the *Lizzie* sailed down the coast, allowing Hamilton, de Robeck and their staffs to observe the situation at Y Beach, X Beach and W Beach. Sailing past V Beach, those aboard the flagship saw the *Cornwallis* lying off Morto Bay. The battleship *Cornwallis* had been assigned to cover the landing at S Beach, in Morto Bay. Captain Alexander Davidson was told that, once the landing had been made, he was to station his ship, with the *Albion*, to support the troops at V Beach. (According to Rear-Admiral Wemyss, anxious about the landing at S Beach, he told Davidson 'before joining the *Albion* he was to stay and support these troops, rendering them such assistance as he could until they had effected [*sic*] a landing.'[112] Davidson decided to send sailors to assist with the landing and personally went ashore with a party of marines to support the attack.) De Robeck ordered the *Cornwallis* 'to go at once to her proper station off V Beach, as she had discharged her mission, and the Morto Bay area was covered by the *Lord Nelson*.'[113] Then the *Queen Elizabeth* returned to V Beach, remaining there for the rest of the day.[114] 'The *Queen Elizabeth*, *Albion* and *Cornwallis* smothered the enemies' defences with high explosive shells at intervals, from various ranges, but were never able to silence the few well sited machine guns and the rifle fire from the deep trenches, which broke out again and again directly our fire was lifted to allow an advance – and so it went on all day.'[115]

'General Hunter-Weston, not realising the impossibility of movement [on V Beach] had continued to urge the capture of the western defences of the beach, to assist the troops from W [Beach] in their advance on Hill 138.' At 2.30 p.m. Carington Smith sent Lieutenant Tony Morse to the *Queen Elizabeth* with a note, written at 2.25p.m., explaining the situation at V Beach. 'Within half an hour of writing this message, Colonel Carington Smith was killed.'[116] Morse boarded the *Queen Elizabeth* with a request:

> For more ammunition for the naval machine guns of the *River Clyde,* which had been provided and manned by the Royal Naval Division; and we learnt from him of the desperate nature of the fighting round the *River Clyde* and the severity of the losses. He told us that the naval casualties included among the killed Lieutenant-Commander [George] Pownall, the commander of the Malta submarine flotilla and Depot ship, who had begged me to get him a billet on one of the beaches. We were all much struck by the bearing of Morse during the recital of his tale, and when he left us to return to the inferno round the *River Clyde* I must confess I never expected to see him again, but I am glad to record he survived.'[117]

ഇന

At his battalion command post about a kilometre inland, Major Mahmut Sabri noted that the shore at V Beach was 'full of enemy corpses, like a shoal of fish. At Seddulbahir pier five boat loads of men were completely sunk.'[118]

ഇന

Tizard said that after Carington Smith's death he took command of the troops on the *River Clyde,* informing William Hutchinson, his 'next senior Major', to take command of the 1st Munsters. 'I had now on board the following as far as I can remember – [As with all of Tizard's reporting, he wrote some words in abbreviated form. While retaining all the information, I have written the words in full. I have used 'and' instead of '&' and I have tidied up the punctuation. In this paragraph only, I have written the unit order in, what I consider to be, a more readable sequence.] No. 1 Hold: W Company, 1st Battalion Royal Munster Fusiliers, one platoon of Y Company, 1st Battalion Royal Munster Fusiliers, about half a company Hampshire Regiment, four machine guns, (as Tizard recorded these after his mention of the Munsters, it seems likely that they belonged to the Dirty Shirts.) No. 1 Hold (Lower): W Company Royal Dublin Fusiliers. No. 2 Hold: One company Hampshire

Regiment. Distributed through No. 2, 3 and 4 holds: One platoon Anson
Battalion, Royal Naval Division, one platoon 4th Battalion Worcestershire
Regiment and three bearer subdivisions Ambulance Corps. 'Every endeav-
our was made to try and locate where the sniping came from. It was chiefly
from the left along high ground and machine guns on board were constantly
searching this ground. The fire power of HMS *Albion* was also directed on
this by Captain [Robert] Lambert R.N. [Beach Master of V Beach] and also
onto various other points to keep the fire down.'

Lieutenant George Davidson, 89th Field Ambulance, said that boats came
to the starboard side of the *River Clyde*. From these the wounded were taken
aboard and treated.

Repeatedly the whole of our floor was covered with wounded and dead men;
a pinnace would arrive from a ship and relieve us of our wounded, but we
filled up again almost at once. Along the water's edge there was now a mass of
dead men, on the sand a mixture of dead and weltering wounded, while a fair
number had reached the sandbank just beyond, where, under an enfilading
fire from the rock [on the high ground to the left of the beach], they scraped
themselves into the recesses … One boat half-way to [the line of rock],
and which had been left stranded, had three men caught in the festooned
rope that runs round the gunwale. Into this they had dived, probably as the
boat heeled over to that side and the rope had floated outwards, and there
they swung for the rest of the day, two not moving a muscle and evidently
dead, but for long I could see the other poor fellow stretch out his arms time
after time, but before evening he too was still.[119]

In response to an order from Major Mahmut Sabri to launch a charge at V Beach,
Platoon Commander Abdul Rahman reported he had only twenty-five men,
and instead appealed for help: 'Send the doctors to carry off my wounded, alas!
alas! My Captain for God's sake send me reinforcements because hundreds are
landing. Hurry up, what on earth will happen, my Captain.'[120]

Unwin said:

I remained on the bridge with [de Lancey] Williams and Doughty-Wylie staring at the beach. Not a Turk did I even see. I thought I saw one once and took a rifle and fired at it and an old vulture flew out of the tree ... The beach was strewn with dead, it was a sight we had before us. I saw a party of 6 men leave the beach and clamber over the ridge evidently with the intention of trying to cut into the wire. They got 10 yards, 5 fell down shot instantly and one ran back and jumped over the heads of the men lying under the ridge. One of those shot turned imploringly round towards us, and rolled about but eventually was still. I know I felt a brute in not going to his assistance ... At about 2 p.m. as the moanings of the wounded lying on [the line of rock] under our starboard bow were more than I could stand, I got a boat under the starboard quarter as far from the enemy as I could get and taking a spare coil of rope with me I got some hands to pay out a rope fast to the stern of the pinnace I was in, and paddled and punted her into the beach, eventually grounding alongside the wounded. They were all soaking wet and very heavy, but I cut off their accoutrements with their bayonets or knives and carried two or three into the pinnace. But, as her side was rather high out of the water, I'm afraid they were not too gingerly put on board, but still they were very grateful. I could not pick up any more, so I got on my hands and knees and they got on to my back and I crawled along the pinnace. Four more I managed like this and then I found a man in his trowsers [*sic*] only, alongside me. He had swum ashore to help me. I found out afterwards his name was [Petty Officer John] Russell and he was one of the R.N.A.S. [Armoured Car Squadron who were manning the machine guns on the *River Clyde*.] We carried one man down together and then [Russell] was shot through the stomach. I tore my up my shirt and bound his wound a bit and got him in the pinnace. I was again beginning to feel a bit dicky, so I got into the pinnace and told them to haul me aboard. On the way across somebody came alongside in the water and wanted to know why I was going back. I replied because I could do no more, and I really couldn't. I was 51, and I had a bit of a shake up in the morning. Anyhow I didn't do any more. The man must, I think, have been young Tizard who got the V.C. for continuing my work. [Twenty-four-year-old Sub-Lieutenant Arthur Tisdall, commanding officer of 13 Platoon, D Company, Anson Battalion, Royal Naval Division, was the only R.N.D. officer on the *River Clyde*.] The poor fellow was killed a fortnight later. I got into my bed and slept till nearly 7.

छछ

Commander Charles Rumney Samson was commanding officer of No. 3 Squadron Royal Naval Air Service. Based at Tenedos, the squadron photographed the Gallipoli peninsula, spotted for naval gunfire and reported on Turkish troop movements.

My duties for [25 April] were to look after all the Helles landings.[121] We were to be up in position over the beaches before the tows left the ships, and we were to spot certain ship's fire on to any guns that were firing on the boats: then we were to shift the fire on to any bodies of the enemy who were resisting the landing. After the landing had been effected [*sic*] we were to spot the ships on to any large bodies moving down to reinforce. In addition long reconnaissance had to be carried out up to Bulair to watch for possible movements of the Turkish reserves.

Most of the squadron's planes made three flights during the day. According to Samson 'we practically all found that the ships took little notice of our signals until too late.'

Samson and his observer Flight-Lieutenant Edward Osmond took off from Tenedos in a Maurice Farman 'at an early hour'. In his memoirs he said 'we were to look out for the Lancashire landing …'[122] He described the landing at W Beach, with the troops trying to get ashore under heavy fire. He continued:

I didn't see much more, as our principal job was to find the Turks in order to signal their position to the ships. They were not easy to find; but we located some Turks and guns quite close to the beach. Osmond signalled their position; but the ships disregarded our message, and kept their fire too far inland. No doubt they did this because they were afraid of hitting our own people. We dropped our bombs at these Turks; but unfortunately missed them. As our time was up and we were relieved by another aeroplane, we returned home, passing over Sedd-el-Bahr, where I could see the landing was held up. The *River Clyde* was fast ashore; but the lighters ahead of her were not in the right position, apparently, and gaps occurred. The lighters were full of corpses; the beach and water close to the shore were strewn with bodies. It was an appalling sight for us to look at from our safe position in the air, and made one think that we were not doing our bit. I could, however, see that some of our men were holding out behind a ridge about 30 yards or so inland. The Turks were keeping up a hot fire on the *River Clyde*, and it seemed impossible for anyone to get ashore from her. Some shells were arriving from the Asiatic side; but undoubtedly the most serious obstacle was the rifle fire from Sedd-el-Bahr village I saw one gallant deed, which impressed itself upon my memory. A Naval steamboat came in right close up to the beach in face of a terrible fire and towed off a cutter which was full of dead and wounded: they did the job as neatly as if they had been taking libertymen off in peace-time. The sea for a distance of about 50 yards from the beach was absolutely red with blood, a horrible sight to see. [123]

ॐ

Lieutenant-Colonel Henry Tizard of the Munsters said that from the time he took command of the troops on the *River Clyde* until about 4 p.m.,:

Things were practically at a standstill. During the afternoon I got a message saying that the Worcestershire Regiment on my left had taken Hill 130. [This was Hill 138.] Later I got another message on shore with Lieutenant [Guy] Nightingale who also took the remainder of Y Company with him [i.e. Tizard sent a message to Nightingale, who was now ashore with the remainder of Y Company] to work along the shore to the left and join up with the Worcestershire Regiment who had taken [Hill 138]. I had seven parties of men on the cliffs to my left. These men were held up by barbed wire, but a small party got as far as the hospital ruins [viewed from the sea, ruins of an old barracks stood on high ground behind the left side of the beach] but were driven back to the original place. This party of Y Company, with some of the Hampshires, whilst getting on shore came under fire and many were hit. I then gave orders to Major [William] Hutchinson, commanding the Munsters, not to try to get his one company ashore with the guns till dark. [124] Previous to this I had sent orders earlier in the day to try and get the wire cut in front of the bank. I thought if this could be done we might get a rush from cover through it although I knew it would cost many men. Five men of my [regiment] went forward and they had not gone more than 15 yards from the bank on the right side when they were all shot down, four were killed and one on the right was wounded. This man got away under cover of dark and came on board. I saw to attempt this was impossible just then.

ॐ

There were at least three doctors aboard the *River Clyde,* Scotsman George Davidson of the 89th Field Ambulance and Irish Surgeons Peter Burrows

Kelly of the Royal Naval Air Service and Arthur Patrick Barrett from the mine-sweeper *Newmarket*. Barrett, from Cork, said:

> I had some of the wounded back on board – chaps whom I had seen half an hour before well and strong – now wrecks for life. It was awful. They were very cheery and dying to be back at the Turks. It was very strange. I would see a poor chap dying, and asking him where he came from, the answer would be 'Blarney Street, Cork,' another 'Main Street,' and one poor sergeant, who had five bayonet wounds in his stomach, came from 'Warren's Place'. He died that night and was cheery to the last. They are fine fellows, and won the admiration of everyone.[125]

Reluctant all day to commit his only remaining reserves, 9th Division's Colonel Halil Sami ordered the 1st and 2nd Battalions of the 25th Regiment to Sedd el Bahr and Teke Koyu (W Beach) at 6.30 p.m. He ordered them to move quickly.[126]

From 5.30 p.m., the battleships *Queen Elizabeth, Albion* and *Cornwallis* bombarded the Valide's fort and Sedd el Bahr village.

> The village broke into flames, and the whole amphitheatre was wrapped in a cloud of blinding dust and smoke. About 7 p.m., profiting by this bombardment, the remnants of the Munsters and a few Hampshires, about 120 men in all, were led by Major Jarrett to the right of the beach, and a fresh attempt was made to effect a lodgement in the old fort. [A footnote says that Major Jarrett was killed by a sniper a few minutes later.] But … the attempt to enter it was frustrated and the invading troops once more took cover on the seaward face of the battlements. So the long day ended.[127]

Tizard said that by 6.30 p.m. he had on shore X, Y, and Z Companies Royal Munster Fusiliers, 'some' Royal Dublin Fusiliers, one company of the Hampshire Regiment under Major Arthur Beckwith and one platoon from the Worcestershire Regiment. He said:

> They all had sustained casualties getting ashore. At this time there was only one signaller who was on the right side under [the Valide's] Fort.

I maintained communication with him during the night. I now formed a plan by which one company Royal Munster Fusiliers was to work to the left, sending a party up a small nulla which ran down to the beach from a road leading into the village across our front. This nulla was on the left of the beach and the remainder were to try and get in touch with the Worcesters on the left on high ground, whilst [two companies of Royal Munster Fusiliers] worked around to the right by the south east corner of the [Valide's] Fort to get us into the village from that side. Then allowing this party time to get the [Company] of the Hampshires to cut the wire and push on up by the left of the village getting in touch with the party on the right through the village if possible supported by the Dublins and Worcestershires. This plan was altered eventually as I found the Hampshire [Company] had moved over to the right. My plan now was as regards the left as before. [It was now about 7.30 p.m.] The company of Hampshires then on board were to get across after dark with [one] platoon of the West Riding Field [Company, Royal Engineers] with wire cutters, cut the wire and move up to the left of the village getting in touch with the right hand party. To leave a signal station near the foot of the fort. The support for this party was [one company Royal Dublin Fusiliers, one platoon Worcesters, three platoons West Riding Field Company, Royal Engineers] whilst the [three companies of Royal Munster Fusiliers and Hampshires] worked around to the right. At about this time W [Company] led by Captain [Charles] Williams and machine guns under Captain [Edward] Dorman [and Second Lieutenant Norman Dewhurst] were sent on shore and did not support very much in doing so. I also gave orders that a message was to be sent to me when the wire was cut but did not get this.

Tizard said that between the time darkness fell and about 12.30 a.m. on the morning of Monday 26 April he had got all the troops ashore with the exception of the three ambulance sub-divisions. The latter 'had their work cut out attending to wounded men which they did without any regard for self. All stores, tools and ammunition was passed across & many of the wounded were brought back on to the boat. At about 11 p.m., the enemy gave us very heavy fire which lasted for some time.' Second Lieutenant Norman Dewhurst said, 'I got my machine-gun party ashore and we built up an emplacement using the dead bodies around us, to give us some elevation to fire over the sandbank.'[128]

According to Sergeant Christopher McCann, (9809) W Company, 1st Battalion Royal Dublin Fusiliers:

It must have been about 7 p.m. that the final order came to get dressed. We filed up out of the hold, where were had been in semi-darkness all of this time, Captain [Herbert] Crozier leading, followed by Company Sergeant-Major C[harles] Smith [6780] (who did splendid work all through the landing), myself, and No. 1 Platoon of which I was in command, there being no officer with the platoon. As we filed out of the holes cut in the side of the old *Clyde* and down the gangway, machine guns opened fire, and we threw ourselves flat where we stood; two of my platoon were hit, and one of them fell headlong into the sea. After about ten minutes we moved on, but had only reached the two [lighters] that formed the landing stage when we came under heavy rifle and machine-gun fire again. We threw ourselves flat on the [lighters] and lay still for some time; I was between two men of the Munster Fusiliers who were dead, but I did not realise this until I asked one of them to make more room, and as he did not move I pushed him with my hand, and then found that his head was blown away. Captain [Herbert] Crozier now passed the word to get ashore; we moved off the [lighters] over the small rowing boat, scrambled ashore through the water, and lined up along the beach. All this time we were under a very heavy rifle and machine-gun fire, several of the company being hit. I was then posted by Captain [he had been promoted to Major] Grimshaw with six men as a look-out post till morning.

Lieutenant Henry Desmond O'Hara, also of W Company, said:

Eventually [Captain Herbert] Crozier, [Lieutenant Lawrence] Boustead, and I got our company ashore about twelve o'clock that night by means of a gangway along the ship's side which connected with some lighters. Crozier went first and got his platoon on shore; Boustead got his into the lighters; and I was on the gangway with mine when suddenly the Turks opened fire, bullets simply whizzing up against the sides of the ship. Crozier shouted to me to take my platoon back into the ship, which I did, though not before three men had been hit, including Redmond, my soldier servant, who was standing beside me: the bullet caught him under the ear and came out just behind the nose without doing him much damage.[129]

According to Captain David French, Y Company, of the Blue Caps:

We lay [behind the sand bank] all day. At night the remainder of the troops disembarked from the R.(iver) Clyde which originally brought along with her 2,000 troops. Never shall I forget that night. Heavy fire incessantly. Drizzling with rain. Wounded groaning on all sides, and, surrounded by dead I admit I thought it was all up. I had only about 20 men with me behind at that part of the beach.'[130] Lieutenant Cuthbert Maffett, X Company, of the *Blue Caps* said 'Night fell at length, and shortly after a large number of men came off the *River Clyde* without mishap; these joined us on the beach, and we formed a sort of defensive line for the night.'[131]

Captain Guy Geddes, X Company, of the Dirty Shirts recorded:

About 8.30 p.m. when it was quite dark [Major Charles Jarrett, Lieutenants Francis Lee, Guy Nightingale and Francis Russell], with remnants of W, Y and Z Companies came over to me without molestation. I suggested to Jarrett that the best thing was to establish oneself in the Fort and get the village of Sedd-el-Bahr. He was killed alongside me and shortly after Lieutenants Russell and Lee were wounded. Suddenly Major[s] [de Lancey] Williams and [Arthur] Beckwith appeared out of the dark with two companies of the Hampshires from the *River Clyde*. Not a shot being fired as they were unobserved. Major [de Lancey] Williams asked me about the situation and I told him all I knew, and that I was going to get my wound dressed. I had been hit then for 13 hours and was rather doubled up with stiffness and feared gangrene. The situation was now in far better hands than mine. I got my wounds dressed on the *River Clyde* and with about 200 other wounded was put on a trawler where we tossed about the whole bitter cold night.[132]

According to Private Robert Martin of the Blue Caps, 'Those who were lying wounded on the shore, in the evening the tide came in and they were all drowned …'[133]

The history of the Hampshire Regiment says that when Major Arthur Beckwith came ashore he 'directed Captain [Richard] Spencer-Smith and the 18 men left out of his 26 to push on into the fort and secure the exit from it to the north. Accompanied by some Dublins and Munsters, the party moved some way to the right, climbed the cliff, cutting many strands of wire, and dashed into the fort, the Turks bolting before them. They then established themselves on the northern face of the fort …' They remained there for the night.[134]

In his summary of the day, Captain Guy Geddes of the Munsters said 'The Turkish fire was opened up on us immediately we debouched from the *River Clyde*. They seemed to have the water edge particularly marked. V Beach formed an amphitheatre about 300 yards in diameter with

Sed-el-Bahr Fort on the right, and on the left high cliffs surmounted by Fort No. 1. In no instance was the range greater than 300 yards … There was little or no fire from [the Valide's fort]. The fire came chiefly from the high ground [to the left] and the village itself.'[135]

While the Commonwealth War Grave Commission officially records only approximately fifty of the battalion as dying on 25 April, the 1st Munsters had only 12 officers and 588 men available for service on 29 April, out of the twenty-eight officers and 1,002 men who had gone to Gallipoli. Like the Dublins, the battalion appears to have had a huge number of wounded men, who would have been immediately evacuated. As with the Dublins, it is not possible to say how many of them died from their wounds aboard hospital ships and in hospitals around the Mediterranean in the days, weeks and months that followed. Neither is it possible to say how many were subsequently unable to return to the battalion as a result of the severity of their wounds.

Among the Munsters who died that day was thirty-year-old Major Charles Jarrett, past-pupil of Stonyhurst College and Boer War veteran. Captain David French of the Dublins said that Jarrett was killed alongside him sometime after coming ashore at about 8.30 p.m. A letter sent to Stoneyhurst by 'a brother officer' said: 'He was shot at 6.00 in the evening and died without pain. I had been speaking to him two minutes before his death … He was buried before dawn by the subaltern by whose side he fell, and who had asked the chaplain to say the funeral service over him. I put a cross on the mound.'[136] Lieutenant Gerald Pollard was shot aboard the *River Clyde*, his promotion to Captain appears to have arrived after his death. He is commemorated by a stained-glass window in a church in Dorset and on the Helles Memorial. Second Lieutenant Timothy Sullivan, who had married the previous month in Coventry, died on 4 May of wounds sustained in the landing. Captain Eric Henderson died of his wounds in hospital in Alexandria on 20 May. Thirty-seven-year-old Boer War veteran, Company Sergeant-Major David Danagher, from Limerick had drawn up his will in Coventry, leaving everything to his wife Margaret. Their son John served as Mayor of Limerick 1964-1965. Twenty-four-year-old Jack Long from Buttevant, formerly of the Irish Guards, left behind his grief-stricken brother William (known as Paddy). John Crowley and Michael O'Sullivan came from the seaside town of Youghal, in County Cork. Peter Frawley from Ennis, County Clare, was one of six brothers serving with the colours. Also from Ennis were Michael Burley and Michael Butler. Adolphus Reuben was born and had enlisted in Burma. James Searles, from the inland town of Bandon, County Cork, had enlisted in the seaside town of Kinsale, County Cork. ('Jimmy Searles was killed on the 25th April and was buried by the seaside.'[137]) Michael Walsh had been born in Springfield, Massachusetts, but lived in Kerry at the time of his enlistment.

ຊຊ

V Beach is located to the right of Cape Helles headland. To the left of the headland, and between it and Tekke Burnu headland, is W Beach. At about 5.30 a.m., the landing there by the 1st Lancashire Fusiliers also met fierce resistance. Amid the chaos of the landing, Brigadier-General Steuart Hare, commanding 86th Infantry Brigade, decided to land on the very left of the beach. Then he and his brigade-major, Royal Dublin Fusilier Tom Frankland, led a small group of Lancashire Fusiliers up a cliff. When more Lancashires climbed the cliff, Hare decided to try to link up with the 2nd Royal Fusiliers who had successfully landed at X Beach, on his left. As the Royal Fusiliers were one of the four battalions in his brigade (with the Dublins, Munsters and Lancashires), he planned to get them to attack the flank of the Turks who were holding up the landing of the Lancashires at W Beach. Meeting Turkish resistance, Frankland grabbed a rifle from one of the men and shot two or three of the enemy. The rest fled. Pushing on towards X Beach, the small party came under fire from a strongpoint on Hill 114. Hare was hit in the leg. He was taken to the beach, from where he was evacuated at about 7.30 a.m. On the beach, Frankland consulted with 86th Brigade's Staff Captain Mynors Farmar. 86th Brigade's objective was to achieve a linkup between the 2nd Royal Fusiliers at X Beach, the 1st Lancashire Fusiliers at W Beach and the 1st Royal Dublin Fusiliers and the 1st Royal Munster Fusiliers at V Beach. Brigade headquarters would be set up in a ruined lighthouse on Cape Helles, between W Beach and V Beach. Frankland wanted to push to the right, attack a Turkish strongpoint on Hill 138, establish brigade headquarters in the lighthouse and link up with his fellow Dublins and the Munsters on V Beach. Accompanied by about fifty Lancashire Fusiliers, from B Company, 1st Lancashire Fusiliers, under the command of Captain Richard Hawworth, Frankland and Farmar began to move towards the lighthouse by way of cliffs on the right of W Beach. They came under fire from a strongpoint, which Frankland took to be on Hill 138. It was in fact coming from a hill which was not marked on British maps. Called Gözcübaba by the Turks, it is the hill on which the Helles Memorial now stands, about 350 yards nearer to V Beach than Hill 138. About 250 yards beyond Gözcübaba is Ertuğrul Tabyasi (Fort No. 1) on the high ground overlooking the left side of V Beach.

Meanwhile, further inland than Frankland's party, Captain John Shaw of A Company, 1st Lancashire Fusiliers led 'the remnants of his command' in an attack on Hill 138. At the same time, Frankland's party attacked Gözcübaba, under the impression it was attacking Hill 138. Neither party made much headway.[138] 'We reached the lighthouse' Farmar wrote:

> ... and pushed on until hung up by a maze of barbed wire. Fortunately there was almost dead ground against the wire for a strip. The Signal Section was established under cover of the lighthouse and they got communication with the Royal Fusiliers, the *Euryalus* and the River Clyde. Frankland left me and went to the ridge on the right to see if there was any way on from there [towards V Beach]. At about 8.45 a.m. he stood up in order to see, and was shot through the heart, neck and head. We buried him two days afterwards.[139]

Thomas Hugh Colville Frankland, Royal Dublin Fusiliers and War Correspondent, and Winston Churchill had been captured together by the Boers and imprisoned in the same camp. Frankland was killed a few hundred yards from his regimental comrades on V Beach.

Captain Mynors Farmar crawled from the lighthouse to a point on the cliff from where he could see the *River Clyde*. At 12.25 p.m. he sent a runner to W Beach with the message, 'Two hundred men have landed on V Beach. These cannot go forward. Connection between River Clyde and shore is very bad and casualties occur as soon as men move from the ship... Landing is easy near lighthouse and cliffs are accessible. If redoubts 1 and 2[140] are taken it would facilitate capture of the village.' Had the message arrived at 29th Divisional headquarters aboard the *Euryalus* in time to be acted upon, the Worchestershire Regiment might have landed at the lighthouse instead of W Beach, thus relieving V Beach early that afternoon, but most of the Worchestershires had landed by the time the message was received. Meanwhile, more troops had landed at the now secure W Beach. Sometime after 10 a.m., a company from the 1st Essex Regiment were held up by fire from the strongpoint on Hill 138. Shortly after 2 p.m. the 4th Worcestershire Regiment arrived. The strongpoint was bombarded for twenty minutes, following which it was attacked and captured at about 3 p.m. The 4th Worcestershire Regiment then advanced towards Gözcübaba. With their officer killed, Gözcübaba was defended by sixty-three men from 12 Company, 3rd Battalion, 26th Regiment, under the command of Sergeant Yahya (Yahya Çavuş). When the Worcestershires broke in and seized part of the trenches, Yahya led a bayonet attack that ejected them. The Worcestershires finally drove Yahya's command off the hill. He lived to tell the tale, was decorated for his actions and is immortalised in a memorial above V Beach.[141]

A detachment of Captain Richard Hawworth's, B Company, 1st Lancashires had been under cover by the lighthouse since going there with Frankland and Farmar.[142] Now, reinforced by some of the Worcestershires, they advanced towards V Beach until they were held up by a belt of barbed wire. While the wire could be seen from the *Queen Elizabeth* and the *Albion*, less than a mile away, neither ship felt it safe to open fire in case they hit their own troops. 'Time after time, plainly silhouetted against the sky-line, a man would be seen rushing up [to the wire], only to fall lifeless across it a few minutes later, when his place would be taken by another volunteer.' Finally a gap was cut and the troops went streaming through. But they were stopped by heavy fire and could make no further progress. Staff-officer Colonel Anthony Wolley-Dod, who had come ashore to take command at W Beach soon after 12.30 p.m., was unaware of the need to assist the troops at V Beach. At 4.35 a.m., hearing that Gözcübaba had been captured, he ordered the 4th Worcestershires to secure the position and bury their dead. At 5 p.m. he received a message from divisional headquarters, saying that V Beach could not be secured until the high ground to the left was captured. The Worcestershires were ordered to advance to the high ground above V Beach. But their commanding officer, Lieutenant-Colonel Douglas Cayley had already learned the situation from Captain Mynors Farmar, who had walked from the lighthouse to meet him and his troops were advancing towards V Beach. But the Worcestershires met considerable fire and were again held up. Making little progress, with his battalion scattered and darkness closing in, Colonel Cayley decided to consolidate the ground won. All hope of assisting the troops on V Beach was postponed until the morning. At 6.30 p.m., Hunter-Weston received a message that the 4th Worcestershires had captured Hill 141, which is behind Sedd el Bahr. This was believed until a message arrived from Calley at 9.15 p.m. saying he had been held up by wire and that his line ran from Hill 138 southwards to a point on the cliff east of the Helles lighthouse.[143]

៷៷

At 1 a.m. on 26 April, messengers from the approaching 1st Battalion, 25th Regiment arrived at Major Mahmut Sabri's command post, about a kilometre behind V Beach. Sabri drew up a plan to recapture Ay Tepe (Hill 138) and Gözcübaba and sent the plan by messenger to the commander of the approaching 1st Battalion. The plan called for the 1st Battalion to be in position by 2.30 a.m., ready to make a night bayonet assault at 3.30 a.m. To assist the reinforcements become familiar with their objectives, Sabri linked the incoming battalion's 3rd Company with his own 9th Company and the newcomers 4th Company with the survivors of his own 12th Company [presumably including Sergeant Yahya (Yahya Çavuş)]. The attack would be supported by two machine guns of the incoming battalion. Sabri ordered his own 11th Company to attack Gözcübaba. The incoming battalion commander was told to station himself with one platoon as a reserve at Harapkale [Hill 141, behind Sedd el Bahr village.] The attack began on schedule, 'but a wall of British rifle fire, machine-gun fire and grenades hit the advancing Turkish infantry. This was soon followed by effective naval gunfire support.' Sabri immediately committed the reserve platoon under the 1st Battalion commander. The battle see-sawed back and forth. Although the Turks recaptured some parts of the strongpoint's trenches, the attack collapsed after about an hour's fighting.[144]

CHAPTER 7

Getting off the Beach

'Gentlemen, we are being killed on the beaches.
Let us go inland and be killed.'
Brigadier-General Norman Cota, at Omaha Beach on D-Day

Just before midnight on 25 April, Hunter-Weston sent Captain Garth Walford, Brigade-Major, Royal Artillery, from 29th Divisional Headquarters aboard the *Euryalus*, to the *River Clyde*. There, he, Lieutenant-Colonel Charles Doughty-Wylie, Major Weir de Lancey Williams and Major Arthur Beckwith of the Hampshires, who was ashore near the fort, took effective command at V Beach. Lieutenant-Colonel Henry Tizard was pretty much sidelined. On Beckwith's orders, Captain Richard Spencer-Smith and eighteen of his Hampshires, together with a party of Dublins and Munsters moved into the fort and establishing themselves on its northern side. There, they spent the night.[1]

Tizard said, about 2 a.m., he received a message by signal lamp telling him that troops had got into the fort, but were held up by snipers positioned high on the walls. The signal asked that the navy shell the fort an hour after daybreak. Tizard said he did not pass the request to the navy as he 'thought the situation would change before then.' He 'heard' that the troops on the left of the beach 'had got in touch with those on the cliff.' Presumably the men on the cliff were from the Worcestershires. Tizard said that the situation at daybreak, at about 5 a.m. on 26 April, was as follows. There had been heavy firing for most of the night. On the left, a small party of Munsters had worked their way off the beach up a nulla, the course of a dried-up stream. They were held up in the nulla. Along the beach, stretching from the foot of the nulla to the shore in front of the *River Clyde*, a group of men sheltered beneath a sandbank. Among them were dead and wounded. About twenty-five yards inland of them a line of thick barbed wire held on posts stretched across the entire front, protecting the Turkish positions. Further inland a parallel line of similar barbed wire also stretched across the Turkish front. A gap had been cut in the wire of the first line and about half a company had got through and were sheltering behind a wall, some of their comrades dead near them.[2]

Before dawn, the *Albion* moved in from the position she had occupied throughout 25 April. By 5.30 a.m., she had taken up station close to the beach. She opened fire ten minutes later. This enabled her to more effectively support the land operations. 'The success of her support on 26 April stands in clear contrast to her failure on the previous day and her ability to destroy from a range of only 600 yards [a] concealed machine-gun post, which could not even be seen from her previous position, confirms that a similarly close station on 25 April might well have provided material assistance to the troops who sheltered during the day under the earth bank.'[3]

Tizard said the majority of the troops ashore were on the right of the beach, near the fort. He could see some, in single file, moving around the corner of the fort, near Morto Bay. Given this, Tizard said that he did not pass on the message requesting supporting naval gunfire. He said that sniping was going on to a considerable extent. Looking at the troops sheltered beneath the sandbank in front of the *River Clyde*, Tizard was unable to see any officer or NCO among them. He said Military Landing Officer Captain George Stoney left the ship to lead this group. At about 6.30 a.m., Tizard saw an officer and a small party of men move from the right front of the fort towards a path which led between the fort and the end of the line of barbed wire protecting the Turkish positions. [Given the fact that Tizard could see them – and the mention of the end of the line of barbed wire – presumably the group moved to the left of the fort.] When the men were 'about half way up along the side of the Fort and opposite 2 windows in an abutment a machine gun opened up on them. None were hit. They jumped a wall on their left and got cover. I immediately sent word to HMS *Albion* who opened on [the machine gun] with good effect. The party then continued the advance and got in among some buildings on the left, where they were held up by some snipers.' About eight men who had been sheltering under the sandbank 'joined up with the first party, getting a little further in. [It was now about 7 a.m.] This party was then seen coming back and another party went up to them from the shore. Fire was then opened by guns onto some house where I had seen snipers and after a time the whole of this party went forward again and got well in to the village on the left side.'[4]

The previous night, Munsters Second Lieutenant Norman Dewhurst had come ashore with his machine-gun party. In order to get the necessary elevation to fire over the sandbank, they used dead bodies to build an emplacement. 'The scene before us in the morning light as we crouched on the beach was horrible and the smell intense.' He said that eleven Munsters officers had been killed the previous day (Battalion Commanding Officer Lieutenant-Colonel Henry Tizard recorded that four officers had been killed and one died of wounds). On source said that W Company had 162 killed, X Company 146 killed, Y Company 156 killed and Z Company 89 killed.[5]

The *Official History* said that, at daybreak, 'the sorely tried troops who had first landed were by this time on the verge of physical collapse'. While Tizard said that the majority of troops were on the right of the beach near the fort, the *Official History* said the "[T]he majority of [the] survivors were on the left of the beach, with orders to attack in the direction of Fort No. 1 [Ertuğrul Tabyasi] and to gain touch with the troops from W [Beach]. On the right of the beach, under the walls of the old fort, Major [Arthur] Beckwith had assembled the fresher troops, who had landed during the night. These, after a preliminary bombardment by the fleet, were to attack the fort and village ... issuing through a small gate which gave on to [a] steep path leading up from the Camber beach [to the village.]. As the result of a night reconnaissance, this route was thought to be the best line of approach to the village, for the main gate had been blocked by the Turks, and it was moreover under point-blank fire from the village itself. But the smaller gate, too, was afterwards found to be under fire from a small Turkish trench on the edge of the cliff, and troops emerging from it were to prove an easy target ... a number of determined snipers were still occupying points of vantage in the fort, and a machine-gun was firing from a hole in one of its bastions.' In the centre of the beach 'the wire was still intact, except for a small gap cut by the troops during the night. One company was to attack by the west of the old fort through this gap [presumably left of the fort]. [T]he remainder were to clear the fort and then to attack the village from the fort's eastern side.' When the fort and the village had been taken, an assault would be made on the Turkish strongpoint at the ruin of the fort on Hill 141 [Harapkale].[6]

'Before dawn Captain [Richard] Spencer-Smith's party [of eighteen Hampshires, together with a contingent of Dublins and Munsters] who had held the ruins during the night were withdrawn, to let the ships bombard Sedd-el-Bahr.'[7] But the fire from the ships was directed against the far side of the village. After waiting in vain for the ships to shorten their range, Beckwith received a message from the *River Clyde* asking why he wasn't advancing. Just as the troops had begun to move again, he received another message from the ship warning him that the navy was again about to fire on the fort. The troops were pulled back, but the ships again fired inland. Beckwith ordered the advance to resume.[8] The Valide's Fort encloses an area of 6.17 acres. The walls average 8 yards in height. Due to the uneven topography of the site, the fort is divided into upper and lower fortresses. The lower section is at sea level. The upper section is almost 18 yards above sea level. The main gate in the upper section faces the village. Only five of the original towers remain. Much of the building has disappeared as a result of harsh weather, earthquakes, war, and the removal of masonry by local residents for the construction of their homes.[9]

As he was awarded a posthumous Victoria Cross, it is a pity that it is unclear whether Doughty-Wylie led or indeed took part in the attack on the fort. His *London Gazette* citation for the Victoria Cross does not mention the attack on the fort. Nigel Steel and Peter Hart said that 'at about 9.00 he decided to land with the Military Landing Officer, Captain George Stoney. Leaving Stoney to organise the troops along the centre of the beach, Doughty-Wylie himself moved across towards the fort and started to assist Beckwith by leading up stragglers and reinforcements.'[10] Stephen Snelling said that Captain Stoney and Doughty-Wylie were aboard the *River Clyde* when, at 8.45 a.m., a message was received from Captain Garth Walford that his advance was slow. Stoney said that, soon after, Doughty-Wylie asked him to accompany him ashore. Dr Peter Burrows Kelly recorded in his diary that Doughty-Wylie 'returned [to the *River Clyde*] and drank a cup of tea' at about 11 a.m.[11] The *Official History* said that 'About noon Doughty-Wylie, who had been assisting Beckwith on the right and had just led 50 reinforcements to that flank placed himself at the head of the Royal Dublin Fusiliers and Royal Munster Fusiliers on the left of the fort' [and attacked the village].[12] Munsters Lieutenant Guy Nightingale is the only source who credits Doughty-Wylie with leading the attack on the fort.

> The Colonel took charge of the situation at once, and after collecting together the whole force, which consisted of the survivors of the Munster Fusiliers, the Dublin Fusiliers and two companies of the Hampshire Regiment under Major [Arthur] Beckwith, he ordered us to charge in one mass into the Castle and occupy it. He led the charge himself with the other officers, whom he ordered to form up in line in front of their respective regiments. The Castle was occupied finally, and the Turkish snipers found in it bayoneted, with very small loss to us.[13]

While sources differ as to whether or not Doughty-Wylie took part in the attack, there is absolutely no doubt as to who was the first man to enter the fort. Private Tom Cullen (10113), 1st Battalion Royal Dublin Fusiliers, was awarded the Distinguished Conduct Medal with the citation 'For conspicuous gallantry on the 26th April 1915 during the capture of Sedd-el-Bahr (Dardanelles). He was the first man to enter the fort.'[14] *Neill's Blue Caps* says that Lieutenant Lawrence

Boustead (who had been fined in Nuneaton for driving a motorbike without a light) also 'distinguished himself' in the attack on the fort. 'Leaving the men, who had momentarily taken cover from the heavy machine-gun fire, he ran fearlessly to the opening in the fort, repeatedly firing his revolver at the enemy within and causing their fire to slacken.'[15] He was mentioned in despatches by Sir Ian Hamilton.[16] Sources agree that the fort was captured quickly. But as soon as the troops reached the exit they were met by accurate fire and for some time were unable to progress. Munsters Lieutenant Guy Nightingale said the exit was:

> ... covered by a deadly fire from machine guns and marksmen hidden in the ruins of the village beyond. Anyone attempting to go through, or even walk past the gate, was killed instantly, and invariably shot through the head. Colonel Doughty-Wylie had a very narrow escape here. He was passing some distance in rear of the gateway when a bullet knocked the staff cap off his head. I happened to be quite close at the moment, and remember being struck by the calm way in which he treated the incident. He was carrying no weapon of any description at the time, only a small cane.[17]

Making no mention of Doughty-Wylie or troops other than the Hampshires, their official history said that further advance was held up by firing from the village on the fort's exit. Then, 'Placing himself at the head of the troops emerging from the fort gateway, Captain [Garth] Walford [Brigade-Major, Royal Artillery], ably assisted by Captain Alfred Addison, [Y Company] Hampshire Regiment, led them up into the village'. According to the Hampshire's history, 'In the village they met desperate resistance, the Turks contested every house and had to be ousted by bayonet. Some lay quiet, concealed in cellars or ruins, till our men passed by and then fired into their backs. Machine-gun fire and rifle fire from Hill 141 was troublesome.' Walford and Addison were killed in the fighting, the latter by 'a bomb'. Walford was awarded a posthumous Victoria Cross. It took nearly three hours before the Hampshires finished clearing the village. They finished with a charge against trenches beyond the village, for which every available man had been collected. Major Arthur Beckwith headed the charge, brandishing an axe with which he cut a cable it was believed led to Kum Kale. Pressing on, the Hampshires cleared a row of windmills on the hill overlooking Morto Bay.[18] Ahead of them, about forty-five degrees to their left front, was Hill 141, on which stood a Turkish strongpoint in the ruins of an old fort (Harapkale).

∞

At 10.15 a.m. the *Albion*'s log recorded that wounded were taken aboard the ship. Meanwhile, on the left side of V Beach, the hoped for assistance from the direction of W Beach had failed to materialise. At nightfall on 25 April, the 4th Worcestershires, commanded by Lieutenant Douglas Calley, had been holding a line from Hill 138 to east of the Helles lighthouse. At 8.45 a.m., Brigade-Major Garth Walford sent a message to 29th Division headquarters. 'Advance through Sedd-el-Bahr is slow. Am receiving no support on my left.' This had been preceded by a message from Calley, at 8.33 a.m., 'Situation unchanged since this morning. Fairly hot fire maintained against my trenches from the direction of Sedd-el-Bahr.'[19]

Major Weir de Lancey Williams had gone to the left of V Beach in an effort to lead the troops there to link up with those coming from W Beach. Unsuccessful in this, at some time prior to 9 a.m., he sent a message to Doughty-Wylie aboard the *River Clyde* saying he was going to W Beach to see conditions there, as further progress at V Beach seemed impossible. (Presumably he intended going to W Beach by sea.)[20]

∞

The Turkish strongpoint on Hill 141 was inland of the mid-point of V Beach. Troops on the middle of the beach, who were preparing to assault the strongpoint, risked coming under fire from the village of Sedd el Bahr on their right. Thus it was vital that the left side of the village – the side nearest to the assault from the beach – be cleared of snipers. While available sources are somewhat lacking in clarity, it would appear that Doughty-Wylie led an attack which cleared the left side of the village before an assault was made on Hill 141. Munsters Lieutenant Guy Nightingale said:

Colonel Doughty-Wylie took me up one of the corner turrets of the Old Castle, and pointed out to me the way he intended to carry out the assault. There was a strong redoubt on the top [of Hill 141], but he decided that the remnants of the three battalions should assault simultaneously immediately after the bombardment. He was extraordinarily confident that everything would go well, and the hill won by sunset, and I think it was due much to his spirit of confidence that he had been able to overcome the enormous difficulties with only such exhausted and disordered troops as he had to deal with. His sole idea and determination was that the hill should be taken that day at all costs. As the time was getting nearer for the bombardment to cease, the Colonel gave his final orders to the few remaining officers before the assault.[21]

Among the few officers who had survived the previous day's landing was Dubliner Major Cecil Grimshaw DSO, of the Blue Caps. Before going into a flashback to tell the story of the troops billeted in Warwickshire and north Oxfordshire, *The Story Behind the Monument* begins with Grimshaw rallying his Dubs. 'The manner in which Major Grimshaw sought to rally his men before their desperate foray is significant. Avoiding recourse to Shakespearean rhetoric he simply asked them: 'Do you want to go back to Nuneaton?' The prospect of returning to the Warwickshire town in which they had been billeted clearly appealed to the Dublins, who cheered in response. 'Very well, then,' said Grimshaw, 'make a brilliant charge and may the best men live to return to Nuneaton.' With that he led his men forward ... Major Grimshaw's rallying cry, which must surely be unique in the annals of British military history, was also, of course, a considerable tribute to Nuneaton and its people – the *Nuneaton Observer* reported the story under the heading 'Nuneaton Immortalised'.[22]

The *Albion*'s log recorded that 'all forenoon' it was shelling trenches to the right of Hill 141. 'About noon [Doughty-Wylie], who had hitherto been assisting Beckwith on the right and had just led 50 reinforcements to that flank placed himself at the head of the Munster and Dublin Fusiliers on the left of the old fort. The advance began to make progress.'[23] According to Lieutenant Guy Nightingale of the Munsters, 'The village was an awful snag. Every house and corner was full of snipers and you had only to show yourself in the streets to have a bullet in your head ... we lost a lot of men and officers ... It was rotten fighting, nothing to be seen of the enemy but fellows being knocked out everywhere. I got one swine of a Turk with my revolver, when searching a house for snipers but he nearly had me first.'[24]

∽∽

Meanwhile, Military Landing Officer, Captain George Stoney had gone to the middle of V Beach. He began to collect groups of unwounded soldiers, who did not have an officer to lead them. Aboard the *River Clyde*, Lieutenant-Colonel Henry Tizard received a message from Doughty-Wylie that he had got through the village and was in a good position to attack Hill 141. Tizard sent a written message to Stoney, informing him of Doughty-Wylie's situation and ordering him to making a supporting attack.[25] 'It was no easy task organising the scattered groups. Any movement along the foreshore invited instant Turkish retaliation, and it was not until nearly 1.30 p.m. that Stoney was ready. Leading the assault [was] a party of Munster Fusiliers with orders to cut a way through the wire.'[26]

Among the Munsters was twenty-six-year-old Corporal William Cosgrove. From Ballinookera, near Aghada, County Cork, he was 6ft 6in in height.

Our job was to dash ahead, face the trenches bristling with rifles and machine guns, and destroy the wire entanglements – that is, to cut them here and there with our pliers. Fifty men were detailed for the work; poor Sergeant-Major [Alfred] Bennett led us, but just as we made the dash – oh, such a storm of lead was concentrated on us, for the Turks knew of our intention. Our Sergeant-Major was killed – a bullet through the brain.[27] I then took charge; shouted to the boys to come on. From the village near at hand [to the right] there came a terrible fire to swell the murderous hail of bullets from the trenches. In the village they fired from doors and windows, and from that advantage they could comfortably take aim. The dash was quite 100 yards, and I don't know whether I ran or prayed the faster – I wanted to try and succeed in my work, and I also wanted to have the benefit of dying with a prayer on my mind. I can tell you that it is not fortunately given to everyone to note the incidents that seem to be the last in your life, and you never feeling better or stronger. Well, some of us got close up to the wire, and we started to cut it with pliers. You might as well try and snip Cloyne Round Tower with a lady's scissors, and you would not hurt yourself either. The wire was of great strength, strained as tight as a fiddle-string, and so full of spikes or thorns that you could not get the cutters between. 'Heavens,' said I, 'we're done'; a moment later I threw the pliers from me. 'Pull them up,' I roared. Put your arms round them and pull them out of the ground!' I dashed at the first one; heaved and strained, and then it came into my arms, the same as you would lift a child. I believe there was wild cheering when they saw what I was at, but I only heard the scream of bullets and saw dust rising all from where they hit. I could not tell how many I pulled up. I did my best, and the boys that were left with me were every bit as good as myself, and I do wish they all got some recognition. When the wire was down the rest of the lads came on like 'devils,' and notwithstanding the pulverising fire, they reached the trenches … [The Turks] gave us great resistance, but we got to their trenches, and won about 200 yards length by 20 yards deep, and 700 yards from the shore … A machine-gun sent some bullets into me, and strange, I was wounded before I reached the trench, though I did not realise it. When I got to the trench I did my own part and later collapsed. One of the bullets struck me in the side, and passed clean through me. It struck the left hook of my tunic, then entered my body, took a couple of splinters off my backbone, but of course did not injure the spinal column, and passed out on

Corporal William Cosgrove breaks through the Turkish barbed wire.

my right side, knocking off the other belt hook. I was taken up feeling pretty
bad, when I came to my senses, and considered seriously wounded. I was
removed to Malta Hospital, where two operations, and the splinters of my
backbone removed [*sic*].[28]

Aboard the *River Clyde*, fellow-Irishman Surgeon Peter Burrows Kelly witnessed
Cosgrove's bravery and noted in his diary: 'The manner in which the man worked
out in the open will never be forgotten by those who witnessed it.'[29] Four days
after the action, Second Lieutenant Hugh Brown of the 1st Munsters reported
to the officer commanding W Company on 'a most conspicuous act of bravery
displayed by Corporal Cosgrove.' His account differs somewhat from Cosgrove's.

I was ordered by a staff captain [George Stoney] to collect all the men of my
battalion that were on the beach, as a general advance at all costs had to be
made to take Hill No. 141. After a great deal of effort I managed to collect
about forty NCOs and men. On a given signal I advanced over very exposed
ground being under the fire of two machine guns and snipers. After we had
advanced 40 yards from the beach we were held up by about 60 yards of
thickly constructed barbed-wire entanglement. Having only one pair of wire
cutters our progress was very slow getting through, though Private [James]
Bryant [8385] was doing his best to cut a passage through the wire. Corporal
Cosgrove, seeing our difficulty jumped into the wire and hauled down the
heavy wooden stakes to which the wire was attached to a distance of about
30 yards long in quite a short space of time. I personally consider he deserves

the height of praise for such a courageous act and was much impressed to see him, though wounded in the back, leading his section shortly before the enemy were driven from their trenches and [Hill 141] captured.[30]

Blue Cap Sergeant-Major George Baker of Y Company said that 'Lieutenant [Robert] Bernard and Second Lieutenant [William] Andrews [both of Y Company] were together with about 20 men of X and Y Companies, and they took cover behind a wall 5ft 6in high. They were being fired at from a house in the village. Andrews stood in a gap made by a shell, and he was directing the fire when he was shot through the heart. Lieutenant Bernard called on the others to follow him, and saying "Come on, boys," he dashed through the gap when he was shot.'[31] While Baker's account does not give the exact location of the two officers, his comment that they were fired at 'from a house in the village' would put them outside the village and thus coming from the beach with the village on their right. Twenty-three-year-old Robert Bernard had been posted to the Blue Caps in August 1912. He was the son of Maud and John Bernard, Church of Ireland Archbishop of Dublin. His father's diaries and other papers survive in Trinity College, Dublin. He wrote 'our dearest boy was killed last Sunday in action. [In fact he was killed on Monday. This would suggest his parents were initially told that he had been killed on the day of the landing.] Poor Maud is broken hearted. My darling Robert – it is hard to believe.' On Sunday 2 May he wrote, 'The [bell] ringers [at St Canice's Cathedral, Kilkenny] rang a muffled peel for our son.' Further on in the same entry is, 'It is heart-breaking to write letters about Rob all day long. Telegram from King and Queen.'[32] Robert Bernard is buried in V Beach Cemetery. As the exact location of his grave is not known, he is commemorated by a special memorial. Thirty-two-year-old William Andrews was the husband of Esther Mary Andrews, 11 Park Road, Polsloe Park, Exeter. According to the *Kildare Observer* of 7 May 1915, he was the son of a former Sergeant-Major at the Dubs Naas Depot. He had been promoted from the ranks in February 1915. He is buried in Grave F.13 in V Beach Cemetery.

Second Lieutenant Norman Dewhurst of the Munsters said that, at 8 a.m., those on the beach were ordered to advance. 'As the day passed men were being killed right and left, we were replenishing our water supplies from the water bottles of our dead comrades. I had a lucky escape when a bullet passed through my pack; all I had at that moment was a slight scratch across the back of my hand. My guns killed a lot of Turks that day – we were taking no prisoners.' He also said that 'Behind us in the cove the *River Clyde* was still the object of heavy fire.'[33]

At 12.52 p.m. the *Albion*'s log recorded that the ship 'fired at enemy seen on left of the castle.' Presumably this was the left side of the village, to assist the force commanded by Doughty-Wylie and Grimshaw. At 1 p.m. the *Albion* recorded that shells fell astern of the ship, presumably counter-fire from Turkish artillery. On open ground west of the village a line was cut through a line of barbed wire that ran roughly south-west to north-east, parallel with the edge of the village. At 1.24 p.m. the *Albion* 'ceased firing at request of the military'. According to Nigel Steel and Peter Hart, 'The final attack began at about 2 p.m. and developed in two separate directions. Led by [Hampshires Major Arthur] Beckwith, the men on the right flank charged northeast, parallel with the cliffs above Morto Bay, towards the edge of the village. At the same time the left flank, led from the front by Doughty-Wylie moved directly to the north against the strongpoint on Hill 141 and linked up with the men led by Stoney.'[34] Guy Nightingale said, 'When the order came to fix bayonets the men scarcely waited for any orders, but all joined up together in one mass, and swept cheering up through an orchard and over a cemetery to the first line of wire entanglement, through which was a way out leading past the deserted Turkish trenches to the summit of the hill.'[35] The troops charging from the village met those assaulting from the beach. Racing across open ground, together they surged towards the ruin of the fort on Hill 141. Captain George Stoney said, 'We did not come under any heavy fire only losing about four men wounded. We rushed the line of trenches and saw the Turks clearing out. Not many getting away alive. The place proved to have been held by only a very few men – certainly if there had been more we could not have got up as easily as we did.'[36] According to Guy Nightingale, 'On the top [of Hill 141] was a flat space surrounded by a moat 20ft deep with only one entrance leading up over it, through which the assaulting troops were led by Colonel Doughty-Wylie and Major Grimshaw.'[37] The *Albion*'s log recorded '1.37 p.m. Troops reached left summit. 1.45 p.m. Troops nearing summit. 1.48 p.m. Main party coming from Seddul Bahr,' suggesting perhaps that the Doughty-Wylie-Grimshaw force attacked the left of Hill 141 slightly before the Beckwith force attacked its right. The log recorded '1.57 p.m. Final assault. 2 p.m. Troops entered [ruins of] old castle.' As the log has an entry '2.07 p.m. Support advancing up hill,' perhaps Stoney's force arrived in the closing stages of the assault.

Both Doughty-Wylie and Grimshaw were killed in the moment of victory. Unfortunately the deaths of both brave men may have occurred due to some recklessness of their part. Private William Flynn of the Munsters said:

[A]fter we took [Hill 141] we dug in a bit of a trench and laid down there and Colonel Doughty-Wylie was with us. He [had gone] all through the village. I never forgot him because he had one puttee on and all he had was a walking stick. I didn't see a revolver and he had come all through the village with us and, he was stood up – I was laid down here with the company – and he was stood up alongside of me, and his orderly and they were shouting to him to get down. 'Get down, sir, you'll get [hit].' Because there was sniping. And he wouldn't and an explosive bullet hit him right here, just below the eye, blew all the side of his face out. And his orderly got killed.[38]

The man described as Doughty-Wylie's orderly may have been interpreter Maurice Constantinidi.[39] In a letter of 15 May 1915, to hospitalised Blue Cap Officer Captain David French, then Dublins Commanding Officer Lieutenant Henry Desmond O'Hara said, '[Captain Herbert Crozier] behaved splendidly in the attack on Hill 141 on the 26th and I sent his name in for gallantry and also Grimshaw's who simply threw his life away by standing up and shouting in the way he always used to do – there was no need for it and we could ill spare him, but he was a real brave man and no mistake.'[40] According to Nigel Steel and Peter Hart '[Doughty-Wylie's] reckless disregard for his own personal safety was perhaps the determining factor of his decisive leadership.'[41] Presumably the same could be said of his fellow leader Cecil Grimshaw. The apparently similar nature of both their deaths might seem to suggest that something was occurring that caught their attention and which they felt needed to be addressed.

Shortly after Doughty-Wylie's death Major Weir de Lancey Williams arrived on top of Hill 141.

I found him lying dead inside the castle on top of the hill. As soon as I real-ised he was dead I took his watch, money and a few things I could find and had him buried where he fell. I had this done at once, having seen such disgusting sights of unburied dead in the village that I could not bear to see him lying there. This was all done hurriedly as I had to reorganise the line and think of further advances and digging in; we just buried him as he lay and I said the Lord's Prayer over his grave and bid him goodbye. I am firmly of the opinion that poor old Doughty-Wylie realised he would be killed in this war; he was rather a fatalist. I am also convinced that he went singing cheerily to his end.[42]

According to Stephen Snelling:

[Doughty-Wylie's death] was, of course, the stuff of legend and, in the hands of the Press, ever eager to find new heroes, that was precisely what it became … So Doughty-Wylie became the Gallipoli campaign's first hero, overshadowing all others involved in the gallant break-out from the beach at Sedd-el-Bahr. There would be no posthumous honours for Grimshaw or Addison … Only the actions of Garth Walford were deemed to rival those of Doughty-Wylie, and their names were linked together in a joint citation for the award of their posthumous VCs which was published in the *London Gazette* on 23 June 1915. They were the first Victoria Crosses of the campaign to be announced.[43]

Brigade-Major Mynors Farmar, said, 'The Royal Munster Fusiliers and Royal Dublin Fusiliers, with a half-battalion of the Hampshire Regiment, organised by Colonel Doughty-Wylie, and led by him and such officers as [Dublins] Majors [Cecil] Grimshaw and [Edward] Molesworth, [and Munsters Captain Thomas] Tomlinson, [Guy] Nightingale, and [Lieutenant Frederick] Waldegrave, did magnificently … The fallen Grimshaw was spoken of as might have been Roland of Charlemagne's day by the witnesses of his deeds in the throes of close combat.'[44] Nigel Steel and Peter Hart said that Munsters Lieutenant Guy Nightingale played a conspicuous part in the clearance of Sedd el Bahr on 26 April and for his actions was specifically named in the *Official History* p. 277. Among Nightingale's papers was a memorandum signed by Guy Geddes, his CO, on 1 November 1915 that states 'from what Colonel Doughty-Wylie said before his death, I am of [the] opinion that Captain Nightingale would have been strongly recommended for the V.C.' Steel and Hart said, 'Instead he was mentioned in despatches.'[45]

Second Lieutenant Hugh Brown's report formed the basis of a recommendation for the award of the Victoria Cross to Corporal William Cosgrove. The VC, however, was not 'gazetted' (announced in the *London Gazette*) until 23 August, two months after the announcements of the VCs to Doughty-Wylie and Walford. The citation read: 'For most conspicuous bravery in the leading of his section with great dash during our attack from the beach on the east of Cape Helles, on the Turkish positions, on the 26th April, 1915. Corporal Cosgrove on this occasion pulled down the posts of the enemy's high wire entanglements single-handed, notwithstanding a terrific fire from both the front and flanks, thereby greatly contributing to the successful clearing of the heights.'[46]

Peter Hart said that, 'the Turks had been ordered to retire towards Krithia in the late morning, but as this would have left them exposed to fire from the Allied ships, they had decided to try to cling on till nightfall.' Major Mahmut Sabri, Commander of the 3rd Battalion, 26th Regiment, recorded that:

> Our soldiers were still active and were pinning down the enemy. The enemy was advancing in rushes, he was unable to assault. Many of those who rushed forward were being hit and there were many casualties. But there was no telling in what strength the landing had been made. Not an inch of ground remained which was not shelled either by the shrapnel of the fleet or by the many machine guns of the infantry.

At about 1.30p.m it was decided that the men in the vicinity of Sedd el Bahr would have to retreat. Just a few survivors of the 10 Company, 3rd Battalion, 26th Regiment remained on Hill 141. 'Their position was desperate indeed: trenches smashed, only a few men left on their feet and fast running out of ammunition.' Major Mahmut Sabri said that:

> Now even withdrawal was very difficult because the enemy fleet's fire was very intense. There was no information from our units, only enemy could be seen at every hand. It was abundantly clear that the enemy would destroy our soldiers as they retreated with the fire of their fleet, his infantry and his machine guns. In fact our line of retreat had had been encircled on right and left. In truth there was no course left but to flee. The distance between us was 500-600 meters.

According to Peter Hart, 'When the final British assault swept up on to Hill 141 at around 2.30 p.m. on 26 April, not many Turks made the final stand. Their wounded had to be left, but they were confident the British would respect them. As they retreated, keeping to ground as best they could, they took every chance to snipe at the advancing British.' [47] Using a report by Major Mahmut Sabri, Tim Travers noted an apparent collapse of Turkish morale.

> [T]he remaining Turkish troops at V, outflanked by the S Beach landing, retreated up the Kirte and Kanlidere stream beds, leaving about 70 wounded behind, who were weeping and complaining. No one, except a stretcher bearer and a trumpeter, followed [Major] Mahmut [Sabri] to the second line of defence because of heavy Allied naval shelling. Although these two men shouted 'The second line of defence is here. The major is

here, come on,' none did so. Eventually Mahmut's men retreated to within about one and a half kilometres from Krithia around 5.30 p.m. on 26 April. Casualties were 5 officers and 570 men.[48]

Lieutenant-Colonel Henry Tizard reported that, '[Hill 141] was taken at 2.25 p.m. and I then moved my headquarters [from the *River Clyde*] through the village to the same spot arriving on the hill at 2.45 p.m.' At 2.32 p.m. 29th Division head-quarters sent a message to Wolley Dodd at W Beach telling him that 'our men from V now swarming into old castle on top of Hill 141. Push forward your right to join up with old castle and consolidate your position.'[49] At about 4 p.m. the Worcestershires advanced to bring their right flank in line with the left flank of the V Beach force on Hill 141. 'By five o'clock the [Munsters were] in [an] out-post position half a mile in advance of the old Fort and connection had been established with the Worcesters on the left.'[50] At 5.19 p.m. the *Albion* recorded that shells were falling on the *River Clyde* 'from southern shore' (i.e. from near Kum Kale). At 5.30 p.m. she 'opened fire on southern shore'. Tizard's report on the landing, dated 28 April 1915, recorded that four of the Munsters officers had been killed and one had died of wounds. (Killed: Major Charles Jarrett, Captain

Window in memory of Gerald Pollard. All Saints' church,
Piddletrenthide, Dorset. (Courtesy of Letitia Pollard)

Edward Dorman, Lieutenant Gerald Pollard and Second Lieutenant Timothy
Sullivan. Died of wounds: Captain Eric Henderson.) He recorded twelve as
wounded (including Norman Dewhurst, who had not been wounded). He said
that about 600 non-commissioned officers and men had been killed.

Captain David French of the Blue Caps, who had been wounded the previous day, recorded that:

> I superintended the wounded being taken off that afternoon and then was
> sent off to the Caledonia – a hospital receiving ship. The wounded had a
> ghastly time – none of the Dublins being attended to – except with field dress-
> ings – by a medical man for 36 hours.[51] Any doctor who [attempted to land on
> V Beach] was immediately knocked out and eventually orders were given to
> them that they were on no account to land until V Beach was 'safe'. [The Blue
> Caps medical Officer Lieutenant Henry de Boer had been badly wounded.]
> We ran terribly short of water as each of us carried three days iron rations –
> a service water bottle filled or a beer-bottle of lime juice and water (in the
> pack) only. Luckily I took a considerable quantity of morphia [*sic*] ashore
> which greatly alleviated the sufferings of those – in some cases smashed to
> pieces. P. [possibly 'pater' i.e. latin for father] kindly sent me weekly a bottle of
> Liq. Brandy after leaving England and I had one of these with me![52]

At 10 p.m. the *Albion*'s log recorded that a boat carrying nine Turkish prisoners arrived alongside. (This contradicts Norman Drewhurst's statement that
no prisoners were taken.) At 10.30 p.m. the log recorded that a boat carrying wounded left the *Albion* for a hospital ship. Meanwhile, as the Dublins,
Munsters and Hampshires were dug in about half a mile in advance of Sedd el
Bahr, French troops began to land on V Beach at 10.30 p.m. They came to take
over the right side of the 29th Division's line. The previous day, 25 April, French
troops had landed at Kum Kale with three objectives: 'to distract the Turks
from the main landings [on Gallipoli], to prevent the Turks from bringing
reinforcements over from Asia to Gallipoli at short notice, and vitally, to stop
the Turks from shelling V Beach [during the landing.]'[53] Having spent the night
of 25 April at Kum Kale, the French force was evacuated on 26 April. At 4 a.m.
General Vandenberg, commander of the Brigade Métropolitaine, presented
himself at Lieutenant-Colonel Henry Tizard's headquarters on Hill 141 and
V Beach formally became part of the French operational area.

Among the Blue Caps who had died on 26 April were twenty-year-old John
Condron from Rush, County Dublin, twenty-four-year-old John Gaskin from
Talbot Street, Dublin, Charles Garvey from Portadown, County Armagh,

Philip Rawlinson from Highgate, London and Andrew Dunne, Patrick Dunne and Thomas Dunne, three non-related men who are commemorated by Special Memorials A. 47, A.48 and A. 49 in V Beach Cemetery. Also killed was Robert Roleston, who a month previously had written to his mother, Elizabeth, in Dublin: 'But I hope I will get out of this war alright. If you watch the papers closely you will know whether I am wounded or killed.'

Among the Dirty Shirts who died that day were James Boyer, from London; thirty-one-year-old Michael Desmond from Millstreet, County Cork; twenty-four-year-old William Gwynne, who had been born in Rawalpindi, India, suggesting that his father, also William, had been a soldier and probably a Munster, Michael McGee from County Clare; Michael Reidy from County Kerry; and Edward Oldall, born in Kent, who enlisted in India, again possibly the son of a Munster. Also killed was twenty-three-year-old Martin O'Malley, from Limerick, of Y Company. After the soldiers were issued with new boots in Coventry, ten-year-old Elsie from the fruit shop in Earlsdon Street had heard him say quietly: 'I expect that these are for my grave.' A photo of Elsie was found among his effects and returned to her family with a covering letter.

Among the men who had survived the fighting that day were Dublin Fusiliers ex-foundlings Stephen Filbey and Harry Fox, Jack Mallaghan, Nicky Smyth, whose grandfather had come in support of the Turks sixty-one years previously and Benjamin Hurt who had arrived in India as part of a draft in 1910 and became a member of the battalion's machine-gun team. He was one of the few members of the machine-gun team to survive the V Beach landing unscathed. Among the surviving Munsters were brothers Bob and Peter Jordan, whose father had come in support of the Turks sixty-one years previously and William (Paddy) Long from Glanworth, County Cork, whose brother, like Sam Mallaghan, had been killed the previous day.

Many Turks were killed defending Sedd el Bahr. Most of their names are lost to history. But a few names are remembered. In 1962 a memorial with some of their names was erected above V Beach. Called 'The Sergeant Yahya Memorial (Yahya Çavuş Anti)', the inscriptions are in Turkish. The one on the north panel reads, 'This memorial was built in 1962 by the Society to Assist the Memorials of the Çanakkale Martyrs'. On the west panel is a poem by Nail Memik, Governor of Çanakkale province in 1962. 'Sergeant Yahya and a hero platoon, Fought with all their hearts against three regiments. The enemy thought these wonderful men were a division, They sought God and joined him in the evening.' The inscription on the south panel (opposite the entrance gate) reads, 'On 25 April in the year of 1915, 63 heroes, under the command of a Sergeant of Ezine, stopped 6 enemy battalions on this shore and held them for 10 hours. They died, but they saved the Dardanelles and became part of history.' The East panel is a roll of honour. It gives the names of eighteen members of 10 Company, 3rd Battalion, 26th Regiment who died. 'Lieutenant Abdürrahim, Commander of 1 Platoon, Halil Ağa from Karacaören, Çanakkale province, Ali Ağa from Özbek, Mustafa from Özbek, Halil from Özbek, Mehmet Ali from Kurşunlu, Big Halil from Saricaeli, Black Hüseyin from Işiklar, Mehmet Ali from Sarik, Black Mehmet from Belen, Mustafa from Kepez, Corporal Kadir from Gökçali, Black Mehmet from Sanbeyli, Hasan from Çinarli, Mustafa from the Ezine village of Akköy, Mehmet from Baliki, Mehmet Ağa from Hayrabolu town in Tekirdağ province.' Seddulbahir village mosque, completed in 1986, preserves the memory of Sergeant Yahya: the Yahya Çavuş Camii or Sergeant Yahya Mosque. On the other side of the track, closer to Ertuğrul Tabyasi (Fort No.1), there is a recently established grave with an inscription in the whitewashed headstone 'Halil İbrahim, ö. 1915' 'The grave is probably not authentic and may in fact have more to do with tourist promotion today than with commemorating the dead of 1915.'[54] The Sergeant Yahya Memorial has the potential to confuse or mislead visitors. Yahya Çavuş (Sergeant Yahya) from Ezine was a member of 12 Company, 3rd Battalion, 26th Regiment. Edward J. Erickson's detailed study of Ottoman military records shows Yahya and his men defended a Turkish strongpoint located on Gözcübaba, where the Helles Memorial now stands. V Beach was defended by the men of 10 Company, 3rd Battalion, 26th Regiment, eighteen of whose, previously quoted, names appear on the Sergeant Yahya Memorial. It is fitting that Yahya Çavuş and his sixty-three men should be remembered for their courage during the fight at Gözcübaba. Given that the scene of their stand is occupied by the Helles Memorial, it is understandable that their monument be located at nearby V Beach and the opportunity taken to also record the names of some of the men from 10 Company who died defending the beach. It is a pity, however, that officialdom has allowed the courage of the men from 10 Company, who actually defended V Beach, to be overshadowed by appearing to incorrectly suggest that Yahya Çavuş and his sixty-three men defended the beach.

Major Mahmut Sabri, Commanding Officer of the 3rd Battalion, 26th Regiment, reported on the evening of 26 April that he had lost six officers and 630 men from his pre-battle strength of 1,128 officers and men. That night, Colonel Halil Sami reported to Brigadier-General Esat of III Corps that the 9th Division had lost ten officers and 1,887 men from the 25th and 26th Regiments.[55] Sabri said, 'I consider [that the battalion's] resistance and tenacity on the Seddulbahir shore on [25/26] April ... is a fine example of Turkish heroism.'[56]

CHAPTER 8

Fighting and Dying

The constant and vicious fighting of the early days of the campaign had taken their toll. "Simply tons of fellows are going off their heads from strain and worry -- mostly fellows who have been wounded and come back. But there are very few now who have gone through from the beginning and are not the worse for it".
Irish Voices from the Great War, *Myles Dungan*

On the morning of 27 April, following 'a somewhat fraught interview with Hunter-Weston', Lieutenant-Colonel Henry Tizard was removed from command of the 1st Munsters, 'for his apparent failure to achieve a quicker success at V Beach.'[1] Norman Dewhurst said, 'Our C.O. Colonel Tazard [sic] who never got ashore from the River Clyde [was] recalled, his age was against him for this type of warfare.'[2] Speaking of Tizard, Unwin had said to Weymss, 'I soon saw he was not the man for the awful position he found himself in, it does not inspire men who don't know what is going to happen to see a little man running about with a papier-mache megaphone in his hands all day doing nothing, and he never landed, till the show was over, but you know about him.'[3] Tizard had taken over from Carington Smith and in turn had appointed Major William Hutchinson to command the Munsters. Hutchinson was now confirmed in this command. While Tizard was criticised for his performance at V Beach, one person has spoken of the benefit of at least one of his decisions. Tony Jordon, whose father Bob and uncle Peter travelled aboard the *River Clyde* under Tizard's command said, 'By chance, I once met him, at a memorial service, fifty years after Gallipoli. To me he did not seem especially prepossessing – a little man, as I recall, a bit like Captain Mainwaring in *Dad's Army*. I did not suspect then, what I suspect now, that I might owe my very existence to one of his unspectacular decisions.'[4] (i.e. to not blindly continue sending the Munsters down the gangplank to face Turkish bullets.)

The Turks withdrew northwards to prepared defences south of Krithia. This allowed the British and French to move inland from the beaches. By the afternoon of 27 April, with the 86th Brigade – including the Dublins and Munsters – in reserve, they had advanced about 2 miles, towards Krithia. The first Battle of Krithia was fought on 28 April, but the Dublins and Munsters were not involved in the fighting. The outcome was stalemate. Beginning the day with between 8,000 and 9,000 men, the 29th Division had about 2,000 casualties, including a high proportion of officers. Out of about 5,000, the French lost 27 officers and 974 men.[5]

On Wednesday 28 April, following the wounding of Major Edward Molesworth and Captain James Grove, command of the Blue Caps passed to Lieutenant Henry Desmond O'Hara, the sole remaining officer. He had gone from commanding a platoon during the landing to commanding a company the next day and then, on or about 28 April, to commanding the battalion. His command did not last for long, however as, on 29 April, due to the losses they had sustained at V Beach, the Blue Caps and the Dirty Shirts were temporarily amalgamated into one battalion under Major William Hutchinson, of the Munsters, with the Munsters making up W and X Companies and the Dubs Y and Z Companies. The Munsters had twelve officers and 588 men. The Dubs had 1 officer and 344 men, by far the lowest numbers of the twelve battalions in the 29th Division.[6] (In one of those discrepancies that often occur whenever numbers are mentioned in connection with historical events, the Munsters history said that, at the time of its formation, the Dubsters had eight officers and 770 men.)

According to *Neill's Blue Caps*, in operations to the end of April, the Blue Caps had lost ten officers and 152 other ranks, killed or died of wounds. Among the officers were Lieutenant-Colonel Richard Rooth, Majors Edwyn Fetherstonhaugh and Cecil Grimshaw, Captains Denis Anderson, George Dunlop and William Higginson, Lieutenants Robert Bernard, Raymond de Lusignan and Reginald Corbet and Second Lieutenant William Andrews. Thirteen officers and 329 men were wounded. The officers were Major Edward Molesworth, Captains Herbert Crozier, David French, James Grove, Arthur Johnson, Alexander Molony and John Mood and Lieutenants Lawrence Boustead, Colin Carruthers and Francis Lanigan-O'Keeffe, and Second Lieutenants Joseph Hosford, Cuthbert Maffett and John Walters. Twenty-one NCOs and men were reported missing. Chaplain Father William Finn had been killed and Medical Officer Lieutenant Henry de Boer wounded. On the day the Dubsters were created, two Blue Caps died of wounds. Private William Conroy was from Portarlington, County Laois. Private John Lambert was from

Milltown, County Dublin. Sergeant Joseph Skerritt from Birr, County Offaly was recorded as killed in action that day. As the battalion was not in action, he may have been shot by a sniper.

According to O'Hara, 'It was an awful time, and at the end I was the only officer left in the battalion, as Grove and Molesworth were both wounded, though only slightly. The Turks made no attempt to follow up their advantage, and we were able to dig in. We remained there for two nights, and on the third the Turks advanced, 20,000 strong, and tried to break through the line.'[7] A question arises around the dating of the Turkish attack. In *Neill's Blue Caps*, O'Hara's account is immediately preceded by the sentence 'Here is [O'Hara's account] of the happenings on April 28th and following days and nights'. This means that if the Turks attacked on the third night, the assault was on the night of Friday 30 April. Yet, the *Official History* of the campaign, the History of the Royal Munster Fusiliers and the other sources on the campaign say that the night attack occurred on the night of 1 May. The point is important because the Commonwealth War Graves Commission record the Blue Caps as having more than eighty men killed on 30 April, a day on which no large-scale fighting occurred. The Commission record no Dublins killed on 1 May, a date on which the Turks made a large-scale attack. The reason might lie in the admitted exhaustion of the Blue Caps senior officer (later quoted), though one might have thought Major William Hutchinson, Commanding Officer of the Dubsters, or his adjutant would have been responsible for signing casualty returns. (a possible contributing factor in the confusion was the fact that Acting Adjutant Edward Dorman was killed on 1 May.) To further add to the confusion, Norman Dewhurst's memoirs, published in 1968, also gives the date of the attack as 30 April.

> The weather was turned wet and cold and some rifle fire was exchanged with the Turks who had their lines about 200 yards away. I took a rifle and telescope and spent the day [April 30th] looking at the Turkish lines for snipers. When I got back into our line I was pleased to receive a piece of bread and butter. It was wonderful after the days on dry biscuits. We had at this period a number of cases where men's nerves cracked, the result of what they had been through, and we had to get them out of the line. That night the Turks launched a night attack about 10 p.m. and at about 11 p.m. I received a wound in the neck (the doctor told me afterwards the bullet had passed within 1/8 of an inch of my spinal cord). They broke through our lines – but they never got back. One of my machine gun teams, a sergeant and six men, was wiped out in one go with a grenade.[8]

He incorrectly said the Dubsters were relieved by the Howe Battalion at 6 a.m. on 1 May. The Munsters war diary said they were relieved by the 4th Worcesters and 1/5th Royal Scots on 2 May.

Saturday, the first day of May, saw the Dubsters in a trench at Kirte Dere (Krithia Nullah), beside the course of a dried-up stream. 'The early hours of the night of the 1st May were quiet, but at 10 p.m. the Turkish artillery opened with a crash. A few minutes afterwards, with cries of 'Allah!', dense masses of Turks assaulted the Allied line.'[9] The first part of the British front to be attacked was the Dubsters trench, where one of the assaulting Turkish columns had outdistanced the troops on either flank. Nightingale recorded in his diary: 'they had crept up through the gorse and bayoneted most of the men in their sleep and swept on. Whatever remained of our (company) retired. I ran up the line shouting to them to get back.' The Dubsters were forced from part of the trench. Westlake (see Footnote 17) quotes/summarises the Munsters war diary as saying, 'It was noted by one witness that many of the dead had been killed while sleeping and their trench ankle-deep in blood.' According to the *Official History* of the Gallipoli campaign, 'A company of the Royal Fusiliers under Captain North Bomford regained the lost trench, and the 1/5th Royal Scots, who were in reserve, succeeded in driving back the Turks, who had penetrated the British line.'[10] A platoon from the Dubsters W Company, composed of Munsters, was in reserve under Sergeant Richard Rice. Fighting with their bayonets, they prevented the Turks taking the Dubsters in the rear. Rice was killed, as was Acting-Adjutant Captain Edward Dorman, who died exhorting his men to hold on and die like Irishmen. Company Sergeant-Major Bertie Hinde 'was found next morning with a ring of dead Turks around him.' Lieutenant Timothy Sullivan – whom Captain Guy Geddes said he had seen wounded on a lighter at V Beach – was mortally wounded and died on 4 May.[11] According to O'Hara, the sole Blue Caps officer:

Henry Desmond O'Hara.

The fight went on from 10.30 at night till 5 o'clock next morning – a desperate fight the whole time. My regiment alone got through 150,000 rounds and they were only 360 strong. The Turks were simply driven on to the barbed wire in front of the trenches by their German officers, and shot down by the score. At one point they actually got into the trenches, but were driven out by the bayonet. They must have lost thousands. The fighting is of the most desperate kind – very little quarter on either side. The men are absolutely mad to get at them, as they mutilate our wounded when they catch them. For the first three nights I did not have a wink of sleep, and actually fell asleep during the big night attack. We had no food for about 36 hours after landing, as we were fighting incessantly.'[12]

According to Peter Hart, 'The myth of the omnipresent German officers malevolently controlling the Turkish troops, so common in British veterans' recollections, is surely nonsense given their very restricted numbers, and indeed relatively high rank.' He suggests the higher quality and cut of Turkish officers uniforms may have led to the belief that they were German.[13]

Brigade-Major Mynors Farmar said, 'the fiercest fighting was against the Irish regiments who were defending the weakest part of the line and bore the greatest weight of the attack.'[14] Blue Cap Joseph Devoy had been a Lance-Corporal on 25 April. While he would go on to be promoted to temporary major, it is not clear what rank he was on 1 May 1915.

Jack Mallaghan.

The 21 men who garrisoned one particular bit of trench died to a man in the trench. One man, I recollect, a signaller, had as many as nineteen wounds. Of course it was hand-to-hand fighting – no quarter was asked or given. Towards morning several of us were using Turkish rifles and ammunition, our own from overwork refusing to function. The following morning a patrol of twelve of us, under Company Sergeant-Major [Samuel] Fergusson, sallied out (it was Fergusson's own idea) to chase away one or two snipers, and if my memory serves me rightly, our total bag of live captives was 38, gleaned from all sorts of holes and corners.[15]

Royal Dublin Fusilier brothers Nicky (standing) and Christy Smyth. Nicky was killed in Gallipoli. Christy survived the war.

In the heaviest fighting since the V Beach landing, the Blue Caps lost over eighty men.[16] Among them was nineteen-year-old Bugler Jack Mallaghan from Newry, whose brother Sam had been killed at V Beach ('I suppose you wonder why [Jack] was shifted from me ... One bugler a company was sent to Bellary to do duty'); twenty-seven-year-old Lance-Corporal Nicky Smyth from County Meath ('My Dear Katie ... I think we are going away next week for certain, we sent all our kit way to France on Monday last'); twenty-eight-year-old Private Richard Richards, who had been a member of the Band and Drum team that won the 1st Battalion Inter-Company Football League in the 1912-1913 season; Private Joe Murphy, the battalion billiards champion; Sergeant James Elliott from Millwall; Privates John Farrell, Christopher Hanlon and Lawrence Kelly from Athy, County Kildare; Private Richard Gorman from Birmingham, who had previously served in the 7th Dragoon Guards; Private Hugh Gribben from Dromore, County Down; the Germanic sounding Private Max Herter from Islington; Corporal Charles Kemp, born in India, who had enlisted in Ahmednagar; Sergeant Robert Ludlow from Galway; and Lance-Corporal William Steven from Brixton.

In the Ridley Chapel in the Parish church of St Boniface, Wyche Road, Bunbury, Cheshire is a brass plaque set into the top of a prie-dieu. The inscription reads: 'In memory of John Lee, brave as a lion. Faithful soldier of the 1st Bn. Royal Dublin Fusiliers. Who fell in action on 28th April 1915, at Gallipoli. The honour of the Regiment never shone brighter then when it was entrusted to him and the other brave men who died with him. Two friends revere his memory, Rev. R. Armitage D.S.O. one-time Chaplain to the Regiment and Capt. T. Mood, his Company Commander.' The inscription contains at least two errors. Commonwealth War Graves records show John Lee as having being killed on 30 April 1915. So he was among the over eighty men killed on 1 May. Captain Mood's first names were John Muspratt. John Lee (6860), was born in Manchester, enlisted at the Dubs depot in Naas, at which time he was living in Dublin. It is not known why a captain and a chaplain erected a plaque to a private. (The Revd Robert Armitage was awarded the DSO for service in the Boer War.)

The Dubsters were pulled out of the line the next day and sent to the reserve trenches.[17] O'Hara wrote home, 'We are now back in the reserve trenches about 1½ miles from the firing line.' The amalgamated battalion returned to the front line on 4 May and went into action on 7 May, advancing 500 yards. But heavy cross-fire forced a withdrawal during the afternoon. On 10 May, the Dubsters were withdrawn to Gully Ravine, where they were formed into two companies, W and X, with the Dublins constituting X. The battalion strength was seven officers and 372 men. Captain Guy Geddes returned, having recovered from his wounds. On 3 April, Sir Ian Hamilton had sent a message to the War Office stressing the urgency of the despatch of his 'first reinforcements', i.e. the 10 per cent drafts of officers and men which customarily accompanied units overseas to replace battle casualties. On 30 April, one officer and forty-six men for each of the regular battalions of the 29th Division sailed from England. (These drafts were approximately 5 per cent.)[18] They arrived in Gallipoli during the first half of May. The Blue Caps draft consisted of Captains Cecil Riccard, Walter Stirling and Adrian Taylor, with one sergeant, two corporals and forty-three privates. Neill's Blue Caps says that five other officers were attached to the battalion around this time. These were Captain G.E. Bruce from the 3rd Battalion of the Dublins and Captain Laurence George, Lieutenant A.G. Cripps, Second Lieutenant Herbert Rogers and Second Lieutenant F.G. Young, all from the 9th Battalion, Somerset Light Infantry. The Somersets were a reserve battalion, based in England. Among the May reinforcements received by the Blue Caps was nineteen-year-old Private Francis McCoy, from Sam and Jack Mallaghan's hometown of Newry, County Down. Coming from a place where religion tended to strongly shape political outlook, McCoy was a Roman Catholic. Also among the reinforcements was thirty-nine-year-old Edward Drohan, who had served with the Dublins in the Boer War. Afterwards he had settled in Carrick-on-Suir, got a job as a labourer in the local creamery, married and had five children. He had re-enlisted after the outbreak of war and now found himself in Gallipoli.

On 15 May, Lieutenant Henry Desmond O'Hara wrote to hospitalised Captain David French.

> Riccard arrived last night with a small draft and told us where you were, so I am sending you a line in the hopes that it may find you somewhere. I hope your wound is getting better. You were reported as very cheerful – is there any chance of you coming back – for your sake I hope not – this is absolute hell this show with precious little chance of coming out alive … I dare say you have heard how we have joined up with the Munsters as a composite battalion, officially known as the 'Dubsters' – it is far from being a satisfactory arrangement and we hope to split up as soon as we get some more officers – we now have Riccard, Taylor, Sterling, Floyd and self. I commanded the regiment for exactly two days before we got Floyd back, he was with the transport.

Lieutenant Henry Floyd did not land at V Beach, but remained at sea in charge of the battalion's transport (he was promoted to captain on 28 April). Continuing the letter two days later, O'Hara said that the Dublins had now been reconstituted as a separate unit and said the unit had been involved in heavy fighting for the first fortnight after landing, but were now in reserve. He said that:

> Hunter Weston gave out that the Dublins and Munsters were the two regiments that had done best of all. It is terribly sad losing all our officers. [Captain James] Grove and [Major Edward] Molesworth are at Malta – they were both wounded on the 28th … We had a desperate night attack on [the night of 1 May – he seems to have had his dates sorted out by the time he wrote the letter] the Turks attacked with the bayonet with a force computed at some 40,000 from 10.30 at night till dawn next morning, and ourselves and the Munsters were in the part of the line where they came thickest – we were some 350 strong and fired nearly 150,000 rounds – there was practically no barbed wire out and they actually got into the machine gun trench where [Sergeant Charles] Emery was at handgrips with two of them but we were re-enforced by the [Royal Fusiliers] and drove them out.

He said that dawn found the retreating Turks about 500 yards away and 'we had a fine time as we simply poured volley after volley into them'. He said there were over 300 dead Turks in front of the Irish trenches. He went on to say that fighting had now developed into the type of trench fighting seen in France.

I have put a cross over Grimshaw's grave [presumably Major Cecil
Grimshaw was initially buried near where he fell[19]] but I can't find where
the Colonel is buried – perhaps you may know – all the rest are in the
same grave except the poor old Major[20] and [Lieutenant] Reginald] Corbet.
[Lieutenant and Quartermaster Michael] Kennedy is having a big cross
made. The French have got V Beach now but there is a small cemetery railed
off. I hope poor old [Captain Herbert] Crozier gets better – he behaved
splendidly in the attack on Hill 141 and on the 26th and I sent his name
in for gallantry and also Grimshaw's. [The rest of the previously quoted
statement about Cecil Grimshaw follows.] I am hoping Crozier will get a
D.S.O. as I wrote as strongly as I could when I sent in my report. You will
be sorry to hear that [Sergeant-Major William] O'Mahony was killed on
the 8th – put his head over the parapet for a second and was shot through
the mouth. Be sure and write soon – you are the only one of my pals in the
regiment now with the Major and Corbet and Bernard all down – it is very
sad indeed – anyhow I don't expect to survive myself …[21]

The following appeared in brigade orders on 19 May. 'From today's date the
1st Battalion Royal Munster Fusiliers and 1st Battalion Royal Dublin Fusiliers,
which were on April 29th organised and known as 'The Dubster Battalion', will
be dealt with as separate units, and resume their correct titles.'[22] On 25 May,
Captain Guy Geddes took command of the Munsters when Major Hutchinson
was promoted to higher duties. According to *Neill's Blue Caps*, for the rest of
May and until the middle of the first week in June battalion operations were
confined to minor raids and trench construction. On 4 June the battalion was
relieved by the 2nd South Wales Borderers in trenches near Geoghegan's Bluff.
Unfortunately, despite the comment of *Neill's Blue Caps* that battalion operations were confined to minor raids and trench construction, Commonwealth
War Graves records show that thirty Blue Caps died on 4 June. Among them
was recently arrived Newry man, nineteen-year-old Private Francis McCoy.
Family legend says a robin flew into the kitchen of his home on the day he
was killed. Further reinforcements had arrived during May. On 5 June the battalion was 750 strong. The following day, reinforcements raised its number
to 850, with nineteen officers, many being new recruits to the army. In early
June the battalion was involved in a number of actions. 'Casualties were daily,
hourly, incurred.' By 30 June battalion numbers had fallen to eight officers
and 595 other ranks. Among the dead were Captain Henry Floyd (28 June),
Lieutenant Lawrence Boustead (29 June) and missing Captain Adrian Taylor
(28 June).[23] On 30 June the battalion was sent into reserve.

After the fighting in the latter part of June, it was decided to withdraw the brigades of the 29th Division by turns to Lemnos for a brief rest. The 86th Brigade sailed for Lemnos harbour on 19 July (per Westlake. *Neill's Blue Caps* puts the date at 16 July). On 21 July the brigade was told to return to Gallipoli. Upon returning the brigade was put in reserve. On 6 August, an offensive was launched against the Turks. Unsuccessful, it was called off at 2 a.m. the following day. Among those killed on 7 August was Edward Drohan from Carrick-on-Suir, the thirty-nine-year-old Boer War veteran with five children who may have re-enlisted to escape life as a general labourer in the local cream-ery. An hour after the offensive was called off, the battalion, now commanded by Lieutenant-Colonel George Ward of the West Yorkshire Regiment, was ordered to take over the whole of the line allocated to the 86th Brigade. Just before daybreak of the following day, the adjutant of the 1st Essex Regiment told Colonel Ward that a party of Essex were still holding part of the Turkish trenches. Lieutenant Hannen and two platoons of Blue Caps went to relieve them. In the Turkish trenches, Hannen's party were shelled and driven back by a Turkish attack. They left about thirty dead and badly wounded men behind. About twenty Turks got into the Dublins trenches. They were driven out by a grenade attack, led by Captain [Colin] Carruthers. As a result of the fight-ing, the Blue Caps had twenty-five men killed, thirty missing and three officers and 150 men wounded. The battalion was relieved and sent to Y Ravine on 16 August.

ॐ

Meanwhile, on 10 May, Sir Ian Hamilton sent a message to Lord Kitchener saying that, 'If two fresh divisions organised as a corps could be spared me I could push on ... with good prospects of success, otherwise I am afraid it will degenerate into trench warfare ...' The following day, Kitchener signalled that he was sending out the Lowland Division and some artillery.[24]

The War Council met on 14 May to consider the situation in the light of developments so far. It was expected that demands for men and munitions from the Western Front were likely to increase. But it was felt that to aban-don the Gallipoli expedition would reflect very badly on British prestige in the Middle East. The view of the War Council tended towards 'sending out sufficient reinforcements for a further effort, but no final decision was reached, except that Lord Kitchener should ask Sir Ian Hamilton what force he would require to ensure success ...' In response to a query from Kitchener, Hamilton, on 17 May, said that 'I shall want an additional Army Corps [in addition to the one he had requested on 10 May], i.e. two Army Corps additional in all.' Unfortunately, a political crisis occurred at this time, which resulted in the Liberal Government having to share power, in a Coalition Government with the Conservatives. The crisis meant that a decision regarding reinforcements was not taken until 7 June.

In the meantime, the membership of the War Council had increased and its name was changed to the Dardanelles Committee. On 7 June, the Dardanelles Committee decided to send Hamilton three new divisions. On 21 June, Kitchener asked Hamilton if he needed a fourth division. Hamilton said that he would not feel justified in refusing one. On 25 June, Kitchener said the Cabinet would like to know if he considered it desirable that a fifth division be sent. Hamilton said he did. The first three divisions would be composed of men recruited and trained since the outbreak of war. The other two divisions would consist of Territorial troops. The reinforcements would arrive between 10 July and 10 August. Hamilton decided to use some of them to support his forces at Anzac Cove, where attempts to break out had become stalled similarly to those at Helles. He would use the rest to make a surprise landing at Suvla Bay, north of Anzac Cove. To distract the Turks, the troops at Helles would launch an attack on 6 August and on the days following. As already described, the Blue Caps took part in the fighting that resulted from this attack.

ନ୍ତ

In May there were no flies. In June they came by armies; in July by multitudes. They came fresh from tins of putrefying food cast into no-man's-land, from blackening bodies in the scrub or on the wire, and from the excrement in the Turkish trenches. These bloated flies alighted on the moisture of your lips, your eyes, your nostrils; they dropped on each morsel of food and pursued it into your mouth and down your throat. Dysentery raged. It became universal. Everybody had it. In any normal campaign every man would have been sent on a stretcher to the base. Yet, in spite of all this, of the heat, the flies, the stench, the disease and the frustration, yes, frustration, for being held up, unable to get ahead, in spite of all this the Army's spirit never faltered.[25]

ନ୍ତ

On 6 August, landings began at Suvla Bay, about 25 miles north of Helles. Among the troops landed was the 10th (Irish) Division, which included, in the division's 30th Brigade, the 6th and 7th Battalions Royal Dublin Fusiliers and the 6th and 7th Battalions Royal Munster Fusiliers. These men were volunteers, who had joined up upon the outbreak of war. Serving with the 6th Battalion Royal Dublin Fusiliers was Private Christy Smyth from County Meath, whose brother Nicky had been killed shortly after the V Beach landing. Christy had been serving with the 2nd Dublins. Wounded at Ypres, he had been assigned to the 6th Battalion upon recovering. Now, like his brother, he had been sent to Gallipoli, a veteran soldier in a battalion of raw recruits. Unlike his brother, he survived Gallipoli and the rest of the war.

Troops of the 29th Division were moved to Suvla to support the landing. On 18 August, the Blue Caps went to W Beach from where they embarked on the *Prince Abbas* for Suvla Bay. They landed early on the morning of 19 August, immediately moving to Chocolate Hill and then to the frontline trenches on Hill 53 (now Dublin Hill), where all ranks worked at improving the trenches. The battalion remained there, in reserve, while the other battalions in 86th Brigade assaulted Hill 112 and Scimitar Hill on 21 August. The following night the Blue Caps were relieved by the 5th Battalion Royal Irish Fusiliers. Among the ranks of the Royal Irish was Newryman Private Herbie Mallaghan, Reg. No. 11567. Like his brothers, he was one of his battalion's musicians, being a drummer. What must have been the thoughts of the young Newry man as he watched the men of Sam and Jack's battalion file past him, knowing his brothers should have been with them?[26]

The Dublins were sent to another part of the frontline at Kuchuk Anafarta Ova. There, on 1 September, they were relieved by their V Beach and Dubster comrades, the Dirty Shirts. Meanwhile, having been wounded at some point not mentioned in *Neill's Blue Caps*, twenty-three-year-old Lieutenant Henry Desmond O'Hara, had died aboard ship on 29 August. On 5 January, he had carried the Blue Caps regimental standard into Torquay town hall. Commanding a platoon during the landing at V Beach on 25 April, he had gone on to command a company the following day and, on or about 28 April, the entire battalion. Awarded the Distinguished Service Order (DSO), he had also been mentioned in despatches by Sir Ian Hamilton. He was buried in Gibraltar.

On the night of 8 September, the Blue Caps marched to the beach for embarkation to Imbros island. There, they went into camp at Kephalos for a rest. The next day it was announced that the battalion was being returned to Suvla. Baggage was sent down to the beach to be put aboard ship, but was returned as it was considered too stormy to sail. The battalion embarked for Suvla Bay on 21 September. Landing at 11 p.m., it marched to Reserve Nullah. The following evening it relieved the 1st King's Own Scottish

Borderers in the firing line between Chocolate Hill and Scimitar Hill. Over the next few days there was intermittent shelling and persistent sniping from the Turks. On the night of 23-24 September, Second Lieutenant John Taylor was killed by a sniper.[27] 'The plague of flies was very distressing, dysentery was rife, and men went sick daily. By the end of September Battalion strength was down to fifteen officers and 608 other ranks, despite the fact that during the last two months upwards of 300 non-commissioned officers and men had reached the Battalion from home.'[28]

In October and November, the Blue Caps continued to serve in the trenches. On 19 November, Captain Hugh de Wolf took command of the battalion. On 27 November, and the four days following, there was a south-west gale and torrents of rain. Piers and landing-stages were destroyed, craft were driven ashore, trenches were filled with water, and streams poured down gullies. Worse was to follow. Suddenly, the wind direction changed and began to blow from the north. For nearly two days and nights snow fell in blizzards, followed by two further days and nights of bitter frost. All of this descended upon the scenes of devastation wrought by the five preceding days of storm. The surface of pools and trenches froze. Soldiers greatcoats, already soaked through with the rain, became frozen. Numbed with the cold, men staggered down from the lines, unable to hear or speak. Sentries in outposts and in the advanced trenches could not pull the frozen triggers of their rifles. About 10,000 sick had to be removed from the peninsula. Many were frostbitten; many lost their limbs; some, their reason. Several of the Blue Caps died of exposure. According to their war diary for 29 November, 'Many men went to hospital and few returned. Impossible to estimate number of sick.' The battalion strength at the end of the month was twelve officers and 332 other ranks. On 2 December, the Dublins received reinforcements of three officers and 168 men.

જ

The force that landed at Suvla was commanded by Lieutenant-General Sir Frederick Stopford, who had served mostly in staff and administrative positions before his appointment, on the grounds of seniority. He had never commanded in battle. While he was finally removed from command by Hamilton, his orders had only stated that he should capture Suvla Bay for use as a base for future campaigns – an objective he achieved. Like the earlier landings at Helles and Anzac Cove, the force at Suvla failed to achieve a breakthrough and became engaged in stalemate warfare with the Turks. On 27 August, the Dardanelles Committee decided that Sir Ian

Hamilton should do his best to hold the ground he had gained and should be asked for his views and requirements. Hamilton replied on 2 September, asking for reinforcements of up to 20 per cent to replace the casualties sustained. He also said, 'There is, in my opinion, no better alternative than to make a fresh effort at Suvla and Anzac … Meanwhile, all preparations are being made for a winter campaign.'[29] On 3 September, Kitchener told the Dardanelles Committee that the French Government had decided to send four divisions to the Asiatic side of the Dardanelles, where a French force had landed on 25 April and withdrawn the following day. They intended using their two divisions in Gallipoli as part of this force and asked that the British replace them with two of their divisions. Kitchener said that he would order that two divisions be sent from France for this purpose. The French troops, however, could not be sent until the outcome of a planned offensive was known. The offensive began on 25 September.

In the meantime, Bulgaria had mobilised its troops and it looked as if an attack on the Allied country Serbia was likely. On 23 September, Kitchener prepared a summary of the situation for the Dardanelles Committee, saying it might be necessary to send troops to Salonika to support Serbia. On 24 September, Hamilton was asked what force he could spare from Gallipoli for Salonika. The Dardanelles Committee (renamed the War Committee on 7 October) was split on the matter of sending troops to Salonika. On 11 October, it was agreed that, as soon as pending operations on the Western Front were over, a force should be sent from France to Egypt, without prejudice to its final destination. Awaiting this, it was agreed that a general would be sent to Gallipoli to report on the situation there and to make recommendations. On 14 October, the government recalled Sir Ian Hamilton. On 20 October, General Sir Charles Munro was ordered to take over command and to report on the situation in Gallipoli. He left England on 22 October and arrived in Mudros on 27 October. Following an inspection of the fronts at Helles, Anzac and Suvla, he reported to Kitchener on 31 October, recommending evacuation of Gallipoli.[30] Kitchener subsequently travelled to Gallipoli. On 7 December, the Cabinet decided to evacuate Suvla and Anzac, but to remain at Helles. The decision was taken on the advice of Kitchener, who had returned from Gallipoli and plans were made for the evacuation.

సు

On 13 December, orders were received for the Blue Caps to leave Suvla the following day. At about 7.30 p.m. on 14 December the battalion marched from Reserve Nullah. Embarking at midnight aboard the transport *Hazel*, they arrived in Mudros harbour the following morning. Remaining aboard the ship all day, they sailed for Helles at 7.30 p.m., where they landed about midnight. About two days later they moved into the firing line at Gully Ravine. On 22 December, there was a very heavy rain-storm. The trenches were 2 to 3 feet deep in mud and water. The Turks shelled the trenches intermittently during the day. Just before dawn on 23 December, the enemy attacked Z Company's part of the trench and took some of it. They were later driven out by a bombing party led by Lieutenant Herbert Ridley. Blue Caps casualties were twelve killed and eighteen wounded. During the day, Major Herbert Nelson of the 1st Border Regiment took command of the battalion with the temporary rank of Lieutenant-Colonel. Unfortunately, *Neill's Blue Caps* makes no mention of how the battalion celebrated Christmas or any happenings for the few remaining days of 1915.

ဢ

On 20 December, on the day the last troops left Suvla and Anzac, Sir Charles Munro telegraphed Kitchener urging the evacuation of Helles on the grounds that this 'would greatly facilitate the reorganisation of the Dardanelles army'. The army, 'when rested and reorganised', would constitute a valuable asset, ready to strike in France or elsewhere. On 22 December, the General Staff also recommended evacuation. On 23 December the War Committee decided on evacuation. The decision was approved by the full Cabinet on 27 December.

ဢ

On 1 January 1916, the Blue Caps were working on defences when orders arrived to embark from V Beach at midnight. Back on the beach were so many of their number had died or were wounded just over eight months previously, they waited for a considerable time, before being ordered to go aboard the *River Clyde*. From there the battalion was transferred by tugs to the *Ausonia*. The ship that had carried the Blue Caps from England to Gallipoli now took them away from the peninsula. The usual difficulties of transhipping at night were aggravated by a choppy sea. The last Dubs boarded the *Ausonia* just as day was breaking. Mudros harbour was reached about noon on 2 January. The battalion disembarked and marched to camp at Mudros East. On 5 January, aboard the *Caledonia*, Captain Colin Carruthers, with ten officers and one hundred other ranks sailed for Egypt as an advance party. The rest of the battalion followed, aboard the *Serangbee*, on 8 January. On arrival the Blue Caps camped 3 miles from Suez. On 13 March the battalion sailed for France aboard the *Minominee*. It spent the rest of the war on the Western Front. Of the Blue Caps who had stormed ashore from ships boats or from the *River Clyde* on 25 April, no officers and only eleven men remained who had served continuously throughout the campaign without having been invalided by reasons of wounds or sickness. Of those who had been invalided for a time and subsequently returned to duty, only one officer and seventy-eight other ranks remained.

CHAPTER 9

From Then to Now

'There is no denying Neill's Blue Caps their place in the annals of the British Army. From the landing at V Beach to the final advances in Ypres in 1918 ... It is one of the great tragedies of Irish history that almost no attempt was made to interview the veterans of the Dublin Fusiliers in the decades which followed.'
Kevin Myers in the foreword to Patrick Hogarty's Remembrance

Though wounded himself, Surgeon Peter Burrows Kelly from Kildare remained treating wounded aboard the *River Clyde* until 27 April. He attended to 750 men, while being unable to walk during the final twenty-four hours of his duty. He was awarded the Distinguished Service Order. He remained in Gallipoli until the evacuation. He later served at the Royal Naval College, Osborne during 'a deadly measles epidemic', before going into private practice in London. Unfortunately his health declined and he died just before the fifth anniversary of the V Beach landing, on 6 April 1920 at his brother's home in Ballitore, County Kildare. He was survived by his wife and daughter.[1] On 26 April 1915, the first man to enter the Valide's fort was Private Tom Cullen of the Blue Caps, from Old Kilmainham. He was awarded the Distinguished Conduct Medal. Transferred to the 6th Battalion of the Dublins, he was killed in Salonika, on 4 October 1916.

On 27 April 1915, Captain John Gillam of the Army Service Corps travelled from W Beach to V Beach.

> [There] I see a sight which I shall never forget all my life. About 200 bodies are laid out for burial, consisting of soldiers and sailors. I repeat, never have the Army and Navy been so dovetailed together. They lie in all postures, their faces blackened, swollen, and distorted by the sun. The bodies of seven officers lie in a row in front by themselves. I cannot but think what a fine company they would make if by a miracle an Unseen Hand could restore them to life by a touch.

He recognised the body of Brigade-Major John Costeker. On 23 May he was back at V Beach. 'We meet with no success in finding Major Costaker's [*sic*] grave, and I can only conclude that he is buried in one of the two large graves down on the beach marked 'Gallant dead of the dead Dublins and Munsters and others.'² Speaking of Father William Finn's grave, the Revd Oswin Creighton said, 'At a chaplain's meeting held some weeks later, two, a Presbyterian and an R.C., undertook to see that Father Finn's grave was properly tended. He was buried close to the sea on V Beach, and a road had been made over the place. I think they managed to get the grave marked off with a little fence.'³ The grave was marked by a cross made from an ammunition box. The inscription read, 'To the memory of the Rev. Capt. Finn.'⁴ On 31 May 1915, 1st Munsters Pioneer Sergeant Denis Moriarty, a carpenter before joining the regiment, made the following entry in his diary. 'At W Beach. Got some carpenters tools and wood and made a large cross to put over the grave on V Beach where 220 of the Munsters and Dublins are buried and who were killed there on the day we landed.'⁵

The cemetery at V Beach was used during April and May 1915. After the Armistice, thirteen bodies were brought for burial in Row O. There are now 696 soldiers and sailors of the First World War buried or commemorated in the cemetery. Four hundred and eighty of the burials are unidentified, but special memorials commemorate 196 officers and men, nearly all belonging to units which landed on 25 April, known or believed to be buried among them.⁶ Lieutenant-Colonel Richard Rooth and Father William Finn are buried side by side in Grave F.4, the only joint grave in the cemetery. Major Cecil Grimshaw DSO is buried in Grave F. 11. Privates Sam and Jack Mallaghan do not have identified graves, but are commemorated by special memorials, Jack at B.45 and Sam at B.46. Similarly, Private Nicky Smyth is commemorated by Special Memorial B.101. His memorial gives his date of death as 11 May, though *Soldiers Died in the Great War* gives his date of death as 30 April, the same date as Jack Mallaghan. A number of men are recorded by the Commonwealth War Graves Commission as being killed on 11 May and by *Soldiers Died* on 30 April. In some cases the Commission went for the 30 April date and *Soldiers Died* for 11 May. The Dubsters were in reserve at Gully Ravine on 11 May and were not involved in fighting. Thus, the 11 May date recorded by the Commonwealth War Graves Commission, and in some cases by *Soldiers Died*, is wrong. For reasons already explained, it appears that the 30 April date is also incorrect and may have been recorded by the sole surviving officer who had not slept for three nights and, according to himself, fell asleep during the attack (on 1 May). Private Richard Richards, one of the quartet of footballing musicians, is commemorated by special memorial B.90, with 30 April given as the date of death. The balance of probability appears

Graves of Father Finn and Lieutenant-Colonel Rooth. (Michael Lee)

to suggest that Jack Mallaghan, Richard Richards, Nicky Smyth and about eighty of their comrades died in the savage fighting on the night of 1 May.

Speaking of Father William Finn, the Revd Oswin Creighton said, 'The men never forgot him and were never tired of speaking of him … I am told they kept his helmet for a very long time after and carried it with them wherever they went. It seemed to me that Father Finn was an instance of the extraordinary hold a chaplain, and perhaps especially an R.C., can have on the affections of his men if he absolutely becomes one of them and shares their danger.'[7] Among other memorials, Finn's name is on Panel 4, east wall, of the Royal Garrison Church, Aldershot. On 8 June 1915, the *St Helen's Newspaper and Advertiser* carried a detailed account of Father Finn's death in action. His story appears to have had an inspirational effect upon the parish priest of the Sacred Heart, St Helen's, Merseyside, Lancashire, where Father Finn had previously served. Although already middle-aged, Father Richard Corcoran was reported to have volunteered to take Father Finn's place. The same newspaper's edition of 9 November 1915 reported on a talk given by Father Corcoran on his return from the Dardanelles. In the interim he had joined up, been posted to Gallipoli and seen action on the Suvla front. The July 1915 issue of the magazine of Ushaw College, Father Finn's alma mater, carried news of his death, his obituary and a poem by J.R. Meagher.

Father Finn's brother, Frank paid for the building, in 1926-27, of the Sacred Heart Church in Hull, Yorkshire in memory of the Blue Cap's chaplain. Frank became Lord Mayor of Hull. An oil painting of Father Finn was presented to Ushaw College, bearing the inscription, 'The Rev. W.J. Finn, C.F. attached to the Royal Dublin Fusiliers, who fell at Sedd-el-Bahr, April 25th, 1915. The first Army Chaplain of any denomination to give his life in the Great War. Presented by his sister.'

On 16 August 1915, the *London Gazette* announced the award of Victoria Crosses to Commander Edwin Unwin, Midshipman George Drewry, Midshipman Wilfred Malleson, Able-bodied Seaman George Samson and, posthumously, to Leading Seaman William Williams. On 31 March 1916, a Victoria Cross was 'gazetted' to Sub-Lieutenant Arthur Tisdall of the Royal

Edward Unwin VC. (Q85893 Imperial War Museums, Public Domain, Wikimedia Commons)

Naval Division. The award was posthumous. On 6 May 1915, Tisdall had been killed in action during the Second Battle of Krithia.

Following the V Beach landing, Commander Edward Unwin was sent to England, where he underwent an operation at the Royal Naval Hospital, Haslar. Early July found him back at Mudros, in command of the cruiser *Endymion*. During the Suvla Bay landings he commanded a fleet of armoured motor-lighters that each carried 500 men ashore at night. He was assisted by George Drewry, who volunteered to join him from the *Hussar*. Between 6 and 11 August, the two *River Clyde* shipmates worked tirelessly to ferry men and equipment from ship to shore. Drewry returned to the *Hussar* on 11 August, but Unwin remained at Suvla. He served there, first as beachmaster and then, during the evacuation, as naval transport officer. In the final days he was to be found day and night on the beach piers superintending the transport of men, animals and equipment. An army officer described him as standing over 6 feet and as broad in proportion and said he roared orders through a megaphone. On 20 December, he was the last man to leave Suvla. Flames from burning stores lit the sky as he left aboard a picket boat. When a soldier fell overboard from a lighter, Unwin dived in and rescued him, for which Rear-Admiral Wemyss recommended him for a Royal Humane Society medal. On 15 January 1916, Unwin received his Victoria Cross from George V at Buckingham Palace. In March 1916, he was created Commander of St Michael and St George (CMG) for his part in the successful evacuation. The rest of his war service was something of an anticlimax. He commanded the light cruiser *Amethyst* on the south-east America station, before serving as principal naval transport officer in Egypt and then for the Eastern Mediterranean. Promoted commodore in 1919, he was made a Companion of the Bath (CB). He retired the following year with the rank of captain, the rank being backdated to 11 November 1918. He enjoyed an active retirement, combining civic duties with sporting pursuits. He regularly attended the annual memorial service for the veterans of the 29th Division at Eltham in Kent. He died on 19 April 1950.[8]

John Kerr, former captain of SS *River Clyde*.

In September 1916, George Drewry was promoted acting-lieutenant on the *Conqueror*. On 22 November, he received his Victoria Cross from George V. By the summer of 1918 he was in command of the *William Jackson*, a decoy trawler. On 2 August, a block fell from a derrick and struck him, fracturing his skull and breaking his left arm. He died the following day.

Despite Edward Unwin's critical comments about him, on 4 August 1915, John Kerr, former captain of the *River Clyde*, was appointed temporary lieutenant in the Royal Navy Reserve and given command of HM Sea Plane Carrier *Anne*. On 21 June 1917, he was given command of HMS *Empress*, having previously received a letter from his commanding officer, dated May 1917, stating that he 'handled his seaplane carrier with immaculate skilled and dash and carried out operations with unfailing accuracy.' Another 1917 note (possibly/probably from the same commanding officer: both signatures are illegible) describes him as 'A loyal, hardworking and reliable officer who has always kept his seaplane carrier in a high state of efficiency. He has invariably handled his ship with unfailing accuracy on operations.' A note in his file in the Liddle Archives says that on 12 February 1918 he was appointed to HMS *Hannibal*. 'Additional for service on shore at Alexandria to assist the Regulating officer of Trawlers.' Another note says that he was appointed to HMS *Wallington* 'Additional for RN Depot, Immingham for "N" duties 20 February 1918.' A letter, from the captain of HMS *Wallington*, says that he served aboard the ship from 26 February to 30 September 1918. It said that 'he has conducted himself entirely to my satisfaction. Has carried out the duties of Lieut. (N) with marked zeal and ability. Recc. [i.e. Recommended] for promotion.' A letter from the lieutenant-commander in command RN Depot Immingham described Kerr as 'a thoroughly efficient and hardworking Navigating Officer'. Lieutenant John Kerr RNR was awarded the Distinguished Service Cross 'for services in command of a seaplane carrying vessel on the East Indies and Egypt Station during the period April 1, 1916-March 31, 1917.' He was demobilised on 18 October 1919. He moved to Vancouver, where he captained the SS *Robert Dollar* and worked for the *Empire Stevedoring Company*. He died on 17 November 1951 and was buried in Mountain View Cemetery.[9]

On 13 May 1915, with the troops only recently ashore in Gallipoli, the *Cork Examiner* published an advertisement. 'Those who know the benefit of Turkish Baths take them regularly at 30 South Main Street, Cork.' On 1 June, the newspaper contained a report that Denis Donovan, a hackney driver of 177 Old Youghal Road had been summoned by Esther Batmazian, 10 St. Patrick's Terrace for abusive and threatening language on 26 May. Mrs Batmazian testified that she was the wife of Harutan Batmazian who manufactured Turkish Delights confectionary under the trade name Hadgi Bay. She said her family were Armenian Christian who had been compelled to leave Turkey due to persecution. She testified that she had three brothers fighting on the Allied side on Russian territory and said that her husband had come to Cork fourteen years previously and invested a lot of money in his successful firm. She said that the defendant had threatened to smash the shop window (in King Street, now McCurtin Street) unless a sign it contained advertising Turkish Delights was removed. The defendant's solicitor asked why the sign could not be removed. In reply, Mrs Batmazian asked why signs for Turkish baths and Turkish cigarettes were not removed. The solicitor tried to suggest there was a Turkish flag in the shop window and said that Hadgi Bay was a Turkish name. Mrs Batmazian denied the allegations, saying that Armenians hated the Turkish flag and that Hadgi Bay was an Indian name. The solicitor said that the name was not fair to the men going to the Dardanelles. Denis Donovan had two sons and four nephews serving in the army. Appointed an NCO and involved in recruiting, he had recruited 72 men. The case was dismissed.[10]

Several survivors of V Beach were killed on the first day of the Battle of the Somme on 1 July 1916. Among them was twenty-one-year-old Lance-Corporal Charles Heatley from 52 High Street in Dublin.[11] On 6 June 1917, as the men of the 1st Royal Munster Fusiliers, prepared to go into action at Messines Ridge, Belgium, they were read a message from their commanding officer, Lieutenant-Colonel Roger Monck-Mason DSO The message began: 'I should like all ranks to know that I have absolute confidence both in the officers and men. A battalion that could land at "V" Beach can do anything ...'[12] Despite all that the battalion had been through in the interim on the Western Front, V Beach was still the totem pole by which everything was judged.

On 15 April 1918, while attached to 42nd Brigade, Royal Field Artillery, Chaplain 4th Class Revd Oswin Creighton, who had written about his time with the 29th Division and about Father William Finn, was killed by a bomb dropped by a German plane. The son of Louise and Mandel Creighton, Bishop of London, he was thirty-four years old.

On 4 October 1917, east of Langemarck, Belgium, Sergeant James Ockendon of the Blue Caps was acting company sergeant-major. Seeing the platoon on the right held up by an enemy machine-gun, he rushed the gun, capturing it and killing the crew. He then led a section to attack a farm, where, under very heavy fire he ran forward and called on the garrison to surrender. As the enemy continued to fire on him, he opened fire, killing four, whereupon the remaining sixteen surrendered. The twenty-six-year-old, who had held the rank of private during the V Beach landing, was awarded the Victoria Cross.

Lance-Corporal Patrick Flanagan, from the parish of St Paul in Dublin, had worked as a messenger before joining the Dubs at Naas on 10 April 1911, aged eighteen. On 11 January 1913 he was sent to India. During the V Beach landing he was wounded in the left shoulder, the right leg and the chest. Having lost movement of his left arm, he was discharged from the army on 25 March 1916. On 23 October 1918, he died at Dr Stephen's hospital, with pieces of Turkish shrapnel still in his chest.

Joseph Berry, from the parish of St Catherine in Dublin, had worked as a farm labourer before enlisting in the Dublins on 10 August 1910. He was wounded in the stomach on the second day of the V Beach landing. Invalided home, he married Jane Grey in November 1915. He returned to service in Salonika, but suffered bouts of malaria and debility and was transferred to the Labour Corps. He died of influenza at his home, 6 Braithwaite St Dublin on 7 April 1919. Patrick Flanagan and Joseph Berry are buried in Glasnevin Cemetery, Dublin.[13]

On 25 April 1915, as Midshipman Haydon Forbes of the *Cornwallis* approached Sedd el Bahr in No. 1 Tow, away to his left he could see boats going in to W Beach. Aboard one of the first boats was nineteen-year-old Private Frederick Wilkinson, A Company, 1st Battalion Lancashire Fusiliers. Hidden in his knapsack was Rags, a sheepdog 'of doubtful parentage.' Wilkinson had acquired the dog in Alexandria. He had smuggled it aboard the troopship and then brought it aboard the *Euryalus*. The dog was 'quite a character and popular with the ships company'. Sadly, Wilkinson was killed within a few minutes of landing.[14] Rags was later taken over to V Beach, 'where he scampered about, cadging food from soldiers and sailors. He loved to swim out and bark at splashes from shell falling into the sea.' Haydon Forbes befriended the dog. 'When the Provost Marshal spoke of having [him] "put down", Rags was welcomed aboard the *Cornwallis* as ship's pet.' Forbes took Rags with him to his next ship the *Aster*, which struck a mine off the coast of Malta. Both owner and dog were saved. When Forbes went to Buckingham Palace to receive the Distinguished Service Cross from King George V, Rags went with him, wearing the ribbon of the General Service Medal attached to his collar. Rags died of old age in Malta on 23 October 1926, where Lieutenant-Commander Haydon Forbes was serving with the Fleet Air Arm. A tablet to the dog's memory was erected in the garden of the Villa Gezira, Sliema, later a Mess for the staff of Queen Alexandra's Naval Nursing Service. Seven months later, on 9 June 1927, Forbes was killed in a flying accident and was buried in Malta not far from Rags.[15]

V Beach survivor Sergeant James Ockendon. He was awarded the Victoria Cross in 1917.

✠

Since bringing Turkey into the war by shelling Russian ports, the German ships *Goeben* and *Breslau* had remained at Constantinople. On 20 January 1918, under cover of a heavy dawn mist, the ships sailed past Sedd el Bahr and the abandoned *River Clyde* and slipped out of the Dardanelles. Sailing northwards, they sunk the heavily out-gunned Royal Navy monitors *Raglan* and *M20* on the east coast of Imbros island. The warships then sailed southwards with the intention of bombarding Mudros harbour. They came under attack by British aircraft, two destroyers and a submarine. The *Breslau* was sunk and the *Goeben* returned to the Dardanelles, listing badly. She ran aground inside the Narrows. On 26 January, she got off the sandbank and sailed to safety. At the end of the war the Turkish navy retained the *Goeben* under her Turkish name *Yavuz* (Ferocious). She remained inoperative for eleven years. Following repairs, she returned to active service in 1929. The next year she became flagship of the Turkish Navy. In 1938 she carried the body of Mustafa Kemal Ataturk, war hero and First President of the Republic of Turkey, from Istanbul to Izmir. The *Yavuz* was flagship of the Turkish Navy until 1950. She was taken out of active service on 20 December 1950. In 1971 the ship was purchased for scrap by MKE (Turkish Industries Machinery and Chemicals). She was scrapped in 1976.[16]

∞

After four years of war, late 1918 saw Germany and her allies requesting peace terms. On 30 October 1918, aboard HMS *Agamennon* in Mudros harbour, Rauf Bey, Ottoman Minister of Marine Affairs and Admiral Arthur Gough-Calthorpe, Royal Navy, signed an armistice, to come into operation at noon the following day. Among the conditions of the armistice was one granting the Allies the right

Royal Dublin Fusiliers V Beach survivors, photographed on 17 March 1920. The officer is Lieutenant Christopher McCann, who had been a sergeant in W Company aboard the *River Clyde*. Moving to the right, the second last man is Stephen Fibley and the final man is footballer Sergeant Michael Ludford.

to occupy forts controlling the Dardanelles and the Bosporus, and the right to occupy any Ottoman territory in case of a threat to security. All ports, railways and other strategic points were to be made available for use by the Allies. The armistice was followed by the occupation of Constantinople. In May 1919, seeking to benefit from apparent Turkish weakness, Greece sent troops to Smyrna (now Izmir) and attempted to conquer the hinterland. In reaction, a revolutionary government came to power in eastern Turkey, under the leadership of Mustafa Kemal. In the war that followed, Kemal drove the Greeks from Turkish territory. An armistice was signed on 11 October 1922. A conference of many of the major powers was called in Lausanne, Switzerland in 1923. This resulted in the Treaty of Lausanne on 24 July 1923. An agreement between Turkey and several major powers, the treaty replaced the provisions of the earlier Treaty of Sévres,[17] between the Ottoman Empire and the Allies.

When the war ended at 11 a.m. on 11 November 1918, the Blue Caps were at St Genois, near Ruddervoode in Belgium. At the time of the ceasefire the battalion had a strength of forty officers and seven hundred and seventy-six men. On 1 December, the Blue Caps were among British troops that crossed the German frontier and occupied part of the country.

On 26 December 1918, led by Captain Alexander Holman, the 1st Battalion Royal Dublin Fusilier Colour Party arrived in Torquay shortly after noon and took up position in front of the entrance porch of the town hall. The rest of the battalion was stationed in Germany, but Holman's men had come to Torquay on an important mission. Almost four years previously, Holman had been among the men who had handed over the colours of the battalion to the Mayor of Torquay. At that time the Woolwich-born man had been a sergeant, a rank he had still held during the landing at V Beach. Now he was a captain. Also in the colour party was Sergeant James O'Leary, a Dubliner who had been a private during the handing over of the colours and during the V Beach landing. In his robes, Mayor Hugh Cumming walked from the Council Chamber, preceded by the mace-bearer, and accompanied by members of the Council. The colours, which the Blue Caps had given to Mayor Towell in January 1915, were carried by Major H.A. Garrett and Lieutenant W.R. Taylor. After mayor Cumming received a salute from Captain Alexander Holman and the Royal Dublin Fusilier Colour Party, he was presented with the colours by Major Garrett and Lieutenant Taylor. Addressing the Royal Dublin Fusilier Colour Party, the Mayor said that it was only by picturing the meaning of the

colours to the regiment, that it could be realised what a great honour had been
bestowed upon the Mayor, the Corporation, and through them, the town of
Torquay, when the colours were handed over four years ago. It was hardly necessary for him to tell Captain Holman and those with him, how proud they had
been to have had those colours in their charge (Applause) and how grieved
they felt to part with them. While Torquay had, with pride, been guarding the
fabric, the regiment had carried the spirit of the colours abroad, and covered
itself with great glory and inscribed the names of further battles on its record.
In giving the colours back, he would like to feel that Torquay might bye and bye
have some reminder, some little record for all time, of the honour bestowed
upon it, when the colours were given into its safe keeping four years ago. (Hear
Hear.) In giving the colours back, he could only say, 'God Bless your gallant
regiment for all time, and wherever it might be.' (Applause.) Captain Holman
and Lieutenant Hinkson then advanced and accepted the colours from the
Mayor. They then retired to their former positions and placed the standards
in their rests. Addressing Mayor Cumming, Captain Holman thanked him for
his kind words. He said that when he returned to his battalion, he would do
his utmost to see that Torquay received a memento which would remind the
inhabitants for all time of the fact that the town had kept the colours so well
for so long. When the colours again passed into the possession of the battalion,
he knew they would show their appreciation in the soldiers' manner, by giving
three hearty, ringing cheers for Torquay. Referring to Former Mayor Towell,
his predecessor, to whom the colours were handed in 1915, Mayor Cumming
said that he would have been present, but for the fact that he was ill in bed.
He said that the former Mayor had made him promise to let him know when
the colours were restored to the regiment. The colour guard then ordered arms.
The colours were rolled and cased and again placed in their rests. To resound-
ing cheers the colour party marched away.[18] On 16 January 1919, the Blue Caps
held a ceremonial parade at Berg Gladbach in Germany to receive the colours
which had returned from Torquay.[19]

British demobilisation commenced in December 1918. By 21 February 1919,
1,848,000 men had been demobilized. Of these, 85 per cent had returned to
industrial occupations. On 17 July 1919, the War Minister announced that nearly
3,000,000 men had been demobilized since the Armistice, leaving 1,200,000 still
in the Army. By 3 September 1919, the 1st Royal Dublin Fusiliers were back in
England and had been reorganised. On 25 October 1919, as well as their alphabet-
ical and numerical designations, each company and platoon was given a name of
an engagement in which the battalion had participated. D Company was to be
known as D Company: Gallipoli. Its platoons were No. 13: River Clyde, No. 14:

Sedd el Bahr, No. 15: Cape Helles and No. 16: Suvla Bay.[20] On 11 December 1919, the battalion was sent to St Lucia Barracks, Bordon, Hampshire.

Neill's Blue Caps recorded sporting successes by the battalion during the period from August 1919 to July 1922. A photograph shows the battalion football team, winners of the Aldershot Command Senior League for the 1920-21 season. Among the team was Sergeant Michael Ludford, who had been photographed at Ahmednagar as part of the Band and Drum team that won the 1st Battalion Inter-Company Football League in the 1912-1913 season. Also mentioned among the sporting successes was that of the battalion boxing team, which had several victories. The officer in charge of the team was the battalion's transport officer, Lieutenant Christopher McCann DCM, who won the Officers Welter-Weight in the Army Boxing Championship in 1920 and 1921. McCann had been a sergeant in W Company in 1915 and had landed from the *River Clyde*.

In August 1921, the Cabinet appointed a committee of businessmen to make recommendations to the Chancellor of the Exchequer on reducing national expenditure in 1922. Known, from its chairman, as the Geddes Committee, it was informally called the Super-Axe Committee. Informed sources predicted a reduction in the size of the army and that, in view of the recently signed treaty establishing the Irish Free State, the Irish regiments in the British Army would be disbanded. On 8 February 1922, the depot of the Royal Dublin Fusiliers was transferred from Naas, County Kildare to Bordon, Hampshire. On 11 March, Army Order No. 78 announced the disbandment, 'as soon as the exigencies of the Service permit,' of all of the regiments that recruited from what was now the Irish Free State and of their depots. The third and fourth battalions of a number of English regiments were to be disbanded, as were the Royal Irish Fusiliers. The latter's recruitment area was comprised of counties Armagh, Cavan and Monaghan. While the last two counties were in the Irish Free State, Armagh was in Northern Ireland. In an act of amazing generosity, the Royal Inniskilling Fusiliers agreed to disband one of its battalions so that the Royal Irish Fusiliers could retain a battalion and thus continue to exist.

On 28 April 1922, the 2nd Battalion Royal Dublin Fusiliers, nicknamed the Old Toughs, arrived at Bordon from India and both battalions began the process of disbandment. On 11 May, Army Order No. 179 announced the procedures for the dispersal of the officers and men of the disbanded regiments. Where officers wished to continue in the army, they were permitted to apply for transfer, giving five regiments in order of preference. A compensation scheme was published, giving the rates of retired pay and gratuities for those who opted to retire. Soldiers serving on normal engagements would be allowed to transfer to other units or to transfer to the Army Reserve.

On 30 May, it was announced that 'His Majesty the King has honoured the Battalion by intimating his intention to receive the Colours of the Battalion and place them in safety in St. Georges Chapel, Windsor Castle. The handing-over ceremony will take place at 11.30 a.m. on June 12th'.

On 9 June 1922, the Committee of Adjustment, Royal Dublin Fusiliers, held a meeting at the Army and Navy Club in London to discuss the distribution of the officers and sergeants mess property. Major David French was a member of the committee. Among items the committee decided to send to the Royal United Service Institution were 'Relics of *River Clyde*'. A photo in *Neill's Blue Caps* shows the starboard light and the binnacle stand of the *River Clyde* with the caption 'Both presented to the Blue Caps by Admiral J. De Robeck.'[21]

On Monday 12 June, colour parties from the Royal Dublin Fusiliers, Royal Munster Fusiliers, the Connaught Rangers, the Leinster Regiment, the Royal Irish Regiment and the South Irish Horse formed up at the railway station in Windsor. As each regiment had two battalions and the South Irish Horse did not have colours, there were ten colour parties, each carrying a King's Colour and a Regimental Colour. Second in command of the 1st Battalion, Royal Munster Fusiliers party was Major Guy Geddes DSO. The King's Colour for the 2nd Battalion, Royal Dublin Fusiliers was carried by Captain John Mood OBE, MC The battalion's colour party was commanded by Captain Colin Carruthers.

The colour parties were met by an escorting party of 100 men from the 3rd Battalion, Grenadier Guards and their band. Preceded and followed by the Grenadier Guards and headed by their band, the column marched up the steep road to Windsor Castle in the following order: South Irish Horse, Royal Irish Regiment, Connaught Rangers, the Leinster Regiment, the Royal Munster Fusiliers and the Royal Dublin Fusiliers. The band played the regimental march of each regiment in turn. At the gateway to the castle the soldiers were met by Lieutenant-Colonel the Marquess of Cambridge, Governor and Constable of Windsor Castle. As the colour parties marched under an archway to St George's Hall, the band played 'Auld Lang Syne'. In St George's Hall the colour parties formed up in line, facing the windows. They were received by the King and the Queen, the Duke of Connaught and other members of the Royal Family. The King addressed the troops. He said that the regiments were called upon to part with their colours 'for reasons beyond your control and resistance'. He said that, 'Within these ancient and protected walls your Colours will be treasured, honoured and protected as hallowed memorials of the glorious deeds of brave and loyal regiments.' The colours were then presented to the King. The South Irish Horse presented him with a Regimental Engraving. Returning to their positions, the colour parties grounded arms and then walked in single file past the King and Queen. The King and Queen shook hands with each member of the colour parties and the King gave each commanding officer a letter addressed to their regiment. The officers then dined with the King and Queen and the others ranks dined in the castle. Afterwards the King spoke with the colour parties for about twenty minutes.[22] The Irish regiments were disbanded on Monday 31 July 1922. *Neill's Blue Caps* said that *War Office Letter No. 20* announced, 'The 1st Battalion The Royal Dublin Fusiliers ceases to exist from this date.' Of course the *Letter* announced the disbandment of all the Irish battalions. In a swipe at officialdom, Captain McCance, in *The History of the Royal Munster Fusiliers*, said: 'On July 31st, 1922, the usual curt official announcement was made that the 1st and 2nd Battalion of the Royal Munster Fusiliers cease to exist from this date.'

Among the officers serving with the 1st Battalion Royal Dublin Fusiliers at Bordon Camp on the day of disbandment was Second Lieutenant Richard Rooth, son of the Blue Caps commanding officer at V Beach. On 12 August, he transferred to the West Yorkshire Regiment. Also serving in the battalion was Major Herbert Crozier (W Company on the *River Clyde*). He transferred to the King's (Liverpool) Regiment at an unspecified date. Serving in the 2nd Battalion, also at Bordon Camp were: Major David French [Y Company at V Beach. He retired on half pay on 27 August 1922], Captain Colin Carruthers (Z Company at V Beach. He transferred to the Border Regiment on 12 August 1922). Captain John Mood (Z Company. Officer in charge of the attack on The Camber. He transferred to the East Yorkshire Regiment on 26 August 1922) and Captain Cuthbert Maffett (X Company at V Beach. He transferred to the Black Watch on 12 August 1922). Attached elsewhere were: Brevet Major Captain James Grove (Battalion Signalling Officer at V Beach. He transferred to the Bedfordshire and Hertfordshire Regiment on 6 September 1922) and Captain Francis Lanigan-O'Keeffe MBE (Z Company at V Beach. He transferred to the Royal Welsh Fusiliers on 7 October 1922). On 16 July 1920, twenty-year-old Richard Goodwin Rooth was commissioned from the Royal Military College Sandhurst as a Second Lieutenant in the Royal Munster Fusiliers. But he must have left the military authorities in little doubt as to the regiment in he wished to serve and, given the circumstances, they must have been very sympathetic. Less than a month later, on 12 August 1920, he was transferred to his father's old regiment, the 1st Battalion Royal Dublin Fusiliers. His seniority in the battalion was backdated to 16 July 1920 'next below Second Lieutenant K.E. Hegan'.[23] On 19 March 1921, the three medals awarded to his father, Lieutenant-Colonel Richard Alexander Rooth, for service in 1914-1915 were issued. The *London*

Gazette of 11 August 1922 said Richard Rooth was to hold the position of lieutenant in the West Yorkshire Regiment from 12 August 1922, with his seniority in the regiment backdated to 16 July 1922. The *London Gazette* of 27 July 1931 said that Lieutenant Richard Rooth was restored to the establishment of the West Yorkshire Regiment as of 26 January 1931. This suggests that he had spent some time attached to a different unit. The *London Gazette* of 14 June 1932 records his promotion to captain on 4 May 1932. The following year, on 3 November, at St Michael's church in Teighmouth, Captain Richard Goodwin Rooth, only son of the late Lieutenant-Colonel Richard Alexander Rooth and Mrs Amy Mary Rooth of Coombe Cottage, Dawlish, married Gwen Mary Watkin of Teignmouth. On 1 August 1938 Captain Richard Rooth was promoted to major.[24] On 24 June 1948, Major Richard Rooth retired.[25] On 21 November 1951, Major Richard Goodwin Rooth (Retired) ceased to belong to the Reserve of Officers, as he had exceeded the age limit of liability to recall.[26]

Neill's Blue Caps said that Captain John Mustratt Mood, Z Company, 1st Royal Dublin Fusiliers, was among the battalion's thirteen officers who were wounded by the end of April 1915. He survived the war and was still serving with the Dubs at the time of their disbandment. On 24 September 1919, at St Luke's church, Chelsea, he married Winifred Wiseman, daughter of the late Sir William Wiseman, Royal Navy and Lady Elizabeth Wiseman. On 26 August 1922 he transferred to the East Yorkshire Regiment. Following the disbandment of the regiment he was given part of the regimental silver. His address at the time was 13 Eaton Rise, Ealing, Middlesex. At the time of his daughter's marriage in 1943, her father was described as the late Major John Mood and her mother was living in Toronto, Canada.[27]

೧೧

It would have been very difficult for ex-servicemen and relatives of those who were killed to travel to Gallipoli in the years following the war. Initially the political situation in Turkey precluded travel. Even when the situation stabilised, expense and distance would have prevented most people from travelling. In 1921, a report on travel to the Eastern theatres, prepared for the British and Australian Governments by Thomas Cook's travel agency, advised that travellers would need to journey independently, as it would not be possible to organise tours similar to those conducted to the Western Front. The report recommended that travellers be warned about the probability of 'uncongenial surroundings' and 'adverse conditions'. Two years later, in 1923, Thomas Cook published *The Traveller's Handbook for Constantinople, Gallipoli and Asia Minor* by Roy Elston.

It was, however, only a matter of time before the difficulties of arranging tours were overcome and at least eight 'pilgrimages' were made to Gallipoli in the 1920s and 1930s. In 1925, the SS *Otranto* landed passengers at Helles and in May of the same year the *Ormonde* arrived with a party of 400 pilgrims who attended the unveiling of the New Zealand Memorial on Chunuk Bair. The St Barnabas Society organised two pilgrimages in 1926 and 1928.[28] An Australian trip was organised in 1929 and a French one in 1930. Ex-servicemen organised trips in 1934 and 1936. In the late 1920s and early 1930s cruise ships from Great Britain, France, America and Germany regularly called at Helles to allow passengers to visit Gallipoli.[29]

Gallipoli was the only battlefield outside the Western Front for which a guidebook was written[30] and many accounts were published about trips to Gallipoli. For instance four books were written about the St Barnabas 1926 pilgrimage.[31] *The Ship of Remembrance* tells of how, in September 1926, a party of almost 300 approached the Gallipoli peninsula aboard 'a big white liner'. The author says that 'Shortly after sunrise a great floating wreath, composed of flowers sent from all over the Empire and decorated with a tiny White Ensign and the flags of the Dominions, was duly blessed and launched overboard, just off Cape Helles.'[32] Later, the ship drew close to the coast. 'Straight ahead certain of the landing beaches were visible, each rendered sadly conspicuous by a military cemetery set on the hillside above it ... We had on board men who had landed on this very peninsula more than eleven years ago – landed in small boats under concentrated fire – and who had now come back, from all over the world, to revive that memory and if possible recapture that ancient hill. And we had with us, too, the wives, sons, and daughters of other men who had affected the same landing and stormed these same cliffs – but had not come back.'[33]

The author said that those on the ship came from all walks of life. Some had paid for their passage, others had made a partial payment, while others still had made no payment '... for that is the principle upon which St. Barnabas works. You give what you can afford; and if your means are so slender that you can afford nothing, St. Barnabas invites you to be his guest.' One of the group was a peeress, who had come to visit her husband's grave at Suvla Bay. Another was 'a poor seamstress from the north of England, who had lost three sons in the war.'[33] The group included a large number of ex-soldiers 'of every grade, men now in the prime of life ... men full of affectionate references to Johnny Turk and Asiatic Annie ... And what is more, a good many of them have brought their young people with them. So, as I say, we are a happy ship: we play deck games; we get up entertainments; we even dance, more or less in the mode of the moment.[34]

… An hour later we were disembarking in small boats on V Beach, of *River Clyde* fame – the merest little sandy cove, closed in on one side by Cape Helles itself and completely commanded on the other by the ancient Turkish fort which stands on Cape Sedd-el-Bahr, only a few hundred yards away. The *River Clyde* is gone now: instead of ending her days as a national monument in some great English seaport she is once more earning her living on the high seas – under a foreign flag, to our national shame – but the great steel barge, or hopper [the *Argyle*], along which the Munsters, the Hampshires, and the men of the Anson Battalion struggled through the tornado of machine-gun fire from Sedd-el-Bahr is still there, half buried in the sand … Above the beach stands Cape Helles lighthouse; above the light-house the Gallipoli (Helles) War Memorial, recently completed. Otherwise the scene is one of complete peace and solitude: there are no reminders of that terrible April morning left, save a few strands of barbed wire rusting among the scrub at the foot of the cliff – and the cemetery above.

Later the group assembled at the Helles Memorial. Their number had now grown to nearly 500. The British Mediterranean Fleet had been cruising nearby and a contingent of officers and men had come ashore in civilian dress. One of them had witnessed the 25 April 1915 landing at V Beach. 'Our exercises were simple enough. A few hymns, a few prayers, an address, then Last Post, then one full minute of silence; then "The King". After that all turned eastward, towards the morning sun, while Reveille rang out, sweet and true. Finally, after the Benediction, all our flowers, from the great regi-mental wreaths to the humblest handfuls of heather and poppy, were laid at the foot of the Memorial, for dedication before removal to their appropriate destinations, and the official part of our day was over. After that we scattered, to more private business. Every cemetery was visited, and every grave sought was found.'[35]

On 20 March 1936, *The Times* had the following item.

Pilgrimage to Gallipoli and Salonika: The liner *Lancastria* will leave Liverpool on May 1 with 600 passengers for Salonika and Gallipoli. The cruise, coincid-ing almost with the twenty-first anniversary of the landings on Gallipoli, will enable some hundreds who fought in the Near East to revisit the scenes of the most eventful years of their lives. Field-Marshal Sir William Birdwood will lead the cruise jointly with Admiral of the Fleet Sir Roger Keyes, and the passengers will include 100 nurses who served in Salonika hospitals or on the hospital ships in the Mediterranean. Arrangements are nearing completion for a meeting en route with the *River Clyde*, which, after deliberate grounding on V Beach

SS *River Clyde* in Malta, *c.* 1919.
(Copyright Stephen Chambers)

on the morning of April 25, 1915, was a familiar sight to all who served in the Cape Helles area. She is now a tramp steamer in the ownership of a Spaniard who cherishes her historic past. Her war-time commander, Captain E. Unwin, V.C., who won his decoration for his services during the landings, will be on board the *Lancastria* to welcome his old ship. Malta, Gibraltar, and Istanbul will be visited primarily for sightseeing and reunion with old comrades still living, and two days each at Salonika and Gallipoli will be devoted to commemoration.[36]

In 1936, the Gallipoli peninsula again became part of Turkey's formal defensive perimeter and for almost three decades foreign visitors to the area required a permit and a military escort. In the 1960s most restrictions were lifted.[37]

✢

The *River Clyde* lay on V Beach for four years.[38] Photographs taken in 1919 show her to have been comprehensively stripped of her fittings by then. In April 1919, Ernest Raymond, who had served in the Gallipoli campaign, was returning from Russia aboard ship. Sailing down the Dardanelles, the ship passed V Beach. 'And there, before Cape Helles, red with rust, listing, empty, and abandoned, was the *River Clyde*, still grounded where we had left her …'[39] In June, within a few weeks of Raymond's seeing her, the *River Clyde* was pulled off the beach by the Ocean Salvage Company's steamer *La Valette* and taken under tow to Mudros harbour in Lemnos.[40] There, temporary repairs were carried out to make her fit for a tow to Malta. Photographs taken at Mudros show the heavy punishment the ship had taken at V Beach. 'There was a very large shell hole at the starboard forward corner of No.1 hatch and another on the poop, where the head of the rudder stock and all other

Shell hole in *River Clyde*. (Copyright Stephen Chambers)

steering gear was missing. The funnel had a shell hole in the after side and the surrounding ventilators were riddled with smaller holes.'[41]

A Royal Naval crew of about twenty were put aboard the *River Clyde*. Seaman Arthur Pearman was among those who volunteered for the job. He said the crew drew rations and climbed on the *River Clyde* to find 'not a rope, hawser, chain or rail [aboard]'. The ship's engines were not working and there appeared to be no habitable place in its interior. For safety's sake the crew sat together in the middle part of the deck, away from the shell holes. As darkness fell, they tried to have a sing-song, but the sea became rough and some of the men were seasick. Pearman said, 'It was as much as we could do to sit together without sliding off the deck'. Their only light came from the matches with which they lit their cigarettes. The *La Valette* towed the ship into Skyros and the crew spent the night on deck in the dark. Soon afterwards the *La Valette* and her charge arrived safely at Malta. Rumours at the time suggested that the *River Clyde* was going to be preserved. Pearman was under the impression 'the ship was to be a museum piece'.[42]

By July, the ship was in the dockyard at Malta. On 18 November 1919, *The Times* reported, 'After being salved at Gallipoli and brought to Malta, it was thought that [the *River Clyde*] would be preserved permanently as a memento. Unless there is a further change in the official view, however, she is to be sold where she lies.' On 20 November 1919, the following appeared in the *Grey River Argus, Australia.* 'The *River Clyde*: Gallipoli Vessel to be broken up. London, Nov, 18. There are many protests from Ireland against the proposal to break up and sell the *River Clyde*, which beached at Gallipoli. It was suggested that the ship should be sent to Dublin as a memorial of the participation of the Irish in the Gallipoli landing. The admiralty replied that an attempt to bring the steamer homeward will probably result in her foundering. It would be better to convert her into cash. Moreover, it says that a prominent commander of the Anzacs might dispute Ireland's claim.' Two days later, the same newspaper published the following.

The *River Clyde:* There is nothing surprising in the Irish demand to have the famous old tramp steamer *River Clyde* sent from Gallipoli to Dublin, to serve there as a memorial of the admittedly most heroic part which the celebrated Twenty-ninth Division (which was mainly composed of Irish Regiments) played in the Gallipoli landing. It may be recalled that the ship was a collier, and that she was run ashore at Cape Helles, Gallipoli, on April 25th 1915, to land troops under fire, was salved recently and towed to Mudros in June by the Ocean Salvage Company's steamer *La Valette*. It was discovered after the *River Clyde* was refloated that she was in much better condition than had been expected. The *La Valette* was employed in carrying out certain repairs to the *River Clyde* to enable her to be towed to Malta. The cables tell us that the official reply to the Irish request from the English authorities is that the old ship must be broken up. She is declared to be unlikely to stand a journey to Ireland. In view, however, of the additional remark that the authorities hint an Australasian claim to the ship might be made, it is possible the breaking up is designed as a solution of a difficulty arising out of conflicting claims. Well, the facts of the case, which might throw light on the merits of the claims, are as follows: [There then followed a lengthy description of the landing at V Beach by the Dublins and the *River Clyde*.] Many famous conflicts, from the dawn of history till now, have been connected with Gallipoli, but none surpassed in heroism the *River Clyde* landing. John Masefield, the historian of Gallipoli, bears striking testimony to this fact. Surely then it is not to be wondered that this relic of a famous fight should strongly appeal to a fighting race, whose sons were so prominently concerned. It would be a wise policy on the part of the authorities to send the old ship to Ireland if it were at all possible.

On 29 January 1920, *The Times* announced that, at auction, the ship had been sold for £11,500 to London shipbrokers Harris & Dixon, acting on behalf of a Spanish interest. Expressing regret that the ship had not been saved, the paper said that Commodore Edward Unwin VC had attended the auction. 'Evidently sentiment brought him to the auction room. His presence lifted the proceedings out of the commonplace.' Two days later, *The Times* reported a British offer had been made to repurchase the ship from her new owner on terms which would give yield 'a very substantial profit'. The Spanish owner was said to be amenable if a suitable alternative ship could be found. Unfortunately, this did not prove possible. On 18 February, Lord Privy Seal Bonar Law told the House of Commons that, the *River Clyde* was sold because the Government did not think it justifiable to incur the heavy expense required to bring the ship to Britain. Nor was it felt that 'preservation at Malta was desirable'. He said that 'It was a very old ship, and had it remained at Malta it would simply have rusted away and have been of no benefit to anybody.' (Completed in 1905, it was hardly 'very old.') On 10 March, Viscount Curzon, the Foreign Secretary, asked why a ship with such historic associations was sold to a foreign owner. 'I, in common with a great many others, would far rather have seen that ship sunk in deep water than it should have been handed over to an alien firm'. In reply Colonel Luke Wilson, Parliamentary Secretary to the Ministry of Shipping and chairman of the National Maritime Board, said if had been possible, the ship would have been returned 'to England', but 'the cost was really prohibitive. It was only a shell-riddled hull and there were no engines.' (According to Denis Stonham 'Wilson was wrong in saying that there were no engines in the ship, although they may have been partially dismantled; *Lloyd's Register* shows her original engines *in situ* until the end of her life.') A member of parliament asked, 'Why not have left her at Malta?' Wilson replied, 'That was considered but we thought we were hardly justified in not, after all, selling her for the very considerable sum of money we got.' Surely a circumlocution of which *Yes Minister's* Sir Humphry Appleby would have been proud.

Sold to Arturo Pardo, of Santander, the *River Clyde* was renamed *Angela*. She was taken to a port in Italy where she was repaired. Three new boilers were installed, in place of the original two. Work for ships like the *Angela* was scarce in the aftermath of the First World War, but Denis Stonham said that 'she would no doubt have been employed on the Spanish coast carrying cargoes of coal from the mines of Asturias'. During the General Strike of 1926, the ship brought at least one cargo of coal to Britain. On 10 November 1927, enroute to Sunderland, she was reported to be in difficulty off Flamborough

Head. A tug was put on standby, but on the following afternoon the *Angela* was reported to be at anchor in the River Humber. *The Times* thought it of sufficient interest to publish this rather commonplace piece of shipping intelligence and gave its report the title *The Steamer River Clyde*. In March 1929, the *Angela* was sold to Gumersindo Junquera Blanco and Vicente Figaredo Herrero, of Gijon, in Asturias. They renamed the ship *Maruja y Aurora*, after the first-born child of each of the partners. In the service of these owners the ship continued to operate around the Spanish peninsula. On 19 May 1936, at the end of the previously mentioned pilgrimage to Gallipoli and Salonkia, the liner *Lancastria* was approaching Gibraltar when she passed the *Maruja y Aurora*. In what appears to have been a previously arranged rendezvous, the two ships dipped their ensigns in mutual tribute.[43]

In August 1937, during the Spanish Civil War, the *Maruja y Aurora* arrived at Santander to assist in the evacuation of Republican forces from the city. Twenty-two hours earlier the Nationalists had captured the port and the ship fell into their hands. Apparently serving as a naval auxiliary, she subsequently made a number of voyages between Gijon and Pasajes during final operations on the northern front. On 22 October 1937, she captured the Republican vessel *Margarita* sailing from Gijon with 400 refugees. Subsequently, the ship remained on coastal duties. In May 1940, she was at Antwerp about the time the city was occupied by German forces. During the Second World War she made her first deep-sea voyages for many years, calling at Santa Fe and Buenos Aires in Argentina and Pernambuco (Recife) in Brazil. In the summer of 1944 she went to Philadelphia. That was her final voyage outside of European and Mediterranean waters. Thereafter she confined herself to coastal service, with an occasional voyage to northern European ports.

On 24 April 1965, the *Daily Telegraph* published a commemorative article by Ernest Raymond on the eve of the fiftieth anniversary of the Gallipoli landings.

Should you one day be on the quays of Barcelona or Castellon you might see a very old Spanish cargo ship bearing the name *Maruja y Aurora*; and should you go on board her you might notice that her bulkheads are still bent as if they'd once known the blast of shell-fire, and her rails still pocked with marks that suggest a storm of bullets. Go down into her heart and you will see a memorial plaque which pictures her as *River Clyde at V Beach, April 1915*. Some of us have always wondered who dared to sell this old collier, with her glory and her story, to Spain, and why she was not brought back to a berth in the Thames, or in Portsmouth harbour, or, better still perhaps, in the River Clyde. Is it too late, even now, to bring her home?

In response, a campaign was started to repatriate the *River Clyde*, with offers of support being made by over fifty individuals and organisations. In June 1965 each received a letter from the 'River Clyde' Preservation Trust. While initially expressing sympathy with the project to preserve the ship, the owners of the *Maruja y Aurora* subsequently said that the ship was due to be withdrawn from service in 1966 and they were awaiting tenders from Spanish shipbreakers. At the time it was believed that the sum of £14,000 would be sufficient to purchase the ship. In August 1965 the ship's owners set the price at £42,500. They said that the price should be guaranteed and that the contract should be signed soon. The sum required was beyond the means of the Preservation Trust. The ship was sold to Desguaces y Salvamentos SA, Aviles, who began demolition at San Juan de Nieva on 15 March 1966.

ಬಬ

In February 1922, *Tell England: A Study in a Generation* was published. A novel by Ernest Raymond, it tells the story of three young men who serve in Gallipoli. The book is dedicated 'To the memory of Reginald Vincent Campbell Corbet who fell, while a boy, in the East and George Frederick Francis Corbet who passed, while a boy, in the West.' Twenty-one-year-old Lieutenant Reginald Corbet, 1st Battalion Royal Dublin Fusiliers, was killed in action on 28 April 1915. Commemorated on the Helles Memorial, he was the eldest son of Eila Corbet and Frederick Corbet, Advocate-General of Madras. He was the grandson of Sir George Campbell, KCMG, Inspector General of Ceylon Police and Lieutenant Governor of Penang.[44] (Second Lieutenant George Corbet of the Welsh Regiment died on 25 January 1916. He is buried in Brookwood Cemetery Z. 177036.) Strangely, Raymond's autobiography did not mention the Corbets or his attempts to save the *River Clyde*. In 1931, *Tell England*, a film of the book, was released. Co-directed by Anthony Asquith and Geoffrey Barkas, it starred Fay Compton, Tony Bruce and Carl Harbord. Asquith's father, Herbert Asquith, had been Prime Minister at the time of the Gallipoli landings and for most of the campaign. Barkas had fought at Suvla Bay. At the time of writing, the film is not available for purchase. A clip from the film, showing a recreation of the V Beach landing, was used in a television documentary about the Gallipoli campaign. Rob Jordan, grandson of Munster Fusilier Bob Jordan, put the clip on YouTube in 2012, under the title *Landing at V Beach, Gallipoli*.

ಬಬ

In 1924, the Helles Memorial was completed. Standing atop Gözcübaba, it is over thirty meters high and can be seen by ships passing through the Dardanelles. It serves the dual function of a memorial for the whole Gallipoli campaign and a place of commemoration for the thousands of Commonwealth servicemen who died in the fighting and have no known grave. Over 21,000 names are inscribed on the memorial.

A memorial to officers of the Royal Dublin Fusiliers, who were cadets at the college, was erected in the chapel of the Royal Military College, Sandhurst. Among the twenty names listed for 1915 are: Captain D. Anderson, Lieutenant R. Corbet, Lieutenant R. de Lusignan, Brevet Major T. Frankland, Lieutenant R. Bernard, Major E. Fetherstonhaugh, Lieutenant L. Boustead, Captain H. Floyd, Lieutenant H. O'Hara, D.S.O. (As the names are not listed according to rank or alphabetically, they may be listed in the order of graduation from the college.) Six stained-glass windows were erected in the Roman Catholic Chapel in Borden Camp: one by the officers of the 1st Battalion in 'memory of their comrades who fell at Gallipoli 1915,' five windows were erected by 'A, B, C and D Companies and Sergeants' Mess in memory of the landing at Gallipoli.'[45]

അ

On 31 August 1936, a lieutenant-colonel in the United States Army, stationed at Fort Shafter, Hawaii, published *The Defense of Gallipoli: A General Staff Study*. The purpose of the study was, 'To examine the methods used in defence against landing operations as illustrated by the Turkish defence of Gallipoli.' The study is easily accessed on the internet. The officer's name was George S. Patton.

അ

Former Dublin Fusilier officer Ewing Grimshaw, who had met his *Blue Cap* brother Cecil at the Suez Canal, was killed in Mesopotamia on 21 January 1916. Before he left England for Gallipoli, Major Cecil Grimshaw DSO was photographed with his sons Tommy and George, the boys dressed in miniature army uniforms. After his death, Violet gave birth to a third son, David, on 13 October 1915. She supplemented a meagre pension by having children, whose parents were abroad, stay during school holidays. She became increasingly involved in Christian activities and in the Oxford Group, which worked to build better relationships between people of different races, religions and economic backgrounds in the hope that ordinary people could positively

influence national leaders and international events. She travelled extensively,
lecturing and leading courses all over
Europe. In 1941, she became ill with cancer
and died two years later. Tommy worked
in engineering, served in the Territorial
Army and played rugby. He died at the
age of thirty-four, leaving a wife and
three children. George, born when the
Blue Caps were stationed in India, was
an outstanding scholar and sportsman.
After distinguished service in the Second
World War, he retired from the army with
the rank of lieutenant-colonel. He subsequently became Regional Secretary of the
Church Mission Society in Kenya. On his
retirement from this post, he settled in

Violet Grimshaw.

Devon, where he was very involved in youth work and local history. He died in
2008, ten days before his 98th birthday. The Oxford Movement set the frame-
work for David's life. In order to foster international understanding, he learnt
Danish, Finnish, French, German and Norwegian. He escaped the Nazi invasion of Norway by posing as a neutral Swede. He served in the Royal Artillery
Regiment during the war. After the war he organised international conferences
to restore shattered relationships. Married, with one son, he died in Sydney,
Australia in 2013, aged ninety-seven. Lieutenant-Colonel Charles Doughty-
Wylie was awarded the Victoria Cross. It is difficult to understand why Major
Cecil Grimshaw DSO who died, in similar circumstances, while leading the
troops with Doughty-Wylie was not given a similar award. He and Violet did,
however, leave an enduring legacy. They have grandchildren, great and great-
great-grandchildren living around the world, including Australia, Botswana,
Chile, England and the United States. They include artists and architects,
conservators, conservationists, an engineer, nursing and health management,
publishers, teachers and lots of parents with young families.

　　Annie Mallaghan died in late April 1915. Family tradition says that she died
'of a broken heart' upon learning of the death of Sam and Jack. But it seems
likely that she predeceased them (or at least Jack). It also seems unlikely that
news of either of their deaths would have arrived in Newry prior to about
mid-May. Family tradition says that John Mallaghan senior was working in
the garden of a local 'big house' when the postman handed him the dreaded

telegram. The story does not say whether the telegram told him of the death of one or both of his sons. Coming soon after the death of Annie, this must have been an incredible blow to the poor man. Hopefully, the family story that his two other sons, Herbie and Willie were home on leave and were helping their father when the news arrived, is true. (Though it seems unlikely that both would have been given leave at the same time, particularly as they were in different battalions of the Royal Irish Fusiliers. Willie was in the 2nd Battalion and Herbie in the 5th Battalion.) On 28 April 1915, at a public meeting in the town hall, the chairman of Newry Urban District Council was presented with Newry's Roll of Honour: A list of the men from the town who were serving in the army and the navy.[46] On 16 May 1915, the Mallaghans next-door neighbour Private Thomas Marshall, 2nd Royal Inniskilling Fusiliers, was killed in France. Jack's few surviving possessions were sent home to his father. These included a knife, fork and spoon stamped with his regimental number, 10741, on the back. The cutlery was in a cloth carrier. Also returned were a New Testament (dated 1907), a book titled *Fragments of Literature:* [containing extracts] *from the most interesting and popular works* (published in 1828), his water bottle and a leather ammunition pouch. On 6 November 1923, the Imperial War Graves Commission wrote to John Mallaghan asking that he pay, at his 'earliest convenience' the sum of 3 shillings and 9 pence for the personal inscription carved on Jack's headstone in V Beach Cemetery, an inscription John would never get to see. John died in August 1949, aged eighty-eight. In 1999, the *Belfast Telegraph* published an article by Dr Margaret Whittock, grand-daughter of Sam and Jack's brother, Herbie. The article told how, only dimly aware of the story of Sam and Jack, she and her husband visited Gallipoli and happened to come upon the boys' headstones. Inspired by her experience, Margaret wrote the novel *Ghost of Gallipoli*, in which Royal Dublin Fusilier Jack Callaghan is killed on V Beach and eighty years later, his great-niece, Ellie McKnight comes to live in Istanbul. Also inspired by their story, Brian Dodds, a grandson of the boys brother Willie, wrote a poem about Sam and Jack.

Sam and Jack and Rupert Brooke

You might have died with Rupert Brook,
but septicaemia took him off
two days before the Churchill madness
that did for both of you; you occupy
some corner of a foreign field
that is for ever Ireland. B45 and 46

Ewan Barlow, great-great-great-nephew of Sam and Jack Mallaghan.

they call them, tiny plots of dead
earth,
lonely graves by Suvla's waves,
land that shelters wasted Irish
bones.

Twenty-seven-year-old Private Nicky Smyth, from County Meath was killed in action not long after the V Beach landing. He was the grandson of Private John Mitchell of the 41st Foot, who had gone to Turkey sixty years earlier to support the Turks against the Russians. Nicky is among a group of soldiers recorded by the Commonwealth War Graves Commission as having died on 11 May 1915, and by *Soldiers Died* as 30 April 1915. As argued earlier, available evidence appears to strongly suggest that Nicky and his comrades were killed on the night of 1 May, in the Blue Caps fiercest fighting since the landing at V Beach. He is commemorated by Special Memorial B. 101 in V Beach Cemetery. His brother Christy, was wounded at Ypres, while serving with the 2nd Dublins (the Old Toughs). Invalided home, he was treated at Jervis Street Hospital in Dublin. Upon recovering, he was sent to Gallipoli with the Dublins 6th Battalion, landing at Suvla Bay on 7 August. He married Julia Lynch. Of their descendants, three sons, three grandsons, a granddaughter, nine great-grandsons and a great-great-granddaughter have served, or are serving in the Irish Army. All of these soldiers can trace their lineage back to Dublin Fusiliers Christy and Nicky Smyth and from them back to Crimean War veteran John Mitchell. Warrant Officer Myles Smyth (retired) is a member of the Royal Dublin Fusiliers Association. When he was in the army, two other men in his unit had relatives who had been killed in Gallipoli, while serving with the *Blue Caps*. The casualties were Private Thomas Monks (9869) from Parnell Street, Dublin. Recorded by the Commonwealth War Graves Commission as killed on 30 April 1915, but recorded on a copy of his will as killed on 25 April, he is commemorated on Special Memorial B. 54. Twenty-one-year-old Lance-Corporal Matthew Kelly (10999), from Malahide, was killed on 6 March 1915. He is commemorated on the Helles Memorial.

Lance-Corporal Edward Nugent was among those in a photograph of the Band and Drum football team at Ahmednagar in 1913. It appears that Nugent was the assistant manager of the team and Harry Fox was the manager. Like Harry Fox, the then Corporal Edward Nugent, survived the V Beach landing and the Gallipoli campaign. Sadly, he did not survive the war. He was killed in action on 29 September 1918, in the final weeks of the conflict. Having had some brush with army officialdom, he had by that time been returned to the rank of private. The footballer-musician is buried in Hooge Crater Cemetery in Belgium.

Giving his occupation as Collier, Benjamin Hurt from Derbyshire had joined the Dubs in 1909. As his career gives a good overview of a First World War Blue Caps soldier, it is worth looking at in brief detail. Sent to the depot in Naas, he obtained a Third Class Certificate in Education, before being sent as part of a draft to the Blue Caps, arriving in Bombay on Bombay in 8 September 1910. He went to Gallipoli as part of the battalion machine-gun team, being one of the few of them to survive the slaughter of the landing. On 22 May 1915, he was shot in the leg. On 9 December 1915, he was promoted to lance-corporal. On 3 March 1916, he was promoted to corporal and, on the same day, to lance-sergeant, shortly before being sent to France with the battalion on 19 March. On 13 May, he was promoted to sergeant. He was posted to the depot in Naas on 5 December and on 6 February 1917 to the Dubs 3rd Battalion at Aghada in County Cork, both postings presumably so that he could train new recruits. While with the 3rd Battalion, he qualified on a Lewis Gun Instructors course at Dollymount, Dublin. On 19 September 1918, as the war on the Western Front was drawing to a close, he was attached to an expeditionary force going to Northern Russia to support the White Russians against the Reds in the Russian Civil War. He embarked at Dundee on 20 September 1918 and disembarked in Archangel on 1 October 1918. He was demobilised on 8 October 1919, being transferred to the reserves. He was called back to the Dublins on 9 April 1921. In response to a miner's strike called on 31 March, the Government had declared a state of emergency and called up the Army Reserve. Troops were camped in different parks around London, so as to be available in the event of disturbance. Among them was a detachment of Blue Caps, twenty-four officers and 445 men, who left St Lucia Barracks, Bordon on 16 April, encamping in Victoria Park, London the same day. There they were joined by 199 reservists. Among the Blue Cap officers stationed in the park were Lieutenant Christopher McCann DCM who had been a sergeant in W Company aboard the *River Clyde* and Second Lieutenant Richard Rooth, son of the Blue Caps commanding

Benjamin Hurt.

officer at V Beach. When the risk of disturbance dissipated and the strike showed signs of ending, the reservists were demobilised. Benjamin Hurt was discharged on 13 June 1921 and again transferred to the reserves. Presumably enjoying his time back with his regiment he re-enlisted, as a private, in the Dubs on 15 July 1921, in Derby. He was promoted to corporal on 19 July. In the run up to disbandment of the Royal Dublin Fusiliers, he transferred to the Northumberland Fusiliers on 18 May 1922. He was immediately promoted to lance-sergeant, the promotion back-dated to 15 May. From 14 July 1922 to 30 January 1926, he served as part of the army of occupation in Germany. He was promoted to sergeant on 11 February 1926 and served in the army until 14 July 1933. He married Mary Catherine Bembridge on 3 January 1922. They had two daughters, Joan (11 February 1923) and Mary (14 September 1925). Both girls were born in Cologne, Germany. Unfortunately, Mary Catherine died after giving birth to Mary. On 25 August 1928, Benjamin married Mary's sister Margaret. A keen footballer, Lance-Sergeant Benjamin Hurt was a member of the Blue Caps battalion team that won the Aldershot Command Senior League for the 1921-1922 season. (Also on the team was Sergeant Michael Ludford, the sole survivor of the quartet of footballing musicians photographed at Ahmednagar in 1913 as part of the Band and Drum team.) Benjamin died on 19 October 1958. His granddaughter (Joan's daughter), Lyn Edmonds is a very active member of the Royal Dublin Fusiliers Association and the Gallipoli Association and has visited Gallipoli several times.

Arthur Wright emerged unscathed from service in Gallipoli and France. When his life began, however, he did not seem to be particularly blessed. He was one of twin boys born to Ellen Wright in Islington, North London on 23 May 1890. Ellen's husband George had died around March 1890, leaving her to raise a daughter and four sons. The family was living in a single room in a boarding house in Campbell Road, Islington. The area was so

impoverished that author Jerry White's 1986 book about the road was titled
The Worst Street in North London. Further tragedy struck the family the following year when twin Francis died at the age of eleven months. The 1891
census gave thirty-nine-year-old Ellen's occupation as charwoman, but it
also recorded her as 'paralysed from waist'. The eldest child Eliza was also
listed as paralysed. No further record of the family has been found until
Arthur Michael Wright enlisted in the army at Fermoy Barracks, Buttevant,
County Cork on 23 November 1905 as a boy soldier. As the fifteen-year-old
gave his previous occupation as musician, perhaps he had spent some time
in an institution where he had been taught music. Three days later he was
posted to the 2nd Battalion Royal Dublin Fusiliers in England. He was
posted to the 1st Battalion in Alexandria 1906 and back to the 2nd Battalion
in 1909. On 11 January 1913 he was again posted to the 1st Battalion, in India.
He went to Gallipoli with the Blue Caps. He was sent to the depot in Naas on
8 November 1915, presumably to train new recruits. He was attached to the
3rd Battalion on 26 May 1916 and sent to the 8th Battalion on the Western
Front on 9 June, presumably travelling out with a draft from the 3rd Battalion.
While with the 8th Battalion, he was promoted to lance-corporal and then
to acting corporal. On 11 January 1918 he was again assigned to the depot.
On 21 May he was sent to the 3rd Battalion in Grimsby and on 16 June to the
2nd Battalion on the Western Front. Again it looks like he travelled out as part
of a draft. He reverted to the rank of private on 18 September 1918 and was
discharged from the army on 20 February 1919. He reenlisted the following
day and was sent to the 2nd Battalion. He was a corporal at the time the regiment was disbanded. Upon discharge, his military conduct was described as
very good. He was said to be 'sober, honest, reliable. Has been employed in
the Drums and is an excellent flute player.' He married in Gravesend in 1924.

Company Sergeant-Major Harry Fox had been evacuated from Gallipoli
with a gunshot wound to the right hand. The wound must have been
severe, because he did not return to the Blue Caps until 23 January 1918.
On 30 March 1918, he was listed as being ill. He was admitted to the 61st Field
Ambulance the following day, with a diagnosis of trench fever. On 3 April,
he was posted to the Royal Dublin Fusiliers Depot in Naas, County Kildare.
On 29 April, he was posted to the 5th Battalion. On 11 May, he was posted
to the 3rd Battalion. His health presumably broken down, he was discharged from the army on 25 July 1918.[47] The following year he obtained
employment as a schools attendance officer in Kent. On 27 January 1920,
the *London Gazette* recorded that he had been awarded the Distinguished
Conduct Medal, an award for bravery. The Victoria Cross was the only

higher bravery award he could have been given. The *London Gazette* made no mention of the circumstances for which the award had been made (See Appendix 2). In 1921, Harry Fox married Margaret Walking, a widow, whose husband had been killed in France in 1918. He was forty-two and she was thirty-one. She had two daughters, a third having died having her tonsils removed. As schools attendance officer, Harry would call to the homes of children who were not attending school. If they did not have shoes, he would tell them to call to his house, expecting Margaret to find them a pair. After twenty-five years' service in the army and little experience of normal family life, he must have found the role of husband and step-father difficult. Being a former musician, he made his step-daughters lives a misery over their piano lessons. He appears to have been over-strict, which he balanced with kindness. He had a frightening temper, but was never physically violent. When he went to the beach, he would always place his deckchair with his back to the sea, presumably haunted by Sedd el Bahr. He had terrible nightmares, during which he would sometimes shout in Hindustani, which he had learned in India. Very patriotic, he always stood during the Kings/Queen's speech at Christmas. He went to church three times on Sundays and sang in the church choir. He was a member of the Royal Dublin Fusiliers Association, a group for ex-members of the Dublins.[48] He wore shamrock on St Patrick's Day, which arrived in the post in a little box. He played tennis, went to dances and attended Remembrance Day parades. At Christmas he wore a fez and shared family life with Margaret's five siblings, who lived nearby. He developed Alzheimer's during the last few years of his life, dying in 1959 at the age of eighty. For three days before his death, he was barely conscious but he mumbled and laughed, as if reliving experiences from his life. He had expressed a wish to be buried in his red army dress coat, but it no longer fitted. With a Union Jack on his coffin during the service, he was buried in Horton Kirby churchyard, near to South Darenth, Kent, where he had lived. After Margaret died, her family found a certification of Harry's birth in an envelope marked 'Strictly Private and Confidential'. When he had applied for the post of schools attendance officer, Kent Council had asked for a copy of his birth certificate. Not having one, he had written to the Foundling Hospital in London. He was sent a statement with the Foundling Hospital across the top, his entry date, his number and his birth date. Kent County Council had returned it to him, with a note saying the matter would be kept strictly private. His step-daughters did not know about his childhood and were unsure if their mother, Margaret knew. In the suitcase where his army items were kept, his granddaughter Pam found a very rough lump of lead with a number on it. She threw it out. Only in recent years did she find out that it was his Foundling Hospital identity tag. It is sad to think that the social stigma of 'illegitimacy' must have haunted the hero all his life.

Wounded on 26 April 1915, Munster Fusilier Corporal William Cosgrove was evacuated to Malta, where surgeons operated on his back. His Victoria Cross award was 'gazetted' on 23 August 1915. He was promoted to sergeant and was sent to Ireland. He remained there for some time, higher command being anxious to exploit his celebrity status. After the war was over he continued to serve in the Royal Munster Fusiliers until the regiment was disbanded. Then, like Benjamin Hurt of the Dublins, he transferred to the Royal Northumberland Fusiliers. Six years later, he transferred to the 6th (Burma) Battalion, University Training Corps, based in Rangoon. In 1934, Staff Sergeant Instructor William Cosgrove retired from the army. Soon afterwards, his health began to fail. It was discovered that splinters of shrapnel, which surgeons had failed to detect during operations on his back in Malta, were slowly killing him. Despite regular treatment at Millbank Hospital in London, he died in the hospital on 14 July 1936, his brother Joseph by his side. During his final months, he was awarded the Meritorious Service Medal and the King George V Jubilee Medal. On 16 July, his remains left London for Fishguard, Wales, where they were placed aboard the City of Cork Steam Packet Company vessel SS *Innisfallen*. The ship left at midnight and docked at Penrose Quay, Cork the following morning. About 300 members of the Royal Munster Fusiliers Old Comrades Association formed a guard of honour and a salute was sounded as the coffin was taken from the ship to a waiting hearse. The funeral cortege then travelled by road to Aghada in east Cork. The cortege arrived in Middleton around midday. 'Not alone from almost every townland south of Midleton, but from distant parts of the county, came sympathisers and friends of the deceased. Conspicuous in the huge gathering were his old comrades and ex-members of the Munster Fusiliers.' When the hearse reached Upper Aghada, the coffin was removed and shouldered to the family grave by members of the Royal Munster Fusiliers Old Comrades Association. The *Last Post* was sounded, while Cosgrove's old comrades stood at attention. Two years after his death, a public appeal raised sufficient funds to place an impressive Celtic cross over his grave.[49]

Royal Munster Fusilier brothers Bob and Peter Jordan survived the Gallipoli campaign. Bob was wounded twice during the fighting. There is a photograph of him in a military hospital, possibly Alexandria. Peter was wounded more severely, though whether in Gallipoli or not, his nephew Tony does not know. He was hospitalised near Stratford upon Avon for almost a year. Unfortunately this did not save him. He was sent back to the fighting. Corporal Peter Jordan, 1st Royal Munster Fusiliers died of wounds on 30 May 1918. Bob Jordan returned to Coventry on leave at Christmas 1916 and he and Elsie Fleming were married. She had gathered together, in her own words, 'a few sticks of furniture' for a home in a room above a shop in Far Gosford Street. Bob returned to the Western Front, where he fought in the Battle of Passchendaele. He survived the war. He returned to Coventry, got drunk at the victory celebrations and had to be helped home. According to his son Tony, 'For the next 27 years, he and Elsie applied themselves to the more congenial work of raising a family in the harsh economies of the Twenties and Thirties.' Their eldest son, nineteen-year-old Ronald Patrick Jordan, was lost when the *SS British Resource* was sunk by a German submarine on 14 March 1942. In 1945, when the war in Europe was over, but the fight against the Japanese continued, a General Election was called. Winston Churchill came to Coventry electioneering. According to Tony Jordan, Churchill 'seemed then at the height of his popularity and everyone wanted to see him. Except my father, who said very firmly: 'I wouldn't cross the road to see him.' He was the least political of men and, as a fourteen-year-old boy, I took this in with silent incomprehension. I did not know then about Gallipoli. Within a month or so Churchill had been defeated by Clement Attlee, one of those who fought at Gallipoli. A few days later my father died suddenly at the age of fifty-seven and, a few days after that, the atom bombs were dropped and another war was over.'[50]

Sub-Lieutenant Johnny Dodge, A Company, Hood Battalion, Royal Naval Division was wounded during the V Beach landing. A cousin by marriage of Winston Churchill, he is the only American known to have landed at V Beach. Invalided to England with his wounds, he was afterwards assigned to training duties. On 8 November 1915, he was 'gazetted' for the Distinguished Service Cross for his part in the V Beach landing. His commanding officer, Bernard Freyberg VC, said, 'When Johnny saw that all was not going according to plan, he led his platoon into the fighting with the utmost gallantry until he was badly wounded and he had to be sent home to recover.'[51] Wishing to get back in action, Dodge transferred to the army, with the rank of captain. He ended the war with the rank of acting lieutenant-colonel, having received two mentions in despatches and been awarded the Distinguished Service Order (DSO) (gazetted 3 June 1919). In 1921, he was arrested in Southern Russia, as a suspected spy. Narrowly escaping execution, he was deported, with an order never to return to the country. While serving on London Council, he made a failed bid to enter parliament as a Conservative. On the outbreak of the Second

World War he joined the Middlesex Regiment. Captured in France he ended up on the prison-camp staff of the Senior British Officer Wing Commander Harry Day. The Germans recorded him as having transferred to the Royal Air Force and he was subsequently treated as an RAF prisoner. Sent to Stalag Luft 111, he broke out of the camp at approximately 1 a.m. on 25 March 1944 as one of the seventy-six 'Great Escapers'. Paired with Flight-Lieutenant James Wernham of the Royal Canadian Air Force, they were recaptured at a railway station later that day. Seventy-three of the escapers were recaptured. Wernham and forty-nine others were shot by the Germans. Dodge and three others were sent to Sachenhausen Concentration Camp, from where they tunnelled out on 23 September 1944. After a month on the run, Dodge was recaptured and held in solitary confinement. Towards the end of the war, because of his relationship with Churchill, the Germans released him through Switzerland with an offer of German surrender to the British and Americans but not the Russians. He was awarded the Military Cross for his activities as a prisoner-of-war (gazetted 18 April 1946). He stood as a Conservative in the 1945 General Election, but was narrowly defeated. Johnny Dodge, the only man to have landed at V Beach and taken part in 'The Great Escape', died of a heart-attack in London on 2 November 1960 at the age of sixty-six.

∞

Referring to Sedd el Bahr, Holt's *Battlefield Guide to Gallipoli* says:

> The local inhabitants were evacuated in 1915 and never returned. The site remained uninhabited until 1934 when, over the next four years, Rumanian settlers moved in and rebuilt the village.

Cook's Traveller's Handbook for Constantinople, Gallipoli & Asia Minor (1923) by Roy Elston, however, suggests a different story.

> The fort at Sedd-ul-Bahr, partly repaired, now contains a garrison of Senegalese [from the then colony of French West Africa] ... In the vicinity of Sedd-ul-Bahr, is a Greek village of some forty houses, many of which were built by the Venezelist Government to shelter returning refugees; in the fields with their oxen, and in the sea with their nets, you may see these Greeks at work from dawn to dusk; and the cafes at evening ring loud with their mirth.

This appears to suggest that, following the Turkish surrender, the original Greek inhabitants returned to the village. Subsequent to the 1922 armistice between Greece and Turkey, there were large population transfers between the two countries. Presumably the inhabitants of Sedd el Bahr were included in the population transfer, being replaced by people from Rumania in 1934.[52]

Between 1999 and 2002, under the direction of Professor Lucienne Thys-Şenocak of Koç University, thirty-one recorded interviews were conducted with residents of the village and of Kumkale. The majority of residents of the village 'were Turks who had emigrated to the village from Romania in the early 1930's, almost two decades after the end of the war.' (The majority of the residents at Kumkale had come from Bulgaria.) While official Turkish history emphasises the War of Independence as the source of Turkish national identity, the study showed that residents of Seddülbahir had an awareness of the area's Ottoman heritage. They were able to recall stories of the foundation of the fortress and the Ottoman village that once existed there. A frequently repeated story was how, in the face of the empire's deteriorating economic circumstances, the Queen Mother Turhan Sultan (the Valide) had financed construction of the fortresses at Seddülbahir and Kumkale by selling a pair of golden slippers. One resident said that, so great was the number of workers brought to Seddülbahir from various parts of the empire to build the fortress, that 'camel loads of cutlery' were brought to help feed them. The most detailed memories were those of Fatma Tuncer, a ninety-five-year-old woman whose father had served as a soldier in the village during the First World War. She recalled how, in her childhood, the village had been so well-to-do, it was known as 'Little Istanbul' and had large bazaars and various shops. Her grandmother had told her of having to stay overnight in the fortress several times after she missed the closing of the gates at 11 p.m. while she was visiting friends. The village was described as having been in ruins at the time of re-settlement. Some residents said that, when they arrived from Romania, the houses in the village were so badly damaged they had to stay in an abandoned military barracks (which appears from photographs to have stood on high ground above the left of the beach, viewed from the sea). Others described finding cannons, rifles, bullets and skulls in the vicinity. As the soil was not immediately suitable for farming, many of the immigrants could only survive by selling ammunition and ordnance for scrap iron and lead. The Valide's damaged fortress became a ready source of masonry for the newcomers as they began to rebuild their lives and homes in the village.[53]

The men who came back to Ireland from the First World War faced a country that soon erupted into the violence of the War of Independence, followed soon after by that of the Civil War. In the climate which followed, remembrance of Irish participation in the First World War was not encouraged.[54] With the regiment disbanded and ex-soldiers dying, the Royal Dublin Fusiliers Association ceased to exist sometime during the 1960s. In the mid-1990s an association was established in Dublin to remember the men who served in the Dubs in particular and the other Irish regiments in general. Like Myles Smyth and Lyn Edmonds, many of the association's members are relatives of men who served in the regiment, or in other Irish regiments. Like its predecessor, the association is called the Royal Dublin Fusiliers Association. While only the 1st Battalion of the Dublins was nicknamed the Blue Caps, the new association decided to publish a journal named after the 1st Battalion's magazine. As the original magazine had ceased publication after three issues, the new association's first journal, *The Blue Cap,* was numbered Issue 4. Since its establishment, the association has hosted lectures on the First World War and gone on tours of First World War battlefields associated with the Royal Dublin Fusiliers. Male association members wear a tie identical to the former association's tie, while female members have headscarves with the regimental colours. The association has its own regimental standard which is paraded on official occasions. Some members have published books, given lectures and been interviewed on radio and television.

ಬಃ

In August 1998, my wife Kate and I visited V Beach cemetery. Coming across the headstones of the Mallagher brothers, I decided to research them with a view to telling their story in an article. It was a decision which set my feet on the path which led to the writing of this book.

On 29 August 2001, in blazing sunshine, a small party of men and women from the Royal Dublin Fusiliers Association entered the little cemetery above the beach about fifteen minutes before midday. While waiting for the Governor to arrive, they spent a few minutes looking at the headstones. Some were looking for particular headstones, but most just wandered, reading headstone inscriptions at random. The headstones for Lieutenant-Colonel Richard Rooth and Father William Finn were quickly located. After a few minutes the Governor of Ecebat Province arrived, accompanied by an army officer and a translator. The little group then stood in front of the cemetery's

Royal Munster Fusiliers V Beach survivors photographed in 1920.

Stone of Remembrance – the cemetery's altar-like point of focus – where they were addressed by Tom Burke, chairperson of the Royal Dublin Fusiliers Association. Tom's voice trembled with emotion. He said that eighty-six years previously many Irishmen had died on the nearby beach and were buried in the cemetery where the group now stood. He told the group that they were making history, because, as far as he was aware, it was the first time in eighty-six years that an association had come from Ireland to the cemetery to represent the people of Ireland at an official ceremony with Turkish officials. He said that the cemetery was 'an important place, an emotional place, a symbolic place.' A wreath was laid on behalf of the Royal Dublin Fusiliers Association at the Stone of Remembrance. The Francis Ledwidge poem 'The Irish at Gallipoli' was read out and 'They shall not grow old' was recited. Then, in keeping long-established Royal Dublin Fusiliers Association practice, each member of the party read out the name and details of a soldier who been killed in the vicinity eighty-six years previously. When it came to my turn, I read out the names of Samuel and John Mallaghan, sons of John and Annie Mallaghan of 48 Stream Street, Newry, County Down. For the first time since they had died, Sam and Jack's names were read aloud to a group of Irishmen and women near the place where they were killed. A short prayer was then read. Tom Burke presented the Governor with a print showing the Royal Dublin Fusiliers Arch at Stephen's Green, Dublin. He said that 1,012 men from 1st Battalion Royal Dublin Fusiliers had landed on the beach on

25 April 1915. In January 1915 only eleven of them were still serving with the battalion when the Allies left Gallipoli. The Governor then replied. Focusing on the fact that old enemies were now friends, he did not make any particular reference to Ireland or the Irish. He wished us well on the remainder of our visit to the Gallipoli peninsula. After the ceremony the group spent further time in the cemetery before going to the beach where so many men had died.[55]

As told in the prologue, on 24 March 2010, Mary McAleese, President of the Republic of Ireland, came to visit the men who rest in V Beach cemetery. Having laid a wreath, she was shown a number of particular graves and special memorials and was told about the men who are buried or commemorated there. I had the great honour of showing her the grave of Father William Finn. The President's visit received huge media attention in Ireland and in Turkey. In Ireland people began to discuss the coverage and some started to speak about their relatives who served in the disastrous Gallipoli campaign.

My pal Jeff Evans, from Holyhead, wrote a verse for my previous book on the sinking of the mail-boat RMS *Leinster*. He kindly wrote the following for this book and I leave the closing lines of the story to Jeff.

V Beach

The plan was simple the General said
But his scheme left hundreds of Irishmen dead.
'We'll use boats, we'll come from the sea
and land on the shores of Gallip-oli'

'The Turks are poor soldiers, they will not fight.'
But they defended their homeland with all of their might.
Now the forgotten Irishmen rest near the sea
Their lonely graves far, from Tipper-ary.

It was 1915 and the world was afire
In France both sides were bogged down in the mire
The trenches ran from Switzerland to the sea
So Churchill said: 'We'll attack Gallip-oli.'

'We'll attack Turkey, she's a German ally'
But the plan caused hundreds of Irishmen to die
They rest at Sedd el Bahr near the sea
A little Turkish village in Gallip-oli.

'We'll use boats, we'll come from the sea
and land on the shores of Gallip-oli
The Turks are poor soldiers, they will not fight.'
But they defended their homeland with all of their might.

The Dublin Fusiliers landed from boats and died
The Munsters shot down near the old *River Clyde*.
Father Finn was killed ministering to the soldier
The first chaplain to die, there was none bolder.

William Cosgrove from Cork was awarded the VC
For his brave actions at Gallip-oli.
Grimshaw from Dublin died rallying his men
His wife and two boys never saw him again.

The Mallaghan brothers from the town of Newry
Lie side by side in graves by the sea.
Some said 'neath an Irish sky 'twere better to die,'
But these men were forgotten, I ask Ireland why?

The Dublin Fusiliers landed from boats and died
The Munsters shot down near the old *River Clyde*.
Why did Ireland forget them, these men so bold?
Their ghosts will not rest 'til their story is told.

APPENDIX 1

The British Battalion

The following information is mostly taken from Chris Baker's excellent website *The Long, Long Trail* at www.1914-1918.net, with the information on the machine-gun section taken from *The World War One Source Book* by Philip J. Haythornthwaite.

The battalion was the basic tactical unit of the British Army during the First World War. At full establishment it consisted of 1,007 men, of whom thirty were officers. It had a battalion headquarters and four companies. The battalion was usually commanded by a lieutenant-colonel. A major was second-in-command. Battalion Headquarters was made up of the commanding officer, second-in-command and three other officers: a captain or lieutenant was adjutant (in charge of battalion administration), a captain or lieutenant was quartermaster (responsible for stores and transport) and an officer from the Royal Army Medical Corps (RAMC), a doctor, was attached to the battalion as medical officer. Battalion Headquarters also included the regimental sergeant-major (RSM, the most senior non-commissioned officer) and a number of sergeants with specialist rolls: armourer (usually attached from the Army Ordinance Corps), cook, drummer, orderly room clerk, pioneer, quartermaster (the quartermaster sergeant reported to the quartermaster officer), shoemaker, signaller, transport. Sixteen privates, from among the musicians, also acted as stretcher-bearers. A corporal and fifteen privates were employed as signallers. Eleven privates acted as drivers for the horse-drawn transport. Ten privates were employed as pioneers (on construction, repair and general engineering duties). Six privates acted as officers servants (batmen). A Corporal and four privates from the Royal Army Medical Corps (RAMC) were attached to Battalion Headquarters for water and sanitary duties. Two privates from the battalion acted as orderlies for the medical officer.

The battalion had four companies. Usually lettered A, B, C and D, those that landed at V Beach were lettered W, X, Y and Z. At full establishment each company had 227 men. Each was commanded by a major or captain, with a captain as second-in-command. Company headquarters included a company sergeant-major (CSM), a company quartermaster sergeant (CQMS), two privates acting as servants (batmen) and three privates acting as drivers. The company was divided into four platoons, each commanded by a lieutenant or second lieutenant. In total the four platoons consisted of eight sergeants, ten corporals, four drummers, four servants (Batmen) and 188 privates. Each platoon was subdivided into four sections, each of twelve men commanded by an NCO (Corporal). Men most-closely identified with their section and platoon. They received orders from their section corporal and lance-corporal or their platoon sergeant. They would also come in contact with the lieutenant or second lieutenant commanding their platoon.

Up to late 1914, each battalion had a machine-gun section consisting of a lieutenant, a sergeant, a corporal, two drivers, a servant (a batman) and twelve privates trained in the maintenance, transport, loading and firing of a Vickers heavy machine-gun. The men made up two six-man teams. By February 1915 the allocation of machine guns to each battalion had been doubled, giving the battalion four six-man machine-gun teams. This and other minor changes led to the full establishment number for a battalion being increased from 1,007 to 1,034.

The machine-gun team was numbered 1 to 6. No. 1 was the principal gunner. He carried the tripod, mounted the gun and fired it. No. 2 carried the gun and supervised the belt-feed of ammunition. No. 3 and No. 4 carried ammunition. No. 4 was also responsible for keeping the gun's water cooling system filled. No. 5 and No. 6 acted as scouts and range takers. Battalion transport consisted of forty-three draught and pack horses and thirteen riding horses. The draught and pack horses were used to draw the six ammunition carts, three general service wagons (for tools and machine guns) two water carts and the medical officer's cart. The signallers had nine bicycles. The divisional train also supplied each battalion with four extra general wagons.

Most men carried a rifle: the Short Magazine Lee-Enfield (SMLE). All those who carried a rifle, except the RSM and other staff-sergeants, also had a bayonet. The only men who did not carry a rifle were officers, buglers, drummers, pipers and the five men in each battalion who carried range-finding instruments.

Apart from the equipment carried by the men, battalion equipment included 120 shovels, seventy-three pickaxes, forty-six billhooks, thirty-two folding saws, twenty reaping hooks, eight hand axes, eight crowbars and a handsaw. Battalion transport carried thirty-two boxes of 1,000 rounds and each man could carry up to 120 rounds. This was supplemented by transport at brigade and divisional level. When added together, the supply per rifle came to 550 rounds per man.

When a battalion went on active service it left a detachment at its depot (e.g. Naas, County Kildare for the Royal Dublin Fusiliers and Tralee, County Kerry for the Royal Munster Fusiliers). The detachment was supposed to consist of a lieutenant/second lieutenant, two sergeants and ninety-one privates to form a first reinforcement for the battalion.

The Adversaries

111 Corps: Brigadier-General Esat.
Headquarters in the town of Gelibolu (Gallipoli).
Made up of 7th, 8th and 9th Divisions.

9th Division: Colonel Halil Sami (about 300 officers and 12,000 men).
Headquarters in the town of Maidos (Ecebat).
Made up of an artillery regiment and three infantry regiments: the 25th, 26th and 27th.

26th Regiment: Major Hafiz Kadri (about 3,000 men).
Headquarters in village of Krithia (Kirte).
Made up of three battalions: 1st, 2nd and 3rd.

3rd Battalion: Major Mahmut Sabri (about 1,000 men).
Headquarters about a kilometre behind V Beach.
Stationed in the Cape Helles-Sedd el Bahr region.
Made up of four companies: 9, 10, 11 and 12. Engineering company attached to battalion.
9, 11 Companies and attached engineering company stationed in reserve.
10 and 12 Companies assigned to beach defence.

10 and 12 companies were assigned to defend X, W and V Beaches.
Each company had two of its three platoons in strong points,
fortified by barbed-wire and trenches, overlooking the beaches.
The third platoon of both companies was positioned in reserve behind the strong points.
V Beach appears to have been defended by 10 Company, with 12 Company defending X and W Beaches, as well as strong points on Hill 138 and

Gözcübaba (where the Helles Memorial now stands). Sergeant Yahya and his men defended the strong point on Gözcübaba.

∾∾

29th Division: Major-General Aylmer Hunter-Weston.
Made up of 86th, 87th and 88 Brigades.

86th Brigade: Brigadier-General Steuart Hare,
Brigade-Major Tom Frankland, Royal Dublin Fusiliers.

Made up of 1st Royal Dublin Fusiliers, 1st Royal Munster Fusiliers, 1st Lancashire Fusiliers and the 2nd Royal Fusiliers. The 2nd Hampshire Regiment was attached to the 88th Brigade. Brigadier-General Henry Napier, of the Royal Irish Rifles, commanded the 88th Brigade, with Captain John Costeker, DSO of the Royal Warwickshire Regiment as his brigade-major.

Blue Cap Distinguished Conduct Medals Awards

The Distinguished Conduct Medal was instituted in 1854, during the Crimean War to recognise gallantry performed by soldiers of non-officer rank. The Victoria Cross was the only higher award that could be awarded to soldiers of non-officer rank. The following awards were made to men of the Blue Caps for bravery during the Gallipoli campaign.

Acting Sergeant Stephen Byrne, 10774, 1st Battalion. For conspicuous gallantry on the night of 2/3 October 1915, on the Gallipoli Peninsula. When a sergeant and one man of a covering party near *Dublin Castle* had been wounded, volunteers were called to rescue them. They were lying between some Turkish snipers and some huts. Acting Sergeant Byrne and two men at once volunteered, and brought the wounded men back safely under heavy fire. (Gazetted 22 January 1916.) Byrne was not among the men who landed at V Beach. He arrived in Gallipoli on 9 August 1915. He was promoted to lieutenant on 4 July 1922.

Sergeant Christopher Cooney, 10256, 1st Battalion. For conspicuous gallantry on 26 April 1915 at Cape Helles (Dardanelles). During the landing Sergeant Cooney, in order to give encouragement to his men in the advance, freely exposed himself, regardless of danger, although the enemy were within 70 yards. His bravery and example had the desired effect and contributed largely to the success of the operations. He has on all subsequent occasions, consistently exhibited great presence of mind and devotion to duty (gazetted 6 September 1915).

Private Thomas Cullen, 10113, 1st Battalion. For conspicuous gallantry on 26 April 1915, during the capture of Sedd el Bahr (Dardanelles) He was the first man to enter the fort (Gazetted 5 Aug 1915). He was killed in action between 2 and 4 October 1916, while serving with 6th Battalion Royal Dublin Fusiliers in Salonika. Recorded on the Commonwealth War Graves Commission online database as T. Cullin, he is buried in Grave 111. D. 11 in Struma Military Cemetery, Greece. Commonwealth War Grave Commission records say that he was the son of William Morrissey, 78 Old Kilmainham, Dublin. Following representations by the author, the Commonwealth War Graves Commission kindly agreed to change the surname spelling of this brave Dublin on their online database.

Sergeant Joseph Devoy, 10335, 1st Battalion. For conspicuous gallantry and devotion to duty on 21 August 1915 at Suvla Bay. The gorse having been ignited by the enemy's shells, Sgt Devoy exhibited great bravery in fighting the flames and thus enabling a stack of reserve ammunition to be saved (gazetted 11 Mar 1916).

Sergeant Samuel Ferguson, 6128, 1st Battalion. On 29 April 1915, during operations near Krithia, for exceptional gallantry and valuable work in action. (Gazetted 3 July 1915).

Private James Ford, 17811, 1st Battalion. For conspicuous gallantry between the 23 and 29 August 1915 at Suvla Bay (Dardanelles) when he volunteered to go out almost every night alone to reconnoitre the ground lying between our trenches and those of the enemy. He brought back accurate reports containing valuable information, in addition he recovered about 60 abandoned rifles. He showed a splendid example of bravery and devotion to duty. (Gazetted 16 November 1915.) Aged thirty-one, he was killed in action on 23 May 1917, while serving with 10th Battalion Royal Dublin Fusiliers. He is buried in Grave South A.25, Albuera Cemetery, Bailleul-Sire, Berthoult. The cemetery is west of the village, 5 miles north-east of Arras. He served under an alias. His real name was James Lantry, son of John and Elizabeth, Portadown, County Armagh.

Company Sergeant-Major Henry Fox 4823, 12th Battalion (Tonbridge) (Gazetted 30 January 1920). 12th Battalion is a clerical error. The Royal Dublin Fusiliers did not have a 12th Battalion. Company Sergeant-Major Henry Fox was a member of the 1st Battalion. No citation was published with the announcement of the award. The award was made under Army Order 193 of 1919. The army order was entitled 'Rewards for Officers and Soldiers for services in the field and for services rendered in captivity or in attempting to escape or escaping therefrom.' It appears to be an order making provision for awards to officers and men whose gallantry had been overlooked when earlier awards had been made. The order included, but was not exclusive to, men who had carried out acts of gallantry while held captive by enemy powers. King's College, London holds papers of General Sir Ian Hamilton under the title 'Papers relating to Hamilton's despatches from Gallipoli and to recommendations for decorations for service on Gallipoli, 1915-1923.' File 7/7/47, covering the period 20 January 1917 to 3 December 1918, relates to 'Correspondence with relatives and friends of officers and men of the Mediterranean Expeditionary Force, seeking Hamilton's help in gaining decorations or mentions in despatches for distinguished service rendered on Gallipoli, including correspondence relating to the cases of [two majors, three captains, sergeant-major Henry Fox, Royal Dublin Fusiliers, a petty officer in the Royal Naval Division and a French Army chaplain].' Presumably someone made representations to Hamilton on Fox's behalf, following which the award was made in 1920, under the provision of Army Order 193 of the previous year. Not having seen the representations made to Hamilton, I would suggest that the person most likely to have made them was Major Edward Molesworth. In a letter held by Fox's family, Molesworth wrote, 'No. 4823 Coy Sergt Major H Fox 1st Bn Royal Dublin Fusiliers X Company, of which I was in command, displayed conspicuous courage and devotion to duty at the landing on V beach Gallipoli on 25th April 1915. When under fire he dressed wounded men, assisted two men wounded in the legs who were in danger of being drowned from rising tide and brought them to cover. He was wounded himself and remained on duty till the following day. He gave much assistance to wounded men. The Medical Officer [Lieutenant Henry de Boer] was himself badly wounded and unable to move.'

Acting Company Sergeant-Major Christopher McCann, 9809, 1st Battalion. For conspicuous gallantry and devotion to duty during the defence of *Dublin Castle* Gallipoli, from 1 to 18 October 1915. He organised the labour, and when any especially dangerous work was at hand, he always personally superintended it, often under galling fire from snipers. He made several valuable night reconnaissances, and on the night of 16/17 October he built a barricade under very heavy fire. His courage and example have been invaluable. (Gazetted 22 January 1916.) Later promoted to Lieutenant.

Corporal Francis McNamara, 10132, 1st Battalion. For conspicuous gallantry on 20 June 1915, on the Gallipoli Peninsula. A machine gun having fallen into the enemy's hands, Corporal McNamara collected a party of sixteen men and led them in a charge against the largely superior enemy numbers, driving them back with loss and recapturing the gun. His bravery and devotion to duty were conspicuous. (Gazetted 6 September 1915.)

Source on the awards: www.royaldublinfusiliers.com

APPENDIX 4

Brevet Major Thomas Frankland, Royal Dublin Fusiliers

Thomas Hugh Colville Frankland was born in 1879, the sixth of eight children born to Colville and May Jay (*née* Dawson) Frankland. He and his older brother Robert Cecil Colville and Robert's twin sister Mary Olive Elsie (1877) were born in Ireland. He was educated at Cheltenham College. When the Royal Dublin Fusiliers were established in 1881, his father, Lieutenant-Colonel Colville Frankland, was commanding officer of the 103rd (Royal Bombay Fusiliers), which became the 2nd Battalion Royal Dublin Fusiliers. Thomas Frankland joined the regiment in February 1899, in time to serve in the Boer War. He fought at Talana Hill, on 20 October 1899.

On 15 November 1899, he commanded a company of Royal Dublin Fusiliers aboard an armoured train that was attacked by the Boers. Also aboard the train were a company of Durham Light Infantry, four sailors from HMS *Tartar*, manning a 7-pounder muzzle-loading gun, a small civilian repair gang and a correspondent for the *Morning Post* named Winston Churchill. The military on the train were under the command of Captain Aylmer Haldane DSO, 2nd Battalion Gordon Highlanders. The train was shelled by the Boers. Some of its wagons were derailed and the rest became uncoupled from the engine. The derailed wagons were cleared from the track and the engine began to steam slowly southwards, with Churchill and some of the troops aboard. More of the troops followed behind on foot, using the engine as cover. One of the soldiers on foot waved a handkerchief in surrender. The Boers ceased firing and a dozen horsemen rode from their lines. The troops became confused and many of them surrendered. As the engine, with Churchill aboard, continued toward the nearby deserted railway station at Frere, he saw Frankland, 'with a happy confident smile on his face,' attempt to rally his men. At the station Churchill got off the train, deciding to return to the soldiers who were making their way to the station on foot. But the soldiers were captured by the Boers, as was Churchill in the vicinity of the station. Meanwhile, the engine and those aboard escaped. The Boers marched their prisoners to Colenso railway station, where they put them in a corrugated shed near the station. Churchill and Frankland spent the night sharing a blanket. On the march the following day an elderly Boer said that he didn't understand what had induced the soldiers to go in the armoured train. Frankland said, 'Ordered to. Don't you have to obey your orders?' That night Churchill, Haldane and Frankland shared a tent, while the NCOs and soldiers shared another. The prisoners and their escorts met several parties of Boers while on the march the following day. An Irishman was with one party. 'He addressed himself to Frankland, whose badges proclaimed his regiment. What he said when disentangled from obscenity amounted to this: 'I am glad to see you Dublin fellows in trouble ... The soldiers felt the sting and scowled back; the officers looked straight before them.'

The prisoners ended up at Pretoria, where the soldiers were put in a prison camp at a racecourse and the officers and Churchill in the Staat (State) Model School, where Lieutenant Cecil Grimshaw of the Dublins was already a prisoner. Frankland was still in the camp on June 1900 when a British force released the prisoners. Promoted Captain in 1908, he subsequently attended Staff College. In May 1914, while he was serving with the Old Toughs, the 2nd Battalion Royal Dublin Fusiliers, in Gravesend, Kent, the military notes of a local newspaper announced that he had been selected to undergo instruction at the Central Flying School at Upavon. Upon the formation of the 29th Division, he was appointed brigade-major, chief-of-staff of the 86th Brigade. Killed on 25 April 1915, while advancing from W Beach in an attempt to linking up with V Beach, he has no known grave and is commemorated on the Helles Memorial.

His brother, Captain Robert Frankland, 3rd Battalion North Staffordshire Regiment, attached to 8th Battalion Lancashire Fusiliers, was killed on 7 August 1915. Like his brother Tom, he has no known grave and is com-memorated on the Helles Memorial. Colonel Colville Frankland died in 1913, aged seventy-four. Mary Frankland died in 1914, aged seventy-one.[1]

On 24 March 2015, my good pal Dave Neenan and I paid our personal tribute to Tom Frankland by following his route from W Beach to V Beach. I believe we were the first in a century to pay such a tribute to this brave man.

Ormond Cook, Owner of the SS River Clyde

Two days after Christmas 1871 James Cook, grocer and wine merchant, of Granville Street, Glasgow and Jessie Ormond were married in Partick, Glasgow. It was the groom's second marriage; his first wife, Agnes Leggat, had died. James and Jessie had five boys: James, Ormond, Crawford, Frederick and George. Ormond jnr was born in 1876. As a young man he was employed by James Hardie & Company, ship owners and brokers, Glasgow and became a qualified shipbroker, specialising in insurance work. At some point he left Hardie's and became self-employed. He appears to have continued work on a claim that he had been processing while working at Hardie's. The claim involved a wooden sailing ship that had touched bottom while inward bound with a cargo of grain for Glasgow. The ship began to leak. This resulted in an expansion of the wet grain, a rupturing of the hull and the sinking of the ship. After failing to settle the case, the owners of the vessel sold the claim to Ormond Cook. To his good fortune, the insurers changed their position and decided to pay the claim. With the resultant windfall Ormond Cook set himself up as a ship owner.[2]

Under the name Steamship River Clyde Ltd, Ormond Cook & Company, Baltic Chambers, 50 Wellington Street, Glasgow placed an order for a ship with the firm of Russell & Company, Port Glasgow. The SS *River Clyde* was launched in March 1905. Lloyd's List shows that she was given the official ship number 121217 and her code letters were HODW. She was 344ft 8in in length; she had a breadth of 49ft 8in and a depth of 17ft 9in. Her tonnage was 3,913, gross tonnage being 3,658 and net tonnage 2,526. The ship was registered in the port of Glasgow. Her Certificate of Registry shows the shareholders as Ormond Cook, George Edie and Thomas Watt.[3]

Two years later, in May 1907, the company's second ship, the SS *River Forth* was launched. By now the firm was called Ormond Cook, Ferguson & Company. As with the *River Clyde*, a separate company seems to have established to own the ship. This company was called the Steamship River Forth Company. Lloyd's List shows that the ship was built by Robert Stephen & Company of Newcastle. Stephenson was the son of the famous inventor George Stephenson. The *River Forth* had the official ship number 124181 and code letters HKQG. With a registered tonnage of 4,413, gross tonnage of 4,109 and nett tonnage of 2,883, the ship was bigger than the *River Clyde*. She was 355ft 4in in length; she had a breadth of 50ft 1in and a depth of 27ft 6in. The ship was also registered in the port of Glasgow. Lloyd's List shows her captain as C.S.T. Hilder.

ಬಿ

In the interim, Ormond Cook had married Charlotte Dimmock in Birmingham in 1903. They had five children, one of whom died in infancy. The others were Doris, Norah, Ormond (his twin, Elaine, died in infancy) and Leslie.

On 3 March 1917, the *River Forth* was torpedoed and sunk in the Mediterranean, 60 miles south-east of Malta, by German minelayer submarine UC35. On a voyage from Barry, in South Wales, the ship was carrying a general cargo and coal. Two crew members were lost in the sinking.[4]

With both of his ships gone, Ormond Cook went into different businesses about which his present day family have little information. He appears to have retired at a relatively young age. During the Second World War, when his brother Frederick's stockbroking firm lost staff to the forces, Ormond made a partial return to work to assist in the company. In the early years of the twentieth century Ormond had moved from Glasgow to the suburb of Lennie. He was a founding member of Lennie Golf Club and Lennie Rugby Football Club (of which he remained a committee member for the rest of his life). During the 1950s he was the Managing Trustee of the Lennie Public Halls Trust and the Senior Elder in the Lennie Union Parish Church of Scotland. He died in May 1958.

Beach Party for V Beach, 25 April 1915

Each major warship contributed men for naval beach parties. These parties would assist in placing buoys and moorings and in getting stores ashore. A naval base station would be established on the beach, from where communications from the Army would be relayed to ships. The following information was extracted from ADM/137/40/2:

Chief Beach Master Captain Richard Phillimore RN

Beach party for V Beach to be sent to *Euryalus:*
Captain Robert Lambert
Commander Neston Diggle
Lieutenant-Commander George Pownall *Blenheim*
Sub-Lieutenant Humphry Sandwith *Wear*
One sub-lieutenant from *Fauvette*
One warrant officer from *Cornwallis* for V Beach
One warrant officer from *Implacable* for V Beach
Three midshipmen from *Cornwallis*
One midshipman from *Implacable.*
Four chief petty officers/petty officers from *Fauvette*
Two leading seamen from *Fauvette*
Eight ablebodied seamen or ordinary seamen from *Lord Nelson*
Eight ablebodied seamen or ordinary seamen from *Agamemnon*
Eight ablebodied seamen or ordinary seamen from *Swiftsure*
Two signalmen from *Swiftsure*
Two carpenter ratings from *Hussar*

Men will land in white rig dyed khaki colour. Blue caps. Each man to carry 50 rounds of rifle ammunition rolled up blankets with blue serge suit.

Each ship providing boats is to send 3 men in each. Ranks and rates [i.e. officers and men] for 1st Squadron to be sent to *Euryalus* for distribution.

Bibliography

Books

Allen, Trevor *The Tracks They Trod: Salonika and the Balkans, Gallipoli, Egypt and Palestine Revisited* London 1932

Aspinall-Oglander, Brigadier-General C.F. *Official History of the War: Military Operations Gallipoli Volume 1* London 1929

Atkinson, C.T. *The Royal Hampshire Regiment 1914-1918* East Sussex 2003

Bandon War Memorial Committee *Bandon District Soldiers Died in the Great War* Bandon, County Cork (undated)

Bandon War Memorial Committee *A Journey of Remembrance: Walks in the Footsteps of Bandon Soldiers* Bandon, County Cork 2005

Bell Davies, Richard *Sailor in the Air* South Yorkshire 2008

Bunbury, Turtle *The Glorious Madness: Tales of the Irish and the Great War* Dublin 2014

Bush, Eric *Gallipoli* London 1975

Callwell, K.C.B., Major-General Sir C.E. *The Dardanelles* Republished East Sussex 2005

Carroll, Tim *The Dodger* London 2013

Carver, Field Marshal Lord *The National Army Museum Book of the Turkish Front 1914-18* London 2000

Chasseaud, Peter and Doyle, Peter *Grasping Gallipoli: Terraine, Maps and Failure at the Dardanelles, 1915* Kent 2005

Churchill, Winston *The Boer War* London 2002 (originally published as two books – London to Ladysmith via Pretoria and Ian Hamilton's March London 1900)

Conway's All the World's Fighting Ships 1906-1921 London 1997

Corbett, Sir Julian S. *Naval Operations: History of the Great War Based on Official Documents Volume Two* Republished East Sussex (undated)

Creighton, Revd O. *With the Twenty-Ninth Division in Gallipoli* London 1916

Davidson, George MA, MD, Major RAMC *The Incomparable 29th and the River Clyde* Aberdeen 1919

Denham, H.M. *Dardanelles: A Midshipman's Diary* London 1981

Dungan, Myles *Irish Voices from the Great War* Dublin 1995

Dungan, Myles *They Shall Grow Not Old: Irish soldiers and the Great War* Dublin 1998

Durney, James *Far from the Short Grass: The Story of Kildare Men in Two World Wars* Naas, County Kildare 1999

Edmonds, H.J. *Norman Dewhurst M.C.* Brussels 1968

Elston, Roy *Cook's Traveller's Handbook for Constantinople, Gallipoli & Asia Minor* London 1923

Erickson, Edward *Gallipoli: The Ottoman Campaign* South Yorkshire 2010

Erickson, Edward J. *Ordered to Die: A History of the Ottoman Army in the First World War* Connecticut and London 2001

Erickson, Edward J. *Ottoman Army Effectiveness in World War 1* London and New York 2007

Fisher, James J. *The Immortal Deeds of our Irish Regiments in Flanders and the Dardanelles. Published in Twelve Numbers. No. 1 The Royal Dublin Fusiliers* Dublin 'Irish Regiments', Dublin undated.

Fromkin, David *A Peace to End all Peace: The Fall of the Ottoman Empire and the Creation of the Modern Middle East* London 2000

Gillon, Captain Stair *The Story of the 29th Division: A Record of Gallant Deeds* London 1925

Handbook of the Turkish Army Eight Provisional Edition, February 1916. Intelligence Section, Cairo. (The book was originally compiled by T.E. Lawrence (later Lawrence of Arabia) and Philip Graves, brother of Robert. Republished in 1996 by The Imperial War Museum, London and The Battery Press, Inc. Nashville, Tennessee)

Gillam, J. *Gallipoli Diary* London 1918

Ian Hay (Major-General John Hay Beith) *The Ship of Remembrance* London 1927

Hart, Peter *Gallipoli* London 2011

Hewson, Eileen *The Forgotten Irish: Memorials of the Raj* London 2004

Hickey, Michael *Gallipoli* London 1995

Hogarty, Patrick *The Old Toughs: A Brief History of the Royal Dublin Fusiliers 2nd Battalion* Dublin 2001

Hogarty, Patrick *Remembrance: A Brief History of the Blue Caps 1st Battalion Royal Dublin Fusiliers 1914-1922* Dublin 2005

Holland, Chris & Jordan, Tony *The Story Behind the Monument: The 29th Division in Warwickshire and north Oxfordshire January-March 1915* Stretton on Dunsmore, Warwickshire 2005

Holloway, S.M. *From Trench and Turret: Royal Marines' Letters and Diaries 1914-18* London 2006

Holmes, Jessie *A Pilgrimage to Gallipoli* London 1927

Holt, Tonie & Holt, Valmai *Major & Mrs Holt's Battlefield Guide to Gallipoli* South Yorkshire 2000

Irwin, Revd Francis S.J. *Stonyhurst War Record* Stonyhurst College, Lancashire 1927

Jerrold, Douglas F. *The Royal Naval Division* London 1923

Johnstone, Tom and Hegerty, James *The Cross on the Sword: Catholic Chaplains in the Forces* London 1996

Jones, H.A. *The War in the Air Volume Two* (The Official History of the Air War) originally published 1928

Keay, John *The Honourable Company: A History of the English East India Company* London 1991

Keyes, Admiral of the Fleet Sir Roger *The Fight for Gallipoli* London 1941

Kinross, Lord *The Ottoman Centuries: The Rise and Fall of the Turkish Empire* London 1977

Layman, R.D. *Naval Aviation in the First World War: Its Impact and Influence* London 2002

Lloyd, David W. *Battlefield Tourism: Pilgrimage and the Commemoration of the Great War in Britain, Australia and Canada 1919-1939* London 1998

Lynch, Michael *The British Empire* London 2005

MacDonagh, Michael *The Irish at the Front* London, New York, Toronto 1916

Masfield, John *Gallipoli* Reprinted Oxford 2002, originally published 1916

Mason, Philip *A Matter of Honour: An Account of the Indian Army, Its Officers & Men* London 1975

Massie, Robert K. *Castles of Steel: Britain, Germany and the Winning of the Great War at Sea* London 2005

McCance, Capt. S. *History of the Royal Munster Fusiliers* Aldershot 1927

McNamara, Patrick J. *The Widow's Penny* Limerick 2000

Messenger, Charles *Call to Arms: The British Army 1914-18* London 2005

Our Heroes: containing the photographs with biographical notes of officers of Irish Regiments who have fallen in action or who have been mentioned for Distinguished Conduct from August 1914 to July 1916, published 1916

Miller, Geoffrey *Superior Force: The conspiracy behind the escape of the Goeben and Breslau* The University of Hull Press 1996

Miller, Geoffrey *Straits: British policy towards the Ottoman Empire and the origins of the Dardanelles Campaign* The University of Hull Press 1997

Miller, Geoffrey *The Millstone: British Naval Policy in the Mediterranean, 1900-14, the Commitment to France and British Intervention in the War* The University of Hull Press 1999

Moorhouse, Geoffrey *Hell's Foundation: A Town, its Myths and Gallipoli* London 1992

Mure, Major A.H. *The Incomparable 29th* Published 1919

Murphy, David *Ireland and the Crimean War* Dublin 2002

Myers, Kevin *Ireland's Great War* Dublin 2014

Pope, Stephen & Wheal, Elizabeth-Anne *The McMillan Dictionary of The First World War* London 1997

Rodge, Huw & Jill *Gallipoli: The Landings at Helles* South Yorkshire 2003

Samson, Charles Rumney *Fights and Flights* London 1930

Snelling, Stephen *VCs of the First World War: Gallipoli* Gloucestershire 1999

Steel, Nigel and Hart, Peter *Defeat at Gallipoli* London 1995

Stephenson, Michael (Editor) *Battlegrounds: Geography and the History of Warfare* Washington, DC 2003

Stewart, A.T. and Peshall, The Revd C.J.E. *The Immortal Gamble* A & C Black, London 1918

Swinnerton, Iain *An introduction to the British Army: Its History, Traditions and Records* Federation of Family History Societies, Birmingham 1996

Taylor, Phil and Cupper, Pam *Gallipoli: A Battlefield Guide* Sydney 2000

The St Barnabas Society *Gallipoli and Salonika* London c. 1926

The Turkish General Staff Ankara *A Brief History of the Canakkale Campaign in The First World War (June 1914-January 1916)* Ankara 2004

Thompson, Julian *The Imperial War Museum Book of the War at Sea 1914-1918* London 2005

Thys-Şenocak, Lucienne *Ottoman Women Builders: The Architectural Patronage of Hadice Turhan Sultan* Hampshire, England and Burlington, Vermont, USA 2006

Travers, Tim *Gallipoli 1915* Gloucestershire 2001

University of Dublin Trinity College War List February 1922

Walker, R.W. *To What End Did They Die? Officers Died at Gallipoli* Worcester 1985

Wedgwood M.P., DSO, Josiah *With Machine-Guns in Gallipoli* London 1915

Weldon, Captain L.B. *Hard Lying: Eastern Mediterranean 1914-1919* London 1925

Wester-Wemyss, G.C.B., Admiral of the Fleet, Lord A.F. *The Navy in the Dardanelles Campaign* Hodder and Stoughton, London 1924

Westlake, Ray *British Regiments in Gallipoli* South Yorkshire 1996

Wild, Anthony *The East India Company: Trade and Conquest from 1600* London 1999

Winter, Denis *25 April 1915: The Inevitable Tragedy* Queensland 1994

Wylly, Colonel H.C. *Neill's Blue Caps Vol. 111 1914-1922* Reprinted Cork 1996

Articles

Caldwell, Michael 'The Landing from the "River Clyde" in letters to Stratford-on-Avon' *The Gallipolian*, Autumn 2006

Chambers, Steve 'Royal Naval Armoured Division at Gallipoli 1915' *The Gallipolian*, No. 96, Autumn 2001

Heald, David 'Gallipoli R. N. D. Personality David Walderne St Clair Tisdall, Anson Bn, Victoria Cross. 1890-1915' *RND*, Issue No. 8, March 1999

Jackson, Pamela 'A Soldier of Ireland: Corporal James Ford' *Journal of the Royal Munster Fusiliers Association*, Autumn 2005

Lecane, Philip 'From Patrick Street to the Dardanelles: The Bernard Mahony Story Dún Laoghaire' *Borough Historical Society Journal*, No. 8, 1999

Molony, Senan 'On the River Clyde, They died, They died' *White Star Journal*, Vol. 9, No. 2, 2001

Stonham, Denis 'Steamship River Clyde-How Britain failed to save a hero of Gallipoli' *World Ship Review*, No. 40, June 2005

Study

Patton, Jr Lieutenant-Colonel G.S., General Staff *The Defense of Gallipoli: A General Staff Study* Headquarters Hawaiian Department, Fort Shafer, T. H. August 31, 1936. This study by the then Lieutenant-Colonel George S. Patton was prepared pursuant to instructions from Major-General Hugh A. Drum, The Department Commander

Notes

Acknowledgements

1 Dr Piotr Nykiel is the author of *Wyprawa do Zlotego Rogu. Azialania wojenne w Darrdanelach I na Morzu Egeskim (sieprień 1914–marzec 1915)* (*Expedition to the Golden Horn. Military Operations in the Dardanelles and on the Aegean Sea (August 1914-March 1915)*).

Author's Preface

1 In 1915, Churchill had taken much of the blame for the fiasco, eventually resigning from government.

2 Australians have undertaken far more detailed research about units of their army's participation in the Gallipoli Campaign than the British have into theirs.

3 The Gallipoli book that comes closest to Ryan's work is *Gallipoli: The Landings at Helles* by Huw and Jill Rodge. It covers the landings at all five Helles beaches on the tip of the Gallipoli Peninsula. Excellently researched and written, it contains the most detail I have come across about the Helles landings. The excellent *Hell's Foundation: A Town, its Myths and Gallipoli* by Geoffrey Moorhouse tells the story of the Lancashire Fusiliers and their regimental home of Bury during and after the First World War. The landing at W Beach – now known as *Lancashire Landing* – forms part of the story.

4 At the time of writing, the National Archives does not have a war diary available for the period in question.

5 While the official history of the Hampshires is titled *The Royal Hampshire Regiment 1914-1918*, the regiment did not have the Royal prefix during either of the world wars.

6 Variations of this spelling were also used by contemporary Ottoman/Turkish sources.

7 I say approximately because it depends on how one does the count. Does one for instance count the Dublin's chaplain Father William Finn, who is recorded in CWGC records as Army Chaplains Department? What about Staff Sergeant

Percival Bonynge who was attached to the Dublin's, but recorded as Army Ordinance Corps? Then there was Captain Thomas Frankland of the Dublins, killed after landing at W Beach, while serving as brigade major of 29th Division's 86th Brigade. While Major Charles Jarrett of the Munsters was killed at V Beach, he will not be located in a search of the records for V Beach cemetery or those of the Helles Memorial to the missing, because he is commemorated at Lancashire Landing Cemetery, where the men killed at W Beach are buried.

8 I do not feel it necessary to cite these sources, as none of those I have read furnished creditable proof to support their particular claim of the song's authorship.

Prologue

1 Private James Fitzgerald from Blarney, County Cork.
2 Private James Searles from Bandon, County Cork.

Chapter 1

1 Research by Tom Burke MBE His figures were derived from the birthplace of the 1st Battalion's casualties during the Gallipoli campaign. In *Military Identities,* David French gave a figure of only 52.7 per cent of Royal Dublin Fusiliers born within the regimental district between 1883 and 1900. Tom Burke's figure of 61.7 per cent from Dublin city and county appears to suggest a change in the composition of the regiment during the early years of the twentieth century.

2 *Military Identities: The Regimental System, The British Army, & the British People c. 1870-2000* by David French, p. 45.

3 While technically 'foundlings' was a word applied to children of unknown parentage, the names of both boys mothers and Fibley's father was known.

4 Research by Liam Dodd.

5 This account is based on Séamus Burke's memoirs, *From the Earth to a Star.*

6 Research by Benjamin Hurt's granddaughter Lyn Edmonds.

7 Research by John Hartley and the author.

8 Michael Ludford had three brothers and two sisters – John b. 1884, Jeremiah b. 1887, Cornelius b. 1890, Mary b. 1891 and Ellen b. 1896. Their parents are believed to have come from Cork.

9 Benjamin Hurt was born in Milford, Derbyshire on 8 August 1884. His parents were William (general labourer) and Mary (*née* Bates). When Benjamin was seven, his brother Charles died at the age of three. Benjamin was living and working on a farm in Chaddesden, Derbyshire at the time of the 1901 census. He enlisted in the Dublins on 7 June 1909 with Reg. No. 10678.

10 The date of the letter was deduced by cross-referencing its contents with *Neill's Blue Caps,* the history of the 1st Battalion Royal Dublin Fusiliers (henceforth *Neill's*). The letter gives the address as Kings Barracks. As *Neill's* always refers to Fort St George, it is unclear if Kings Barracks is used in the sense that it was literally the King's Barracks and was locally known as such. As with many

soldiers' letters of the time, Sam's letter does not contain punctuation or capital
letters at the start of each sentence. To make it easier to read I have put in
punctuation and started each sentence with a capital letter. Sam spelt the word
'too' as 'to' and the word 'wee' (i.e. little) as 'we'. I have written them as 'to[o]'
and 'we[e]'. No other changes have been made. I have left the misspellings
of 'pice' (i.e. lunch. Piece meant a sandwich, derived from 'piece of bread')
and 'tobbacco'. Apart from explaining that Coy stood for company and owl
meant old, I refrained from making comments so as to avoid breaking the
flow of the letter. The letter implies that Jack Mallaghan was a bugler. 'On the
tack' meant abstaining from alcohol. The reference to Albert looking at Ethel
(Sam's sister, aged three years and nine months in Ireland's 1911 census) meant
looking at her photograph. The comment 'Me and him goes home together'
would appear to date the letter prior to late 1914, when the whole battalion was
ordered to prepare to move to England for wartime service. Minnie was Sam's
sister, a twenty-year-old mill worker in the 1911 census. Sam's father was John
Mallaghan, a forty-year-old gardener in the 1911 census. Willie and Herbert
were Sam's brothers. Willie was not at home for the 1911 census. Herbert was
aged thirteen at the time of the census. Jack Mallaghan's regimental number
appears to have changed from that he held in the 2nd Battalion. 'Dr' is Drummer.
Londoner Albert B. Bowsher Reg. No. 10190, was subsequently transferred to
the Royal Irish Fusiliers with Reg. No. G/234 and to the Leinster Regiment with
Reg. No. 4009. He survived the war and later served with the Wiltshire Regiment
with Reg. No. 7178253. (This is a post-war regimental number). Research by Liam
Dodd. 'pc' meant postcard.

11 The Rooths were married on 25 June 1895. Richard jnr was born on 7 June 1900
and Nancy on 23 May 1908. Research by Mary Long, family historian and by the
author and information from the *Morning Post* of 4 May 1915 and wording from
unnamed and undated 1915 newspaper clipping on www.grimshaworigin.org/
Webpages2/CecilGrimshawNewsSuppl.htm

12 Gazetted to the Dubs as Second Lieutenant in 1901, William Frederick Higginson
had served in Aden (1903) and had subsequently been promoted to Lieutenant
(1906) and Captain (1912). While stationed at the regimental depot in Naas,
he won the County Kildare Lawn Tennis Championship in 1911. He was also
'a fine exponent of Cricket and Hockey'.

13 'Monsieur' refers to his father, John Grove. The R. and W. in his own name stood
for Robert and Wood.

14 According to the *University of Dublin Trinity College War List* February 1922, Cecil
Grimshaw was awarded a BA in 1895. The 1895-1897 editions of *Thom's Directory*
show Lieutenant C.T.W. Grimshaw in the 5th Battalion. The 1898 edition shows
him as second lieutenant in the listing of officers for the 1st and 2nd Battalions.
The following year, he is again shown with the same rank.

15 'Then the next thing that occurred of note was Churchill's escape. This he did as all
the world knows, but they do not know that he did it contrary to the agreement of
his mates, who were to escape with him; and so instead of twenty officers getting
away, as they might easily have done, as there was no one to know whether they
were there or not, except myself; he was the only one from the School. After his

escape all sorts of restrictions were put on, newspapers stopped etc.' Hilary Tulloch put the information on Cecil Grimshaw on the Grimshaw family history website www.grimshaworigin.org/Webpages2/CecilGrimshaw.htm.

16   Thomas Grimshaw was born on 16 November 1839 in County Antrim. Qualified as a physician in Dublin, he practiced there until 1879, when he was appointed Register-General for Ireland. He investigated the causes and distribution of water-borne diseases in Dublin and authored a pioneering public health paper in 1872. He married Sarah Elizabeth Thomas on 11 April 1865. They had twelve children. Thomas died in Dublin on 23 January 1900. Sarah Elizabeth (known as Settie) lived to be 102.

17   Churchill was first cousin to the 9th Duke Malborough. His father, Randolph Churchill, was the younger brother of the 8th Duke.

18   *In Pretoria Prison: The Diary of An Officer,* an undated clipping from an unidentified newspaper held by Hilary Tulloch.

19   The Delhi Durbar meant the *Court of Delhi.* The Durbars were mass assemblies to proclaim the Kings and Queens of Britain as Emperors and Empresses of India. Durbars were held in 1877, 1903 and 1911. The 1911, Durbar was held in December and was attended by George V and Queen Mary. 26,800 Delhi Durbar Silver Medals of 1911 were awarded, mostly to officers and men of the British regiments who took part. A small number of gold medals were awarded to Indian princes and high-ranking government officials.

20   Research by Tom Burke MBE.

21   There were five infantry battalions stationed in Egypt/Sudan, five in Malta, four in South Africa, two each in Gibraltar and China (excluding Hong Kong) and one each in Bermuda, Mauritius, Aden, Singapore and Hong Kong.

22   On 1 April 1908, Britain established a new army for home defence. Called the Territorial Force, it comprised of part-time volunteer soldiers. Men enrolled for four years. They attended regular drills and a fourteen to eighteen-day camp annually. There were no units in Ireland, the force being confined to England, Scotland and Wales. The Territorials were only liable for home service. They could not be ordered to go overseas, but could volunteer. Many Territorial units volunteered to serve abroad. Thanks to Ronald Clifton, Historical Information Officer, Western Front Association for this information.

23   *Superior Force: The Conspiracy behind the Escape of Goeben and Breslau,* by Geoffrey Miller, gives an excellently researched and well-told account of the events surrounding the escape of the German ships. Millier's *Straits: British Policy towards the Ottoman Empire and the Origins of the Dardanelles Campaign* is also worth reading.

24   Lucknow Week commemorated the participation of the battalion, under its earlier name the 1st Madras Fusiliers, in the initial relief of Lucknow during the Indian Mutiny.

25   The light cruiser SMS *Emden* virtually paralysed trade and troop transport in the Indian Ocean for three months, before being put out of action by the Australian cruiser HMAS *Sydney* on 9 November 1914. A fragment of a shell fired at Madras by the SMS *Emden* is on display in the Fort Museum in Fort St George.

26   Heffernan (twenty-nine) died on 7 October. Presumably his death followed

an illness. Regimental Number 11128, he was a member of B Company. Born in Belfast, he enlisted in Dublin. The son of Edward and Jane of Kilmainham, Dublin, he is buried in St Patrick's Cemetery, Madras. Coughlan (twenty-three) died of cholera on 17 October. Regimental Number 10432, he was the son of John and Mary Ann. Born in Tipperary, he enlisted in Aldershot. He is buried in St Mary's Cemetery, Madras.

27 Battalions usually had two colours i.e. flags. One bore the battalion emblem and battle honours. The other – known as the King's/Queen's colour – was the Union flag i.e. the British flag.

28 This would appear to suggest that, despite the reformation into four large companies, the old eight-company lettering was still in use.

29 Weighing 7,896 tons, the British India Steam Navigation Co. Ltd ship was built in 1913. On 25 August 1917, she was sunk in the Atlantic by U-70 with the loss of sixty-four crew.

30 Edwyn Fetherstonhaugh was born on 2 November 1867. The fourth son of Stephen and Jane Fetherstonhaugh of Rokeby, Howth, County Dublin, his father was Clerk of the Peace for County Westmeath and his brother Godfrey was a barrister and MP for North Fermanagh. Educated at Chard Grammar School, Somerset, Edwyn joined the 2nd Battalion Royal Dublin Fusiliers from Sandhurst in 1888 with the rank of Second Lieutenant. Subsequently promoted (lieutenant 1891, captain 1898 and major 1900), he was mentioned in despatches during the Boer War and also served in action in Aden. He later transferred to the 1st Battalion.

31 Weighing 6,810 tons, built by Caird & Company, Greencock in 1899 for the Peninsular & Oriental Steam Navigation Company, she was employed for most of her life as a troopship.

32 Presumably death was due to illness. Regimental Number 10593, Adams was born in Kirkdale and enlisted in Liverpool. He is commemorated on the Hollybrook Memorial, Hampshire.

33 A sentence in a February 1915 letter to his sister Katie, however, appears to suggest that he did get home at some point (*see* Chapter 3).

34 Two photographs survive from Stephen's youth. One appears to have been taken shortly before George Underwood's death in 1899. In the photo, George is seated and Ellen is standing beside him in the front garden of their home. A horseshoe is nailed above the front door. The other photo shows Stephen, aged about fifteen, Ellen Stevens, and a young boy and younger girl (possible foster children or nephew and niece), two pigs and a slop bucket. At this time, 2nd Battalion Royal Dublin Fusiliers was based at Aldershot, a few miles from Ottershaw. Presumably Stephen would have visited his foster parents whenever possible. By late 1914, all that he had left of his foster parents were two photographs, his memories and Ellen Stevens.

Chapter 2

1 In an illustration of official attitudes at the time, the letter makes no reference to the fact that the four boys were also Annie's sons.

2 Patrick Hogarty's *Remembrance* p.12 records that Corporal Thomas Sloan, born

in Liverpool in 1891, joined the Dublins on 11 May 1909. With four other Blue
Caps, he was billeted in the Dale family home, on Iletham Road. His best mate
was Private Joe Murphy, the battalion billards champion. Sloan was wounded at
V Beach and later on the Western Front. Discharged on 6 June 1921, he returned
to Torquay, married Alice Nellie Dale from the family where he had been billeted.
He lived and worked in Torquay. He wore his medals and Royal Dublin Fusiliers
cap badge at Armistice Day parades. He died in March 1962.

3   O'Hara was born in Ballyduff, Thomastown, County Kilkenny on 21 May 1892. He was
commissioned into the Dublins on 4 September 1912. His mother Cecilia was the
seventh and youngest daughter of Peter Connellan JP DL of Colmore, County Kilkenny.
His grandfather was Revd James Dunn O'Hara of Portstewart, County Antrim.

4   George Dunlop was born on 13 January 1889 at St Helens, Holywood, County
Down, son of Archibald and Bessie Dunlop. He was gazetted second lieutenant
in the Royal Dublin Fusiliers on 6 February 1909 and lieutenant on 15 June 1910.
A lieutenant at the time of the Torquay ceremony, he was promoted to captain
shortly afterwards, backdated to 14 December 1914.

5   The Royal Dublin Fusiliers suffered their first casualties of the war on 27 August 1914,
when twenty-eight-year-old Second Lieutenant John Gunning Moore Dunlop and
twenty-six other ranks from the 2nd Battalion were killed at Le Cateau, France.

6   Of the twenty-eight divisions previously formed, the 9th to the 26th inclusive were
composed of men who had joined up since the outbreak of war. Among them were
the 10th (Irish) and 16th (Irish) Divisions.

7   The other battalions were the 1st Royal Inniskilling Fusiliers, the 1st Lancashire
Fusiliers, the 1st Kings Own Scottish Borders and the 2nd Royal Fusiliers

8   The other battalions were the 1st Border Regiment and the 4th Worcestershire Regiment.

9   The 1st Essex Regiment from Mauritius and the 2nd South Wales Borderers
from Tianjin.

10 Steuart is not a misspelling. Thomas Frankland was a brevet major. This meant that
he held the rank of major in the army, but if he returned to his battalion – the 1st
Royal Dublin Fusiliers – he would revert to being a captain.

11 The Bengal European Regiment was established from soldiers at the company's
post at Fort William, Calcutta. In 1805, while on campaign, the Bengal Europeans
were inspected by General Lake. Apologies were made to the general because
the regiment hadn't had the opportunity to change their shirts for several weeks.
Calling them his Dirty Shirts, Lake said that their shirts were a badge of honour
and showed that the men put duty ahead of comfort. The regiment immediately
adopted the nickname and it was used until they were disbanded in 1922.

12 Weighing 11,419 tons, built by Barclay Curle, Glasgow for the Allan Line. Slightly
damaged in a collision with an iceberg in 1912. Wrecked near Cape Race,
Newfoundland in 1923.

13 Gazetted second lieutenant in the 2nd Royal Dublin Fusiliers in September 1885
and promoted to captain in 1895, he served in the Nile Expedition of 1898. (He was
twice mentioned in despatches and was awarded the Order of Medjidieh, 4th Class.)
Promoted to Major in 1900, during the Boer War he was seconded to serve as Assistant
to the Military Governor of Pretoria. He later commanded Robert's Horse and served
with the South African Light Horse. On 31 March 1900 he was wounded at Sannas Post

while attached to Robert's Horse. On 23 June, while back with the 2nd Royal Dublin Fusiliers, he was wounded at Heidlberg. He was twice mentioned in despatches during the Boer War. In 1903, he went to Aden with the 2nd Royal Dublin Fusiliers.

14 Because the 67th South Hampshire Regiment had served in India from 1805-1826, King George IV authorised the carrying of the Bengal tiger and the word 'India' on their Regimental Colour. Hence the Hampshire Regiment's nickname of 'The Tigers'.

15 Built 1911 for Union-Castle Mailsteamship Company. 8,006 tons. Sunk 15 July 1942 off south-west Africa by a Japanese raider. Sixty-one people were taken to Japan as prisoners. Two of them died in captivity.

16 The Congregational Hall stood in Chapel Street, Nuneaton. The Congregationalists were a non-conformist group.

17 Private Michael Byrne (17369) was buried in Naas (St Corban's) Catholic Cemetery: E. 13.39, Naas, County Kildare.

18 *Norman Dewhurst M.C.* by H.J. Edmonds, p.20 (henceforth *Norman Dewhurst*).

19 'Billet' was derived from the French word for ticket and referred to the form used in billeting troops. According to the *Coventry Graphic* the word 'billet' had gone out of use before the war (presumably because there was sufficient barrack accommodation available for soldiers in the pre-war period).

20 *Norman Dewhurst*, p.20.

21 *With the 29th Division in Gallipoli* by Revd O. Creighton, p.7 (henceforth *With the 29th Division*).

22 NAI, 2002/119, E/75663/1, Soldier's Will of Private Thomas Hughes. The author gratefully acknowledges the permission of the director of the National Archives to publish the letter. 'We are out of this on the 20th of this month': presumably October, when the battalion moved to Sittingbourne. The letter seems to suggest that the army was stopping some of his pay and sending it to his wife.

23 An unusual surname, 1901 and 1911 census records list it only for the city of Cork and the village of Carrigaline, County Cork.

24 Information on John Sullivan from Seán Connolly, Royal Dublin Fusiliers Association.

25 Reg. No. 17077, he was the son of James McCluskie McGhee and Elizabeth McGhee of 114 Sister Street, Glasgow. Commonwealth War Graves Commission records show him as being a member of the 3rd Battalion Royal Dublin Fusiliers. When recalled to the colours he would have reported to the 3rd Battalion in Cork, from when he was sent with his sixty-nine colleagues to Nuneaton.

26 The colonel of a regiment was an honorary post. Appointed for life from among serving or retired senior officers, he acted as the unpaid titular head of the regiment.

27 *With the 29th Division*, pp.10-11.

28 Private William Raffery, Reg. No. 10931. He was later promoted to corporal. (As Nicholas Smyth was Regimental Number 10935, presumably he and Rafferty joined up at the same time.)

29 Note the suggestion that Smyth had been home on leave and the fact that the decision to send the 29th Division to Gallipoli – taken by the War Council two days previously – had not yet been communicated to the men of the Royal Dublin Fusiliers.

30 Before the passing of the Anatomy Act of 1832, there were insufficient cadavers available for the study of anatomy. William Burke and William Hare were tried for

a series of murders in Edinburgh in 1828, committed for the purpose of supplying bodies to a surgeon. In return for non-prosecution, Hare testified against Burke. The latter was convicted and hanged.

31 Dyball worked as a lift attendant for the Liverpool Investment Building Society, Lord Street, Liverpool. He enlisted in 1909, served two years at home and three in India. He was discharged from the army in June 1915. Research by Conor Dodd.

32 According to the *Kildare Observer*, 7 May 1915, he was the son of a former sergeant-major at Naas Depot. Giving his rank as second lieutenant, the paper said that he was promoted from the ranks in February 1915

33 Walters was Welsh, born in Carmarthenshire. He served an apprenticeship as a printer. Leaving because of poor pay, in July 1908, he joined the 1st Welsh Regiment. He was put in charge of the battalion printing press. In January 1914, the battalion was sent to India. In a letter to his mother he talked about the 'awful' job of loading the printing press. He was promoted to sergeant. In late 1914, his battalion was called back to England. Walters was promoted to second lieutenant and transferred to the Dublins. Research by Tom Burke OBE.

34 Many doctors joined the British Army at the outbreak of war. They were assigned to the Royal Army Medical Corps (RAMC) and given temporary officer rank for the duration of the war. Father William Finn was born in Hull on 27 December 1875. The 1881 census and local research shows his father, Austin, and mother, Catherine, came from Aghamore, Ballyhaunis, County Mayo. Austin and Catherine had nine children, all born in Hull. The children were John, Sarah, James, Kate, Austin, Mary, William, Agnes and Francis. In 1889, William entered the seminary at Ushaw, Durham. On 5 August 1900, he was ordained at Middlesborough Cathedral. From 1900 to 1908 he was curate at the Cathedral Church of St Mary's, Middlesborough and from 1908 to 1909 at St Hilda's, Whitby, Yorkshire. From 1909 to 1913 he was Parish Priest at All Saints', Thirsk, Yorkshire. At the outbreak of war he was serving at the Holy Family church, Houghton Hall.

35 *With the 29th Division*, p.18. Rooth's servant was Private John Jackson (Reg. No. 9327) of A Company. His second servant was Private James McCormack (Reg. No. 9993) of C Company. (*Neill's* gives his Reg. No. as 19993) McCormack was later promoted corporal and served in the Labour Corps Reg. No. 444927. (Note: The men's title was 'servant,' not batman.)

Chapter 3

1 The Committee for Union and Progress (CUP) was nicknamed the Young Turks, after its journal *La Jeune Turquie*.

2 Turks at the time did not have surnames. The honourary title Pasha was given to those of high rank in the Ottoman political system, such as governors, generals etc. It was equivalent to the British title of Lord.

3 The treaty was signed the day after Germany declared war on Russia and several days before Austria-Hungary declared war on Russia. As Germany had not been

required to declare war by the terms of her treaty with Austria-Hungary, the treaty with the Ottomans – if read literally – did not require them to enter the war.

4 WO 106/1463.

5 Sources on Esat *Ordered to Die: A History of the Ottoman Army in the First World War* and *Ottoman Army Effectiveness in World War 1*, both by Edward J. Erickson and *Brothers in Arms: Turkish officers in the Çanakkale (Dardanelles) Campaign* by Dr Mesut Uyar, paper presented to conference *Gallipoli in retrospect 90 years on* Onsekiz Mart University International conference Çanakkale 21-23 April 2005.

6 Each Turkish Army Corps consisted of three divisions. Each division comprised of three infantry regiments, each of which had three battalions. In 1914 a full-strength Turkish division had nine infantry battalions and three artillery battalions. It had 12,239 men, twelve heavy machine guns and between sixteen to twenty-four artillery pieces.

7 The 8th Division, however, was assigned for service on the Sinai front and it immediately began preparation for departure. (The Corps did not receive a replacement division until March 1915, when the 19th Infantry Division arrived.)

8 The website www.turkeyswar.com says that Sami was born in 1866 and that during the Balkan Wars he first commanded the Volunteer Regiment from Izmir and was subsequently second-in-command of the 31st Division.

9 Ece Limani: Port/Bay of Ece. Halil Ece was an Ottoman commander who captured the Gallipoli Peninsula in 1354, during the reign of Sultan Orhan. The Turks renamed the town of Maidos, on the peninsula, Eceabad (town of Ece) after him. Ece Bay was also named after him. He was buried on a hill named Ece Baba. My thanks to Tosun Saral for this information.

10 On 13 September, the Bursa Field Jandarma (Gendarmarie) Battalion, the 9th Division Mountain Howitzer Battalion and a cavalry troop were attached to the 9th Infantry Regiment. Formed under a French training mission after the 1878 war against Russia, the Jandarma's role was border control and internal security. It was deployed throughout the empire. Each province – and many large cities – had a Jandarma unit. Upon mobilisation control of the Jandarma was transferred from the Ministry of the Interior to the Ministry of War.

11 The 8th Battery, 3rd Mountain Howitzer Battery and a 105mm howitzer battery.

12 The circumstances of the explosion were retold by a survivor who visited Sedd el Bahr with a group of veterans several years after the event. Turkish historian Sahin Aldogan was told that the incident was also related in the privately published memoirs of a Turkish officer in the 1930s. Unfortunately, to date, he has been unable to locate a copy of the memoirs. A memorial, surmounted by a shell, was erected in 1915 where the Ilk Sehitler Anti (the First Martyrs' Memorial) now stands. It was destroyed during the subsequent fighting. The present memorial was erected in 1986. It commemorates Captain Sevki, Fort Commander, First Lieutenant Cevdet, Deputy Fort Commander, First Lieutenant Hasan Pala, First Lieutenant Riza, First Lieutenant Esref and eighty-one privates. (*Major and Mrs Holt's Battlefield Guide: Gallipoli*, p.112.) My thanks to Eric Goossens and Bill Sellers for contacting Sahin Aldogan on my behalf.

Chapter 4

1 It would appear that the expedition was at sea before the rank and file were informed of their destination.

2 *A Peace To End All Peace* by David Fromkin, p.151.

3 NAI, 2002/119, E/80828/1, Soldier's Will of Private Robert Roleston. The author gratefully acknowledges the permission of the director of the National Archives to publish the letter.

4 His brother William, aged eleven in the 1911 census.

5 Regimental Number 9843, he was a single man, who was born and had enlisted in Dublin. He was the son of Peter Kavanagh, 16 Verschoyle Place, off Mount Street, Dublin. He is commemorated on the Helles Memorial at the tip of the Gallipoli peninsula. The memorial commemorates all those who were lost in the Gallipoli campaign and have no known grave.

6 Research of the medal rolls by Liam Dodd established that 9845, the missing Reg. No. in the sequence, was not issued to the Royal Dublin Fusiliers.

7 Strangely, *Neill's* records that the *Ausonia* docked at Gibraltar on 20 March so that Lanigan-O'Keeffe could be sent to hospital. The War Diary records him being sent to hospital in Alexandria on 30 March. The latter source, written by the battalion Adjutant Captain William Higginson as events occurred, must be regarded as more reliable.

8 Fort Mex was part of the defences of Alexandria. During the two world wars the area around the fort was used as a transit camp.

9 Letter from Seán Connolly.

10 War Diary WO 95/4310. *Neill's* gives the figure for other ranks as 953.

11 Figure per War Diary. *Neill's* gives the figure for other ranks as thirty-eight.

12 War Diary WO 95/4310, compiled by the adjutant, Captain William Higginson, gives the number of horses as 66.

13 War Diary WO 95/4310. *Neill's* gives the date as 9 April.

14 War Diary WO 95/4310. *Neill's* says the ship docked the following afternoon.

15 *The Incomparable 29th and the 'River Clyde'* by George Davidson pp.23 and 27 (henceforth Davidson). *Neill's* and Davidson disagree on the departure and arrival dates of the *Ausonia*. The former has it leaving at 11 a.m. on 9 April, the latter leaving at 10.45 a.m. on 8 April. The former has the ship docking at Mudros in the afternoon of 11 April, while the latter puts it at about noon on 10 April.

Chapter 5

1 In attendance were Vice-Admiral de Robeck and Rear-Admiral Wemyss of the Royal Navy, General Hamilton, Lieutenant-General Birdwood, Major-General Braithwaite and Captain Pollen of the Army.

2 *Official History of the War: Military Operations Gallipoli* by Brigadier-General C.F. Aspinall-Oglander, p.111 (henceforth *Official History*).

3 Abbreviation of the latin words *Deus vult*, meaning God Willing.

4 Instructions to Birdwood (in AMW 45, bundle 3 at the Australian War Memorial)

said that because Helles was the chief landing, it had been decided that the regular 29th Division would land there.

5 *Official History* Appendix 3 said that, while dated 13 April, the Force Order was not issued until the following day.

6 Of the two undated accounts, one is addressed 'Dear Admiral'. Given its contents – and the fact that, in his book *The Navy in the Dardanelles* (published in 1924), Wemyss quotes from the letter – there is little doubt that this account was sent to Wemyss. In the account to Wemyss, Unwin says that he had never before put an account of the landing from the *River Clyde* on paper. This means that the other account was written later. As Unwin's account to Wemyss refers to walking in a Victoria Cross holders' procession some years after the landing, it seems likely that Wemyss requested the account at the time he was writing his book.

7 IWM 13473 05/63/1.

8 IWM 13473 05/63/1. Unwin did not name Guépratte, merely calling him 'the French Admiral'.

9 'Steamship River Clyde – How Britain failed to save a Hero of Gallipoli' by Denis Stonehan, published in *World Ship Review: The Journal of the World Ship Trust*, No. 40, June 2005 (henceforth Denis Stonham).

10 SS *River Clyde*'s date of completion, date, place of departure and destination for first voyage: Denis Stonham. Research on the captain and first mate, Simon Riches, Brian Ellis and the author, from documents in the Liddle Archive, *Lloyds List* and the ships log.

11 *Lloyds List*.

12 IWM 13473 05/63/1.

13 ADM 137/3134.

14 ibid.

15 William Alfred Bowskill, No. 101914, was born in Church End on 24 September 1883. I am grateful to James Bowskill for the information on his father. He only became aware of his father's work on the *River Clyde* within the last few years, when he discovered that, after the V Beach landing, a local newspaper published a letter from his father to his mother, mentioning his work on the *River Clyde*. As the *Bacchante*'s log makes no mention of a workparty being sent to the *Reliance*, it seems likely that any work party sent from the cruiser was small.

16 IWM 10946 P216.

17 Eric Bush served in the Royal Navy at the time of the landings. His excellent book *Gallipoli* (henceforth Eric Bush) gives the most detail on the sally ports and gangways I have come across. Unwin said that eight holes were cut in the side of the ship, four on each side. Munsters officer Norman Dewhurst said that the holes in the side of the ship were covered by doors. I arrived at the estimate of the 45° angle on the hinged extension from Charles Dixon's painting of the *River Clyde* that adorns the front page of every edition of *The Gallipolian*, the journal of the Gallipoli Association. Paintings and drawings of the landing from the *River Clyde* – presumably based on research by the artists – show the gangways on both sides of the ship extending towards the shore, thus providing two separate pathways ashore. An account of the landing, by Private William Flynn of the Munsters, appears to suggest, however, that the two gangways may have met somewhere near the bow

of the ship, thus allowing only one pathway to the shore. His is the only account
I have come across that appears to suggest this.

18 In *The Fight For Gallipoli* by Sir Roger Keyes (henceforth *The Fight For Gallipoli*)
the author says 'Captain Unwin of the *Hussar* had suggested using the *River Clyde*
as a means of rapidly reinforcing the first flight of boats, and had begged to be
given command of the ship ...'

19 *VCs of the First World War: Gallipoli* by Stephen Snelling, p.46 (henceforth Stephen
Snelling).

20 IWM 13473 05/63/1.

21 ibid.

22 IWM 13473 05/63/1. Unwin's remark about petty officers is puzzling, given that
Williams was an able seaman.

23 IWM 13473 05/63/1.

24 ibid.

25 Eric Bush and *The War in the Air: Volume Two* also said there were eleven maxims,
as did Unwin's second-in-command Midshipman George Drewry in a letter to his
father dated 12 May 1915 IWM 10946 P216.

26 *With Machine-Guns in Gallipoli*, by Lieutenant-Commander Josiah Wedgwood,
MP, DSO.

27 Davidson, pp.28–29 and 32.

28 *Norman Dewhurst*, p.24.

29 Weldon, Captain L.B., *Hard Lying: Eastern Mediterranean 1914-1919*, p.55.

30 The current at Anzac Cove was stronger than believed.

31 Winter gives his source as AWM44, draft of the *Official History*.
(AWM signifies records at the Australian War Memorial).

32 Unwin's report to Wemyss IWM 13473 05/63/1.

33 Davidson, p.40.

34 ADM 137/40/2.

35 IWM 10946 P216. In his undated account to Wemyss – which may have been written
to assist Wemyss with his memoirs, published in 1924 – Unwin said he selected
six seamen, six engine-room ratings, the ship's carpenter and the warrant engineer.
He also said Wemyss later supplied him with 'some' petty officers. As Drewry's
account was written on 12 May 1915 – and because midshipmen were required to keep
diaries – it seems reasonable to suppose that his details are more likely to be accurate.

36 A relative of former Arthur Balfour Conservative Prime Minister (1902–1905).

37 Davidson p.41. De Robeck's orders said that each transport ship was to tow four
lighters. Davidson's diary says that the *Ausonia* was towing three.

38 WO95/4319.

39 Davidson p.41.

40 IWM 13473 05/63/1. Some sources, including Unwin, give de Lancey-Williams' rank
as lieutenant-colonel. He was a member of the Hampshire Regiment and *Hamphshire
Regiment* p.469 shows that his promotion to this rank was dated 28 April 1915.

41 The interpreter is mentioned, though not by name, by Stephen Snelling, p.66.
His relative, Michael Constant, supplied me with his details.

42 IWM 13473 05/63/1. According to Ian Hamilton's Force Order No. 1 'Two staff officers
of G.H.Q. will be landed with the covering force [i.e. the first wave of troops] to

select and mark out forming up places for rendezvous.' *Official History*, Appendix 3.

43 Stephen Snelling, pp.66–67 and 75–77. The fact that he was in the Intelligence Section: *Official History*, p.249 (Footnote 2).

44 www.angloboerwar.com.

45 Unwin's comment regarding towing the hopper and lighters and the fact that two donkeys were carried IWM 13473 05/63/1.

46 IWM 10946 P216.

47 IWM 13473 05/63/1.

48 Tenedos lies 3 miles west of mainland Turkey and 11 miles south-south-west of the entrance to the Dardanelles.

49 *The Navy in the Dardanelles Campaign*, p.66 and p.68.

50 IWM 10946 P216. According to orders issued by Vice-Admiral de Robeck, both the *River Clyde* and the *Fauvette* were to have assigned positions on the north side of Tenedos. ADM 137/40/2. The *Fauvette* (2,644 gross tons) was built in 1912 and owned by the General Steam Navigation Company Ltd, London. In March 1915 she was requisitioned by the Admiralty and used by the Royal Navy as an armed boarding steamer. On 9 March 1916, she was sunk by a mine laid by UC-7, off North Foreland, Kent.

51 Davidson, pp.41–42.

52 WO 95/4319.

53 IWM 929 99/62/1.

54 Appendix 4 of *Official History* is titled 'Instructions for Helles Covering Force'. Headed 'G.H.Q. 19th April, 1915', p. 13 shows that the 1st Royal Dublin Fusiliers (less the company on the *River Clyde*) was, with one platoon of the Anson Battalion, Royal Naval Division, to transfer from the *Ausonia* to a minesweeper called *Fleet Sweeper No. 1*. Page 14 of the appendix says troops were subsequently to go ashore from *Fleet Sweeper No. 1* (V Beach), the *Euryalus 1* (W Beach) and the *Implacable* (X Beach). *Official History* recorded a number of changes to the plan. This does not, of course, prove that the book recorded all changes of plan. The book does not record any change of the plan for the Royal Dublin Fusiliers and the Anson men to travel on one Fleet Sweeper. However, *Neill's* says that the men of the Royal Dublin Fusiliers were aboard two sweepers, which it names as the *Clacton* and the *Newmarket*. For reasons outlined later in the text, I believe that the *Newmarket* was *Fleet Sweeper No.1*. This means that the *Clacton* was *Fleet Sweeper No. 2*. Eric Bush said the Dublins were landed from the *Clacton* and the *Newmarket*. Because he cites it as one of his references, he appears to have had access to *Neill's*. He did, however, say the *Clacton* and the *Newmarket* were ex-Eastern Railway Packets, a fact not mentioned in *Neill's*. Without naming them, *Naval Operations: History of the Great War Based on Official Documents: Volume Two* by Sir Julian S. Corbett (henceforth *Naval Operations*) refers to 'the fleet sweepers' that carried the Dublins. The mystery is further compounded by the fact that while the *Newmarket*'s log shows that she took aboard and disembarked troops during the landings, the *Clacton*'s log ends in February 1915 and recommences in May 1915. An account by Midshipman Hayden Forbes of the *Cornwallis*, however, shows that he took ashore men of the Royal Dublin Fusiliers from the *Clacton*. So, despite what is published in *Official History*, there is evidence

to suggest that the Dublins may have been aboard two sweepers rather than one. Built by Earle's County, Hull, before the war the twin-screw minesweepers had been Great Eastern Railway Company mail packets travelling between Britain and the Continent. The *Clacton* (820 gross tons) was built in 1904 and commissioned as a minesweeper on 7 October 1914. The *Newmarket* (833 gross tons) was built in 1907 and commissioned as a minesweeper on 8 October 1914. Both ships were lost to German submarines. On 3 August 1916, while going alongside the cruiser *Grafton,* the *Clacton* was sunk by U73 off Kavalla Bay in the Aegean Sea. Five crewmen were lost. The *Newmarket* was sunk by UC38 on 17 July 1917 off Nikaria Island in the Aegean Sea.

55 RNR was the Royal Naval Reserve, created by an Act of Parliament in 1859. The RNR was comprised of officers and men from the Mercantile Marine (now called the Merchant Navy) who received regular training and were immediately called up in time of war. The Naval Forces Act of 1903 established the Royal Naval Volunteer Reserve (RNVR) to supplement the RNR. The RNVR was comprised of volunteers who came from all walks of life, apart from the Mercantile Marine.

56 Author's copy of ship's plans for the SS *Gibraltar,* a ship of similar dimensions to the *River Clyde,* built by the same shipbuilders, Russell and Company.

57 It is unclear whether the separation of No. 1 Hold into upper and lower decks was done at the time the ship was built, or if it was carried out at Mudros. While the former seems more likely, such separation does not appear on the plans of the SS *Gibraltar.*

58 *The War at Sea 1914-1918* by Julian Thompson, p.246 (henceforth *War at Sea*). Thompson called Rickus an unidentified sailor, but by cross-referencing another statement made by the sailor with one quoted by Peter Hart in *Gallipoli*, it is clear the sailor was Ricus.

59 Davidson, p.43.

60 He appears to be talking about the men of 89th Field Ambulance, rather than all the troops aboard ship.

61 As Munsters Officer Captain Guy Geddes slept on the floor of Wedgwood's cabin, perhaps the officers mentioned here were those from the Field Ambulance and the Engineers.

62 Davidson, p.48.

63 IWM 13473 05/63/1.

64 Letter dated 12 May 1915 from Lieutenant George L. Drewry VC to his father, IWM 10946 P216.

65 IWM 134 05 05/63/1.

66 IWM 134 05 05/63/1.

67 WO 95/4319.

68 IWM 10946 P216.

69 IWM 13473 05/63/1.

Chapter 6

1 WO 106/1463. British military intelligence report September 1914.

2 *Gallipoli: A Battlefield Guide* by Phil Taylor and Pam Cupper, p.75 (henceforth *Gallipoli: A Battlefield Guide*).

3 *Ottoman Women Builders: The Architectural Patronage of Hadice Turhan Sultan* by Lucienne Thys-Şenocak, p.108 (henceforth *Ottoman Women Builders*).

4 Born in Russia, Hadice Turhan Sultan was captured by the Ottomans at the age of twelve. Brought to the Ottoman harem in Istanbul/Constantinople, her duties included service to Kösem Sultan, mother of the reigning Sultan. Rising through the ranks of the harem, she bore a male child to Sultan İbrahim. Upon his death she became *Valide Sultan* (Queen Mother) in 1648. As her son Mehmed IV was only six years old when he became sultan, she became the de facto ruler of the Ottoman Empire for many years. She died on 4 August 1683. During this time she was patron of large-scale architectural works. Her first architectural patronage was the extensive repair of the fortresses at Kilitbahir and Kale-I Sultaniye at the narrowest point of the Dardanelles.

5 *Ottoman Women Builders*, p.165.

6 ibid, p.163.

7 ibid, p.166, Footnote 127.

8 *Major & Mrs Holt's Battlefield Guide to Gallipoli*, p.104.

9 *Naval Operations: History of the Great War Based on Official Documents: Volume Two* by Sir Julian S. Corbett, p.173.

10 WO95/4290. Accounts in January 1920 edition of the *Globe & Laurel* by Lieutenant John Richards, No. 4 Company Plymouth Battalion, and *Britain's Sea Soldiers: A Record of the Royal Marines during the War 1914-1919* by H.E. Blumberg. Marine casualties: Colour-Sergeant Alfred Barnett Baldwin, PLY/4690, the son of Alfred and Julia Baldwin of Southsea, Portsmouth and husband of Alice Baldwin, 2 Walkham Terrace, Horrabridge, Devon. He is commemorated on the Plymouth Naval Memorial. Twenty-year-old Private William George Dyter, PLY/17661, son of John William and Kitty Calista Dyter, 22 Elm Road Walthamstow, London. A native of Barnes, London, he is commemorated on Plymouth Naval Memorial. Private John Jones, PLY/305 (S) is commemorated on the Helles Memorial. Lance Corporal/Acting Sergeant William Ernest Dickinson was hit in the leg, but was safely evacuated. Royal Navy casualty: Petty Officer William John Eagle Newland, 189635 (Chatham), brother of Mrs A. Broom, 4 Deptford Ferry Road, Millwall, London. Buried at sea on 5 March 1915, he is commemorated on the Chatham Naval Memorial.

11 *Gallipoli: The Ottoman Campaign* by Edward J. Erickson, p.39 (henceforth *The Ottoman Campaign*). On 4 March 1915, some of the landing party found fowl and eggs in one of the houses in Sedd el Bahr. This would appear to suggest that at least some of the locals were still in residence and had hastily evacuated their home prior to the landing.

12 While the entire division had about 300 officers and 12,000 men, this total included its artillery component as well as its three infantry regiments.

13 Information on the Turkish preparations: *Ottoman Campaign*, pp.65–67.

14 Source for Unwin's comments about Drewry: IWM 13473 05/63/1.

15 The steam-powered picket boats were 55ft long, with a funnel one third of the way back from the bow. There was a protected wheel house aft.

16 Information on the tow from *The Immortal Gamble* by A.T. Stewart and

C.J.E. Peshall, pp.109–114 (henceforth *Immortal Gamble*). Thirty-eight men from the battleship *Cornwallis* were assigned to crew picket boats and tows. Supplemented by a picket boat from the battleship *Agamemnon,* under the command of Midshipman Banks, all of the ship's lifeboats, two cutters and a sailing pinnace were assigned to troop-landing. Lieutenant John Anthony (Tony) Morse was in charge of the *Cornwallis's* boats. Midshipmen Edwards, Voelcker and Denis Last were operating picket-boats. Midshipmen Arthur Hardiman, Maurice Lloyd and Howard Weblin were beach party, under the command of Lieutenant E.E. Madge, RNR. *Dardanelles: A Midshipman's Diary* by H.M. Denham, p.88 and *Immortal Gamble*, p.68.

17 The official military and naval histories call them 'fleet sweepers'.

18 *Neill's*, p.34

19 Information on the Dublins from *Neill's*. While *Neill's* gives Brennan's first initial as F., a search of the medal index cards (WO 372/11) shows Company Quartermaster Sergeant Thomas Brennan, Reg. No. 9050.

20 *The Irish at the Front* by Michael McDonagh, p.109 (henceforth *The Irish*).

21 While *Neill's* gives his first initial as G., WO 372/11 shows Michael Joseph Kennedy.

22 Shown in photographs of tows setting off for the beaches.

23 Eric Bush, p.118.

24 Observers often give differing accounts of the same events. Lieutenant-Colonel Henry Tizard, commanding officer of the 1st Munsters, was on the bridge of the *River Clyde* with Unwin and Carington Smith. He said that as the *River Clyde* passed close to 'a battleship' Unwin called out, asking if the tows had gone in. The reply was 'Don't know but go on in!' Major Weir de Lancey Williams wrote the following notes for his diary: '6.10 a.m. Within half-mile of the shore. We are ahead of the tows … It must cause a mix-up if we, 2nd line, arrive before the 1st line. With difficulty I get Unwin to swerve off and await the tows.'

25 Eric Bush, p.117 and IWM 13473 05/63/1: two accounts of the landing by Unwin.

26 *War at Sea*, p.246.

27 Eric Bush, p.118.

28 Forbes mistakenly called them Munster Fusiliers in his account, published in *Immortal Gamble*, pp.109-114.

29 *Immortal Gamble*, pp.84-86.

30 *The Dardanelles* by Major-General Sir C.E. Callwell KCB, pp.84-85.

31 *Official History*, p.233.

32 ibid., p.235, Footnote 1.

33 *Naval Operations*, p.335.

34 Eric Bush pp.119-120.

35 *The Fight for Gallipoli*, p.103 and *Naval Operations*, pp.165-166. According to a footnote on this page, 'For his services on these two days and his mine-sweeping work Lieutenant Sandford was awarded the D.S.O.'

36 WO 339/9257. The statement was taken by a Miss Lowe. His medal card shows Finnigan was discharged 23 January 1919.

37 ibid.

38 Letter in private collection.

39 The reference to Johnson is a bit of a puzzle, Captain Arthur Johnson was in Y Company, as was Captain David French. The letter would appear to suggest that

Johnson (who was wounded before he could get ashore) had orders to move from the beach to link up with the force at the Camber.

40 *Ottoman Campaign*, p.70.
41 ibid.
42 ibid.
43 Service No. 172227, Taylor was the son of Mrs Mary Taylor, 23 Ruthlin Street, West Derby Road, Liverpool. He is buried in the (Capuccini) Naval Cemetery: Prot. 251, Malta. The story of the third boat in No. 4 tow is told in *Immortal Gamble*, pp.88-90.
44 *Immortal Gamble*, pp.88-90.
45 *War at Sea*, p.246.
46 *The Irish*, pp.62 and 63.
47 *The Irish*, p.62.
48 *Gallipoli* by Peter Hart, p.146 (henceforth Peter Hart).
49 *Neill's*, p.29.
50 *The National Army Museum Book of the Turkish Front 1914-18*, by Field Marshal Lord Carver, pp.31-33 (henceforth *Army Museum Book*).
51 See later account by Midshipman Wilfrid St. Aubyn Malleson.
52 *Immortal Gamble*, pp.105-108.
53 The most likely candidate for the 'Sub-Lieutenant' would appear to be Petty Officer James Whitehead, Clyde 1/1853, RNVR of the Anson Battalion, Royal Naval Division. Killed on 25 April 1915, he is commemorated on the Helles Memorial.
54 *Sailor in the Air* by Richard Bell Davies, pp.120-121.
55 The fact that Maffett, from X Company, landed at the extreme left of the beach would appear to support my thesis that X Company were in tows No. 5 and No. 6.
56 *Neill's*, pp.30 and 31.
57 Petty Office William Medhurst, Reg. No. 158162, was born on 14 May 1875 at Ripe, Sussex. He is commemorated in V Beach Cemetery on Special Memorial B. 49.
58 *Immortal Gamble*, pp.90 and 91.
59 Eric Bush, pp.118-119.
60 ibid, pp.109-110.
61 He was not the first British chaplain to die in the war. Forty-seven-year-old Roman Catholic Canon Robert Basil Gwydir, Order of St Benedict, was drowned when the Home Fleet hospital ship *Rohilla* struck Whitby Rock, a reef south of Whitby at about 4 a.m. on 30 October 1914. Eighty-five lives were lost of the 229 aboard.
62 *Cork Examiner*, 20 May 1915. Colgan wrote from hospital in Malta to his wife in England. He is quoted in *The Irish*, p.62. The newspaper and book gave his rank as sergeant. His medal card shows he was a corporal. WO 372/4. Before quoting him, the book says that he was in the same boat as Lieutenant-Colonel Rooth, Adjutant Captain Higginson and Father Finn, though Colgan did not say that in the newspaper extract. Neither did he say 'One fellows brains were shot into my mouth as I was shouting to them to jump for it,' which the book quotes instead of 'Two bullets went through my pack'.
63 *The Dodger* by Tim Carroll, p.59.
64 Letter held by Harry Fox's granddaughter Pam Smith. Private Henry Thompson wrote the letter from the Royal Hospital Netley on 4 December 1915. He apologised for not writing sooner, but said that he had developed pneumonia on the boat

bringing him home and had been bedridden for three months.

65 Letter held by Pam Smith.

66 *Neill's*, p.34.

67 *Official History*, p.233, Footnote 1. Able Seaman Lewis Jacobs J 4081 (Ch) is commemorated on the Chatham Naval Memorial. This means his body was not recovered.

68 Snelling, p.35.

69 Eric Bush, pp 119-120. Midshipman Arthur Hardiman (aged seventeen), HMS *Cornwallis*, son of Eugenie and the late Joshua Hardiman, Osborne House, The Hoe, Plymouth, Devon. Commemorated on the Chatham Naval Memorial. This suggests his body was buried at sea.

70 Snelling, pp.35-36.

71 IWM 13473 05/63/1.

72 *Official History*, p.232.

73 Commonwealth War Grave Commission records show that twenty-year-old Sapper Walter Duckenfield, Reg. No. 1028, 1st (West Riding) Field Company Royal Engineers was killed on 25 April 1915. Commemorated by Special Memorial A. 43, V Beach Cemetery, he was the son of Lily and the late George E. Duckenfield, 25 Woodgrove Lane, Penistone Road Sheffield. The records show the date of death for twenty-two-year-old Sapper John C. Mulligan, Reg. No. 629, 1st (West Riding) Field Company Royal Engineers as 26 April 1915. The son of Joseph and Annie E. Mulligan, Sheffield, he is buried in Grave K. 8 of V Beach Cemetery.

74 IWM Sound SR 4103.

75 *Norman Dewhurst*, pp.25-26.

76 *Neill's*, p.32.

77 *Far from the Short Grass: The Story of Kildare Men in the Two World Wars* by James Durney, p.37 (henceforth *Short Grass*).

78 IWM 76/107/1. Apart from one sentence, I did not quote from the letter, as it is difficult to read.

79 While Unwin does not mention the rock in either of his accounts, Drewry said that 'the Capt decided to make the connection with a spit of rock …'

80 Stephen Snelling, pp.33-34.

81 Author's copy of ships plans for the SS *Gibraltar*, a ship of similar dimensions to the *River Clyde*, built by the same shipbuilders, Russell and Company.

82 It is unclear whether modifications to Hold No. 1 had created an upper and lower hold.

83 WO95/4319.

84 WO95/4319.

85 ibid.

86 The part inside the brackets is crossed out in the original account. (Note: Sullivan did not have an 'O' in his surname.)

87 IWM Sound SR 4103.

88 *History of the Royal Munsters Fusiliers*, p.11.

89 *Short Grass*, p.37.

90 Some of the officers on the *River Clyde* expressed critical opinions of others: Drewry appeared to be critical of Ellard, Unwin appeared to be critical of Drewry

on one occasion and Wedgwood appeared to be dismissive of Unwin, Drewry and the *River Clyde's* Warrant Engineer.

91 A younger brother, Lance-Corporal Gilbert Grace Kelly, Reg. No. 10/2986, 1st Battalion Wellington Regiment, enlisted in the New Zealand Army from Barrett's Hotel, Wellington. A member of the Wellington GPO staff, he was killed in action on the Somme on 26 September 1916.

92 X Company (Captain Guy Geddes) and Y Company (Captain Eric Henderson) had been detailed as assaulting companies. Y Company (Major Charles Jarrett) was supporting company and W Company (Major William Hutchinson) was reserve company.

93 *Norman Dewhurst*, p.26.

94 IWM 10946 P216.

95 *Neill's*, p.33.

96 Davidson, p.51.

97 *Official History*, p.238.

98 ibid, pp.239-240 and footnote 1, page 240. *The Royal Hampshire Regiment 1914-1918* by C.T. Atkinson p.72 (henceforth *Hampshire Regiment*).

99 Peter Hart, p.153.

100 *Hampshire Regiment* pp.72-73. A footnote on page 73 says that 'Some 15 were hit.' Neither of the officers was killed that day and Commonwealth War Graves records do not show any 2nd Battalion Hampshire Regiment non-officer deaths for 25 April 1915.

101 *Ottoman Campaign*, pp.70-71.

102 ibid, p.71.

103 *Hampshire Regiment*, p.72. Captain Caryl Lermitte Boxall (twenty-seven) died on 27 April 1915. The son of Sir Alleyne Alfred and Lady Boxall, 14 Cambridge Square, London W.2, he is commemorated on the Helles Memorial. None of the men who were hit are recorded by the Commonwealth War Graves Commission as dying on 25 April 1915.

104 *Hampshire Regiment*, p.72.

105 This statement is puzzling. *Hampshire Regiment* p.72 says that Beckwith commanded Z Company and that Boxall, among the group who left the ship, was from Y Company. p.73 says 'Before it was dark, Major Beckwith went ashore to take over command.'

106 *Official History*, p.240.

107 Peter Hart, p.153.

108 Brigadier-General Henry Edward Napier (fifty-three), Commanding Officer of 88th Brigade, 29th Division was the son of Charles George and Susanna Napier, the Acacias, Bury St Edmunds. The husband of Mary Ida Napier, 13 Stanley Place Chester, he had served with the Cheshire Regiment and the Royal Irish Rifles. He is commemorated on the Helles Memorial to the missing. His brigade-major, Captain John Costeker, who was killed about the same time, has a grave. This would appear to suggest that when Napier was shot he fell into the water and his body was not recovered.

109 Peter Hart, p.154.

110 Captain John Henry Dives Costeker DSO (thirty-six) Royal Warwickshire Regiment was attached as brigade-major to 88th Brigade, 29th Division. Son of William and Clara Costeker, 46 Evelyn Gardens, South Kensington, London;

husband of Margaret Picton Grant Poole (formerly Costeker), 6 Mallord Street, Church Street, London. He is buried in Grave F.10 of V Beach Cemetery. Had he returned to his regiment he would have reverted to his rank of captain. He is recorded on Commonwealth War Graves with the rank of major.

111 Lieutenant-Colonel Herbert Carington Smith is commemorated on the Helles Memorial.

112 *The Navy in the Dardanelles Campaign*, p.74.

113 *The Fight for Gallipoli*, p.119. 'Sharp criticism [was later] meteted out to Davidson for allowing his unofficial support [of the S Beach landing] to distract him from his proper role. Once the [troops] were ashore [at S Beach] the *Cornwallis* should have moved to V Beach to add her weight to the supporting fire there. But Davidson and the beach party did not withdraw from S Beach until after 10.00. The censure he later incurred overshadowed any recognition of the value of his increased support for the [S Beach landing].' *Defeat at Gallipoli* by Nigel Steel and Peter Hart, p.97. 'It is not clear whether bringing in another supporting battleship would have made much difference to the pattern of events at V Beach. But by then it was too late.' Peter Hart, p.132.

114 *The Fight for Gallipoli*, pp.115–125.

115 ibid, p.125.

116 *Official History*, p.247.

117 *The Fight for Gallipoli*, pp.124–125.

118 *Gallipoli* by Tim Travers, p.57 (henceforth Tim Travers).

119 Davidson, p.52.

120 Tim Travers, p.57.

121 Presumably 'my' meant 'my squadron' and 'we', in the next sentence, also referred to the squadron.

122 It is not clear if a particular plane was assigned to V Beach and if not, why not. No mention of one has been found in any of the published accounts.

123 *Fights and Flights* by C.R. Samson, pp.233–234. It is a pity that Samson did not give even an approximate time of his flight over V Beach. Given that planes were still a rare sight, it is surprising that none of those who left accounts of their participation in the landing mentioned Samson's flight over the beach.

124 It is unclear if the 'seven parties of men' were the men from Y Company, and the Hampshires, as he refers to his orders to Hutchinson not to go ashore immediately after the comment that men from Y Company and the Hampshires were hit. If they had got ashore as far as the hospital ruins why would Tizard wait until then to order Hutchinson not to go ashore? Perhaps the sentence beginning 'This party of…' should have begun with 'A party of …'

125 *The Irish at the Front* p.66, The *Cork Examiner* 4 June 1915 and Researcher Jean Prendergast.

126 *Ottoman Campaign*, pp.72–73.

127 *Official History*, p.248.

128 Norman Dewhurst, p.26

129 McCann and O'Hara *Neill's*, p.33.

130 *Army Museum Book*, p.32-33.

131 *Neill's*, p.31.

132 WO 95/4319.

133 Peter Hart, p.146

134 *Hampshire Regiment*, pp.73–74.

135 WO 95/4319.

136 *Stonyhurst War Record* by Revd Francis Irwin SJ, p.136. Jarrett's grave must have subsequently been lost, as he is commemorated in Lancashire Landing Cemetery. His brother, Captain Aylmer Jarrett DSO, 2nd York and Lancashire Regiment was killed near Ypres on 22 June 1915.

137 Undated letter from Lance-Corporal John Walsh of the Munsters in *Bandon District Soldiers Died in the Great War* (no page numbers).

138 *Helles Landing Gallipoli*, pp.90–92 and *Official History*, pp.229–230.

139 Eric Bush, pp.133–137.

140 Possibly Hill 138 and Gözcübaba, though a number of British officers appear to have mistaken the latter for Hill 141, behind Sedd el Bahr village. When Gözcübaba was captured, it was reported to divisional headquarters that Hill 141 had fallen.

141 *Ottoman Campaign*, p.73 and *Gallipoli: A Battlefield Guide* by Phil Taylor and Pam Cupper, pp.106-107 (henceforth Taylor and Cupper).

142 Hawworth had been severely wounded at 11.30 a.m., but refused to leave his company.

143 The movements of Captain Farmar, the Worcestershires etc. *Official History*, pp.241–243.

144 *Ottoman Campaign*, p.75. The British *Official History* does not mention the attack. Nor does it mention naval gunfire. It says, 'After midnight a few bold parties of Turks pushed up to the British lines, but nothing in the nature of a counter-attack was attempted. Nevertheless the night was spent by some of the British units in heavy and continous firing, and frequent messages were received at W Beach to the effect that ammunition had run out, or that units were being heavily attacked and could not hold on without reinforcements.' A footnote says messages that the Turks were attacking in 'German mass formation' were twice received at headquarters. 'Not till morning, when it transpired that the night casualties had not exceeded half a dozen, was it realised that most of the disturbance had been due to overwrought nerves.' Yet another footnote says, 'During the night, when every available fighting man had been sent into the line, midshipmen and even captains R.N. were carrying boxes of ammunition up to the troops.' All in all, there was an amazing amount of activity on foot of what the *Official History* suggests was merely 'due to overwrought nerves.' *Official History*, p.250 and footnotes 3 and 4.

Chapter 7

1 Nigel Steel and Peter Hart, pp.113, *Hampshire Regiment*, pp.73–74.

2 WO95/4319.

3 Nigel Steel and Peter Hart *Defeat at Gallipoli*, p.114 (henceforth Defeat at Galliopli) and the *Albion's* log on www.naval-history.net.

4 WO95/4319.

5 *Norman Dewhurst*, p.26.

6   *Official History*, pp.275–276.
7   *Hampshire Regiment*, p.74.
8   *Official History*, p.276.
9   *Ottoman Women Builders: The Architectural Patronage of Hadice Turhan Sultan* by Lucienne Thys-Şenocak. Advance draft of Chapter 3.
10 Nigel Steel and Peter Hart, pp.114–115.
11 Snelling, p.70.
12 *Official History*, p.277.
13 Peter Hart, p.162.
14 *Edinburgh Gazette* 13 August 1915. *Neill's* said it was published in the *London Gazette* on 5 August 1915.
15 *Neill's*, p.36.
16 Supplement to *London Gazette*, 5 November 1915.
17 Peter Hart, pp.162–163.
18 *Official History*, p.276 and *Hampshire Regiment*, pp.74–75. Captain Alfred Addison (thirty-two), Y Company, 2nd Hampshires, Son of Annie Kate Addison, 'St Lawrence,' Queen's Crescent, Southsea, Portsmouth and the late Albert Addison. Captain Garth Walford VC (thirt-two), Brigade-Major, Royal Artillery, 29th Division. Son of the late Colonel Neville Walford, Royal Artillery. Both men are buried side-by-side in V Beach Cemetery, Walford in Grave O.1. and Addison in Grave O.2.
19 *Official History*, p.277 and footnote 1 on the same page.
20 Nigel Steel and Peter Hart p.114 and Snelling p.70.
21 Peter Hart, pp.164–165.
22 *The Story Behind the Monument*, pp.6–7.
23 *Official History*, p.277.
24 Letter by Nightingale dated 4 May 1915. Quoted by Nigel Steel and Peter Hart p.115 and footnote 104.
25 Nigel Steel and Peter Hart p.115 and WO95/4319.
26 Snelling, pp.81–82.
27 Company Sergeant-Major Alfred Bennett, 6426, was born in Ballyseedy, County Kerry. He enlisted in Tralee, where he was resident at the time of his enlistment. Having no known grave, he is commemorated on the Helles Memorial.
28 Snelling, pp.82–84.
29 Snelling, p.84.
30 ibid.
31 *Neill's*, p.30.
32 *Kilkenny People* website, accessed 28 July 2014.
33 *Norman Dewhurst MC*, pp.26–27.
34 Nigel Steel and Peter Hart, p.116.
35 Peter Hart, p.165.
36 ibid, p. 165.
37 ibid.
38 Nigel Steel and Peter Hart, p.117.
39 Maurice Stuart Constantinidi's medal card lists him as 1st Battalion Royal Dublin Fusiliers, Rank: Interpreter. His address is given as 8 Elgin Road, Sutton, Surrey. His medal card says that application for his medals was made through a member

of parliament, which would suggest he was dead. His death is not recorded by the Commonwealth War Graves Commission, possibly because he was a civilian. His name was on a Red Cross Enquiry list on 14 August 1915, page 123 and 4 September 1915, page 118. Research by Mal Murray of the Gallipoli Association.
40 *Army Museum Book*, p.46.
41 Nigel Steel and Peter Hart, p.117.
42 Peter Hart, p.168.
43 Snelling, pp.84–85.
44 *Neill's*, p.36.
45 Nigel Steel and Peter Hart Footnote 104, pp.429–430.
46 Snelling, pp.84–85.
47 Peter Hart, pp.166–167.
48 Tim Travers, p.47
49 WO 95/4319 and Nigel Steel and Peter Hart, p.117.
50 Nigel Steel and Peter Hart p.118 and *History of the Royal Munsters Fusiliers*, p.51.
51 Medical Officer Captain Lawrence Wedderburn, who served on the *Caledonia*, noted in a letter written on 8 May 'We set off doing our best for [the patients] but horribly understaffed; only twenty RAMC orderlies and badly equipped', *Army Museum Book*, p.38.
52 *Museum Book*, p.39.
53 *Helles: The French in Gallipoli* by Eleanor van Heyningen, a paper for *The Joint Imperial War Museum/Australian War Memorial Battlefield Study Tour to Gallipoli*, September 2000, p.3.
54 Taylor and Cupper, pp.106–107.
55 *The Ottoman Campaign*, pp.76–77.
56 Nigel Steel and Peter Hart, p.118.

Chapter 8

1 Nigel Steel and Peter Hart, p.168.
2 *Norman Drewhurst M.C.*, p.28.
3 IWM 13473 05/63/1.
4 *The Story Behind the Monument*, p.59. While Tizard has been forgotten outside a small circle of present-day 'Gallipolians', Tony Jordan has grandchildren.
5 *Official History*, p.294.
6 Figures for the Dublins and Munsters *Official History*, p.316. *British Regiments at Gallipoli* by Ray Westlake, p.228, gives the Dublins 1 officer and 374 men.
7 *Neill's*, p.39.
8 *Norman Dewhurst*, p.28.
9 *Official History*, p.318.
10 ibid.
11 This suggests either that Geddes was mistaken or that Sullivan was not badly wounded on 25 April.
12 *Neill's*, p.39.
13 Peter Hart, p.210.
14 *Neill's*, p.41.

15 ibid.

16 From a 'work in progress' database, Mal Murray of the Gallipoli Association gave a total of eighty-three *Blue Cap* casualties for 30 April, i.e. 1 May by my adjusted calculation.

17 Ray Westlake's book *British Regiments at Gallipoli* summarised battalion war diaries for the campaign. As the Blue Caps war diary is unfortunately not available for the period in question, Westlake and *Neill's* are the sources on the activities and movements of the battalion that are outlined in this chapter. According to the summary in Westlake, the Dubsters were relieved on 1 May. But the *Official History* of the campaign and the war diary of the Munsters show the attack occurred on the night of 1 May and the war diary shows the Dubsters were relieved on 2 May.

18 *Official History*, p.301, Footnote 1. 'At the time of this expedition the rule [of sending ten per cent reinforcement drafts] had fallen into abeyance in the case of units going to France, the distance being short and communication rapid. Although the troops for the Dardanelles were to operate at a distance from England, Lord Kitchener would not allow the additional 10 per cent to be sent with them.' *The Dardanelles Commission 1914-16*, p.141–142.

19 *Cook's Traveller's Handbook for Constantinople, Gallipoli & Asia Minor* (1923) by Roy Elston p.119 says that a cemetery at Sedd el Bahr was 'removed to V Beach'. So, with the exception of Doughty-Wylie, presumably Cecil Grimshaw and those killed in the fighting of 26 April were buried near the village and later moved to V Beach Cemetery.

20 A footnote in the *Army Museum Book* says that this refers to Fetherstonhaugh.

21 *Army Museum Book*, pp.45–47. Regimental-Sergeant Major William O'Mahoney (thirty-one), son of Humphrey and Hannah (*neé* Kelleher), 26 Mary Street, Cork. 9 May 1915. Commemorated on the Helles Memorial.

22 *History of the Royal Munsters Fusiliers*, p.53.

23 Twenty-five-year-old Floyd was the son of Revd Canon James and Mrs A.C. Floyd, 30 Norfolk Crescent, Edgware Road London. He is commemorated in Twelve Tree Copse Cemetery (Sp. Mem. C.121). Twenty-one-year-old Lieutenant Lawrence Clive Boustead from W Company, was the son of Lawrence Twentyman and Ethel Margaret Boustead of 'Gray Wings', Astead, Surrey. He is buried in Grave VII. B.3, Twelve Tree Copse Cemetery. All that is known about Captain Adrian Taylor is that before the Gallipoli campaign he had been seconded from the Royal Dublin Fusiliers to the Egyptian police. With no known grave, he is commemorated on the Helles Memorial.

24 *The Dardanelles Commission*, p.141.

25 Eric Bush, p.200. The surgeon-general told the Dardanelles Commission there was a lack of materials such as wood and corrugated iron to enclose the latrines and make them fly-proof and to provide fly-proof kitchen shelters. A major cause of the deficiencies was the belief that the campaign would be of short duration and no provision was made for long-term occupation of the peninsula. *The Dardanelles Commission*, pp.244-245.

26 Medal Card WO 372/13/92759 and Newry's Roll of Honour in *Newry's War Dead*, Newry and Mourne Council, 2002, p.152.

27 He is commemorated in Azmak Cemetery, Suvla.

28 *Neill's*, p.55.

29 *The Dardanelles Commission*, p.195.

30 While many accounts credit Munro's report as the final deciding factor to evacuate Gallipoli, a number of high-level attempts were made to continue the campaign. Rear-Admiral Wemyss, who took over command when de Robeck went on sick-leave on 25 November, argued for a further naval assault. To counter the effect on British prestige of a withdrawal from Gallipoli, Kitchener argued for a landing at Ayas Bay, near Alexandretta in the Eastern Mediterranean. On behalf of 'several colleagues', Lord Curzon argued against evacuation. *The Dardanelles Commission,* pp.200-205.

Chapter 9

1 *London Gazette,* 13 August 1915. He was a member of the Kelly family of Ballintubbert, County Laois. An ancestor, Revd Thomas Kelly, wrote the hymn 'The Head that Once was Crowned with Thorns' and founded the short-lived religious sect, the Kellyites. Peter Burrows Kelly was educated at St Vincent's College Castleknock, County Dublin. He was working in Charing Cross Hospital, London, on the outbreak of war. He served with the Royal Naval Air Service during the siege of Antwerp in October 1914 and was 'the only medical man to escape when the Germans swept into the Belgian city'. *The Glorious Madness: Tales of the Irish and the Great War* by Turtle Bunbury, pp.164 and 175.
2 *Gallipoli Diary* by J. Gillam, pp.46–47.
3 *With the 29th Division in Gallipoli,* p.67.
4 *The Irish at the Front,* p.110.
5 www.ww1.osborn.ws.
6 From the website of the Commonwealth War Graves Commission.
7 *With the 29th Division in Gallipoli,* p.67.
8 Snelling, pp.46–49.
9 Information on Captain John Kerr from his file in the Liddle Archive. My thanks to Simon Riches for sourcing the file.
10 The author's paternal grandmother, Monica Higgins, used to babysit the Batmazian children while their parents manufactured Turkish Delight.
11 *Remembrance,* p.149.
12 *The 16th (Irish) and 36th (Ulster) Divisions at The Battle of Wijtsscate-Messines Ridge,* 7 June 1917 by Tom Burke MBE, pp.115.
13 Information on both men from an exhibition at Glasnevin Cemetery.
14 Private Frederick Wilkinson (nineteen), Reg. No. 2599, 1st Battalion Lancashire Fusiliers, is commemorated on the Helles Memorial. He was the son of William and Sarah Wilkinson, 5 Paper Street, Burnley.
15 Eric Bush, p.139. Forbes was married to Cicely Armitage. They had a daughter Pamela, born in 1925. Forbes was a descendent of Robert 111 of Scotland.
16 Information supplied by Mr Selcuk Unal, Third Secretary of the Embassy of the Republic of Turkey and the *Dún Laoghaire Borough Historical Society Journal,* No. 8, 1999, article 'From Patrick Street to the Dardanelles: The Bernard Mahony Story' by Philip Lecane.
17 Named after the commune in the south-western suburbs of Paris where it was signed, the treaty had been signed on 10 August 1920.

18 *Remembrance*, Patrick Hogarty, pp.151–154. My thanks to John Tucker, local and family librarian, Torquay Library for Mayor Hugh Cumming's name.

19 *Neill's*, p.127

20 Information on the final years of the 1st Royal Dublin Fusiliers is from *Neill's*.

21 *History of the Royal Munster Fusiliers*, p.52. Letter 22 June 1916 from Major P.T. Chute, DSO to Lieutenant Colonel R.H. Monck-Mason DSO Commanding Officer of the 1st Royal Munster Fusiliers. 'I am pleased to inform you that I have this day received from Vice-Admiral Sir John de Robeck a case containing the steering wheel and a mast-head lamp of the famous River Clyde in memory of the landing of the 29th Division at Sedd-el-Bahr on April 29th 1915.' In 1927, when the Munsters history was written, the items were in the Royal United Services Institution, Whitehall. In 1955 they were placed in the Munster Room at Sandhurst. At some point they were moved to the National Army Museum. At the time of this book going to publication, they are on loan to the National Museum, Collins Barracks, Dublin.

22 *History of the Royal Munster Fusiliers*, pp.89–91 was a particularly good source for this paragraph.

23 *The Times* and the *London Gazette* of 12 August 1920.

24 *London Gazette*, 5 August 1938.

25 ibid, 25 June 1948.

26 Email to author from Torquay Reference Library, 1 December 2009.

27 Research by Liam Dodd.

28 The St Barnabas Society was founded by New Zealander Revd H. Mullineux, who had served with the New Zealand forces during the war. During the 1920s the society took parties of pilgrims to Gallipoli, Palestine, Greece and Italy.

29 IWGC Annual Report 1930/31, p.33.

30 Thomas Cook's *The Traveller's Handbook for Constantinople, Gallipoli and Asia Minor* (London 1923).

31 *Gallipoli and Salonika* by the St Barnabas Society (London *c.* 1926), *The Tracks They Trod: Salonika and the Balkans, Gallipoli, Egypt and Palestine Revisited* by Trevor Allen (London 1932), *The Ship of Remembrance* by Ian Hay (Major-General John Hay Beith) (London 1927) and *A Pilgrimage to Gallipoli* by Jessie Holmes (London 1927).

32 pp.19–20.

33 pp.8–9.

33 pp.9–10.

34 p.13.

35 pp.20–24.

36 Of interest to Irish readers is the fact that, in 1934, The Catholic Boy Scouts of Ireland chartered the *Lancastria* for a pilgrimage to Rome. Among the scouts were future Taoiseach (Prime Minister) Liam Cosgrave and future Tainiste (Deputy Prime Minister) Brendan Corish, James Plunkett, future author of *Strumpet City* and Cornelius Ryan, future author of *The Longest Day* and *A Bridge Too Far*. Source: Lecture at the National Museum of Ireland on *The Catholic Boy Scouts of Ireland* attended by a man who was one of the scouts on the pilgrimage.

37 General information on the pilgrimages: *Battlefield Tourism: Pilgrimage and the*

Commemoration of the Great War in Britain, Australia and Canada 1919-1939 by David W. Lloyd and *Gallipoli: A Battlefield Guide* by Phil Taylor and Pam Cupper.

38 The major source for this part of the story is Denis Stonham's excellent, previously cited, article.

39 *Daily Telegraph*, 24 April 1965.

40 *Grey River Argus* (Australian newspaper), 22 November 1919.

41 Denis Stonham.

42 Papers of A. Pearman IWM Documents 6593.

43 On 17 June 1940, two weeks after the Dunkirk evacuation, the *Lancastria* was attacked and sunk by German bombers off the French port of St Nazaire, while evacuating troops and civilians.

44 *The Straits Times*, 14 July 1915.

45 *Neill's*, pp.203–204.

46 *Newry's War Dead* pp.175–180.

47 Information supplied by Ian Gillian, Great War Forum from Fox's records.

48 The association was founded in 1910. My thanks to Liam Dodd for the information that Harry Fox was a member of the association. I am very grateful for the very extensive information on Harry Fox provided by his granddaughter Pam Smith.

49 Snelling, pp.86–87. The *Cork Examiner* 18 July 1936. The sailing time of the *Innisfallen* was taken from an advertisement in the paper. Cosgrove's brother Joseph, who was a farmer, was among the mourners. In a sign of the times, the report merely identified his widow as 'Mrs Cosgrove', while it gave her brothers names William, Martin and David Mulcahy.

50 *The Story Behind the Monument*, p.74.

51 *The Dodger*, p.60.

52 *Holt's*, p.113. *Cook's*, p.115.

53 *Ottoman Women Builders: The Architectural Patronage of Hadice Turhan Sultan* by Lucienne Thys-Şenocak. Advance draft of Chapter 3.

54 Recent studies have shown that commemoration services in Ireland were strongly supported during the 1920s. During an August 2014 discussion on RTÉ television, one panellist suggested that 'forgetfulness' surrounding Irish participation in the First World War only occurred following the country's neutrality in the Second World War.

55 Recounting of the ceremony was facilitated by Nick Broughall's film of the event. The Royal Dublin Fusiliers Association party consisted of Dr Tim Bowman, Nick Broughall, David Buckley, Tom Burke, Joe Gallagher, Philip Lecane, Betty Mullen, Gillian Mullen (Betty's daughter), Dr David Murphy, the late Tony Quinn and Christian Taylor.

Appendix 4

1 Sources for this appendix: *Thom's Directory of Great Britain and Ireland* (various years), *The Times* 4 May 1915, *London to Ladysmith via Pretoria* by Winston Spencer Churchill, pp.43, 50 and 56, *The Old Toughs* by Patrick Hogarty, pp. 45 and 52 and information from Pam Stephney, who has researched the Frankland family.

Appendix 5

1 Information on Ormond Cook and family from his grandson Captain Howard Cook.

2 Captain Howard Cook said that maritime historian and researcher Denis Stonham was unable to find any mention of a ship sinking in the manner described during the period in question. But, while the story may be in error in the detail, Captain Cook says that the finance he obtained from a claim enabled his grandfather to set himself up as a ship owner.

3 As Captain Howard Cook is aware that Lord Inverforth (founder of the Bank Line) invested in the *River Clyde,* it is possible that Eadie or Watt held his shares in their name.

4 The crewmen were Fireman A. Creighton (twenty-six), born in Mayo. Fireman Joseph Freeman Boreham (forty-one), son of John Freeman Boreham and Elizabeth Boreham, husband of Annie Boreham, Bakehouse Yard, Haggersgate, Whitby, born in Whitby. UC35 was commanded by Kapitänleutnant Ernest von Voight. The submarine fired a single torpedo from about 300m range. The *River Forth* sank quickly. My thanks to Michael Lowry of www.uboat.net for the information about the sinking.

Index

Note: As men's ranks often changed in the time period covered by the story, ranks are not given in the index.

Also from The History Press

IRELAND
AT WAR

Find these titles and more at

www.thehistorypress.ie

Printed in Great Britain
by Amazon

56663967R00192